DEATH
BY
EDUCATION

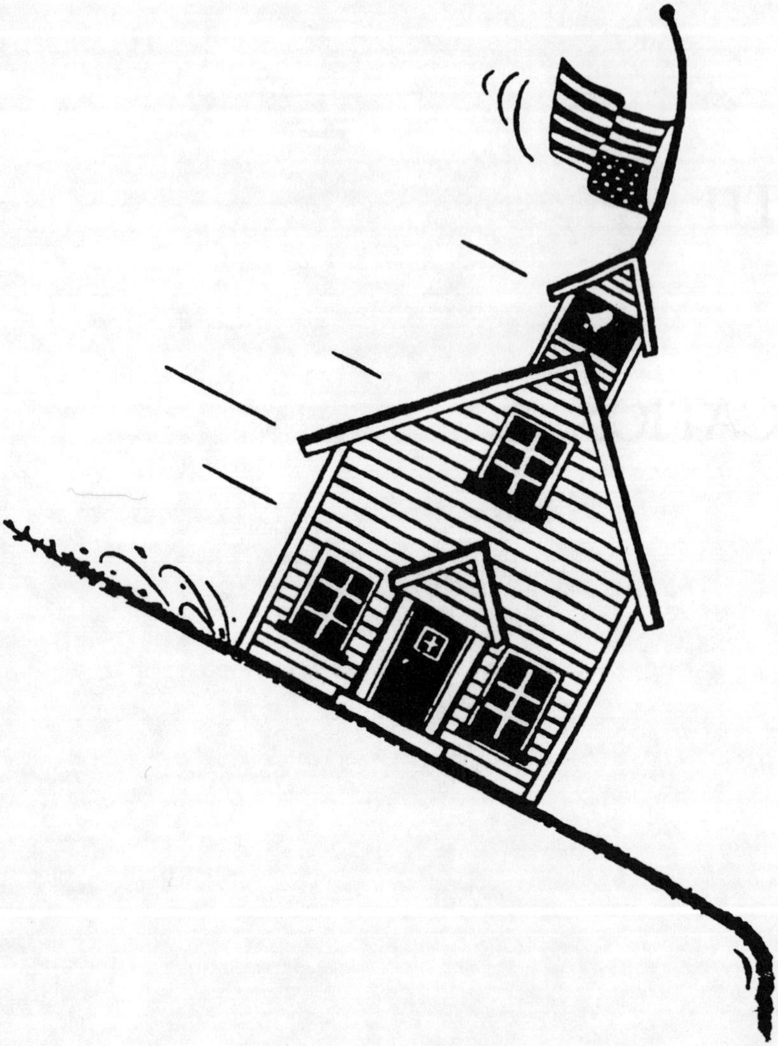

DEATH
BY
EDUCATION:
An American Autopsy

By William Wieser

WISER ENTERPRISES
Tampa, Florida

Death by Education

Copyright © 1993 by William Wieser
All rights reserved. In conjunction with the International Copyright Convention, no part of this book may be reproduced or transmitted in any form or by any means, electronic or mechanical, except for brief quotations in reviews, without permission in writing from the publisher.

Wiser Enterprises
Post Office Box 272346
Tampa, Florida 33688-2346

First Edition
Published January 4, 1993 in 49 states except Florida
(Florida publication release—July 4, 1993)
Printed in the United States of America on acid-free paper
Illustrations, jacket and book design copyright by William Wieser 1993

Library of Congress Cataloging-in-Publication Data

Wieser, William, 1943–
    Death by education : an American autopsy / by William Wieser.—
1st ed.
     p. cm.
  ISBN 0-09634543-5-8 (alk. paper : $25.00
    1. Education—Florida—Hillsborough County. 2. School management and organization—Political aspects—Florida—Hillsborough County.
3. School management and organization—Florida—Hillsborough County—
Moral and ethical aspects. 4. Wieser, William. 1943–
I. Title.
LA259.H55W54 1993
370′.9759′65—dc20   92-96913
                                                                                        CIP

REAFFIRMATION   2 4 6 8 10 9 7 5 3 1

"We are not afraid to follow the truth wherever it may lead."
—Thomas Jefferson, President
and renowned educator. 1820

"Let's not be afraid to follow truth, wherever it may lead."
—George Bush, the Education President
quoting Jefferson during the
Education Summit. 1989

To Peg and Hans, who taught me the values of family, life and education.

And to Dr. Camm, my professional mentor who taught me never to forget any of the fundamental purposes of education.

CONTENTS

PROTASIS   v

    CHAPTERS

1. I Gotta Be Me   1
2. All American City   6
3. A Crash Course in Ethics   10
4. It's Not *What* You Know...   14
5. Program Assessment   17
6. Lesson Number One   22
7. The Cryptic Memo   27
8. Equal Pay Please   30

    Beginning of School Year 1986–87

9. All Hell Breaks Loose   32
10. Subordinate Shakedown   47
11. Attorney Number 1   53
12. Perceiving, Behaving, Becoming   58
13. Power Hour   66

    Beginning of School Year 1987–88

14. The Big Black Book   78
15. Now What?   81
16. Hello "Deep Throat"   83
17. Attorney Number 2   85
18. CEO and Me   88
19. The Commissioner's Code of Ethics   94

CONTENTS

20.	Protect Thyself	102
21.	Tap Tap Tap	104
22.	Grievance Level I	107
23.	Grievance Level II	111
24.	Okay...Don't Anybody Move	124
25.	Whistleblower Protection Program	143
26.	Attorney Number 3	145
27.	Yes...Ah...No!	147
28.	Who's The Boss	153
29.	Probation Equation	168
30.	A Rare Happening	174
31.	The Commissioner's Ethics	178
32.	Power Play	200
33.	Umbilical Discord	203
34.	Read My Lips...Not My Memos	207
35.	See You in Court	210
36.	A.C.L.U....Help?	214
37.	Going Public	217
38.	Money Means Power	222
39.	I Did My Best	227
40.	Last Day On The Job	230
41.	Hearing Number One: Motion For Temporary Injunction	233

Beginning of School Year 1988–89

42.	Don't Beat a Dead Horse	235
43.	This Soapbox Didn't Remove The Stains	240
44.	One Down, One To Go	254
45.	No Fury	257
46.	Hearing Number Two: Motion to Dismiss	262
47.	Hearing Number Three: Summary Judgement	264
48.	Two Down, A Pyrrhic Victory?	267

CONTENTS

49.	What "Right To Work"	275
50.	Unappealing Appeal	279
51.	Your Friendly Credit Union	283
52.	The New Superintendent	286
53.	Attorney Number 3½	290

Beginning of School Year 1989–90

54.	Hearing Number Four: The Appeal	293
55.	Appeal Appeal	296
56.	Degrade Charade	299
57.	Attorney Number 3¾	308
58.	Hearing Number Five: Contempt of Court	310
59.	Reinstatement?	318
60.	United States Court	332
61.	Hearing Number Six: Final Judgement	339
62.	Cammaratta Retires	346
63.	Lessons in Class	348
64.	Go Directly To Jail	361

Beginning of School Year 1990–91

65.	Healthy Time-Out	367
66.	Attorney Number 3⅞	373
67.	184/120 Hypertension	375

Beginning of School Year 1991–92

68.	Attorney Number 3¹⁵⁄₁₆	381
69.	Jailbird	384
70.	Attorney Number 3³¹⁄₃₂	404
71.	Cut! That's a Print	407
Epilogue		413
Epitaph		417
Appendix		419

PROTASIS

Our nation is still at risk. American students test below average in math and science as compared with other industrialized nations. As we approach the 21st century, the solution to bring us to the top of a world-class ranking is, nonetheless, still not explicit. And the whole world is watching and waiting.

Allow my story to take an innovative approach in identifying a problem in public education that has quietly remained undiagnosed and in the background: poor management. Before we can organize a solution to the education crisis, we must agree on the causations and then set problem-solving priorities.

This American autopsy is a true story about one person's experiences inside the infrastructure of a large public school system. This post-mortem study of my career will attempt to reveal the cause, manner, and mode which contributed to our education crisis. See if you will be able to identify the vital signs. This gross inspection will cover a thirteen year period, and dissect it into 71 bite-sized passages. Instead of strictly writing chronologically, I actually began writing about my status in the middle of the story, then continued from the beginning and wrote topically as events arose. Therefore, some passages will naturally overlap.

May the data from this autopsy provide for advances in educational management and, accordingly, may you and your next of kin achieve a greater intellect in your educational responsibilities to the community, state, and nation.

The school bell tolls for America. Until there is a change in the dynamic politics in education, we will not solve the national education crisis because we have an entrenched educational bureaucracy.

The characters in this examination are many. The main ones are capsulized in a hierarchy on the following page. Their names and positions in the Hillsborough County Public School System, Tampa, Florida, are real.

...Scalpel?

HILLSBOROUGH COUNTY PUBLIC SCHOOL SYSTEM
Tampa, Florida

ADMINISTRATIVE ORGANIZATIONAL CHART 1987
(Showing *main* positions related to this story)

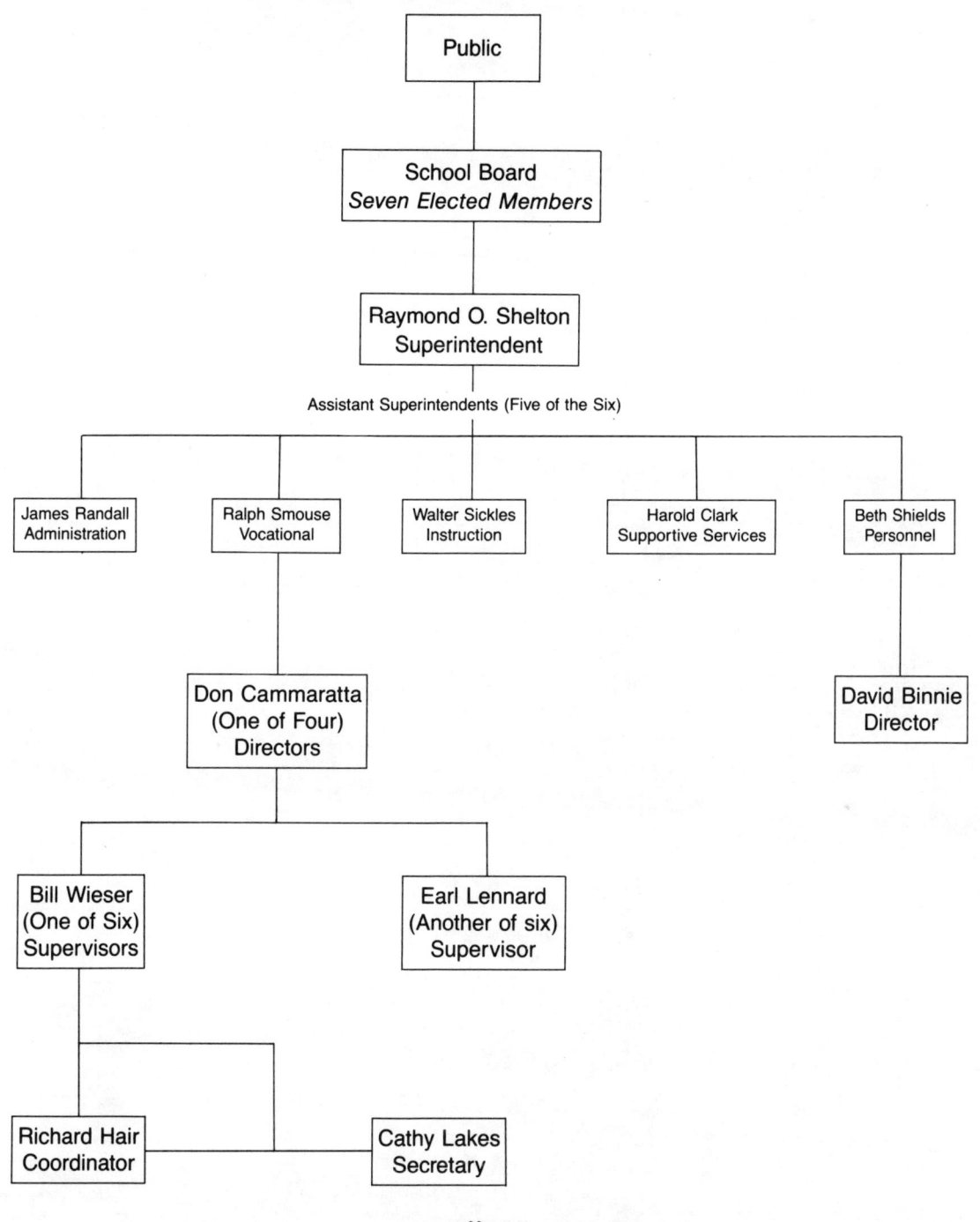

```
                          ┌──────────────┐
                          │    Public    │
                          └──────┬───────┘
                                 │
                       ┌─────────┴──────────┐
                       │    School Board    │
                       │ Seven Elected Members │
                       └─────────┬──────────┘
                                 │
                       ┌─────────┴──────────┐
                       │ Raymond O. Shelton │
                       │   Superintendent   │
                       └─────────┬──────────┘
              Assistant Superintendents (Five of the Six)
   ┌──────────────┬──────────────┬──────────────┬──────────────┐
┌──────────┐ ┌──────────┐ ┌──────────┐ ┌──────────────┐ ┌──────────┐
│ James    │ │ Ralph    │ │ Walter   │ │ Harold Clark │ │ Beth     │
│ Randall  │ │ Smouse   │ │ Sickles  │ │ Supportive   │ │ Shields  │
│ Admin.   │ │ Vocational│ │Instruction│ │ Services    │ │ Personnel│
└──────────┘ └────┬─────┘ └──────────┘ └──────────────┘ └────┬─────┘
                  │                                          │
          ┌───────┴────────┐                          ┌──────┴──────┐
          │ Don Cammaratta │                          │ David Binnie│
          │ (One of Four)  │                          │   Director  │
          │   Directors    │                          └─────────────┘
          └───────┬────────┘
        ┌─────────┴─────────┐
  ┌───────────┐       ┌──────────────┐
  │ Bill Wieser│       │ Earl Lennard │
  │(One of Six)│       │(Another of six)│
  │Supervisors │       │  Supervisor  │
  └─────┬──────┘       └──────────────┘
        │
  ┌─────┴──────────────────┐
┌──────────────┐      ┌──────────────┐
│ Richard Hair │      │ Cathy Lakes  │
│ Coordinator  │      │  Secretary   │
└──────────────┘      └──────────────┘
```

vii

1
I GOTTA BE ME

"Hey Mom, I want to be a teacher like you were," I declared. During my last year of high school, I decided to be a teacher because of the influence of my mother. Over the years, I remember her talking about the enjoyment she had teaching fifth grade. Because of her rewarding experiences and being raised as a teacher's son, I guess my choice was a kind of "birth by education." I had the opportunity to take over the family flower farm, in the Garden State, but I turned it down, as did my older brother. He became a policeman.

After high school, I attended college in New York; however, after the first year, I lost some enthusiasm for higher education and lost direction in my life. I broke up with my girlfriend, dropped out of college, and went to work in the trades.

While working as a mechanic, I had the urge to vindicate my drop-out status to my family and myself. I had the dream to design and build a car from the ground up. It would be a hot-rod roadster with two Corvette engines. I planned to drive it on the street and race it at the drag strip, quite a status symbol in the early sixties. All my friends said it wouldn't work and my parents were apprehensive too. Well, it did work; it worked great; I have the trophies to prove it. The most valued trophy was not a statue, but the educational and technical challenge that I conquered in building and racing the car. Most of all, I had a reborn confidence in myself and a renewed desire to teach, specifically in the vocational field. Within five years, I had completed a B.S. degree in industrial arts at the University of Wisconsin—Stout. A year after that I received an M.A. in Industrial Education from the University of South Florida. It now was time to begin my teaching career.

In 1971, I got my first teaching assignment with Hillsborough County Public Schools in Tampa, Florida, the twelfth largest system in the nation. I taught a special vocational program for drop-out students at the Lake Magdalene

Juvenile Home. Since then, my other teaching experiences included the high school, community college and the university levels. Then, in 1988, while working with the Hillsborough County school system again, this time as a supervisor, my career took a turn for the worst. My dream of being an educator was dismantled; I was fired.

A year after I was fired, feeling worthless, depressed, and dejected, I spoke with an old friend who knew my predicament. He suggested that I write my experiences down; it might help me feel better. He added that if I was going to write a book about my experiences, I should do it while it's happening rather than after it's resolved. So, on June 14, 1989, Flag Day, a day celebrating the American experience under the Education President, still unemployed, my law suit against the school board for wrongful termination pending in the courts, I began to write.

JUNE 14, 1989. FLAG DAY.

I felt like I died: I had no job, no income, no self-worth, no self- esteem, no job security, no health coverage, and no get-up and go. I sold my new Chevy Blazer and motorcycle, as well as furniture, cellular phone, antiques, and tools in three garage sales. I didn't like myself.

I had lost my educational identity. I had no occupational title. When I'd meet new people and they asked "What do you do?," I didn't know what to say. I'd say, "I used to be an educator." Then, "What are you doing now?" And I'd say "Nothing." Their response: "Oh, it must be nice!" Then I'd say, "I am in between jobs," and the exchange would go on. It wasn't nice. It wasn't fun at all.

While writing about this identity crisis, I was reminded of a speech that I made to the Van Buren Junior High School, American Industrial Arts Student Association (AIASA), Florida Chapter 39, in 1981. The organization was installing officers at the first meeting of the school year. Over 100 dues-paying students were there. Most of them had just started their first year in a shop class in vocational education. I was asked by the club advisor, Bob Lawson, to give comments to the AIASA club from the county office. I congratulated all the eighth and ninth-grade students, boys and girls, on joining the club and for signing up to take a vocational course. I then asked if it was okay if they played a game with me for a moment.

I would name some people and the students would identify them. I told them they didn't have to raise their hands; they could shout out their answers. I said to them, "Ronald Reagan?" A few students raised their hands, but the majority said, "President!" After a pause, I said, "Mr. John Alfano?" They all said in unison, "Principal!" I said, "Johnny Bench," they said, "Baseball player!" "Mrs. Kay Mc Kinnis?" "Counselor!" "Mr. Bob Lawson?" "Our teacher!" Thanking them for helping me to play this game, I explained to them the results of their score. When I asked who these people were, they said: president, principal, ball player, counselor, teacher. I said to the students, "You identified these people by their jobs." I didn't tell them how to identify these people. Correct answers could also have been father/mother, husband/wife, citizen/resident/neighbor, hunter/fisherman, coin/stamp collector, or friend. I told those students that people are identified first by the jobs they have, just as they had identified those people that day. Then I worked backwards, explaining that the job(s) we will have in our life, most likely, will be based upon the education we have. Our education depends on what we do in classes each day and the rest of the year. Finally, I emphasized to them that they must decide who they wanted to be and work toward that goal.

This philosophy of education and job identity was given to me by my father when I was a teenager. And because I still regard it today, I have lost my identity. Since I am without employment, I am also without health insurance. It has been years since I have needed to see a doctor. I haven't been to a dentist in over five years, but now a filling falls out and he tells me that other teeth need treatment. I need new glasses. No insurance for this either since I'm not employed. I can't afford insurance now. When you have the insurance, you don't need it. When you don't have it, everything goes wrong. I sure hope I don't end up in the hospital because of an accident!

During National Education Week, I got the urge to buy a computer to write this book. I looked at several types, and I liked the Apple. I had heard previously that teachers received big discounts. I picked up an Apple Educator Buy order form at my local dealer, and the salesman asked me if I was a teacher. I said that I was a supervisor with the school system, but not really now. He said that I needed to certify that I was a full-time employee; I would need an authorized signature. A teacher friend of mine offered to order the computer for me under his name; then, I would pay him. I considered it, said no, and thanked him for his thoughtfulness. I was not employed by the school system, but I expected to return to my job sometime. I considered myself an educator, but it was meaningless.

I was depressed; I was sad; I felt like crying. I was trying to cope with the events in my life and the actions taken by Hillsborough County schools over the last three years. I was making an attempt to adjust to the necessary changes in life style. It's not easy. It's not something that I expected to be doing.

I had often felt lethargic and slept late because I stayed up late thinking about what had happened. I felt like a mannequin in a store window: he looks like he is doing something, but in fact he is doing nothing at all. We're dressed up on the outside with nothing on the inside.

I know of one solution: I have played the Florida Lottery as a means to dream away the struggle that I am going through. The jackpot is always in the millions. It is fun talking about what I would do if I won. Believing that you can win is part of the fantasy relief. I don't play every week, but a dollar ticket buys better daydreams than the ones I have at night.

My family and close friends have stood by me during these distressful times. They can't solve the problems in education, but they lend their ears and provide hope for the future. I am in debt to them. It's easy to count my blessings. With all that has happened, I only have a ramble-scramble vision into my occupational future.

I wonder if I will win my law suit and get my job back. I contemplate what I should do if I do win. What do I do now? Must I plan for an alternative career? I'm not getting encouraging results from the job resumés I'm sending out. My experiences in educational administration have left a bad taste in my mouth. I still hope to stay in my chosen field and contribute to the education of the youth. I care about students.

I thought about a longtime dream to open a restaurant. I had a special atmosphere planned, and I consider myself a good cook. Woodworking is also my forté. I could go into specialized wood craft or wood carving. I had worked for my uncle in his sign shop and always thought that I could go into my own sign business. Maybe I could specialize in hand-carved wooden signs for golf courses or restaurants? There I am, back to restaurants again. Maybe I should make my own sign and go into the restaurant business! I enjoy fishing and often considered going into the charter boat business in the Florida Keys. You need to enjoy what you do for a living. I know that I could always return to the classroom because I loved teaching and really missed it. Then again I could move to the Keys, teach school, and do charter boat trips on the weekends and during the summer. Then I could hire students to work as the mates on my boat. However, I would have to start with a small boat. My brother buys old houses and fixes them up for resale. I could offer to go into business with him; I have experience in home repair. I knew I could successfully perform in these occupations, but the transition would be difficult and uncertain.

Additionally, I thought about being a screenplay writer. I took a night course in creative writing to see what it would be like. I wrote a short story and submitted it for critiquing by the class. I thought the story was good. The class didn't. It was devastating! I questioned if the writing field and I had any overlapping qualities. I was still looking for a career shift with a purpose. I needed some form of therapy to cut this albatross from my neck. However, I still had the desire to work or contribute to my career in education. I still needed a sense of achievement or recognition.

I joined a writing club and continued to learn about communicating. Slowly, I became sure that writing could fill my void. My confidence in writing improved. Then, one day, I just said that I was going to write a book. This book was to become my form of therapy to tell my story and to contribute something to the field of education without the benefit of a professional outlet. My only outlet was to be my self-expression in book form.

Here was my catharsis, a regurgitation of the experiences that were not digestible. I became aware that, in writing the book, I would relive every moment of grief without the assistance of any anesthetic. The rote pain could only be endured by the release of my emotions into a script format for all to see.

No more "back to the drawing board." I have a purpose, a purpose greater than myself. This is my therapy route. Bad air out—good air in. I now will set my albatross free and contribute this true story to the field of education. May we both be better for it!

2

ALL AMERICAN CITY

From the many 250 million American citizens, I am only one.
From the many 3½ million educators in America, I am only one.
From the many 13 million residents of Florida, I am only one.
From the many 825 thousand residents of Hillsborough County,
I am only one.
From the many 300 thousand residents of Tampa, I am only one.
From the many 22 thousand employees of
Hillsborough County Schools, I am only one.
From the two educators in my family, I am only one.
To many, I am one dedicated educator.
E Pluribus Unum.

The good old United States of America, relatively speaking, is a young country that has come a long way in today's world, proud and always willing to fight for what we believe is right. Americans have achieved freedom and shown an active vigil to maintain the land of the free and the home of the brave. The words "E Pluribus Unum" are inscribed on every piece of currency. From the many came the creation of one great nation out of thirteen colonies. "E Pluribus Unum" is on the Great Seal of the United States. All for one and one for all.

Florida is the fourth most populated state in the Union and is predicted to be third by the year 2000. Tourism is the number-one industry with sun and fun emphasized. Theme parks such as Walt Disney World, Sea World, Universal Studios, and Cypress Gardens attract millions each year. Agriculture is the second largest industry with citrus production as the leader.

Betty Castor is the 17th person to serve as Chief School Officer (now called the Commissioner of Education) of the State of Florida. She taught school in

Uganda, East Africa, and at Holmes Elementary School in Dade County. She served as a Hillsborough County Commissioner from 1972 to 1978. She was President of the League of Women Voters 1969 to 1970. She served as Director of Governmental Relations for the University of South Florida in Tampa from 1979-81. Commissioner Castor was named Outstanding Legislator of the Year by the Florida Education Association in 1977, 1983 and 1986. The Florida Association of School Administrators (FASA) and the Florida School Boards Association have awarded her their highest honor.

Hillsborough County can be described as a cross-sectional slice of the American apple pie. The sunny climate attracts tourists to Busch Gardens, the state's third largest theme park. Sport fans can enjoy the NFL Tampa Bay Buccaneers, Tampa Bay Rowdies soccer club, or the spring training of the Cincinatti Reds. Plus, the National Hockey League expansion team, the Tampa Bay Lightning faced off in 1992. In addition, the Tampa Bay Storm, World Champions in the new Arena Football League, started their second season in 1992. The annual Strawberry Festival, in Plant City, has topped the attendance of the Florida State Fair which is also held in Hillsborough County. The county has pride in its 130 parks and recreation areas, seven museums and the revitalized Lowry Park Zoo. Not only is Port of Tampa Florida's largest; it is the seventh largest in the nation. The Tampa Museum of Art and a state-of-the-art Performing Arts Center demonstrate the cultural aspects of the county.

You can light up a good hand-rolled cigar, sip a cup of Cuban coffee, and savor the authentic atmosphere of historic Ybor City in Tampa, the "Cigar City." Que' Pasa? However, a study reported in the November, 1988 issue of *Psychology Today*, which rated stressful conditions in American cities, gave the Tampa-St. Petersburg-Clearwater area a rating of 268; New York received a 267. The rating which indicated the most stressful condition was 286.

Tampa, the largest city in Hillsborough County, was host to Super Bowl XVIII and then the silver anniversary Super Bowl XXV in 1991. Chamber of Commerce had adopted a slogan to help build economic development: "Tampa, America's next great city." The city is proud of its new Tampa Convention Center and renewed downtown area. If you have ever flown into Tampa, you surely understand why we are so proud our state-of-the-art international airport.

In 1990, the National Civic League gave Tampa its "All American City" award. Tampa was one of ten cities awarded out of 113 nominated. One of Tampa's celebrated residents is General H. Norman Schwarzkopf of MacDill Air Force Base, command operations center for operation Desert Storm. The

University of South Florida, University of Tampa, Florida College, and Hillsborough Community College are the institutions of higher learning.

Tampa was chosen as the Gold Medal Celebration Send-Off city for our athletes in the 1992 Summer Olympic Games in Barcelona, Spain. Compliments to Busch Gardens (Anheuser-Busch Entertainment) and Tampa resident George Steinbrenner, vice president of the U.S. Olympic Committee, for their efforts to bring the official send-off to Tampa. General Norman Schwarzkopf gave a pep-talk and the command for the athletes to depart.

Tampa houses the district offices of the Hillsborough County School Board, which provides public education services: early childhood education, kindergarten, elementary, secondary, adult, vocational, exceptional, and alternative education programs. The Board is comprised of seven elected members and an appointed Superintendent of Schools. The system has 150 schools and a total enrollment of more than 162,000 students. It is the twelfth largest school system out of 15,000 in the nation. It employs 22,000 people including 8,100 full-time teachers. The budget for the 1991–92 school year was $940,000,000. In 1987, Superintendent Raymond Orris Shelton was identified as one of the 100 "best and brightest school executives" in North America by the National School Boards Association.

The Hillsborough County Schools received national attention in 1988 when a Federal Judge, Elizabeth Kovachevich, ordered that Eliana Martinez, a 6-year-old mentally handicapped child with AIDS, be placed in a special classroom chamber. The national news media called it a "glass cage." The school board had refused to allow the child to attend school and the federal suit followed.

On June 24, 1987, an editorial in *The Tampa Tribune* argued that the Hillsborough County School System needed a "credibility check." The paper reviewed 20 years of the Superintendent's performance and then reported some criticism of the state auditors about financial practices. Even though the *Tribune* was careful to note that more information was needed to examine the criticism and determine its accuracy, the editorial concluded:

> Even the best public servants, even the sharpest executives, reach a plateau in performance. Perhaps the longevity of Shelton's tenure has tempered his zeal to keep tabs on the nitty-gritty of the school district's operations. Or perhaps—as we have suggested before—he needs to revise his longtime philosophy of implicitly trusting his lieutenants until provided with irrefutable proof that they have erred.
>
> Whatever the problem, there needs to be a solution. And the buck stops with School Board members, the elected guardians of our tax money. It is up to

them to see that local public schools not only educate our youngsters but also adhere to the law and to sound financial practices.

Shouldn't our "elected guardians" communicate with each other? Can issues be "hidden" in a School Board agenda which pass by the Board members or the public? If the Board is the one ultimately responsible to the community, then shouldn't all of its members know all the details about the superintendent's practices?

Elected officials have a fiduciary responsibility to their constituency. The least they could do to honor it is to stay informed. That's the American way.

Tampa has so much going for it: tourist attractions, four professional sports teams, two universities, an international airport, an Air Force Base, many museums, and an unparalleled atmosphere for fun in the sun. It is, in so many ways, at the heart of America.

3
A CRASH COURSE IN ETHICS

For now, I need to provide a short crash course review of "Ethics 101" for this book to have meaning, direction, and afterthought.

We don't have to look far to remember the Senate Ethics Committee hearings on the so-called Keating Five, nor does it take long to recall Ivan Boesky's involvement in Wall Street trading. Let me also recall Watergate back in 1972 or the Iran-Contra scandal in 1987. Let me also note the number of times our government purchased a $165.00 tool such as a "rotational fastener controller," which in reality turned out to be a $3.00 screwdriver. And for heaven's sake, let's say a short prayer for ex-PTL minister Jim Bakker. This brief list causes us to recall our impressions about these people's ethics. We look at the behavior we expected from them and compare it to what we would expect of ourselves, if we had been in their shoes. And after our judgement of their ethics—or actually our own ethics—we go on with our lives. Sometimes these examples change our ethical behavior, and sometimes they don't. In addition to these national examples, all of us can name some state and local examples of questionable ethical conduct.

We don't have a national educational system because, according to our Constitution, each state is left with the responsibility to educate its residents. Therefore, each state develops its own code of ethics or just has none at all. The Florida Department of Education has a Code of Ethics for The Education Profession, which includes a three-part code of ethics and a five-part principles of professional conduct.

I'm going to crank the microscope down one more notch to look at the local school system, which is really made up of individual people, with individual names, performing individual jobs. Put all together, we call it a system which has the purpose of providing meaningful education to our community. These individual people who make up our school systems have different personal and

A CRASH COURSE IN ETHICS 11

professional ethics. To corral these ethics into a cohesive operating system, local school systems rely on the ethical character of each employee *along with* input from state guidelines and professional education associations, such as one of the largest and oldest in the nation, the American Association of School Administrators.

In 1991, I received an information packet from the AASA, headquartered in Arlington, Virginia, which, in part, read:

> The American Association of School Administrators (AASA) is the professional organization for top-level educational leaders from across the United States, Canada, and other nations. Current membership is nearly 19,000. Founded in 1865, AASA cultivates a climate in which quality education will thrive. The association works to ensure the development of highly qualified leaders to support excellence in educational administration, promotes activities focusing on leadership for learning, and initiates and supports legislation, policies, research, and practices that will improve education. Through AASA, members distinguish themselves as leaders who care deeply about education.

In addition to a variety of timely publications to keep the membership informed and current, AASA has published books relevant to educational administration. In 1985, the AASA published a book titled *Ethics—A Course of Study for Educational Leaders*, developed by Ralph B. Kimbrough. Their "textbook" is used as the main reference in the review of "Ethics 101" which is pertinent to the meaning of my story. The Foreword of this book states, in part:

> From the beginning this has been a cooperative endeavor of the American Association of School Administrators (AASA), the University Council for Educational Administration (UCEA), and the University of Florida. Subsequent discussions resulted in formal approval for this publication by the AASA Ethics Committee and the AASA Executive Committee...AASA believes firmly that ethical behavior is an important part of the administration profession. Actually, ethics marks the cornerstone of many professions. For that reason, AASA published a Code of Ethics, originally in 1966, with a revision in 1976...and the Association continues to encourage its members to follow such precepts in their professional capacity....

The "Introduction" of this book examines the true nature of ethics:

> To many, the mention of ethics may conjure up acts of immorality that sometimes include sex or money, but acts of immorality frequently mask

underlying sins. In commenting on a television movie, *The Thornbirds,* a Catholic bishop observed that, wrong indeed as the main character's sexual behavior was, his most serious act of immorality may have been his selfish, opportunistic pursuit of power and authority regardless of the feelings and welfare of those in relationships with him.

As you can see by this quotation, ethical breeches are sometimes more subtle than they seem. On the surface, actions may be perceived as unethical; more fundamentally unethical, however, are the motives that give rise to those actions. Apparently no one, not even those in the noble profession of teaching, is immune to questionable ethics. Unfortunately, bad apples exist and have the power to spoil bushels.

If administrators are going to effectively cope with all the problems in education, there should be some type of training on how administrators ought to conduct themselves. The AASA book says:

> School administrators who have an insufficient sense of right or wrong may be dangerous both to themselves and to others as well. Moreover, achieving a binding code of ethics marked by altruistic, public service overtones is essential to a truly professional status. Initiating formal preservice training and inservice training programs in administrative ethics is an important step in this direction. Moreover, formal training in administrative ethics would better prepare school administrators to cope with the difficult leadership problems faced on a daily basis. (46)

Perhaps predicting the corrupting potential of power, the AASA calls for a strict adherence to an ethical code:

> Administrative ethics includes the broad perspective of legal obligations. Administrators are obligated to see that the law is followed, that local board policies are carried out, and that state board rules and regulations are observed. This also includes a responsibility to observe organizational rules. For members of AASA there is the obligation to live up to the AASA Code of Ethics.

My crash course in ethics wouldn't be complete without quoting some authority's code of ethics. I have included the entire AASA Code of Ethics and the Florida Code of Ethics for the Educational Professions in the Appendix. The majority of the ethical standards will directly relate to my story, but I will highlight the following now:

A CRASH COURSE IN ETHICS

AASA Code

[Administrators] Makes the well-being of students the fundamental value of all decision making and actions.

Fulfills professional responsibilities with honesty and integrity.

Supports the principle of due process and protects the civil and human rights of all individuals.

Implements the governing board of education's policies and administrative rules and regulations.

Florida Code

[Educators] Shall not intentionally make false or malicious statements about a colleague.

Shall not use coercive means or promise special treatment to influence professional judgement of colleagues.

Shall seek no reprisal against any individual who has reported a violation of Florida School Code or State Board of Education Rules.

The AASA book of ethics cites several committees and expresses appreciation to those who contributed to the book. "Members and corresponding members of the AASA Ethics Committee reviewed the manuscript and made valuable suggestions." The first committee to be acknowledged was the current (1985) AASA Ethics Committee. One AASA Ethics Committee member had the role of Executive Committee Liaison, and he was Raymond O. Shelton, Superintendent, Hillsborough County Public Schools, Tampa, Florida. In 1989, Dr. Shelton became the President of the American Association of School Administrators. I can't say that Superintendent Shelton "wrote the book" on administrative ethics, but I can say he did participate in its development. Dr. Shelton was obviously aware of AASA ethical standards before my story started to unfold.

This crash course in "Ethics 101" is complete. It will help to give direction and afterthought to this book. After reading this book, it may be prudent to reevaluate the title of this chapter as "we are on a crash course with educational ethics in America."

4
IT'S NOT *WHAT* YOU KNOW...

I had taught industrial arts for several years in Hillsborough County schools before I was promoted out of the classroom and into the position of County Coordinator of Industrial Arts and Industrial Education back in 1979. I had received the highest score in the interview and I was recommended for the promotion by Dr. Don Cammaratta, General Director of Vocational Education. I had never met Cammaratta before the interview.

The Coordinator's position is subordinate to the Supervisor of Industrial Arts and Industrial Education and, therefore, is considered a "training position" for promotion to the supervisory level. During my first two years as his "assistant," B.H. Blankenbecler, Supervisor of Industrial Arts and Industrial Education, had spoken about taking retirement. Five years later, he had no intentions to retire, and I felt my career was due for a promotion. I accepted a position as principal in Pasco County which is contiguous to Hillsborough County.

In 1985, I was in my second year in Pasco at a new, but small, vocational center with only nine teachers. Back in Hillsborough County, Blankenbecler, with 38 years of service, suddenly and unexpectedly retired. He always told me about the ideal time to retire; it was the last day of December, because you would get paid for all your vacation time accrued during the present year and you could arrange for your accumulated sick time pay-off for next month in January—a new tax year. Many long-term administrators had several hundred sick days accumulated, which almost equaled a full year's salary pay-off. For some reason, Blankenbecler chose to retire in the middle of the summer. The vacant position created by his departure in Hillsborough was enticing for several reasons: it would give me a chance to return to a system that I had previously worked in for eight years; it paid $1,000 more than I was earning as principal in Pasco; and since I lived in Hillsborough and commuted to Pasco, it would be much more convenient.

The Hillsborough school system was much larger than Pasco's and, therefore, potential for future promotion was high. I had left Hillsborough County under good terms; I now felt this was an excellent opportunity to come back "home" to Hillsborough because I saw that my future in vocational education was here.

I submitted my application and I was ready for the county screening process, which included 30 minutes of inquiry for each of the four applicants by a committee of seven administrators and teachers combined. Each applicant would be evaluated on a scale of forty points maximum with a minimum of thirty points to pass. After the scores were totaled, the committee was dismissed and the decision to recommend an applicant came from the "higher ups" in the vocational division. My name was recommended to and approved by the School Board for the position of supervisor in October of 1985. Dr. Cammaratta became my immediate boss.

Shortly thereafter, I told Dr. Cammaratta about a welcome letter sent to my home by Ralph Smouse Jr., Assistant Superintendent for Vocational, Technical and Adult Education. Smouse was Cammaratta's immediate boss. They were in the opposite positions ten years ago when the superintendent transferred them into the positions they currently held at that time. In the letter, Smouse welcomed me back to the vocational family in Hillsborough County and indicated that he was pleased to have me on board and looked forward to a long and productive working relationship. While I was pleased at receiving the letter, a couple of the things Smouse wrote concerned me: "Look and act like a professional," and "Form a steering committee of teachers, administrators, industry and labor people." I expressed concern to Cammaratta about these directives since I had worked in that office for five years. Didn't Smouse think I knew how to do the job? Why was I being asked to do things that the other vocational supervisors were not asked to do? Dr. Cammaratta tried to explain that I needed to understand that I was not Smouse's choice for the job. He said Smouse had just lost a battle and that I should not worry about it, that I should do the job that I was hired to do and also do the extra things that Smouse asked. I accepted what he said, but I knew things weren't right.

During my first year on the job, Smouse didn't show any appreciation of me, and for the job I was doing. I tried to stay out of his way. Then, at the end of my first year, Smouse started to make serious accusations about my job performance.

Concerned about these actions, I asked Cammaratta to tell me more about what happened when I was appointed as supervisor. He said that after the screening, he and Smouse met in Smouse's office downtown. Cammaratta recommended me because I had five years experience as a coordinator as well as experience as an administrator (principal), and because I received the highest score during the screening. Smouse disagreed and wanted Richard Hair. Hair took my place as coordinator when I left two years ago. Neither man would budge. But, apparently, Hair was not squeaky clean. And when Cammaratta made Smouse aware of some concerns he had about Hair while on the job, Smouse blinked; he would check on them right away.

Smouse tried to degrade me and put Cammaratta on the spot by asking "so what did Wieser do as coordinator for five years?" That was an elusive question because, as coordinator, I did what ever the supervisor told me to do. The credit for achievement in that office goes to the supervisor, not the subordinate coordinator. I did a good job as coordinator and my yearly evaluations proved it. Smouse himself had written numerous letters of congratulations and compliments to me, as did others, because of my "contributions to our vocational division" during my tenure as coordinator. Now, he could not recall any of these. When I left Hillsborough County in 1984, my personnel file contained a collection of letters written to compliment my job performance. These letters somehow disappeared.

A few days later, Smouse called Cammaratta back for another meeting. Smouse said they would go downstairs and discuss the matter with his boss, Superintendent Shelton. Cammaratta related his rationale to Shelton. Smouse had checked on the veracity of Cammaratta's statements of concerns about Hair and found them to be true. The superintendent agreed with Cammaratta that I should be recommended for approval.

I knew that it must have been a big embarrassment for Smouse to have to pull Hair's name from the school board agenda after it had already been sent for preview by the board.

Little did I know, the battle was over, but the war had just begun.

5
PROGRAM ASSESSMENT

It was October, 1985; I was the new supervisor and I was excited to finally have the opportunity to apply my style of supervision to the industrial programs throughout the county. I dreamed of this day during the five years while I was coordinator.

The first thing I did was to visit most of the schools and re-introduce myself to the principals that I had worked with before and introduce myself to the several new principals that were promoted in the last two years. I did receive a warm reception at all of the schools. The principals liked my direct approach and said they were glad to see me avail myself to them—an approach which established immediate and positive communication between my office and the schools and enabled me to assess each program and renew teacher contacts. I was confident that I would be an asset to the vocational programs.

My rounds of the schools and programs gave me immediate and factual information, and identified potential programs that might not meet state program standards. From my previous experience in the county, I had a general idea that some programs would need help; however, little did I know that I would be overwhelmed by calls from principals for help with their industrial programs. My immediate job activities were outlined by these school needs, to name only a few:

> Ms. Janelle Wade, Principal at Greco Junior High, called me to visit the shop because she felt the teacher was unsafe. I visited the shop and saw there was gross lack of classroom management, no structured curriculum, and equipment that was in need of repair. The shop was messy, and safety was ignored.

> Mr. Rodney Osborne, Principal at Dowdell Junior High, called me for help because his teacher was teaching unsafely. Osborne had to shut off the main

power switch because students were in danger of injury. Minor accidents had already occurred. Shop housekeeping was by-passed.

Mr. Ed Ballas, Principal at Jefferson High School, called me because of his concern for the automotive mechanics curriculum. The teacher had a welding project (a big trailer) in the auto shop which should have been constructed as a project in the welding shop. Ballas was also concerned about the morale of the instructor. The instructor complained that no air conditioned classroom was provided as reported in the SACS (Southern Association of Colleges and Schools) five-year study.

Principal John Alfano called me to help out with a shop in disarray at McLane Junior High. The shop was very sloppy and in need of painting. Much of the equipment was old and broken. Electrical hand tools needed repair. The previous teacher commented about the equipment, in a newspaper article, and said "all that stuff there...was junk."

Later, Frank Scaglione, principal at King High School, requested my assistance in upgrading and improving the metals lab. His letter indicated that he felt "the lab had been woefully neglected in the past, a fact which was further emphasized by the new instructor" he had hired to teach Metals.

In addition to principals' requests such as these, I accumulated an overview of the program needs during my rounds. Some of the main findings I discovered were as follows:

Two months after I was on the job, several industrial programs were due for a State Department of Education program review. Two of these programs failed the review and were labeled "out of compliance," reducing the funding on these two automotive programs. Later that year, these programs were closed and teachers laid off.

Even though the Superintendent frequently boasted that all county classrooms were air conditioned, many industrial classrooms—auto mechanics, printing, metals, and carpentry—were not, even though much of the high-tech electronic equipment required in today's vocational classes requires proper climate control to avoid damage.

Many shops had old and broken equipment sitting around which needed to be transferred or disposed of. This accumulation of old equipment created a "junk yard" image for some programs and unsafely cluttered the work space.

PROGRAM ASSESSMENT

Several graphics arts programs did not have required dark rooms to accommodate the photography part of the curriculum.

The required county semester exams were incomplete. A typical year-long program was divided into two parts for the exam, but an outline was not provided as to how it should be divided. For example, an auto mechanics teacher might teach transmissions and brakes during semester one, but the exam would cover tune-up and alignment. The teacher had no idea what subjects would be on the exams.

No one had applied for federal funding to support the annual Vocational Industrial Clubs of America student competition that year in Tampa. The previous supervisor should have applied for these federal funds the year before when Hillsborough County Schools volunteered to host the student competition. I had to apply for these funds in a last-minute undertaking.

Generally, I saw that equipment at the Erwin Center was most complete, while other schools, like Tampa Bay Tech had less, and the other high schools had still less.

In concluding my assessment, I saw that many industrial programs didn't meet state standards in reference to facilities, equipment, and curriculum. Substantial funding was necessary to purchase needed equipment so that curriculum could be met.

As a courtesy after my assessment, I wrote a progress report to Smouse and Cammaratta after I had been on the job for three months. My memo summarized my activities and specifically responded to the directives outlined in Smouse's letter of October 2, 1985. I expressed that I was grateful to have been hired and gave a summary report of my program assessment findings. I told Smouse that I had formed a Steering Committee as he had instructed and requested his approval of the membership list. Furthermore, I spoke about other activities such as developing inservice programs with the University of South Florida, being a support team member for two teachers in the Beginning Teacher Program, a "PRO" resource leader for a teacher participating in the Florida Adult Extern Program and becoming an Advisory Committee member for our Vending Machine Repair program.

My work load rapidly became more demanding than that of any other vocational supervisor. Before I became supervisor, the course listing for the industrial department was listed on four pages. However, greater curriculum definition and computer listings in Tallahassee required more extensive computer reporting. As a demonstration to compare program course listings and to show the diversity of my industrial department to Smouse, I simply listed the number of new computer pages which were developed and monitored.

Computerized Course Listings 1986–87 Program

Program	Number of Pages
Marketing	1.0
Health	2.0
Home Economics	2.0
Business	2.5
Agriculture	3.5
Industrial	**11.0**

It was board policy that semester exams be developed for each course. Each of the 176 industrial courses was to have its own exam. The exams were given twice each semester, a mid-term and a final; therefore, four exams were required each year for each individual course. My volume of work in preparing and developing course examinations was overwhelming when compared to the workload of other supervisors for the same task.

Because the majority of the industrial education instructors were hired directly out of industry for their technical skills and therefore were not required to have a teaching degree, special attention had to be given to these non-degree instructors in reference to inservice teacher training and classroom management. Extra work.

Another way to show the work load in the supervisors office is through the number of "Full Time Equivalency" (FTE) students enrolled in the different vocational programs. The Annual Report for 1986-87, of the Vocational Education Division, shows a total of 9,253 FTE's earned in vocational education in grades 7 to Adult. Of these, the largest FTE earned was 2,396 in the Industrial area. The next largest area was 2,026 FTE in Business with the other programs having less.

Since it was economically feasible to maintain a warehouse full of the most common teaching supplies used by the variety of industrial teachers, one unique responsibility of my office was stocking the county warehouse with industrial classroom supplies. My office would solicit three vendors for prices and then purchase the lowest priced supply at a quantity discount. The savings were passed on to the classroom teacher. It was a good concept, but it did require additional responsibilities in my office.

The summer session was always a time when the number of programs offered is reduced because vocational education courses are optional for secondary school students. The number of teachers in summer school programs can also imply supervisory work load. In the 1986 summer school session, the following number of teachers were reported in vocational teaching positions; Industrial 44, Business 21, Marketing/Work Experience 20, Home Economics 11, and Health Occupations 0. The Agriculture programs (about 40) by state law are all twelve month positions and, therefore, these teachers are employed year round. Compared to other supervisors, my office had the most active programs during the summer extended-year session.

More so than any other supervisor, my major responsibility was shop safety. No other vocational programs had the potential of student or teacher accidents as did shop programs. Classroom safety was consistently a number-one priority of my office.

After assessing the program's strengths and many weaknesses, I realized that, to do a complete job, I needed some help. I was inundated with continuous requests for program services which already required me to work beyond the normal workday. Therefore, I requested additional full time staff (a coordinator) to remedy the concerns found in my assessment, a request—I found out later—which had been made every year for the past nine years. We needed additional supervisory assistance for this diverse industrial office, even though we were attempting (and having some success) to perform well even under these conditions. My request was ignored.

6

LESSON NUMBER ONE

As an educator, I teach lessons and I learn them too. We don't always realize it at the time, but some days, months or even years later something happens to remind us about what we have learned and how we learned it.

My first contact with Ralph Smouse was in 1979, long before I attained the position of Supervisor. I had been a classroom teacher at Brandon High School, and I was just promoted to the position of County Coordinator of Industrial Arts and Industrial Education in August under the supervision of B. H. Blankenbecler, Supervisor. Blankenbecler reported to Cammaratta, who was immediate supervisor of the six vocational program supervisors. In September, at one of Cammaratta's bi-weekly staff meetings, Smouse spoke to the group of supervisors and coordinators about an update on the building of the new Erwin Vo-Tech Center, an old Sears Roebuck building the school system had purchased and was renovating into a vo-tech center. Smouse told a funny story about a horrid smell somewhere up on the second floor. He said that they just found out what that rotten smell was. In a humorous way, he stated that they tore apart a wall and found a dead animal, so badly decomposed that they couldn't even tell if it was a dead pigeon or a dead cat, and he laughed and so did everyone else. As the laughing began to cease, I said that they should have counted the legs; if they got to three, they might as well stop counting. And everyone laughed harder and longer. Everyone except Smouse. I didn't really pay attention to Smouse because my intent wasn't to insult him, and I'm not sure that I did. My upstaging Smouse seemed to get me off on a wrong foot. Today, I look back and speculate that this could have been my first lesson in educational administration.

Lesson Number One: In a meeting, don't tell a joke that is funnier than your boss's boss's boss's joke.

LESSON NUMBER ONE

In 1979, I brought a coffee cake into one of Cammaratta's bi-weekly staff meetings. I heard that the meetings started at 8:30 a.m. and lasted about four hours without a break. At the end of the meeting, Cammaratta said, in a serious but humorous way, the rule is that the newest staff member brings in coffee cake for one year. And all the other staff members agreed and I acquiesced, bringing cake faithfully each and every meeting.

When I was selected to go to a national conference in California to represent the group, I knew the staff would miss my refreshments. The next week's meeting was in the east county office of the agriculture supervisor, Earl Lennard. I knew they would have some special refreshments for the staff, but I didn't want the group to think that I was neglecting my duty. I bought an Entenmann's gourmet coffee crumb cake. I opened the back of the white and blue box with a razor blade and replaced the soft, moist cake with a wooden block replete with real crumbs and chocolate swirl icing to make it look authentic. It looked delicious. I glued the box back together and gave it to RoseAnne Bowers, business supervisor, and told her to take it to the staff meeting because I wanted the staff to be *sure* to think of me while I was gone.

When I returned, I waited a few days and no one said anything about my fake cake or the staff meeting. Then there was a knock on the door. I was told by the receptionist that a lady was there from a church and she wanted her money back for a cake. Cammaratta escorted me to the reception area. He said that they had too many home made refreshments at the meeting, so Earl Lennard donated my cake to his church bazaar. The lady who bought it was here asking for her money back. I became concerned and asked how much did she pay? Then everyone laughed because they pulled one over on me. I laughed. I found out later that RoseAnne Bowers had put the cake in her refrigerator for two days prior to the meeting. On the way to the meeting, she held it on her lap so it wouldn't fall. When she found out the truth, she laughed the hardest.

The next month was my birthday. Three guesses what I got from the staff. We all got plenty of mileage out of that fake cake. Let me note, that we all did our jobs first and *then* found time to enjoy our cooperative working relationships.

Some time later, Cammaratta was directed, by Smouse, to meet with me. I was told indirectly that Smouse didn't like my humor. I think he was jealous.

Lesson Number Two: Humor can be an effective management catalyst to bring a group together. However, someone might disagree.

In the fall, I was made chairman of the office social committee. I planned our Thanksgiving office luncheon. A sign-up sheet gave everyone a job to do or food to bring in. I cooked the turkey at home and carved it at the office. We had food left over for several days in the office refrigerator. That was the good news. The bad news was that the committee that I worked with felt, as I did, that we should not invite Smouse to our social activities because we would have alienated others in the vocational division that would not be invited simply because we didn't have enough room to accommodate everyone. We wanted to keep it small, within our own group of supervisors. Smouse's office was in another building several miles away, and we all felt that if he wanted a party for the vocational division, his office staff should plan it. Cammaratta was one of four directors under Smouse's supervision. I think "downtown" felt we were discriminating against them. Since I was chairman of the committee in Cammaratta's department, I took the brunt of it.

As social chairman, I continued to provide entertainment for the staff. We all talked about time away from the office when we could visit without the pressures of the job. We had weekend beach parties, picnics at state parks, runners in the Gasparilla 5K race, Christmas parties and dinner socials. Our first dinner social, at the home of Richard Powell, Supervisor of Marketing, included a surf and turf dinner with a "show and tell" time when supervisors shared something from their personal lives: hobby, craft, sport, or card trick. At our first Christmas party, at the Old Swiss House at world-famous Busch Gardens, I got decked out in my Santa Claus outfit and made a special presentation to the supervisors. As Santa Claus, I looked back into the "letters to Santa" files and found old letters from the supervisors when they were little children. Of course, each letter had the characteristics of the individual supervisor in his/her current job expertise. I read them aloud and we all laughed. It was a time when we could let down our guard and enjoy the evening. People talked about that party for a long time. We were working as a successful group. We were almost "family."

Lesson Number Three: Don't forget to invite your boss's boss's boss to all parties, no matter what.

The following year, 1980, Cammaratta and his staff moved into the new offices in the new Erwin Vo-Tech Center. We were experiencing daily parking problems in our reserved lot. We didn't get much help from the administration at the vo-tech center. The vo-tech director was considered a close friend of Smouse and some even said that he was advising Smouse. The problem of students and visitors parking in the reserved supervisor's lot continued. The supervisors/coordinators were required to leave and return often each day on their visits to various schools, and were frequently carrying curriculum, supplies, books and other materials to and from the cars. Proximate parking was relished.

After getting approval from Cammaratta, I went to work one weekend in November and painted "reserved" on the numbered parking spaces for Cammaratta's staff, which helped for a little while. However, the daily parking problem reappeared, and was starting to affect the temper of the staff. One day I was in the parking lot putting mock parking tickets on unauthorized cars when Smouse drove up, parked in a supervisor's reserved numbered space, and asked, "Who gave you the authority to do this?" When I told him that I was just trying to do my job, he ignored my explanation and demanded again, "Who gave you the authority to do this?" Concerned that Cammaratta would suffer from this fallout, I took full responsibility for the parking ticket caper. He then told me to get back to doing something useful. Because of insignificant happenings like this confrontation with him in the parking lot, I believed that my political standing with him had already been blueprinted.

Lesson Number Four: Don't "stand up" to the boss's boss's boss.

However, my efforts did not go overlooked by the supervisors and Cammaratta. For my birthday, a few months later, they gave me a plastic police badge, handcuffs and a certificate. The certificate read:

Be it resolved that

WILD BILL WIESER
after issuing the minimum required parking
tickets has attained the notable degree of
DOCTORATE OF PARKING ENGINEERING

They all thanked me for my bold efforts to try to solve everyone's parking problem. The Erwin Center soon had a full-time security guard making rounds in the parking lot. Tough times brought the staff together. Cammaratta's staff was a strong cooperating team with a common sense of purpose. Smouse was envious.

I never could nail down the whys and what-fors of the erosion process between Smouse and myself to any one substantial event. I wonder if it was simply the "political temperament" that I happened to come upon. It probably was a combination of the political temperament and Lesson Number One, Lesson Number Two, Lesson Number Three, and Lesson Number Four.

Why does educational administration have to be so difficult, especially when personalities and the pursuit of power and authority take precedence over educational ethics and philosophy? What rules of administration, if any, did Smouse or I break? Did Smouse react to a situation that he should have reasoned with? Regardless, programs and students suffer when administrators decide to bicker rather than administer.

7

THE CRYPTIC MEMO

Several supervisors had requested an additional coordinator's position for their individual department, including myself. However, in January of 1986, Cammaratta received approval to hire an additional coordinator for his department who would work with the vocational student organizations in all six of the supervisor's areas and on the Division's five-year vocational plan. He wanted this person to be housed in the office next to his. However, because of the usual demand for office space, the Health Occupations Coordinator, Joy Henderson, was already in that office. The question then became where do we move Henderson. One option that was considered was using Steve Cannella's office for Henderson and her secretary and moving Cannella downtown. Cannella's office was between the Supervisor of Health Occupations, Dr. June Saltzgaver's, and mine. Cannella's position as Statistical Supervisor was the only vocational supervisor position not under Cammaratta's supervision and evaluation. He was under the supervision of Mr. Richard Roland, Director of Student Services, whose office was in the downtown administration building, next to Smouse's office in a four-office pod. The other two offices were vacant and it seemed logical that Cannella be downtown because he covered all vocational programs and he worked closely with Roland and Smouse.

If Cannella moved downtown, Henderson could be moved in an office adjacent to her immediate supervisor in health occupations and Cannella would be next to his immediate supervisor, Roland. Thus transferring Henderson into Cannella's office was not only logical, but also convenient for logistics and communication. But Cannella didn't wanted to give up any space, nor did he want to move downtown next to his boss. Of course, no other supervisor wanted to give up any space either.

Guess who saved the day: nice guy Bill Wieser. My industrial office had an empty desk because there were distant plans to expand this office and add another coordinator because of the work load. To solve the problem, I offered to give up some space. My office space consisted of three rooms: the main room with three desks; a reception area with a secretary's desk and a small storage room. My secretary moved into the room where my coordinator and I were, and I gave my reception area to Henderson and her secretary, (a loss of about 30% of my space.) With the three of us now in one common room—unlike any other supervisor's office, privacy was non-existent. Phone and all other conversations were noisy and easily overheard by both health and industrial people. Outside visitors were greeted by my secretary in the same room where I worked, allowing them to overhear my conferences or phone conversations while they were waiting to meet with me. We were over-crowded and were not operating under the best office management conditions. However, by giving up some space, I solved a problem that was facing all of us and I was glad that I could help out. I made the best out of the new situation.

Then, in March, 1986, Cammaratta asked Saltzgaver and myself to meet with him in his office. He indicated that he had received a letter from Smouse concerning a memo from Steve Cannella in which Smouse articulated concerns that Cannella had about us. Cammaratta told us that a copy of Cannella's memo was not enclosed and that he was not able to show us the memo from Smouse. He asked us to explain our motives for considering to move Cannella to the downtown office pod. Smouse wrote that my "statements indicated a total lack of professionalism." When I asked what Smouse wrote, Cammaratta said he was not permitted to tell me.

Saltzgaver and I both wondered why we could not see Smouse's memo and why a copy of Cannella's memo wasn't included. We were being asked to offer an explanation for third-hand accusations about our alleged motives. I wondered why a fellow supervisor, Cannella, whose office was ten feet away from mine, would have to send a written complaint to the Assistant Superintendent at the downtown division office. I thought we had a better working relationship with Cannella and his office staff than that. Why didn't Cannella first speak to Saltzgaver or myself or at least speak to our immediate boss Cammaratta, before anything was put into writing? Did Smouse make a poor administrative decision to write a memo directing Cammaratta to resolve the "inappropriate remarks" that I allegedly said before Smouse verified that indeed these remarks were said? Did Smouse have some alternative motives? Our meeting ended with Saltzgaver and me both asking Cammaratta to request a copy of

Cannella's memo so that we could respond specifically to what was written. We never received a copy of the "cryptic" memo from Cannella. For a while, I forgot about this issue and went on with doing my job.

My decision to give up space showed that I was a team player. However, Smouse's actions make me feel that doing something good for the group would get no recognition, but being accused of doing something wrong gets you nailed to the wall. This treatment wasn't fair.

8

EQUAL PAY PLEASE

In Hillsborough County schools, supervisors and administrators are paid on a salary schedule based upon achieved academic degrees and years of experience in a position. For each year of experience, there is a set increase in salary. For example, in the school year 1987-88, a supervisor that was on a 260 day contract was placed within a salary schedule that increased approximately $1,220 per each additional year of service.

When I was appointed as supervisor, I asked Robert Gardner, Personnel Supervisor, for two years of credit on the supervisor salary schedule for my experience as a principal. He refused, saying that it wasn't the same kind of experience. I believed that many of the experiences as a principal were similar to those of a supervisor and that salary credit was viable. But I didn't want to push the issue since I was newly hired.

Toward the end of my first year as supervisor, I found out from several elementary school principals that, when they transferred from their principal's positions to county supervisory positions, they were given salary credit for their years of experience, easy to calculate because the pay scale for elementary principals was the same as for county supervisors, dollar for dollar, years of experience for years of experience. So when a principal transferred to the district office, to maintain salary, he was automatically put on a higher experience level. It had become a routine and automatic process; they didn't have to ask for it. My interest to request salary credit for my administrative experience as a principal was renewed.

On June 5, 1986, still within my first year of experience as a supervisor, I sent a memo to Dr. Walt Sickles, Assistant Superintendent for Personnel. I asked for supervisory salary credit for my two years of experience as principal. I waited several months for an answer from Sickles, but heard nothing. Some time later, he was transferred to the position of Assistant Superintendent for Instruction.

Eight months after my letter to Sickles was sent, I called for an appointment with the newly-appointed Assistant Superintendent for Personnel, Beth Shields, and met in her office on February 25, 1987. I told her about the letter to Sickles. Remembering that she had recently seen Sickles writing a memo to me about that request, she said that she would speak to Sickles about it.

Still not hearing anything a month later, I called Sickles directly and asked if Shields spoke to him. He said yes and asked if I had received his memo. I told him I didn't and he said he would send another copy. Nine months after I sent my original memo, I received an answer.

Sickles turned down my request for salary step consideration, writing "If you had been employed as a principal when you returned to our system, you would have received two years' experience on our salary schedule because of the two years of experience you had at that level. However, you had no previous supervisory experience, so you received no experience on the supervisory salary schedule." He also stated that he reviewed the issue with Dr. Binnie, Director of Personnel and Mr. Dobbins who was the previous Director of Personnel, and as far as they could determine, they must deny my request.

Since then, I have heard of other principals transferring to a supervisory position and receiving full salary credit for years of experience, even in 1991. I also heard this is true for supervisors who transfer to principal positions.

Some questions still remain. Why did it take Sickles nine months to answer my request for salary credit considerations? This was a very important issue to me since it affected my pay check. Why was there a double standard? Why do some employees, who have no experience, get salary credit automatically and others, who have the experience and request it in writing, don't? Why am I being treated differently? These questions bothered me, and made me wonder if the inequity had anything to do with the situation with Smouse when I was hired. I never received any salary credit for my experience. This was discrimination.

BEGINNING OF SCHOOL YEAR 1986–87

9

ALL HELL BREAKS LOOSE

On September 22, 1986, two significant letters were written to me. The first letter was from Ralph Turlington, Commissioner of Education, Florida Department of Education, thanking me for agreeing to participate on a team to review a new list of competencies and skills used to certify beginning teachers. Commissioner Turlington wrote:

> I am grateful that you have consented to be a member of the group that will review a preliminary draft of the new list of competencies and skills. Participation of professionals, such as yourself, will make possible this valuable element in the continuing development of the Florida Teacher Certification Examination and in the future training of Florida teachers.

It was an honor to be selected and participate on this state project at the University of South Florida. I have always felt that my varied background has given me the experience to be a valuable contributor to special projects such as these. A copy of this letter was sent to Smouse by Commissioner Turlington.

A second letter was sent to me on September 22. This letter started a chain of events and paperwork that has lasted almost six years, a chain that revealed the private thought process and deepest character traits of the major parties involved. It took educational procedures to ridiculous lengths and has stretched human endurance past the point of resilience. I believe it caused things to happen that had nothing to do with the advancement of education or with the respect, worth and dignity of persons involved, including students.

The letter was to Dr. Don Cammaratta by Mr. Ralph L. Smouse Jr. The Subject was: "LACK OF TIMELY ACCOMPLISHMENT AND OTHER PROBLEMS WITH REGARD TO WILLIAM F. WIESER, SUPERVISOR OF INDUSTRIAL ARTS AND INDUSTRIAL EDUCATION." Because of its significance, I have quoted it in full.

ALL HELL BREAKS LOOSE

This is to review, confirm, and expand on several conversations we have had over the past several months with regard to the apparent inefficiency and ineffectiveness of William F. Wieser, Supervisor of Industrial Arts and Industrial Education.

As a result of my visits to school sites and conversations with teachers, department heads, and administrators, it has become apparent that there is a serious deterioration of service to the programs and therefore a rapidly developing lack of confidence in the office of Supervisor of Industrial Arts and Industrial Education.

It has been noted that Mr. Wieser has spent an inordinate amount of time pursuing visits of a personal nature which have little if anything to do with his responsibilities as supervisor. Two examples are the amount of time spent arranging for the construction of a boat cover, and the amount of time and number of visits with the Print Shop instructor at Tampa Bay Vo-Tec Center. Mr. Wieser never seems to have enough time to carry out the responsibilities of his position; however, he always seems to have plenty of time to take care of personal business during the day.

I am beginning to receive a number of complaints with regard to the lack of county-adopted textbooks for the industrial education programs and some complaints have come to me through members of the School Board. This does not build a good image for this division, your department, nor Mr. Wieser's section.

Three examples of Mr. Wieser's lack of attention to the urgency of timely response are contained in the following examples:

On July 19, 1986 my office returned to Mr. Wieser a field purchase order to Brodhead-Garrett for repair of a pilot press in the graphics laboratory at Adams Junior High School with instructions to resubmit for payment from the 1986–87 budget. The deadline for 1985–86 field purchase orders was June 13, 1986. It took Mr. Wieser's office two and one-half months, until 9/15/86, to respond with a refiling of the field purchase order. This does not provide for timely payment of bills for repair work.

On July 7, 1986 Mr. Wieser's office was contacted with regard to a discrepancy in a travel reimbursement claim form for Frank Zeitler. It took several telephone calls before the requested information was provided on August 12, 1986. This was a response time of 37 days.

On September 8, 1986 my office requested Mr. Wieser to provide information with regard to a travel reimbursement claim form for Jack Campbell, automotive instructor at Tampa Bay Vo-Tec Center. As of this date I have not received a response to the request. From September 8 to the current date is 15 days.

Last February both you and I had to get involved to get Mr. Wieser to move on expediting a project for the materials needed for the VICA contest which were held in this district. Mr. Wieser had not successfully initiated the processing of the project until you intervened.

Next month Mr. Wieser will have served as our Supervisor of Industrial Arts and Industrial Education for one year. When he was selected for this position, you, he, and I had a conference wherein the expectations of his assuming the supervisory position were thoroughly discussed. At that time Mr. Wieser assured both of us that he would carry out the responsibilities of the position in a manner which would be efficient and effective and that program improvement would be a top priority. As of this date the efficiency and effectiveness have declined appreciably and I have seen no examples of program improvement. I am beginning to observe in my visits to school sites a decline in program morale because of dissatisfaction with the performance of Mr. Wieser and his office.

I am requesting that you meet with Mr. Wieser and outline a plan to address the aforementioned deficiencies in his performance. The plan should provide for greater attention to the responsibilities of the supervisor's position as well as closer supervision and follow-up by Mr. Wieser of those activities delegated to others. Your closer supervision and documentation of Mr. Wieser's performance should also be provided.

In order that I may be fully informed with regard to progress or lack thereof, it is requested that Mr. Wieser maintain a daily log of his activities. In order that I may remain current with regard to improvements or future problems, please prepare a monthly report to me on this subject. A copy of Mr. Wieser's daily log should be an addendum to your report.

Smouse sent copies of this letter to Dr. Shelton, Superintendent of Schools, Dr. Sickles, Assistant Superintendent for Personnel and me.

Cammaratta asked me to meet with him in his office and he read Mr. Smouse's letter to me and gave me my copy. I was devastated! I took it personally. I knew this was serious. I wondered why all the hard work I was doing to improve programs wasn't mentioned by Smouse. "Program improvement" was the priority he set before I started my first week of employment. I carefully shared my thoughts with Cammaratta about each point that Smouse made in the letter. At first, I was puzzled and couldn't rationalize why Smouse wrote this type of letter. I told Cammaratta that I would write a memo in response. I thought about this letter every day and night.

Smouse's letter hit me hard because of his position in a system that I was loyal to. I viewed and respected him as an officer at the top. Imagine standing on a cliff overlooking the ocean shoreline and lining up 100 people on the beach from left to right. Count these people one at a time. Then, extend this line to the right until there are 1000 people and count them again. Extend the line once more until it reaches 22,000 people and try to visualize the line. Now, come back to the beginning of the line and put the superintendent of schools there, with his six assistant superintendents next in line with some 21,000 plus employees after them. Smouse was one of the six, which meant to me that he was tied for the second place position in this very large "company." I would place myself somewhere around the 400 mark, but still, I had to strain to see all the way up to his position. He had my sincere respect and attention. His position of power scared me.

My memo in response to Smouse's letter was dated September 29, 1986. I addressed the statements in his letter. It was difficult to address his conclusions since they seemed so opinionated. It was difficult for me to challenge an assistant superintendent because of the respect I had for that position, but I had to defend myself.

Smouse stated that I was spending an "inordinate amount of time" pursuing visits of a personal nature. His examples included time spent arranging for the construction of a boat cover and time spent visiting the print shop instructor. I stated that I did not arrange to have a boat cover made, but that I personally made a small 2 foot by 4 foot console cover. I purchased the material and a spool of matching thread and then used the sewing machine in the upholstery shop on my lunch hour. I did all the labor; no students did any work. I did admit that this could be considered a misuse of vocational equipment, but I have heard of similar practices throughout our school system. I was taught that this was acceptable. However, I told Cammaratta that I would not do it again. I clarified that I had a 20 foot, full length commercial boat cover made at a local boat top shop and I wondered if Smouse had confused the two covers. I also suggested that Cammaratta check with the upholstery instructor and he did. I said to him that it seemed evident to me that no investigation was done by Smouse to verify his information prior to putting it in writing.

The only people that knew that I went down to the upholstery shop to use the sewing machine were my secretary, my office coordinator, and the upholstery instructor, Frank Murgado, who allowed me to use the sewing machine. I wondered who Smouse was relying on for information to draw his conclusions in his letter.

In reference to the "inordinate" time with the print shop instructor, I wrote, "...time spent with individual teachers is based upon program improvement, teacher inservicing or by request of the teacher. I have spent a lot of time at Tampa Bay Vo-Tech since our largest number (28) of industrial teachers is concentrated there. I do not believe that I have spent an inordinate amount of time with the print shop instructor." I wondered how much time was "inordinate." As a standard practice, when I would visit Tampa Bay Vo-Tech, I would first check in at the principal's office, inform him why I was on campus, and then make my rounds with teachers. I wondered if someone was keeping a stopwatch on me. Again, where was Smouse getting his information concerning "inordinate" time? It had to be someone at Tampa Bay Vo-Tech.

In reference to the complaint about lack of county-adopted textbooks, I cited a three-page memo sent to Smouse from Cammaratta on September 29, which reported that, when the new state list came out, several books were dropped and therefore could not be ordered from the county list. Cammaratta stated in his report:

> The original orders for numerous schools totaled $22,000.00. Less than 25% have been ordered through the book depository. What happened to those funds that were encumbered for all the books that were not ordered?...
>
> There were no contingency funds this year [1986] for emergencies. It appears that our present system has some flaws. Additionally our staff had numerous experiences that we did not receive the information in the appropriate time frame noted to phase in our request.

Furthermore, Robert Godwin, principal at Tampa Bay Vo-Tech, told me that the textbook problem at his school was a shortage in the automotive mechanics class for beginning students because they had more students enroll than they expected. Plus the diesel instructor wanted a supplementary class textbook for his program, but due to limited funds, only the original classroom set could be purchased. Godwin further explained that his shop coordinator, Rich Roberts, told Smouse that there was a big textbook problem at Tech, but Godwin told me that there wasn't really a problem. Godwin also said that he informed Rich Roberts not to be communicating things like this to Smouse because it was his responsibility as principal to speak to Smouse. That made me speculate if Roberts was communicating other things to Smouse like the amount of time that I spent at the tech center.

It is also interesting to note that several months after Smouse's memo of September 22, 1986, and according to newspaper reports, the school system's textbook supervisor was suspended and eventually charged with embezzling $875,000.00 from the school district by operating a phony textbook scam and collecting payments from the school system's book fund over several years since 1981. The Textbook Scam, as it became known, set up phony companies and payments were made to an outside business associate for books that never existed. I was interviewed by special agent Ellen W. Plough, Florida Department of Law Enforcement; I was shown a copy of several textbook purchase orders allegedly issued from my office when I was coordinator, and was asked if the initials were written by me. It was obvious to me that the handwriting was not mine; although, the description of book titles were exactly the same as the orders from the industrial arts and industrial education office, just the company names were different. More on this Textbook Scam later in this chapter.

The urgency of "timely response" was another example of Smouse's presumed problems in my office. In his first example, about a purchase order for the repair of a printing press, Smouse stated that it took my office two and one-half months to respond in refiling the field purchase order. I responded to Smouse by stating that repair funds were "frozen" because a lack of county funds at the end of the year. I said that the repair order was placed in a folder to hold for processing. After awhile, I was able to look back at what had actually happened. My secretary originally told me that she had placed the repair order in a folder and lost it on her desk for over two months. The person that I placed in charge of equipment repair work in my office was my assistant, Richard Hair, a job he did for two years before I became supervisor.

You might recall that Hair was Smouse's choice to be supervisor instead of me. Hair sent in the repair purchase order and it was returned to him by Smouse. Then Hair gave it to our secretary, and that's when she lost it. He never told me it was returned. When she found the purchase order, she submitted it to Smouse on September 15, without informing me. I guess if you put 2 and 2 together, you get September 22, the day he wrote his noted letter, one week after my secretary found the purchase order. Coincidental timing? When Smouse used the term "timely response," he hit the nail right on the head.

Smouse's second and third examples of timely response were about two teachers who claimed travel reimbursement through my office. All travel forms are prepared by my secretary from my instructions. I sign them and then they are processed by her through Smouse. His office handles all travel requests. As usual, she obtains all the receipts at the end of the teacher's trip and forwards the completed forms. This has been the standard practice in this office for at least the last eight years. For some reason, she was having trouble getting the information from teachers Frank Zeitler and Jack Campbell, and she asked me to get the information.

I wrote the following to Smouse and informed him that Zeitler was not teaching summer school and he was on vacation and therefore he was difficult to contact. I stated the following:

> After securing Mr. Zeitler's information, I made several visits to Jean Ippolito to explain Mr. Zeitler's reimbursement request. Mr. Zeitler's ticket cost was actually $661 because his students were considered to be traveling as his children for a single package price. This ticket savings did save Tomlin Junior High School VSO several hundred dollars in airline fees.... I felt that I needed to contact the school bookkeeper and principal to confirm this ticket purchase so that a check could be made directly to the school. The bookkeeper was on two weeks' vacation then and the principal was at a week-long principal's workshop. These events caused the response time to be so long.

Jack Campbell's request for reimbursement was unusual too. He had gone on a two week auto mechanics workshop and we planned that he would stay overnight in a motel. After one day at the workshop, Campbell decided to commute each day rather than stay in a motel and be away from his family. This was permitted and it gave a savings to the county. Campbell kept forgetting to submit this hotel receipt, however; I had to remind him several times before he was able to find it. He said that he was in no hurry to be reimbursed. Smouse then asked me to confirm that Campbell actually did attend the workshop. After several long distance calls, I contacted the workshop instructor and he confirmed that Campbell was there for the entire time.

I can understand Smouse wanting this detailed information right away. But I can't make teachers respond when they are on vacation or when they are unable to find receipts and are in no rush to be reimbursed. I wondered again why my secretary was unable to get this travel information like she had done for several years.

Another point that Smouse makes in his letter was about me not successfully initiating a project for the VICA contest until my immediate supervisor intervened.

The Regional VICA contest (Vocational Industrial Clubs of America) is held every February as a skills competition among vocational schools in a fifteen county region. Each year a different county hosts the contest and coordinates the many different hands-on skill contests. A state grant of $4,000 is provided for the cost of contest materials and the host county must apply through the Federal funding process to get the money. The previous supervisor of this office, who retired in July, 1985, after 38 years of experience in this school system, was responsible for applying for this funding grant when Hillsborough County accepted the responsibility of hosting the contest. He did not do this; he retired.

Alfred Gonzales, Specialist-Industrial Education, Florida Department of Education, stated in a letter that "a school district is told by the Regional VICA Advisor a year in advance that they will be hosting the VICA Regional Conference for the next school year." When I took over the supervisor's office in October, no one in my office, nor my immediate supervisor, was aware that Hillsborough County was responsible for hosting the next year's VICA contest in February. When I was told in November by a teacher that we were going to be the host, I picked up the blank application forms along with some old sample forms from Alfred Gonzales in December and submitted them. The funds were received before the contest began.

Why was Smouse blaming me for the lack of application of Federal funds by the previous supervisor? I had informed Smouse about the programs that I found in disarray. Why couldn't he realize that I could not instantly correct all the problems that I had found in the Industrial programs, especially the ones left over from last year that I was not aware of? Why wasn't Smouse more understanding about my office situation?

Reviewing Smouse's letter, it is difficult for me to comment since these statements are of his opinion and carry no specific facts as to who, what, when, where and how. In his second paragraph, he states that "it has become apparent that there is a serious deterioration of service to the programs and therefore a rapidly developing lack of confidence" in me. Why didn't Smouse allow me to give my facts before he put his conclusions into writing and into my personnel file? Where was Smouse's evidence to back his statements of "deterioration" and "lack of confidence?"

Toward the end of Smouse's letter, he says that he has seen no examples of program improvement. Again, what facts did he use to draw this conclusion? There was program improvement, but he just couldn't see it. Where were my due process rights in Smouse's scrutiny of my performance?

Further on, Smouse said he was beginning to observe a decline in program morale because of dissatisfaction with my performance. How did he evaluate the topic of morale? Did he take a survey? How many people did he interview? Where was his supporting criteria? I can understand the teacher morale being lower than normal at that time because of budget cuts. Less than one month before Smouse's letter of September 22, I had announced to the Industrial teachers, during the first week of school, that my equipment budget was reduced from $240,000 last year to zero for this coming year because of a county-wide budget crunch. However, I didn't tell the teachers that Smouse cut the budget. The new equipment budget is very important to the industrial shop teachers because the majority of the curriculum is hands-on activity.

In his last paragraph, Smouse requested that I maintain a daily log of activities. I wondered what was the purpose of a daily log. What conclusions was he going to draw from my daily log? What would he compare it to?

When Smouse sent copies of this letter to Dr. Shelton and Dr. Sickles, I wondered if they believed Smouse's conclusions or if they generated the same questions as I did about the lack of supporting evidence.

In my response memo of September 29, I stated that "I feel that I am a dedicated professional. This is my tenth year in this school system. I make every effort to work closely with teachers, administrators and all my colleagues. I try to put forth every effort for an exemplary program."

I felt that I had addressed the major factual issues in Smouse's letter with my response memo. But who was going to judge this? Did I have my "day in court?" Did Smouse have a greater understanding of the operations of my office? Did it matter? Whose move was it now?

Well, Smouse made the next move. On September 30, 1986, he called Cammaratta to meet with him downtown. Smouse had just received my memo of September 29. After the meeting, Smouse wrote a memo to Shelton and Sickles. He stated that my memo "contained several inaccuracies and differences of opinion with the documentation currently on file." Of course, he didn't say what the inaccuracies were, nor did he say what the differences of opinion were. What authority was going to say whose opinion was correct? He could not be persuaded to reconsider, no matter how much the preponderance of evidence called for it. If he states that I was inaccurate, then where were his facts? Where was his proof? Was this justice...or a vendetta? In his last paragraph, he writes "In view of Mr. Wieser's failure to recognize the inefficiencies and ineffectiveness previously documented, it will be necessary for Dr. Cammaratta and me to follow closely on Mr. Wieser's future activities. Dr. Cammaratta and I will continue to keep you informed as to Mr. Wieser's progress or lack thereof."

There was a note to Sickles at the end of the memo. It asked him to place this correspondence in my personnel file. I could foresee my file growing in the future.

I couldn't understand why this was happening. What prompted all this? First of all, it sounded like Smouse wasn't going to accept my response to anything he already stated. Second, it seemed far-fetched that Smouse was evaluating me, when it wasn't his job to do so. It was the job of my immediate supervisor, Cammaratta. Third, why was Smouse so adamant about reporting all this to the Superintendent of Schools and to the Assistant Superintendent for Personnel? It seemed to me that he was reaching over his head for an issue that was beneath his position. Was he trying to show the Superintendent and others that I could not do the job that I was hired to do eleven months ago? Was he trying to prove that he was right and that Cammaratta was wrong in selecting me? Was I caught in the middle of a political cross-fire between Smouse and Cammaratta?

One month later on October 27, 1986, Smouse called Cammaratta and me to meet with him in his office. He summarized his last meeting with Cammaratta and told me that he was displeased with my performance. And then his face and bald head became flushed in red and he stated that if I worked for private industry rather than public education "that he would have fired me already." This statement and his physical reaction told me the direction of his intentions. His message was evident that things were most serious. I could not comprehend that, before I completed my first year on the job, Smouse concluded that I should be fired. I believed that I was doing a good job considering all factors. My yearly evaluations clearly showed my above-average performance. I didn't think that I was being treated fairly or honestly.

On the next day, October 28, Smouse wrote another memo to me. He summarized the previous day's meeting for the record and stated "I also indicated that you would be given several months to move the activities of the Supervisor's office in a positive direction. I also indicated to you and Dr. Cammaratta that in the event major improvements were not forthcoming, steps would be taken to remove you from your current position." I knew I would see this in writing sooner or later. But it did not discourage me in doing my job to the best of my ability with the resources that I had. I even looked forward to maintaining my daily log because it would truly reflect my daily activities and my office workload.

Since Smouse requested that I maintain a daily log, I decided that I would keep it most complete, detailed, accurate, and factual; Smouse would have no doubt of the activities and workload in my office. I planned to present all the facts and would rely on truth as my best defense for my job performance.

I started my daily log on October 1st, 1986. It was a minute by minute accounting of my daily activities including evenings and weekends. The posted work day schedule for vocational supervisors was 8:00 a.m. to 4:45 p.m.. I usually came in early and often stayed after hours. Supervisors don't get paid overtime.

I submitted my monthly report to Cammaratta for support of his required monthly report to Smouse. I organized my monthly report into four sections. The first section was a cover memo to Cammaratta stating this was my monthly report. I requested that copies be sent to the Superintendent and the Assistant Superintendent for Personnel who received the original letter from Smouse. They received Smouse's original letter and now I wanted them to see the facts that I had to present. Also, this would place a copy of *my* support data in my personnel file for future reference.

The second section was a summary memo of the month's activities. The third section was an assortment of support data that showed my activities, such as: workshop attendance, contest judging, state/regional/area meetings, conferences, appreciation letters, speaking engagements, student activities, industry visits, TV interviews, inservice training and advisory committee meetings. The fourth section contained the actual daily log. My complete monthly report, typed in single spaced format averaged 31 pages each month. To give an idea of my typical day and the format that I used, I will quote one day from my log.

My Daily Log of Activities

Daily Log – November 21, 1986

Arrive office, 7:30 a.m.

Continue work on vicinity travel and comp time for October and November.

Call from Al Gonzales, State Consultant, OK to meet at TBVT with diesel next week or week after.

Visit Herb Carrington, Hillsborough, to check on plans for north campus. Pick up all plans to bring back to the office.

Call Industry Services, Erwin, to inform them I will be unable to attend the last session of the program today.

Visit Tom Blackwell, talk with him about the due date for north campus plans. Also reviewed memo from Jerry Miller to Dr. Wagers. Told him that some information was misleading.

Stopped to see Dr. Larry Wagers about Mr. Miller's memo. He was out of his office, left a message that I would call him.

Talked with Ben Knox, Erwin, about two pieces of office equipment available to be donated to his program.

Confer with Richard that the plans for north campus at Hillsborough were never sketched by him as I asked him to do. He took plans to Herb Carrington to do the layout with the other teachers there. I told him I specifically indicated for him to sketch the plans and ask if the students could draw a formal print. Gave him the unfinished plans and told him to sketch these by 12:00 noon next Tuesday, November 25.

Attended annual supervisor's Thanksgiving luncheon.
Call Frank B. Hall, Insurance Company, to accept the office machines for donation to the Erwin Center.
Review with Dr. Cammaratta the schedule for the due date for the plans for north campus of Hillsborough.
Confer with Dr. Cammaratta about a memo from Dr. Wagers about plans for Hillsborough north campus.
Memo to Boyd Wilborn about equipment donation.
Call from Wanda Tidwell, Plant City, she would like to go to the VICA advisors workshop.
Call from Bob Jarlinski, Brewster Advisory Committee, information on a food service recommendation for his workshop in December.
Note from RoseAnne Bowers who recommends the Family Sandwich Shop for catering.
Letter from Augie Martinez, Gaither, requesting the transfer of three cooling fans to him for his computers.
Memo to Augie Martinez, Gaither, OK to transfer computer cooling fans to your school.
Call Bob Ball, Armwood, questions about program review. Made appointment for December 4, 9 AM to visit with him.
Call from Al Gonzales, State Consultant, he can meet with me at TBVT in early December about the diesel curriculum.
Received membership verification in sick leave bank.
Sign claim for sick leave, Cathy Lakes.
Deliver purchase order change (cost) to Mr. Smouse's office.
Review and sign request for bid to Henry Morbach, 59 items.
Sign memo to Mr. Smouse about Richard Crofutt's travel.
Roseanne Miller, Gaither, called and needs a printer repaired and wants to write a letter to Betty Easley about the six period day.
Glenda Lovell, Land-O-Lakes, called and wants to teach in Hillsborough County. I requested that an application be sent to her.
Sign request for quotes for warehouse.
Bill Moore, Hillsborough, stopped in to give information about the plans for Hillsborough north campus.
Sign and send several memos as listed above.
Review VISTA information memo from Dr. Walt Sickles.
Read and review memo from Mr. Smouse about Federal Funds application. Read School Board Digest, November 18.
Call Bill Troutman, Principal- Dorothy Thomas, let him know his instructor, Mike Julian, can drop off the tools to be repaired anytime.

Ted May, Armwood, called and would like to go to the General Motors workshop in Sarasota.

Memo from Barbara Anderson about follow-up information from November 19 meeting. Review.

Call from Augie Martinez, Gaither, set up meeting to review 3rd year project exam.

Memo to Jeff Hurst, property control, to transfer a welder to Jefferson High.

Sign purchase order for books from DOE Dissemination and Diffusion.

Sign repair order for Brewster.

Sign repair order for King.

Sign field purchase order for AVA posters and pins.

Deliver program review self study forms to the DOE Regional Office.

Talk with Al Gonzales about the diesel mechanics questions at Tampa Bay Vo- Tech. Set meeting date.

Leave Regional Office at 5:15 pm.

There were many nights when I would go back to the office to catch up on paper work. I usually was the only one there at night except for Joy Henderson, health coordinator, who was teaching an evening course. It was clear to me that I put in more office time than any other supervisor. It was also clear to me that my office was over worked, especially with the extra duties required of me by Smouse. Never once did Smouse challenge anything that I wrote in my daily log. It was all fact, and it could be verified if necessary.

In the middle of January, 1987, Cammaratta told me that Smouse talked with him about my daily log and said that I should discontinue the extensive daily log and in place do a general summary of each week's activity for my monthly report. Why did Smouse assign the daily log in writing and then verbally change it to a weekly summary? Did Smouse learn anything about my job performance based on the facts in my daily log over the last four months? What was Smouse going to do with my daily logs? What good did my daily logs do for the school system? How did Smouse use my daily logs in his evaluation of me? Did Smouse really assign the daily log to me as a means of busy work and punishment?

I continued my daily log on a weekly summary until July, 1987, when Smouse wrote a memo indicating that I should discontinue my daily log. He never gave me any feedback as to his approval or disapproval of my reporting of my daily log. Needless to say that it was an extra burden in time and paperwork since my office was already very busy. The log consumed quality time that could have been given to the teachers and programs.

ALL HELL BREAKS LOOSE

I found out in the Fall of 1987 that several of my copies of the daily log and monthly report were not in my personnel file as I had requested of Smouse. Were my daily logs providing information that was contrary to the statements and conclusions previously made by him? Why weren't these placed in my file when I requested it? Why didn't Smouse provide me with any feedback about my daily logs or Cammaratta's monthly reports of my performance? What was the purpose of Smouse requesting the daily logs in the first place?

Looking back, I see that one letter, written on September 22, 1986, caused events that dramatically restricted my ability to do my job effectively and efficiently. In this one letter, with no prior documentation, he concluded that I was performing below his expected level and then passed judgement on me by directing me to keep a daily log of activities even before I had a chance to respond. I was sentenced before I was even accused. Even after I had a chance to respond to his statements, he held stead-fast on his conclusions which were based upon his undocumented opinions and on several of his "facts" about my "lack of timely accomplishment." How could he conclude that, based only on the facts about my reported slow response time (three examples in eleven months of work), I would be removed from my job if major improvements weren't forthcoming? Did Smouse have a predetermined agenda concerning my future?

I didn't really know what job performances I did or did not do that would justify removing me from my position. I began to work closer with my immediate supervisor, Cammaratta, to be sure that he had good visibility of my activities and performance. I was anxious to hear from Smouse on any feedback about my job performance or his greater understanding of my office responsibilities.

Does this kind of leadership and experience, from Smouse, promulgate positive education delivery to our students?

I was at the psychological point where I needed some personal therapy. So, I went shopping for a new car since my eight year old Chevy Malibu station wagon had over 80,000 miles on it. I always wanted a sport vehicle and therefore purchased a brand new 1987 Chevy Blazer K-5. It was black, four-wheel drive, and had all the accessories of a luxury car. The $22,000 window sticker made it the most expensive car I ever purchased, thanks to the teacher's credit union. The excitement of the purchase was soon doused when I drove it to work and got the comment; "How many textbooks did I have to sell to buy that one?" Since I was under scrutiny from Smouse, I didn't want to give the wrong impression, so I'd still drive the old station wagon on a daily basis and only use the new Blazer occasionally. I was disappointed that I couldn't enjoy my new toy.

The Textbook Scam centered around the textbook supervisor, Benicio "Benny" Martinez who was in that position for 15 years. Martinez and his outside associate, Armando Blanco, purchased four Gulf of Mexico beach front condominiums in neighboring Pinellas County with some of the $875,000.00. A newspaper report in October, 1986, quotes three school system vocational officials, including myself, stating we cannot account for books ordered from the phony textbook companies. The two other school officials were Don Cammaratta, director of vocational education and Marvin Skinner, assistant director for administration of Erwin Vocational Technical Center. No one from the academic side of the system was quoted in the report. It is interesting to note that Skinner was the supervisor of industrial arts and industrial education while B. H. Blankenbecler was the coordinator. Blankenbecler was promoted to supervisor when Skinner transferred to the Erwin Center in 1979. That's when I became coordinator.

10
SUBORDINATE SHAKEDOWN

Since my office was being put under the microscope of evaluation, I felt that it was incumbent upon me to review operating procedures and working relationships with my subordinates: Richard Hair, coordinator and Cathy Lakes, secretary.

My assistant or coordinator, Hair, had been with the school system for about 29 years. He was promoted out of the classroom in 1984 to the vacant position created by me when I left to work in the Pasco school system. He was married with grandchildren and his wife was a teacher at an elementary school.

I met with Hair on October 3, 1986, and told him that this office was being looked at in reference to efficiency and effectiveness. I gave him the example about the repair purchase order he handled that was lost for over two months by the secretary. I informed him about additional textbook orders that he completed which sat around for several days on the secretary's desk. He knew that these books were needed in the schools. He did not tell the secretary to put a priority rush on them. In these two examples, I told him that his assignment responsibilities were complete when his work leaves this office, not just when it leaves his desk. I emphasized to him that all correspondence from this office would go out under my name and title, not his, and I reminded him that I had mentioned this to him before indicating that it is an effective way for me to be informed of all office activities. I wrote in a memo to Hair:

> You need to keep me better informed than in the past concerning your activities. In reference to the eight day blue enrollment forms, Dr. Cammaratta asked you to complete a low/high enrollment list since I was out of the office. Dr. Cammaratta questioned me about this on the next work day and I was not aware of what you did. Besides, the memo to Dr. Cammaratta had my name on it, but not my initials. You should have told me right away what you were asked to do or write me a note so I would be informed as soon as I

returned to the office. In addition, your report was inaccurate because eight teachers did not send in their blue forms and you did not mention this in your memo to Dr. Cammaratta or to me when I returned to the office. Sloppy reports like this which bear my name give everyone in this office an inefficient reputation.

I wanted total communication in this office; I thought that we must work together as a team. The importance of this office, simply by its size and diversity alone, was demonstrated by the services that we provide to all the schools and various county level personnel. Finally, I asked for Hair to provide me with a weekly itinerary of his daily work and school visits, previously done verbally. This record would help me to be fully aware of any activities or problems that might affect this office.

Then on November 25, 1986, I wrote two memos to Hair. In the first memo I had to reprimand Hair for his failure to follow directions to complete plans for a new school building. After checking on these plans, it became evident that Hair's assignment was incomplete, which placed us behind schedule in meeting the county deadline date for construction plans.

In the second memo, I again had to take Hair to task for his poor office communications as enumerated here:

I have recently indicated that for this office to perform efficiently and effectively, communication among this office is a high priority.

Recently, on several occasions, it has come to my attention that messages for me are not passed along by you. Example: the Erwin Center called you and told you about a newly hired full time drafting instructor. I found out this information a few days later when Cathy asked me if I knew how to pronounce her name. I didn't even know who she was.

Again, Dick Keller, a teacher at Hillsborough High, called about an auto mechanics workshop that was planned in his classroom. He said that Chuck Holland, Principal, cancelled the campus workshop and now it would be held at the NAPA store on Habana Avenue. He said he told you the week before to let me know of this change and I received no communication from you. I am embarrassed when a teacher calls and asks why I didn't know about something.

I returned a call to Mr. Gallagher at the warehouse and he told me that a decision was made to ship all new equipment directly to the new Bloomingdale school and not to the warehouse. Since you are assigned to work on equipment, I immediately told you this new policy and you said that Mr. Gallagher already told you about it. Again you had information that should have been shared with me.

In a memo to you on October 6, 1986, I talked about "total communication from you in this office. I suggest you use an informal note pad system to alert me to any items of concern." I say again, I need you to communicate office information to me. I have a concern about other information that you may not have shared with me. This office cannot operate as it is expected if these gaps continue.

I encourage you to work closely with me in order that these negative events do not occur. I want to assist you in improving our communication and hopefully rectify these discrepancies.

The lack of communication also extended to my oral instructions to Hair. I had set up a mail tray for communication from me to him. I asked him to check it daily. The tray went untouched for days at a time. Why wasn't he more cooperative? If he was Smouse's original choice to be the supervisor, then how come he wasn't performing at that level of competence?

Cammaratta told me that in the past, Hair repeatedly communicated directly to Smouse instead of going through Cammaratta's office even after he was told not to do so. Why was Hair trying to avail himself to Smouse and avoid Cammaratta? Was Smouse promoting this practice? Why didn't Smouse discipline Hair when he was originally informed about Hair's improprieties? Once, after Smouse broke his hip chasing a purse snatcher while he and his wife were at a conference in California, Hair lent him a walker. Their relationship appeared to be more than professional.

When I was on the job for two months, at Christmas time, and since it was traditional to exchange gifts in the vocational offices, Hair approached me and asked if I wanted to purchase gifts separately for our secretary or join together for one gift. Since the office was so busy, I decided it would be easier to get one gift. He said he could find out what she wanted and then buy the present. I asked him how much was appropriate for each to contribute and he said around $25. I thought it was a bit much, but I said okay. He never showed me the gift before he wrapped it and I didn't get to sign the card. My secretary did say thank you to me "for the gift." When I found out later that the gift was an very expensive bottle of perfume, I felt awkward about the gift procedure and decided that we should buy individual gifts after that. I was befuddled by the gift giving ruse which seemed to garner favor from my secretary for my coordinator at my expense.

My next meeting was with my secretary, Cathy Lakes. She had been with the school system for about ten years, the last five in this job. She was a 30 something divorcée (no children) tall and thin and blond. She lived alone in a house in the suburbs east of Tampa.

The job description for the position of Secretary II, states: "Detailed instructions are given at beginning of work but usually the employee is expected to work independently of supervision and is required to exercise initiative, tact and good judgement in carrying out her duties."

On October 8, 1986, I wrote a memo to Lakes summarizing the meeting that I had with her about office procedures. A copy of the memo went to Cammaratta and Hair to be sure that they were included in all aspects of my office procedures. In this memo, I stated my concern about the office procedures and performance that were pointed out by Smouse. I reiterated to her that this office has been reviewed because of slow response time for paperwork. I told her to double check all travel forms that went out of this office, the same travel forms that she had been doing for years, and that I expected that they would be complete and accurate when they are given to me to sign. I also spoke to her about her filing system and the "lost" files. I stressed that things to be typed on a priority order would be told to her. And if she wasn't sure about these priority items, she should ask.

I told her to be very careful when typing, because she had an odd propensity for typos. She had typed "Connecticut" as "connection." She also had mislaid dates. I have to note that even after this memo of October 8, 1986, she made another typing error. On the first line of the memo to her, she failed to capitalize the letter "L" in her last name. Apparently, my secretary has developed the habit of making minor typing mistakes even when I alerted her to the review Smouse was doing. I stressed to her that accuracy was more important than speed. I relied on an experienced secretary who had performed satisfactorily in this job for years; however, I still was obligated to check over her work: word for word, letter for letter. Her errors placed additional pressure on my position, because, as supervisor, I was responsible for all correspondence that left this office. In conclusion of this memo to her, I said that I was disappointed in the negative responses this office had received and that my expectations of this office and the people in it were high, but so far performance has been less than expected. Finally, I stated that I must be informed in a timely manner of any concerns or problems. The efficiency and effectiveness of this office must increase to an acceptable level.

As I monitored the office performance of Lakes over the next several months, I noticed a pattern of sick days that became evident. Since absenteeism does affect overall office performance, I decided to look into the number of days she had called in sick. In the last twelve months of work she had an equivalent of 20 sick days with 10 of these days on Mondays. I wondered if she was calling in

SUBORDINATE SHAKEDOWN

sick on Mondays because she was really sick or just wanted a three day weekend. Looking at 20 sick days per year and add a couple of weeks of vacation and you have about a month and a half of time away from the job. In a conference with her, I told her that these sick days may be beyond her control; however, Mondays are an important day to begin the work pattern and I believed her absences may have contributed inadvertently to inefficiency in our office operation schedule. I told her to work on any extenuating circumstances and to change this pattern. I questioned her dedication to the job. Her response to all of my input?: "This isn't fair that you're doing this to me." I guess it is debatable if it's fair or not, but I wasn't absent; she was, and it did affect office operations. Over the next twelve months the number of sick days were almost as high as the previous year. However, the frequency of being sick on Mondays did change and her sick days were spread throughout the week including Fridays. She used more sick days per year than she earned. Later in the year, on a day when she was absent, I collected the day's mail and opened and date stamped it. Hair usually did this when she was out, but that day he was out sick too. In one day's mail, I found seven pieces of personal mail sent to her at our office address. The letters were from a seed company, two from a million dollar winner contest, an organic gardening company, a clearing house millionaire contest, a national retirement association and a national family publisher.

In April of 1987, yearly evaluations were due for secretaries. In the previous year, I had evaluated her much lower than she had been evaluated by the previous supervisor. I was not pleased with her work even before Smouse did his critical review of my office. But this year I had more supporting facts to support an evaluation that was poor. In the evaluation conference with her, I explained my evaluation ratings and also told her that I was not pleased with her work and I suggested that she look for another job. She started crying, feeling that I was too hard on her, but said she would look for another job.

My eleven months on the job were filled with turmoil and apprehension, especially in my office. Oftentimes, I would return to my office and the conversation between my secretary and coordinator would stop abruptly when I entered the room. I paid little attention to it then, but the frequency of these interrupted conversations increased after Smouse's letter. One day, I returned early to my office and Rich Roberts, Shop Coordinator at Tampa Bay Vo-Tech, was conversing with Lakes and Hair, but stopped talking immediately when I entered. My gut feeling told me that the conversation was about me. The principal at Tampa Bay Vo-Tech, Bobby Godwin, later told me the original plan was that Hair would get the supervisor's job and Roberts would get Hair's coordinator's job. Did my return to Hillsborough County upset the apple cart?

It was uncomfortable to be in charge of an office where such a strained atmosphere dominated. Hushed conversations and expensive bottles of perfume caused me to look more closely at the office relationship between my secretary and coordinator. I felt that she would have liked to have seen Hair receive the promotion rather than me. I also think Hair gave her support to remain after I had asked her to look for another position. I had the feeling that Hair wanted to be the supervisor even if he didn't get the promotion, because he had the support from Smouse. I also had noticed that Hair and Lakes went to lunch together more frequently than any other supervisor or coordinator and secretary.

My subordinates' actions have caused me to look at the perplexity of their relationships: Lakes to Hair, Hair to Smouse, and Lakes to Smouse. In spite of these overtones, I had to do my job, respond to the accusations of Smouse, and ride shotgun over my office. My candle was burning at both ends and now in the middle.

11
ATTORNEY NUMBER 1

In January of 1987, my thinking towards Smouse started to change in an uncoupling and disassociating manner, and I hired an attorney to rectify the inequity. I now realized that a dichotomy existed which I hadn't perceived before, and I was now to use "chop logic" and differentiate between Smouse as a person and Smouse as a top-level administrator, one of my superiors. I didn't seek legal relief to degrade him or raise myself to his level. I hired a lawyer to help me recover my integrity and self-respect. I have always had the highest respect for all educational positions, (including students!). I respect the position of Assistant Superintendent; I did not respect the man who held it.

With the detachment between the person Smouse and the professional Smouse, I was able to view my job position in a new light. This being most significant to me because now I didn't feel that I was "standing up" against my employer, the school system, but that I was taking issue with what was right and wrong in the processes and conclusions raised by Smouse, another person like myself.

In January of 1987, it had been four months since I heard anything at all from Smouse about his memos of last September and October. I was very concerned about the statements the memos contained and I took them home with me every day, thought about them in the car, thought about them while watching TV, and often fell asleep with them on my mind. Needless to say, the next day began with the same, even if it was on the weekend. I strongly felt that it was time that I received feedback on my current status since it appeared that my job was on the line. He had three monthly reports of the daily log that he required me to maintain and to submit to him. I wondered if he could have forgotten about me?

According to the new administrative/supervisor evaluation format, the Manager Performance Appraisal System states that "Managers should receive feedback on their performance." The document later says that:

> Feedback and coaching may occur at any time during the year. However, as a minimum, it will occur any time the supervisor notes that the manager's performance in any area is falling below the level of minimal acceptable performance. When the supervisor identifies an area where a manager is below expectations, the supervisor will provide the manager with coaching in addition to feedback.

Worrying about the pressures of my job, not knowing if I would be removed from my job, not getting the feedback I should have, listening to my close personal friends asking about my job status, and not knowing where my career was going, all caused me to seek the advice of a lawyer. A friend told me that he knew a law firm that had some experience litigating cases with educational institutions. I consulted with Fritz Gray of Cohen, Gray and Reback and told him of the events since I was appointed as supervisor and showed him copies of Smouse's memos and my daily log. He agreed that there appeared to be a "pipeline," carrying personal information about me to Smouse. Gray advised me to keep quiet to everyone about my personal life, whether it was lunch time, at a coffee break, or whatever. When I asked about the possibility of filing suit against Smouse, Gray did not recommend it, saying it would be difficult to win. I told him that I was looking for some way to stop Smouse's vindictiveness.

Gray suggested that I draft a letter to Smouse, with copies to the original three people that Smouse sent his first memos to, (Shelton, Shields, and Cammaratta). The letter (in part) read:

> It has been several months since I have heard from you concerning your memoranda of September 22, 1986.... Since I have not received any feedback from you concerning the subject matter of the memoranda, or the performance of my job as reflected in my daily log sheets, I felt it incumbent upon myself to request of you to provide me written feedback....
>
> Due to the fact that these memoranda are in my permanent personnel file, I feel compelled to request of you one of two things. You can provide to me supporting documentation and specific facts to support your conclusions of my alleged ineffectiveness and inefficiency in my job performance. This would include the specific names, places and dates which demonstrates my alleged ineffectiveness and inefficiency so that I can assess the merit of your claims and determine the accuracy of your sources. Alternatively, you could remove the three memoranda and all related material from my files. I think it only fair that when one accuses another of incompetence in the performance of their job, that they have specific facts to support their claims. To date I have not seen

any and I will assume that your inability to provide such specific facts and documentation as requested within ten (10) working days will indicate that your conclusions in said memoranda clearly lack merit.

It was a good feeling to write the memo, and know that the pressure was off me now and that I was going to get some specific information or have these memoranda removed from my file. Did I smile too soon?

Well, eighteen (18) working days later, Smouse sent his two-page response with copies to Shelton, Shields and Cammaratta. My first question for additional facts of specific names, places and dates was answered by his statement, "If you will refer to copies of my correspondence to Cammaratta dated September 22, 1986, you will find a number of specific examples of inefficiency and lack of timely response." I felt he was side-stepping my question by referring me back to the original memo. I wondered if he didn't want to tell me who was providing him with information, if anyone at all. I asked only that my accusers be placed in front of me so that I could defend myself. I still want to know when Smouse had "conversations with teachers, department heads and administrators," as he detailed in that original memo. Whom did he talk to and specifically what did they say? Was Smouse placing my job on the line based upon rumors and gossip?

He mentioned nothing about removing these memos from my personnel file. As a matter of fact, my request to remove the letters generated even more paperwork for my file. While Smouse didn't provide any clarification to the previous memos, he did enumerate some new accusations to show that I wasn't doing an effective job: for example, that there was a non-expenditure of $20,000 in categorical budget for vocational equipment. He wrote that "This $20,000 had not been encumbered as of the final deadline date of January 31, 1987. Therefore the funds were withdrawn and reassigned to other vocational areas that had expended funds within the allocated time." This is true, but the $20,000 was returned to a pool in Smouse's office and redistributed. I applied for an additional $15,000 and got it. So, what was the big problem that Smouse was attempting to magnify? My total funds for categorical equipment was $165,000 at the beginning of the year. I wonder if anyone in the vocational division overspent their budget. That, it seems to me, would be a problem worth monitoring.

I drafted the letter to Smouse to find out, in his opinion, just where I stood in my job performance. Smouse's memo continues:

You also state that you have been spending a great amount of time in the performance of your position and I agree that a review of your daily logs bears this out. However, one of the traits of a good manager is not how much time you put in but what you put in the time and the results that are achieved. The fact that you are putting in so many hours and not achieving the results which other people with similar responsibilities achieve with less hours may indicate a lack of time management and organization. I feel there has been some improvement compared to the manner in which you were carrying out your responsibilities a year ago and I would hope that more improvements will follow. However, your correspondence indicates disagreement with my conclusions based on facts previously stated....

Within the last year Dr. Cammaratta and I have spent more time with you in this regard than we have with all of our other supervisory personnel combined...

When you accepted the position of Supervisor of Industrial Arts and Industrial Education, you assured Dr. Cammaratta and me that you had the qualities to be a good supervisor. Let's begin to see less evidence of your disputing the judgement of Dr. Cammaratta and me and more evidence of those qualities which make a good supervisor.

When my lawyer saw Smouse's memo, his first concern was that Smouse and Cammaratta were in concert with their evaluation of my performance. Yet, Cammaratta rated my mid-year performance evaluation as "exceeds standards." I told Grey that Cammaratta worked closely with me and approved of my performance. For the next several months Smouse continued to send memos with "specific facts" that I'm sure he felt answered my original question. It is interesting to note that the original memo from Smouse on September 22, 1986, was the only basis for drawing conclusions that I was not doing an acceptable job. Now, four, five and six months after the fact, Smouse is gathering data to support a decision he made six months earlier. He was putting the cart before the horse in his evaluation of me.

I still wanted some type of legal solution to be implemented. Gray felt that I would be better off to put the money (an estimated $25,000 to pursue the case in court) into a savings account rather than into a law suit which only had an estimated $50/50$ chance of success.

My close friends told me that they understood what I was going through and that I should consider a different type of attorney. I told them that I appreciated their concerns and that I would think about it. I would look for attorney number two.

My body weight was steadily increasing and I was growing out of my clothes. I only wore my larger suit sizes. When I drove my car, I had to take off my suit coat and put it in the back seat because it was too bulky now to get in and out of the car. I felt fat and I didn't like it because I always could carry my weight well. The stress was mounting.

I heard a rumor that the state investigation in the Textbook Scam was looking at B. H. Blankenbecler, retired industrial supervisor, because of his sudden retirement and his proximity to industrial textbook orders over the years.

12

PERCEIVING, BEHAVING, BECOMING

During the two months of March and April, 1987, no less than eleven letters/memos were exchanged between Smouse, Cammaratta and myself concerning my performance. The yearly evaluations were due on May 1.

The process of Smouse's documentation of my performance reminded me of a paper I read during graduate school at Oregon State University. The paper, written by Arthur Combs, appeared in the Association for Supervision and Curriculum Development's Yearbook in 1962 and was titled "Perceiving, Behaving, and Becoming." It explored how teachers look at students with preconceived notions. These notions can also serve as an analogy to the way a top administrator (Smouse) perceives a mid-level administrator (me). The following quotes from the paper help to tell Combs' message.

> Whatever we do in teaching depends upon what we think people are like. Teachers who believe children can, will try to teach them. Teachers who believe children are unable, give up trying or spend their days on a treadmill, hopelessly making motions they never expect will matter. The beliefs we hold about people can serve as prison walls limiting us at every turn. They can also set us free from our shackles to confront great new possibilities never dreamed before....
>
> I believe we are guilty by virtue of the fact that our own perceptions are so selective. We choose that which the self feeds upon; those things that suit our purpose and fit into our own past experiences. We cram and twist things to fit our carefully constructed pigeonholes. We care more about our own psychological health than the psychological health of the children we teach. Granted, we do not wish to do so, nor will we readily admit guilt, but the irrefutable evidence lies in the premium we place on such things as intelligence, good

behavior, respectability, and even cleanliness. We almost wish the kids were carbon copies of everything we value....

School for many children is not a friendly place. There are too many teachers who are arrogant and self-seeking, demanding and unfair, tactless and insensitive. Even one is too many....

Last October, Smouse stated that if major improvements weren't forthcoming, steps would be taken to remove me from my job. Keep in mind that he had only two months left now, before the year-end performance evaluations were due. Looking back, I wonder what Smouse was doing during the months of November, December, January, and February when no documentation of my performance was made by him until I wrote a letter requesting feedback.

The documentation process continued with a memo about my performance from Smouse on March 31, 1987, pointing out a "Need for Better Planning and Time Management." This memo started what I have come to call The Mike Grego Affair. The memo was sent to Cammaratta with copies to Shelton, Shields, and me. The memo started out like this:

> On the afternoon of March 20, 1987, Mr. William Wieser, Supervisor of Industrial Arts and Industrial Education, brought to my office an SB-77 travel authorization for Michael Grego to travel to the National Industrial Arts Conference to accept an award as the "Teacher of the Year." The travel form was for Mr. Grego's travel on 3/21/87. The SB-77 has no account coding, no allocation for substitute, no budget transfer, and was three days late for arrival in the Personnel Department as required by county policy.
>
> As I was out of the office attending a meeting, it was necessary for my office to contact me to seek approval to process the authorization for the travel expenditure. The SB-77 should have been in my office on or before Tuesday, March 17, 1987 with all information correctly filled in on the form and with all necessary accompanying documents such as the budget transfer and substitute form. The support documents were furnished by Mr. Wieser before the close of business on 3/20/87.

On the surface this does sound like I didn't know what I was doing. And I think the other people who read the memo probably thought the same. As I have said before, it appears that it is of Smouse's administrative manner to put things like this in writing before he checks to confirm the facts and details. Smouse concluded his memo to Cammaratta this way:

> Please counsel with Mr. Wieser regarding the continuation of his failing to do his work in a timely manner as evidenced by the foregoing and in similar

instances documented in previous correspondence. Summarize in writing to Mr. Wieser your comments to him and send a copy to me. Please have Mr. Wieser acknowledge by signature my memorandum of March 17, 1987 (copy attached), this memorandum of March 31, 1987, and the memorandum which you write to Mr. Wieser on this subject. Send copies with original signatures to me.

Your prompt attention to this matter will be sincerely appreciated.

If Smouse would only have checked into this situation just a little more before he put it into writing, then six additional memos on this one subject probably would not have been written. Perhaps he had a different agenda.

After I received this memo I double checked what happened and I explained the situation to Cammaratta and gave him a follow-up memo. He responded with a memo to me and a copy to Smouse. I explained to Cammaratta that I believed that Smouse's memo should have been directed to Grego, not me, because I was not sending him to the conference in Oklahoma, his principal was. My memo to Cammaratta stated these facts.

Mr. Grego was selected as the Florida Industrial Arts Association (FIAA) "Teacher of the Year" and was given $500 toward attending the National convention. It was suggested by the President of FIAA that the local school district pick up any additional costs for this teacher to attend. Mr. Grego called me and asked if I could pay for any additional costs for him to travel. I told him that I could not provide a substitute or pay additional cost because I had no budget for this type of travel.... Because of these funding restrictions, I told Mr. Grego I could not send him and that he should ask his principal if she would cover his classes with a substitute and pay any expenses over $500.00.

Then on the afternoon of March 20, my office received a travel authorization form for Mr. Grego which was signed by his principal.

At this time I took the travel request to Mr. Smouse's office to see what could be done. There it was noticed that the request was incomplete as to account coding and no substitute allocation. It was decided at this time by Mr. Smouse's office, that Mr. Grego should attend since he is "Teacher of the Year" and that travel funds be taken out of my industrial budget.

I tried to contact Mr. Grego from Mr. Smouse's office to ask about final details, but he already left school and was not at home. I left a message to call Mr. Smouse's office.

To summarize, since I was not sending Mr. Grego from my office, I do not feel I should be responsible for this teacher's travel request. I took the travel request to Mr. Smouse's office to offer my assistance and to seek a solution to a county problem.

When I received the travel form, I wondered whether I should return it to the teacher because it was past the deadline date, or take it to Smouse's office to see what should be done since the teacher was leaving the next day, not knowing if it was approved or not. I did not know at that time that Grego's principal had agreed to send him.

I agree with Cammaratta about forwarding incomplete travel forms. However, I didn't forward the travel form, I brought it to Smouse's office in an attempt to find a solution to a problem that I did not generate. There I was with possession of this incomplete form and the teacher was traveling on the next day. Next time, I will return the travel form to the teacher instead of trying to assist in a solution. What if I did return it to the teacher, but he left before he received it? Would he be gone on unauthorized travel? Would the school system be covered under insurance if the teacher was involved in an accident? These were my concerns. Now, I have been taught to return it and then it just wouldn't be my problem anymore. However, I originally thought it would be better to try and solve the problem, rather than to pass it back to the sender.

Two days after Cammaratta's memo, Smouse responded to him. A copy went to Shelton and Shields. No copy to me. Why? Part of the memo went like this:

MICHAEL GREGO'S TRAVEL FORM

Please refer to the items numbered and my comments:

1. Michael Grego did not walk into the office with the SB-77 form in hand; Mr. Wieser did. Michael Grego reports to his principal; Mr. Wieser reports to Dr. Cammaratta, General Director, Vocational-Technical Education. My statements refer to Mr. Wieser's actions only.

2. Why did Mr. Wieser pursue the request for approval of out-of-county travel funds for Michael Grego if he had already told Mr. Grego that no funds were available? Why did Mr. Wieser fail to inform Mrs. Ippolito that he had already told Mr. Grego that no funds were available?

3. Why did Mr. Wieser hand-deliver to my office an incomplete SB-77, knowing that it was incomplete?

4. It is not considered a "solution" when the supervisor merely brings to my office an incomplete document, knowing that it is incomplete, and not having attempted to complete the form before handing it over to the secretarial staff. This merely transfers the problem from Mr. Wieser to my office.

Mr. Wieser's memorandum offers considerable detail on his involvement with the SB-77 travel form for Michael Grego. Nowhere in his memorandum does he acknowledge that he knew the form was incomplete, yet he purposely handed it over to my office without complete information and without the support document.

At the end of his memo he said "Please counsel with Mr. Wieser further and give me a written reply."

Some of the questions that Smouse asked in his memo were appropriate, but should have been asked before he wrote the first memo. It would have saved a lot of confusion in his office, Cammaratta's, and mine.

Again, I responded to Cammaratta in response to Smouse's follow-up memo of April 15, 1987. Some of my explanations in my memo of April 27, are as follows:

> Michael Grego submitted a travel form...to the wrong person....If the principal was sending him as I told him to check into, then the travel form should have been sent to the Area Director....
>
> This form and its authorization was not initiated by my office....I now feel that when I discover a situation like this again, that I will not try to assist the teacher, but instead I will return the travel authorization form to the principal who originated it....
>
> Since it was not initiated by me and submitted late to me, I took it with me to Mr. Smouse's office seeking direction. I am sorry for the subsequent results for trying to get information....
>
> In summary, I am sorry that my responses have repeatedly been misinterpreted in such a negative manner....Hopefully, these misunderstandings can be resolved in a positive and professional manner.

Cammaratta's response memo to Smouse was sent on April 28. He indicated to Smouse that he discussed and counseled with me about Smouse's comments of April 15. He also said that he asked me to respond and give my rational in reference to Grego's travel form. He attached my memo to his memo to Smouse.

Repeatedly over the months, Smouse has closed his memos with a statement such as: "If there is anything that I or anyone else can do to assist you, please let us know." So, as per his instructions, I went to his office for assistance on what to do with a form that I didn't originate or sign, that was sent to me by mistake, and instead of assistance to solve a problem, I get my head cut off because he overreacted. I felt like the messenger in the old story who brings bad news.

Smouse wrote another memo to Cammaratta on May 4, and indicated that in my last memo I misspelled two words and had used incorrect grammar. He asked Cammaratta to review this with me and obtain my signature.

Now it is time to set up the "punch line" for this Mike Grego affair. Several months later, during the summer, Grego was visiting Cammaratta and I happened to walk by his office. I saw Mike and congratulated him again on being "Teacher of the Year" in Florida. During our conversation in Cammaratta's office, the topic of his travel form came up. In talking to him about it, Grego stated that when he returned from Oklahoma, he called Smouse's office because I had left that message for him when I tried to contact him on March 20, the day I took the travel form to Smouse's office. When Grego called Smouse's office on Thursday, March 26, he made that office aware that his principal, Alene Mahin, at Leto High School, had authorized him to go, that she provided a substitute for him, that she agreed to pay the additional cost, and that she originated the travel form and signed it.

The "punch line" to this story is that Smouse's office was told of this information on March 26, *five days before* Smouse wrote his first memo of March 31, criticizing me for bringing in a form that had no coding, no substitute, no budget transfer and was three days late. How could he make me and my immediate supervisor go through all this paperwork when he *knew* that the error was that of the principal and not mine? Why did he write all those memos, with copies to the Superintendent and the Assistant Superintendent for Personnel, request my signature on them and place them in my personnel file? Was this just "filler" for my file, or was it something to keep me busy, as though my office wasn't already busy enough? Was it a method to drive a wedge between one of my teachers and myself? I was offended.

There is one more interesting occurrence in the Mike Grego Affair that I found out in the above same conversation with Grego. I originally thought that my office received his travel form on Friday, March 20. But in the conversation, Grego told us that he tried to get the form to my office on Monday, five days before he left on his travel. To do this, he asked a colleague in his department, Bobby Harrell, an electronics teacher, to bring the form to my office on Monday, March 16. After school, in the late afternoon, Harrell brought the form to my office and put the it on my secretary's desk because everyone had left for the day. My secretary had gone home at noon on that day, Monday, March 16, and was also absent on March 17, 18 and 19. She returned to work on Friday, March 20. She did not present the travel form to me until the afternoon of March 20. And that is when I took it to Smouse's office to seek advice on what could be done to ensure the teacher was covered to travel.

The procedure for receiving the daily mail in my office when my secretary was out sick was for my coordinator, Hair, to collect the school mail and the U.S. Mail from our box in the hall and then to open, date stamp and distribute it to me, him or our secretary. He always sits at her desk to do this because the letter opener and date stamp are there. I'm surprised that he didn't notice the travel form on her desk during those three days that she was out sick. Did he really find it and put it aside?

I was disappointed that this commendable occasion of Grego being named state "Industrial Arts Teacher of the Year" became so tarnished.

After observing all of Smouse's actions over the last year, I started to become bold and courageous. When he requested that I sign his memos, he would always type this statement at the end.

> I acknowledge receipt of this memorandum. My signature does not necessarily mean approval.
>
> _____
> William F. Wieser   Date

I knew that he was putting all this into my personnel file and I knew that I better start to stand up for myself. When I would sign these memos, I would cross out the words "not necessarily" and add the letters "dis" in front of the word approval. The statement would then read: "My signature does mean disapproval." On one hand, it made me feel valiant, but on the other hand it made me feel disrespectful because I felt I was standing up to my employer, to whom I was dedicated. Graduate school never taught me about things like this.

Was Smouse caught in the syndrome of "Perceiving-Behaving-Becoming" about evaluating me? Did he first perceive how he wanted me rated and then set out to prove it (in his opinion)? Finally, in his mind, did I become what he perceived because he had all the "extensive and convincing" documentation? Yes? It may have been convincing to him, but not to me, my supervisor, and many other educators. Were his steps in the evaluation process valid and reliable according to professional ethics and School Board policy? Was Smouse going to be the judge, jury and executioner? God help us!

Cammaratta and I were spending a lot of office time together because of the directives from Smouse. We usually came into the office half an hour early and often stayed late when others got to go home. I'm sure these long work days took a toll on Cammaratta's wife and his family, not to mention the stress he took home over the weekend when you are supposed to relax. If I were still married, I'm sure this job stress would have lead to marital problems, not to mention a divorce.

13

POWER HOUR

It had been a long, busy, and most active year for my office as Supervisor of Industrial Arts and Industrial Education. There were many positive achievements that year in spite of all the attention given to my office by the Assistant Superintendent for Vocational, Technical and Adult Education. It was April now and the end-of-the-year performance evaluations were being completed. Under the new manager performance appraisal system, there was a two-step process of evaluation including a formative evaluation in mid-year (December) in which progress is evaluated and a year-end summative evaluation (April) which evaluates overall performance.

My formative evaluation was completed on December 19, 1986. The rating is based upon a scale from 0 to 4, with 4 being "Exemplary." I completed the self-rating part with a rating in the five categories of 4,3,3,3,3. My immediate supervisor, Cammaratta, rated me with 3,3,3,3,3. Both ratings are recorded on the form. A rating of 3 is "Exceeds Standards."

Two months before the formative evaluation, Smouse had written his memo of October 28, 1986, in which he stated, "you would be given several months to move the activities of the Supervisor's Office in a positive direction. In the event that major improvements were not forthcoming, steps would be taken to remove you from your position." This formative evaluation by my immediate supervisor, Cammaratta, obviously showed approval of my job performance since Smouse had written his memo. I had hoped that it would satisfy Smouse, who did not acknowledge Cammaratta's approval, but then again, did not object either in writing or verbally. I felt good, but I did not know what Smouse was thinking and that bothered me. At my option, I had attached comments to my formative evaluation which had become part of my permanent record in the personnel files. My comments spoke about the size of my department as the largest of the six vocational supervisor departments in the county. I pointed out other items for the record, making sure that interested people had information to make clear judgements about my performance. I had written:

> This department is currently understaffed, causing me to work beyond the normal workday to meet the required support services requested by the schools. I find that I am "spreading myself thin" to complete all the office responsibilities, and therefore I have evaluated myself lower than what I am capable of performing. I have requested additional staff members to be added to this department.
>
> A concern that I have about equipment is that it is difficult to monitor the maintenance, repair, and safe operation of all the different machinery at the various sites. It is also important that funding becomes available to purchase new and replacement equipment so that we may keep programs abreast with state-of-the-art training and safety.

Funding is important to any department, especially to industrial programs because they require a lot of high-priced equipment, more than any other program. I had readily known that teacher morale was hurt when I had told them of the drastic reductions from $240,000.00 for equipment for the last fiscal year to zero this year. The effect on my programs and my image were devastating.

I was apprehensive where the $240,000.00 was going. We were never told specifics other than there was a "budget crunch." I wondered if there was another type of textbook scam.

Cammaratta, as directed by Smouse, had worked closely with me and was ready to complete my year-end summative evaluation. In doing so, Cammaratta had gathered information from others who had worked directly with me. Such information would support his final evaluation. According to board policy B-45.5, the person directly responsible for the supervisor will make the evaluation. Policy A-31.1 states that "the General Director will evaluate supervisors," and that was Cammaratta. To support his evaluation, Cammaratta knew he must cover his backside in his evaluation of me because of the manner in which Smouse was behaving.

In April, Cammaratta, met with all the supervisors to complete their evaluations. On the 0 to 4 scale, I did my self-rating in the five categories as 4,3,4,3,4. Cammaratta evaluated me as 3,2,3,3,3. The 2 rating is "Meets Expected Standards" and unofficially is considered average. The supervisor evaluations were complete, and Cammaratta made an appointment with Smouse so that he could review them.

On Monday afternoon, May 4, 1987, I drove Cammaratta, who was having trouble with his old car, to Smouse's office so that he could present his completed evaluations of his staff. Our supervisory offices are about five miles from the county offices downtown, so I decided to wait for him in the cafeteria, clearing up some paperwork. He had expected his meeting to last less than one hour. When he came to get me, after an hour exactly, he looked haunted with apprehension.

I drove slowly back to work and he told of the "threats" that Smouse made to him. They sounded like threats to me.

The next sequence of events included some critical happenings. Because of Smouse's reactions to my year-end evaluation, Cammaratta made the professional and prudent decision to write the following statement for the record:

THE ISSUE OF THE EVALUATION PROCESS AND RALPH SMOUSE'S REACTION

To Whom It May Concern:

Since Mr. Smouse elected to write Mr. Wieser the memo of September 22, 1986, I have continuously worked with Mr. Wieser almost on a daily basis. I am familiar with his responsibilities, program development, and the goals of the Industrial Arts and Industrial Education department. This year Hillsborough County Schools initiated a new evaluation system. During the first semester, due to the sensitivity of Mr. Smouse's memo of September 22, 1986, I carefully researched the major evaluation items. Having monitored Mr. Wieser's professional activities, I followed policy in determining the rating for the first semester (formative evaluation phase).

During the second semester, it is required to observe and evaluate the second phase of the new evaluation system. The summative evaluation (phase two) was completed on April 24. Much time and effort was spent in this process. In order to develop perceptions and judgement in all areas and levels, I involved three different groups in the evaluation process. They were: principals (junior and senior high), peer colleagues (supervisory staff), and industrial classroom teachers.

The above research substantiated my own evaluation in working with Mr. Wieser on a daily basis. Once I had completed my detailed study of Mr. Wieser's evaluation, I proceeded to make an appointment with Mr. Smouse. After several attempts to set an appointment, Mr. Smouse agreed to review the staff's evaluations on May 4. It is important to note our completed evaluations were due May 1. We met to discuss the evaluations on Monday, May 4 at 2:00 PM. I presented all the staff evaluations, holding Mr. Wieser's for the last item since I expected there would be a lengthy discussion of Mr. Wieser. He accepted my evaluation of the entire staff except for Mr. Wieser. When we were discussing Mr. Wieser's evaluation, I outlined the lengthy and time-consuming qualitative and evaluative process that I had developed in arriving at Mr. Wieser's summative evaluation. During the entire discussion at several intervals, he made the following statements:

1. At the inception of the discussion when he saw my evaluation of Mr. Wieser, he indicated that he wanted me to rate Mr. Wieser on a very low scale in order to place him on the remediation track and probation. (See Mr. Smouse's attached form.) I did not agree with his evaluation. I felt it was my responsibility to evaluate Mr. Wieser since I am his immediate supervisor and work with him daily. Then he specifically made the comment that he had not discussed my own evaluation at this point indicating my evaluation was in jeopardy.

2. During the ensuing discussion, he became more adamant when he insisted I change my evaluation and found out that I was not willing to change. He stated that he would have me before an administrative hearing if I did not change. At this point, I began to be more concerned of his statements. I felt I could not professionally, ethically, and morally change my evaluation since I had conducted an intense study on this evaluation.

3. Mr. Smouse had commented that he had discussed this issue with Dr. Sickles and that in order for Mr. Wieser to be put in a remediation track, that Mr. Wieser's rating would have to be in the one and zero levels. Mr. Smouse also stated if this were to be done, that next year if Mr. Wieser did not show a major improvement, he would be terminated. I was most concerned about his intended evaluation, and since he had made two previous threatening remarks, I became deeply concerned about the discussion. I then repeated I could not in good conscience change my evaluation. He became angry and stated to me in no uncertain terms "that your job is on the line." Mr. Smouse's statement completely undermined all the evaluation work I had done. Since I saw he was not going to accept my evaluation of Mr. Wieser, I told Mr. Smouse that I would need a few days to think about his demands. I felt I was being held hostage.

After I left his office, I decided to confer with Dr. Shelton, but I found that he was out of town. Due to the urgency of the discussion with Mr. Smouse, I felt I had to talk to someone. I then decided to speak to a board member, to seek advice. I discussed the entire issue with this board member on May 5. I was advised to meet and discuss the issue with the superintendent, Dr. Shelton. On Wednesday, May 7, I met with Dr. Shelton and discussed the entire issue. I also mentioned to him that since he was out of town, I had felt obligated to discuss the issue with a board member who I knew would give me advice. When I had fully informed Dr. Shelton of the situation with Mr. Smouse, Dr. Shelton asked me to meet with Mr. Smouse again and attempt to resolve the issue. Then I was to make an appointment with Dr. Shelton to inform him of progress.

Knowing Mr. Smouse would be out of town on Thursday and Friday, May 7 and 8, I called his office and made an appointment for Monday, May 11 at 8:30 a.m. I then called Dr. Shelton's secretary at 9:29 AM and left a message about my meeting planned with Mr. Smouse. During this meeting Mr. Smouse told me he would not accept Mr. Wieser's evaluation. Also, he gave me my own evaluation form to complete for the formative phase, a form that had been due in December, 1986. The following Tuesday I made an appointment with the superintendent for Wednesday, May 13, at 1:30 p.m, the day Mr. Smouse also wanted to see my evaluation and Mr. Wieser's evaluation. At this time, he cast further aspersions and indicated insubordination. On Wednesday, May 13, Mr. Smouse had indicated I was to meet in his office first. When I went to his office, his secretary told me that he had already gone to Dr. Shelton's office and the meeting had been changed to 1:45 or 2:00 PM I then went to Dr. Shelton's office and waited in the reception area. Dr. Shelton's door was closed. Later when the door opened, Dr. Walt Sickles, Assistant Superintendent for Instruction and Ms. Beth Shields, Assistant Superintendent for Personnel came out of the superintendent's office, leaving only Mr. Smouse in Dr. Shelton's office. Finally summoned to meet with them, Dr. Shelton asked me to review the issue. I told Dr. Shelton my reasoning for Mr. Wieser's and how I had arrived at the evaluation after a year's study and input from principals, teachers, and a peer group.

These evaluations were consistent with my own evaluation. I also told Dr. Shelton of my meeting with Mr. Smouse on Monday, May 4. I told him that Mr. Smouse threatened me on three occasions during that meeting. They were:

1. My own evaluation was not done yet.
2. Threatened me with an administrative hearing.
3. My job was on the line.

I noticed at this time that Dr. Shelton became concerned about our discussion. Dr. Shelton told Mr. Smouse and me to go back and try to resolve the issue amicably so as to continue the good working relationship. I also told Dr. Shelton that prior to this problem, my office had a good working relationship with Mr. Smouse's office and that I was concerned about the developments in this case. At this point, Dr. Shelton knew that it was my responsibility to evaluate Mr. Wieser. He confirmed that it was my job to do the evaluation. At this point, Mr. Smouse heard Dr. Shelton in reference to the evaluation and stated that he would attach a letter of disagreement to my evaluation. Dr. Shelton again reiterated that we should resolve the issue.

In summary, I am submitting again my rationale for Mr. Wieser's evaluation in reference to Mr. Smouse's memo of June 2, 1987, stating his disagreement with my evaluation.

> Dr. Don P. Cammaratta
> General Director

Many questions were generated after I had learned of this sequence of events. When I tried to answer some questions, new and additional questions arose. Most of my questions still remain unanswered today. I could only speculate on what I believe was happening to me and why.

However, there was one further "threat" Cammaratta did not put in writing. I will let it remain silent too.

I worked closely with Cammaratta over the last year and felt that I really got to know my boss as a professional leader and as a person. I saw him just about daily. But, I never saw him as I saw him after that meeting; hearing him talk in my car. I could easily tell that things were most serious. I wanted this confrontation to stop. I just wanted to get back to doing my job. I enjoyed my work; it was most important to my life because it was my identity and fulfillment!

It had been professionally prudent of Cammaratta to include feedback from other professionals about my performance at various schools. My job as supervisor, according to the job description, was to "assist principals and county staff in planning, developing and administering the industrial programs and facilities." Also to "assist teachers in curriculum planning... and act as a liaison between teachers and principals." I worked with principals and teachers at sixteen high schools, about thirty junior high schools, three vocational schools, and several special education centers. Cammaratta had asked the principals, at a meeting, to please give him feedback on my performance at their schools. Eight principals even put their comments in letters. Along with letters from some industrial teachers, these combined letters represented a cross-section of my school-site contacts. In reflection of Cammaratta's evaluation, I offer the following comments he received.

> Thank you William Wieser for your extra efforts that has helped to provide a positive learning experience for our students. I especially appreciate Mr. Wieser's willingness to spend time needed with my assistant principal for curriculum in planning for the 1987-88 school year and giving requested assistance to our faculty members.
>
> Edward J. Ballas, Principal
Jefferson High School

> Mr. Wieser...has been so very instrumental in providing the kind of support necessary for programs like ours to be successful. He not only communicates well with Mr. Julian, our Industrial Arts teacher, but keeps the administrative office appraised of current business. His flexibility and understanding of our unique needs lends itself to keeping the morale high at our center.
>
> William I. Troutman, Principal
Dorothy Thomas School

> Thank you for your help in getting our shop here at McLane Junior High School in top-notch shape. The enthusiasm that you displayed in helping us accomplish this task is greatly appreciated.
>
> John Alfano, Principal
McLane Junior High School

> Let me take this opportunity to express to you our thanks for the fine job that Mr. Bill Wieser...has done in working with our vocational program. Mr. Wieser has been more than willing to give of himself and aid us in our every request.
>
> Ronald L. Allen, Principal
Gaither High School

Upon my request he has made frequent shop visits to observe and assist the new shop teacher in teaching methods and implementation of better safety practices. As a result of our combined efforts, improvements are evident in this teacher's program. I have found him to be thoroughly professional in all contacts....

> Rodney R. Osborn, Principal
> Dowdell Junior High School

I called Mr. Bill Wieser...for the purpose of making recommendations for upgrading the lab....Within a matter of days, Mr. Wieser had responded by making an on-site visit, followed by suggestions, recommendations and, most importantly, follow-through.

> Frank Scaglione, Principal
> King High School

I want to express my sincere appreciation to you for the expedient way in which you have helped this administration in dealing with some of our shop problems. Your assistance in our Beginning Teacher observations has helped tremendously, and I appreciate your continued support of our programs.

> Robert E. Godwin, Principal
> Tampa Bay Vocational -
> Technical High School

In addition to the above principals, several teachers expressed their views about my working relationship with them and their programs.

I can say without reservation, that Mr. Wieser performed his duties to the utmost. He has always gone the extra mile to afford his time and experience whenever I have called upon him. As department head, he has kept me informed with any and all new information which I have in turn been able to pass along to my department members.

> Augie G. Martinez
> Department Head
> Gaither High School

In my workings with Bill, I have found him more than helpful in areas of equipment, purchasing, travel, repairs, supplies, or perhaps the most important is simply being able to call and talk.

> Michael Grego
> Department Head
> Leto High School

I wish for it to be known that Bill has handled his duties with both dedication and sensitivity. I have seen him handle personnel on an individual basis. I have had the opportunity to experience Bill's leadership in both intimate and large group settings.

>Rodney Arthur Norris
>Greco Junior High School

I have taught industrial arts for 17 years in Hillsborough County. I have worked with seven different supervisors, and I have found Mr. Wieser to be extremely intelligent, articulate, and innovative. As past president of the Hillsborough County Industrial Arts Teachers Association I am in constant communication with my colleagues. The message and tone is clear. Mr. Wieser is always accessible when teachers call for help.

>Denis Binder
>Department Head
>East Bay High School

Cammaratta told me that no principal or teacher who spoke to him indicated any dissatisfaction with my job performance. He also stated that Smouse presented no letters from anyone indicating displeasure with my performance.

Cammaratta had expanded the input for my evaluating, he told me, by asking each of the other five vocational supervisors to evaluate me in writing on the new form. He told them that to do so was optional. I had worked with them for two years as a fellow supervisor and for five years before as a coordinator. All five agreed, filled out the form, and signed it. Cammaratta totaled the evaluations and the average came out to be a 2.9 rating, again, 2 "Meets Expected Standards" and 3 "Exceeds Standards." These results were similar to Cammaratta's evaluation.

Cammaratta used last year's evaluation form as a starting point for a more comprehensive look at my performance. Last year's form had eight main categories and a total of forty-two sub categories to rate as compared to this year's new form, which had only five general ratings. Last year's rating scale was the same: 0 to 4 rating. Cammaratta's rating on last year's form had averaged 3.18. He felt his rating correlated with the supervisors' 2.9 rating and reflected the letters of evaluation by principals and teachers. He had pointed out many of these details in his meeting with Smouse and Shelton. With all this input from Mr. Smouse, principals, supervisors and teachers, Dr. Cammaratta then arrived at my evaluation ratings. I truly thought that Cammaratta did an honest, professional, and accurate job in evaluating me.

There were so many little things that happened during Cammaratta's meetings. When I would ask what was my status, he would share specifics of what took place. Smouse had prepared, for Cammaratta, a sample evaluation form specifically showing him how Smouse wanted me rated. A copy showed Smouse's handwriting, in a shaky style, rating me in the five categories as 2,0,1,1,1, a rating that would have placed me in "Track 3" for remediation and possible, or probable, termination at the end of next year. Smouse had never observed me in my office, had never accompanied me on any of my weekly visits to schools; furthermore, Smouse had no responsibility to evaluate me, according to board policy. Why did he try to take over? Did he have a motive?

After the first meeting with Smouse on May 4, Jean Ippolito, secretary to Smouse, had commented to Cammaratta about my situation. "Don't you think it is time to give in and call a truce to all of this? You should know that Mr. Smouse has involved Dr. Sickles, Beth Shields and Dr. Binnie in this too." Cammaratta told me that he had replied that my evaluation had become a matter of principle and that he felt that he would be professionally, morally, and ethically wrong to change anything.

Was Smouse holding Cammaratta hostage. He had not completed Cammaratta's year-end summative evaluation. He didn't complete Cammaratta's mid-year formative evaluation last December. Why did Smouse wait to complete Cammaratta's mid-year formative evaluation until the end of the year with the summative evaluation?

During the last meeting between Smouse, Shelton and Cammaratta, Superintendent Shelton had said that it was Cammaratta's responsibility to evaluate me. Then Smouse had stated that he would attach a letter of disagreement to my evaluation. The letter, actually a memorandum dated June 2, 1987, was sent to Cammaratta, three weeks after their conference, with copies to Shelton, Shields, and me.

> This is in confirmation of the conference we had with Dr. Shelton last week regarding your evaluation of William F. Wieser. I did not feel that the evaluation which you completed for Mr. Wieser was compatible with the factual information which was accumulated since last September regarding his performance. It was my opinion that the evaluation should have been somewhat lower than you have indicated in the areas of Organizational Skills, Management Skills, and Judgement Skills.
>
> I have discussed this with Dr. Shelton and I am writing this in order that there be a record of my disagreement with the evaluation. Please have Mr. Wieser acknowledge receipt of this memorandum by signing a copy and returning it to me.

In Smouse's first sentence he said that the conference was "last week." He was wrong. The conference was on May 13, and his memo was written on June 2, which is about a difference of three weeks. I question Smouse's accuracy. Did the superintendent put a memo in Smouse's file because of a technical mistake like this one? Smouse states that he "discussed this with Dr. Shelton," but he didn't say if Shelton gave his approval of him writing this memo. I am concerned because if someone reads this memo in my file and sees Dr. Shelton's name, that it would give a connotation of "approval." Also, Smouse states he "did not feel that the evaluation...was compatible with the factual information." But, the "factual" information included my mid-year evaluation and the back-up documentation from principals, supervisors and teachers. This made me wonder if Smouse refused to recognize any opinion inconsistant with his own? Why didn't Smouse object to my mid-year formative evaluation back in December and write a memo indicating his opinion? More inconsistency.

Because of Smouse's memo, it had became vital that I too write for the record. My memorandum to Cammaratta was dated June 10, 1987.

> I have told you that I don't mind anyone telling or sending information to you about my job performance whether it be positive or negative, since you are the one authorized and responsible for my evaluation. But I feel Mr. Smouse has exceeded his responsibilities when he tried to change your evaluation of me and more so now when this evaluation memo is attached to my permanent evaluation. If the superintendent accepted my evaluation, then I feel Mr. Smouse should accept it.

At this point I began to wonder about the role of the Superintendent of Schools. I couldn't understand why the superintendent had told Cammaratta to go back for a second time and try to resolve the issue amicably. I believe, in my best professional judgement, that the superintendent personally should have resolved it since the School Board had already been informed about the conflict.

I experienced so much frustration at the end of this busy year. I became concerned about all these memos filling my personnel file. If someone saw these memos and they didn't know the whole story, what would they think of me? Would all these memos affect my future promotions?

It was one hell of a year right up to the end. I look back through all the documentation trying to understand just what transpired. In what way did it benefit our educational system? Why had it come so far. Is it over? Can I breathe easy now and put all my energy into doing my job?

In summary of this chapter I will quote the last paragraph in my June 10, 1987, memo to Cammaratta about Smouse's memo where he felt my evaluation should be somewhat lower.

I feel Mr. Smouse has been biased and revengeful in launching an unprovoked blitzkrieg which will affect my professional career. I am presently searching for appropriate action to take to renounce recent unethical and unprofessional action from him and to relinquish future occurrences of the same.

I have heard the oft-quoted remark made by Lord Acton one hundred years ago in 1887: "Power tends to corrupt and absolute power corrupts absolutely." I'm starting to believe this sentiment is true.

BEGINNING OF SCHOOL YEAR 1987–88

14

THE BIG BLACK BOOK

After a long, busy and active year with a dark cloud hanging over my yearly performance evaluation, I was disenchanted, perplexed and looking for an abatement. I felt that things had happened over the last year that should not have happened. My goal was to look for a way to stop these actions once and for all. I wanted to resolve the conflict between Smouse and myself now.

The story that took place over the last year was already too big and complex to tell quickly and easily in a verbal manner. The best way to tell this story was in written format with all the accompanying documentation. This would be an organized method to put all of the correspondence and facts together in a logical and understandable sequence. Numerous documentation on my performance had already been placed in my personnel file by Smouse. My documentation compilation could also serve as support information on my job performance, if I needed it. I wasn't sure what might happen in the future in reference to my performance evaluation. I was skeptical.

I organized the "book" into a chronological manner showing dates, facts, letters/memos, events and people that were involved. As I compiled the data, its size grew to fill a three-inch ring binder. My office had several extra binders and I chose one that was black. The paper and section tabs were all from office supplies. I titled it "A Data Documentation" and gave it the nickname "The Big Black Book." I divided its contents into seventeen sections with a total of 414 pages. It weighed seven pounds. To ease the rigorous and tedious reading of this 414 page fact book, I developed an "Executive Summary" consisting of three pages to give an overall view of the content and sequence.

The contents started from my appointment as Supervisor in October, 1985 and continued through the yearly evaluation process in June, 1987. It was most complete. I even met with my immediate supervisor, Cammaratta, and asked him several specific questions about events when I was hired and since evaluated. I took notes during these meetings and included the information in the book. I also added an appendix that included job descriptions of the Supervisor, Coordinator and Secretary II, plus a copy of the new county administrator and supervisor evaluation procedures and the Code of Ethics and Principles of Professional Conduct for the Education Profession in Florida.

I asked Cammaratta if it would be all right if his secretary typed some pages for my documentation during her lunch time or after work. I felt I couldn't trust my secretary to keep this data documentation confidential, and I knew I needed confidentiality because the situation was so delicate. He said it was Okay with him if it was Okay with his secretary. She said yes because she understood my office situation. Because I considered this to be extra work for her, I paid $150 for her efforts. I still wasn't sure what I was going to do with the book, if anything at all.

One day, I was assembling the book in my office at my desk, I was called out of the office for a few moments and left the documentation open and on top of my desk. As I returned to my office, my secretary looked up to see me coming down the hall and turned to say something to Mr. Hair, my coordinator. As I entered the office, where we were all housed in one room, Hair was by my desk looking for a place to go. He started mumbling and stumbling in his speech to my secretary and then turned and went into the storage room by my desk. Collusion? When you work with someone in the same office for two years, you can tell when something is abnormal. I had a strong feeling that he was looking at the papers on my desk. They knew I had been doing something and my secretary knew I wasn't sending any typing to her. Curiosity was expected. I became more discreet.

The Big Black Book was finished in July, 1987. It was ready for possible use in some manner. It was aimed at resolving the conflict between Smouse and myself. I felt it was packed with so much information, that it was like a loaded cannon ready to go off. I was prepared for a recoil that I may have to sustain.

The book was loaded. Where should I aim it? Should I pull the trigger?

According to the newspapers, the Textbook Scam was expected to reach a settlement. Money and condominium properties would be given up by the suspended textbook supervisor. The school system was expected to recover between $70,000 and $200,000 according to W. Crosby Few, School Board attorney. Some of the cash was in 12 accounts across the state. The tentative settlement would place the school board in a position of owning resort condominiums. Could one person do all this by himself without the knowledge of any other school system officials?

15

NOW WHAT?

Did you ever go to the store and pick out something you didn't really need, and once in the check-out line, wanted to get rid of it? This is the quandary that I'm in since I have compiled The Big Black Book.

Back in Chapter 13, Power Hour, Cammaratta stated in his memo that Superintendent Shelton said to Smouse and him, "go back and try to resolve the issue." This happened twice. Because the issue had grown from a normal evaluation process to one that included the Superintendent and the School Board, I believe that the Superintendent should have resolved the issue there and then. It already had gone too far. Did the Superintendent have a hot potato thrown at him and he didn't know what to do, so he threw it back? These actions by the Superintendent told me that, if anything equitable was going to be done, then it had to be started by me. I still felt there was a fire smoldering between Smouse and Cammaratta. When it finally erupted, I would be the one who was buried in ashes. The ones that will suffer from this situation are in the Vocational Division, all the way down to the students in the classroom.

I have compiled The Big Black Book and the big question is "Now what?" Then the next question is "What will happen if I present the book to someone?" Will the conflict between Smouse and myself be resolved, or will it create a greater irritation? Will I be looked at as a whistleblower or someone who cares about the education of students? Will I be able to return to giving my full time and attention to the needed services of the vocational programs under my supervision or will I be hampered in my office duties? What consequences could I personally suffer? Will I be putting my job on the line? Will my immediate supervisor, Cammaratta, eventually be over-powered or out-flanked in his evaluation of me? What risk will I be placing on my future career? Will I be labeled as a nonconformist? All of these possibilities were considered before I could make a decision as to what to do. I also considered what had been happening to me because of Smouse's actions. I felt his approach was wrong; it had gone too far and had to be stopped!

The options that I saw I had at the time were:

1. Do nothing and hope that things would get better with Mr. Smouse.
2. Go public to the newspapers and TV stations and tell my story.
3. Meet with Mr. Smouse to try to bury the hatchet.
4. File a grievance against Smouse with the school system.
5. File suit against Mr. Smouse in court.
6. Meet with the Superintendent to try to solve the issue quietly.
7. Tell my story to the School Board during a public meeting.
8. Physically attack Mr. Smouse to put a scare into him. But this wasn't my way.

The decision on which option I should take was difficult because I had mixed emotions. It had been a long year and I was anxious to get things resolved. I saw my future in Hillsborough County Schools and I wanted to protect that aspiration. I was confident that I could ask a favor of Cammaratta. I said that I wanted to talk to a School Board member informally for advice. I asked for his recommendation. He recommended Mr. Sam Rampello. I had already shown the book to Cammaratta and he was aware that I was in a quandary as to what to do. I asked Cammaratta to attend my meeting with Rampello to introduce me and to confirm my story.

The meeting took place during the summer of 1987, at Pach's Place restaurant in Tampa. The three of us had breakfast and I generally summarized my problem with Smouse. I told Rampello that this was an informal meeting and that I was looking for advice. So that he could understand the extent of the problem, I gave him The Big Black Book to review. We met again a few weeks later and he returned the book to me. His comment was that I had a pretty good case. I asked for his advice and he said that I should meet with the Superintendent.

I knew that I should also get advice from legal counsel. My current attorney, Fritz Grey, did not have a background in educational matters and several months earlier he had recommended that I not file suit against Smouse. I had the feeling that I should consult with a different attorney who would recommend filing suit if my attempts within the school system didn't work out.

It was time to meet with the Superintendent and have an attorney with me who would recommend filing suit if a solution wasn't reached. I felt that I needed this clout when I met with the Superintendent.

I had a feeling of satisfaction because it looked like I would be able to resolve the issue in a quiet and professional way without having to go public. The feeling of satisfaction turned out to be superficial. My loss again.

16

HELLO "DEEP THROAT"

In the book *All The President's Men* by Bernstein and Woodward, Bob Woodward tells about a source of information involved in their investigating and reporting of the Watergate situation. Their source was dubbed "Deep Throat" after a celebrated pornographic movie. "Deep Throat" only met with them on limited occasions. The agreement was not to identify him, but to use his information to do their jobs as news reporters. "Deep Throat" preferred not to talk on the phone, but to meet in a parking garage late at night. He cautioned them to take care when using their telephones. He would give Woodward and Bernstein advice and confirm other information they found. Woodward considered him a wise teacher because he seemed committed to the search for truth. "Deep Throat" also had a working knowledge of politics and had access to information from the White House.

In my story about the politics of education, there was a "friend" that I met that had characteristics similar to "Deep Throat." I too will keep this person's identity confidential. I will not reveal the person's sex or professional background. I also will not say if the friend was only one individual or a mixture of several. This source had a strong knowledge of the educational system, a caring attitude for quality education, a direct line of communication to the State Commissioner and a knowledge of activities in the Superintendent's office. I nicknamed my source the "Professor." I thought this title would give things an educational flair. Plus, in the following Chapters, I'll refer to this person as the "Professor" or I'll use the pronoun "he/him" to make the writing easy.

I saw that I could use the Professor's advice and information to help resolve the problems with Smouse. Plus I could double check that what I was doing was ethically and professionally right.

I, too, met with the "Professor" on limited occasions. We did talk on the phone sometimes, but we spoke briefly and in code. We would meet at one of several restaurants. We usually met at Denny's, called the big "D" or "the same place," and we would wait to sit at a special table in the corner so we could talk confidentially. We were prepared so that if I saw someone that I knew, I would introduce the "Professor" without using a title or last name. There were times when the "Professor" left early so we would not be seen together. We often "cased the joint" to see who, if anyone, was there.

The "Professor" soon proved his creditability. He had contacts in the "big office downtown" and in the state Department of Education. He sometimes shared detailed information from the office of the state Commissioner of Education. Later this information turned out to be exact and true.

I soon confided in the "Professor" and showed him The Big Black Book. He said my reputation had been damaged. Also he commented that he never saw a case so well documented. Since July, 1987, the "Professor" and I shared thoughts and ideas about solving my immediate problems and improving the quality of education in Hillsborough County.

17

ATTORNEY NUMBER 2

I was ready and anxious to resolve all issues between Smouse and myself in one way or another. It didn't appear that he was letting go of his stand. After Dr. Cammaratta's evaluation meeting with the Superintendent, where my evaluation was accepted (Chapter 13), Smouse still wrote a letter of disagreement with my rating and placed it in my personnel file. Because of Smouse not yielding to the Superintendent's inclination in this matter, I felt that the Superintendent should put a final stop to it. People were starting to talk about the happenings in the Vocational Division between Smouse and me. Rumors were being spread. I saw the division as being wounded and in need of first aid.

The best plan now seemed to be a meeting with the Superintendent. He should be presented with a factual and documented "case" that should be handled directly by him. If he balked at this type of approach, then I would go to plan B with an attorney who was ready to take legal action.

Cammaratta told me about a Tampa attorney who knew a "headhunter." Cammaratta said this attorney was suggested to him by the Professor. I knew what a headhunter was in a job search, but I wasn't sure what he was referring to. In the legal field, a headhunter digs up all kinds of "dirt" about people to help prove that they are no good. Most of the information that I knew about Smouse was regarding how he reacted in the evaluation of my performance. I thought this was the way to go to stop Smouse's actions. I planned to use whatever information was dredged up only if necessary.

I knew that this problem between Smouse and me was already serious because he had placed all those letters and memos in my permanent personnel file. I was sure that it would affect my chances for future promotion or application to another employer. I also knew that, by Board policy, Smouse had access to the School Board attorney, W. Crosby Few, if he wanted it. Therefore, I too should be on an equal level and have legal counsel for advice.

ATTORNEY NUMBER 2

The attorney recommended to me was Jack Joseph Craparo. He had graduated from high school in Tampa and I felt that was to my advantage because he would be from the grass roots. During my first appointment with him, I generalized my conflict with Smouse and he said that he would take the case. I gave him all the specifics about my situation. I pointed out that Cammaratta was supporting me and I told him of the letters from the principals and teachers. Then, I gave him a copy of The Big Black Book and he said it wouldn't be necessary to contract with the headhunter because he would handle it himself. He encouraged me by stating in the last several years the liable suits in Tampa were successful and were increasing in frequency, which made it look good for my chances if we ended up going in that direction.

I was game for the concept of the headhunter approach, which was the appetizer that brought me to Craparo, but he threw me a curve ball when he said that he would handle my case instead of the headhunter. I wasn't sure that I fully understood his pitch.

We talked about my options. He said we could also blast the Superintendent at a School Board meeting like *The Tampa Tribune* was doing. I wasn't sure that would solve anything, but it was another option to consider. I listened and learned about the law.

We had several planning sessions over the summer as to how to handle the problems with Smouse. I mentioned my informal meeting with Sam Rampello and his recommendation to see the Superintendent. One of the first specific options that came up was filing a grievance against Smouse with the school system. We talked about the strategy of this move. It could be a way to solve things and that was good. But, it would be under the control of the school system and that was dubious. In addition, we wanted to settle things quickly and quietly. The grievance could be a drawn-out process. Plus, we were concerned that over this duration, everyone downtown who handled the paper work and those involved in a possible hearing would know of all the problem issues. Then, through normal office gossip, harm might be brought to me, the Vocational Division and the overall school system. According to policy, the grievance process was to be kept confidential, but there was no guarantee. The grievance process was not our first choice for a quick and quiet resolution. I alerted Jack Craparo to the Code of Ethics of the Education Profession in Florida. We both were sure that Smouse had violated the Code. It was decided that we would approach the problem of Smouse's actions from two fronts. First, to meet with the Superintendent and request a hearing for Smouse violating the Code of Ethics and the Principles of Professional Conduct. Second, to file a complaint with the Professional Practices Commission in Tallahassee about

Smouse violating the Code of Ethics and Principles of Professional Conduct. But first we would both meet with the Superintendent and request that he have a hearing concerning Smouse and ask for his permission to file a complaint with the Professional Practices Commission. The meeting would be requested at the Superintendent's office, behind closed doors, to avoid all unfavorable publicity that would make the school system look bad.

A letter was drafted to the Superintendent and was to be hand delivered at our meeting. Attached to it was a statement of my current status, recommendations for a solution and a copy of the Code of Ethics and Principles of Conduct for Educators in Florida. The Big Black Book would also be given to the Superintendent for his study.

I called Raymond Shelton's office to set up a meeting with Jack Craparo and myself for September 18, 1987.

18

CEO AND ME

The stage was set for the meeting with the Superintendent of Schools, Dr. Raymond O. Shelton, a.k.a. Chief Executive Officer, on September 18, 1987. Upon my attorney's advice, this was selected as the best approach to resolve my problems with Smouse because we thought it had the possibility of being handled quickly and quietly. Plus it was also recommended by School Board member Sam Rampello.

We entered the reception area at the Superintendent's office. I was carrying The Big Black Book and the letter to the Superintendent stating our request in writing. My attorney, Jack Craparo, said that he would do most of the talking and I would present the letter and the book for the Superintendent's review.

Superintendent Shelton greeted us in his office and came around his desk to sit with us. We exchanged small talk: Jack apologized for his voice being hoarse because he was just getting over a sore throat and he just moved his office across town; the Superintendent said he too was busy with the challenge of bringing the budget into balance as priority number one. A TV crew had just left his office from a live on-camera interview about the budget and the new school year. To be cordial, Jack, a former teacher himself, commented to Dr. Shelton on the importance of the Superintendent's job.

Then the small talk ended. Jack said, rather directly, that he perceived a problem with Assistant Superintendent Smouse. In no uncertain terms, Jack told it like it was. He requested that the Superintendent have a hearing about the actions of Smouse and asked if we could file a complaint with the state Professional Practices Commission. Jack then gave the letter to Dr. Shelton to read while we read copies. Dr. Shelton responded with a recommendation for the grievance process because it was already in place.

Jack told me to give The Big Black Book to Dr. Shelton for his review and we would be in contact again in the near future. We thanked him for his time. On the way to the car, Jack noted that we left a problem in the lap of the Superintendent and we should get back to him in one week. We both felt good about having the meeting but we were disappointed that the Superintendent didn't offer to take the bull by the horns and handle the problem immediately.

To assist in summarizing this significant meeting, I'll quote the letter that we submitted to Dr. Shelton.

September 18, 1987

Re: Request for Hearing for violating the Code of Ethics and Principles of Professional Conduct.

Dear Dr. Shelton:

As a member of your staff in vocational education and after careful review of all of the facts of which I have documented, hereby, submit same to you for your review and appropriate action.

Upon your review of the facts, it will be apparent that Mr. Ralph Smouse has made, on several occasions, attempts to discredit me by clearly violating the Code of Ethics and the Principles of Professional Conduct for the education profession in Florida.

These overt and unethical acts have created a false condition by which future opportunities for job promotion would be impossible. He has embarrassed me and other colleagues in the presence of others. His conduct has interfered greatly with my mental and physical ability to function within my professional job.

In support of this, I have prepared a summary, making reference to documentation that I have compiled in book form, together with the applicable Code of Ethics and Principles of Professional Conduct rules for the education profession which Mr. Ralph Smouse has violated. The book contains a chronological log of such conduct which includes the dates, facts and witnesses who will be willing to testify at the hearing.

I desire to avoid all unfavorable publicity that will reflect negatively on the school system and prefer that the problem be handled administratively pursuant to our system's administrative policies, the Code of Ethics, and the Principles of Professional Conduct for the education profession.

I respectfully request that you consider this matter by reviewing the summary, carefully reviewing the facts in the documented book in light of the enclosed Code of Ethics and Principles of Professional Practice, and take all steps required by and to adhere to the Code of Ethics and the Principles of Professional Practice in the education profession in Florida.

Sincerely,

William F. Wieser

In an attached status statement, I said, "I feel his (Smouse) harassment activities have tainted and besmirched my professional career and have caused some of my colleagues to view me in a negative context....I believe that documentation of my office personnel has alienated me within my own operating office."

Another attachment was a list of recommendations to be considered in seeking a solution. Some recommendations were the following:

- Require that all future statements of job performance be based upon factual data and not on hear-say information, stories, opinions, bias, personal preference, and/or rumors.

- Remove all defamatory correspondence from William F. Wieser's personnel file.

- Immediate transfer of the Coordinator and Secretary in the industrial office.

- A letter of apology be sent from Mr. Smouse to William F. Wieser for his unprofessional actions.

- Recognition of William F. Wieser's achievements by the Assistant Superintendent for Vocational, Technical and Adult Education.

A copy of the Code of Ethics and Principles of Professional Conduct of the Educations Profession in Florida was also attached to the letter. These appear in the appendix of this book.

The next week I met with Jack Craparo again who recommended we retrieve this request from the Superintendent. Since the Superintendent recommended the grievance, he wasn't going to do anything else about it. It was up to us to do something. Jack told me to meet with Shelton and ask to take the matter directly to the School Board and the Professional Practices Commission. He additionally told me to ask for The Big Black Book back. This would get the Superintendent out of the bind that we put him in.

I called and made the appointment for September 29, 1987. I arrived about ten minutes early. My appointment time came and I got up and went into Shelton's office. We were interrupted by his secretary because someone else had to see him immediately. I went back to the reception area and waited about another ten minutes and was offered a cup of coffee. I said no. My thoughts were on business, not refreshments. My hands got clammy because of the delay, but I regulated my breathing and then all systems read out normal again. Yes, I was nervous, but I could handle it.

Then, it was just the "CEO" and me in his office. I had my notes on my lap of what Jack told me to say. I started by saying we had additional thoughts in reference to our last meeting. Jack Craparo had just received a copy of the Code of Ethics, before our last meeting, and he didn't have much time to review it because he was ill and was busy moving his office. Since then, he reviewed it in depth and he and I agreed it would be better if we asked permission to take this matter directly to the School Board and the Professional Practices Commission. I told him that Jack feels it is best to remove this matter from the Superintendent's office. Shelton said that I didn't need his permission to go to the School Board or to the Professional Practices Commission. He went on to say that if I filed a complaint with the Code of Ethics, I placed myself in a position to have a complaint filed against me. I took that as a threat, simply by the look in his eyes. He said that he still recommended the grievance process as a way to take this matter to the Board, but he couldn't advise me on what to do.

I also said that Jack Craparo wanted me to ask him if he was informed of these events last year. Then I stated I knew he was sent all the correspondence from Smouse's office and mine. I told him that Jack Craparo said if he was informed, something should have been done at that time. The Superintendent didn't comment on that statement, but started to question me and put me on the defensive. He asked me if Cammaratta wrote the "appointment page" that was in The Big Black Book. I told him that I went to Dr. Cammaratta to verify exactly what happened, and I took notes as he told me specifics about my appointment and other happenings that I directly asked about. Shelton then stated, quite clearly, if Mr. Smouse had recommended Richard Hair, he (Shelton) would have gone with it and Hair would be the supervisor today. He looked at me and shook his head to emphasize what he was saying. This is contrary to what Cammaratta said happened in the meeting between Shelton, Smouse and him in reference to Hair's nomination.

Shelton then asked me if I thought it was appropriate to use school board materials, like the cover, paper and tabs, for personal use. I said I didn't consider it as personal use, but that I thought it was all job related. I had hoped that he would be glad that I assembled all the facts for his finger-tip access in solving this problem. However, my hopes and good deeds were now out the window. Then, in a cranky voice, he asked how long it took me to do this fact book. I sensed that he was looking for me to make a commitment in hours. So I answered him as sincerely and truthfully as I could and said "Over a year." I saw that he knew I was in a defensive stance. I had to stand up for myself because I sensed I wasn't getting a fair shake. In all good intentions, I came to him to solve a problem that he had in his administration. I wanted to do it as professionally as I could within the system to which I am dedicated. He said it seemed there were innuendos in the fact book and he wondered if there was a hidden agenda too. He then reminded me that I did not have tenure. Because of his consistent questioning of my actions and not Smouse's, I became more convinced that coming to the Superintendent for assistance was the wrong choice.

I requested that he return the book of facts to me now and allow us to go directly to the School Board about Smouse with reasons why he should resign. This was the last note on my meeting agenda and I placed a star by it because Craparo told me to get it back. The Superintendent said he didn't have a chance to go through all of the material in the book and he wanted to keep it for awhile. He showed me where he had made some notes in pencil in the margins. He said he would return it soon. He then asked me if this was the only copy of the book and I wondered what that had to do with trying to solve this problem. So, I answered by saying "I have parts of the book." I think the Superintendent was glad he kept the book because, I sensed by his manner, he thought it would take me over a year again to make another copy. To be honest, I did have parts of the book, ... all the parts. On my way out of the office, he stated again that he could not advise me what to do. The meeting had lasted 45 minutes. I now was totally disgusted with this attempt to resolve a problem. I came in good faith to help with a problem that was out of control and in return, I am made out to be the culprit. Now, at least we each knew where the other stood. As for that book, I never got it back.

I immediately met with Jack and went over my notes that I made after the meeting. Jack said that we would handle it by working within the system and file the grievance and take it all the way to the School Board to Level III, if necessary. We would also file a complaint with the Professional Practices Commission in Tallahassee.

When I returned to my office, I met with Dr. Cammaratta and told him of my meeting with Shelton. I wanted to be sure he was kept abreast of all these happenings because he was my immediate supervisor and he should be aware of my actions. Besides, he already had several meetings in the last year with Shelton and Smouse about my performance.

I picked up the grievance form from Kenny Allen, the new Supervisor of Affirmative Action. I discussed the procedures and the pro's and con's of filing a grievance. I studied the information and gave a copy to Jack Craparo. I started to organized my notes and materials that I would use in the grievance.

I also spoke to John Miliziano, Director of Pupil Administrative Services, who previously was the Supervisor of Affirmative Action for several years. I too asked him about my concern in filing a grievance. I wanted to be sure this was the right thing to do. He said that I would probably be perceived as the bad guy who went against the system or as a hero for standing up for what I believed to be right. I appreciated him sharing his candor and experience.

I was still most apprehensive that I didn't get any assistance or even some comprehension from Shelton about my concerns to come forward and quietly work together to resolve a problem that would end up damaging everyone if not curtailed immediately. I went in to help solve a problem and I came out being the problem. They didn't teach about this topic in graduate school.

Was the Superintendent wishing that this problem didn't occur now because of his election as President of the American Association of School Administrators? Was he afraid that I was going to rain on his parade? Was he being protective of his waning image with the community because of other events?

I put many hours of thought into why the Superintendent refused to handle the problem with one of his Assistant Superintendents. The more I thought, the farther away I moved from an understanding of his reaction. I was glad that the meeting was over. I did what I had to do.

19
THE COMMISSIONER'S CODE OF ETHICS

All new instructional employees of Hillsborough County Schools are required to read, sign and agree to adhere to the Code of Ethics of the Education Profession in Florida. I first signed it in 1971 when I started my first year teaching (which happened to be in Hillsborough County).

In the 1986 Annual Report of the Florida Education Practices Commission, the Chairman, Richard N. Rich, wrote the following "Introduction" that describes the commission:

> In 1980, the education profession was granted the right and responsibility of policing its own ranks. By an act of the Florida Legislature, a thirteen-member commission was established and empowered to authorize punitive action against those educators who either were incompetent or who engaged in illegal, immoral, or unprofessional activities.
>
> The Education Practices Commission, which was conceived in controversy and implemented through compromise, has functioned with compassion and understanding. The Commission members have shown a level of professional expertise which has earned them the respect of both the legal and educational communities.
>
> The Education Practices Commission is gaining national recognition. It is being viewed as a model system. States who wish to upgrade their regulatory systems are looking to Florida for creative alternatives.
>
> The success of the Education Practices Commission is due to its members and staff. Their unrelenting commitment to quality education and their strong sense of duty and responsibility has transformed a complex set of rules and procedures into a functioning commission dedicated to preserving the integrity of the teaching profession.

The events that take place in this book may throw a blanket of doubt on some of the statements made in this introduction. The Educational Practices Commission, in conjunction with the Commissioner of Education, may attract national attention as a model regulatory system. However, a poor decision in just one case can hurl what appears on paper as a theoretical model system into a dishonorable showcase with one tarnished trophy. At first sight, everyone sees the tarnished trophy and it casts a dim light on the others.

The Educational Practices Commission is an autonomous quasi-judicial agency administratively assigned to the Department of Education. The Commission operates like a circuit court and is not responsible for investigations and prosecutions. These functions are the responsibility of the Commissioner of Education, Betty Castor, through the staff of Professional Practices Services which functions somewhat like the State Attorney's office. The Education Practices Commission is the final agency to hear certificate disciplinary cases and to render decisions in regard to penalties. In addition to revocation or suspension of the teaching certificate, the Commission has the authority to deny the application for a teaching certificate, impose an administrative fine not to exceed $2,000, place the educator on probation, restrict the authorized scope of practice or reprimand the educator.

The Education Practices Commission can take disciplinary action based upon rules of the State Board of Education, 6B-1.06, which are called the "Principles of Professional Conduct." There are twenty-nine rules listed under three sections categorized as an obligation to the student, public and profession.

A publication by the Education Practices Commission in September, 1985, lists the advantages of the Commission to the profession. Several of these are listed below:

1. Unlike most states, the education profession in Florida truly sits in judgement of its peers through the Education Practices Commission.

2. The Education Practices Commission removes politics from the arena of decision making.

3. The profession's public image is raised by demonstrating its ability to set rigid standards and to enforce them.

As a result of my meeting with the superintendent to seek a quick and quiet remedy to the problems with Smouse, my attorney, Jack Craparo, advised me to file a complaint with the Commissioner of Education in addition to filing a grievance with Hillsborough County Schools.

I called the Educational Practices Commission in Tallahassee and requested information to be sent to me on the Code of Ethics and the current membership of the Commission. When I received this information, I began to study it in detail. I immediately felt that Smouse had violated several rules of conduct. I also reviewed the current 1986–87 membership list and quickly noted that of the thirteen members, three were from Hillsborough County Schools. There are sixty-seven counties in the state of Florida; each is a separate school district. How come there was such a large representation from Hillsborough County on the Commission? The three members on the Commission from Hillsborough were Helen Juares, Walter Sickles and A. Leon Lowry; Helen Juares was a teacher at Oak Grove Junior High School; Walter Sickles was Assistant Superintendent for Personnel (and was mentioned in Chapter 8—"Equal Pay Please"). A. Leon Lowry, Sr. was a School Board member and Vice Chairman of the Education Practices Commission.

When I called Tallahassee again about filing a complaint, a worker in the Commissioners office told me that it is usually the superintendent that files, but anyone could report a violation with the Commissioner. The worker told me to state the alleged misconduct and give details and the witnesses who would testify.

My letter to the Professional Practices Commission was written on October 7, 1987, two weeks after my meeting with the superintendent. It was addressed to Karen B. Wilde, Executive Secretary and read as follows:

> As an individual who holds a valid Florida teacher's certificate and after careful review of all of the facts of which I have documented, hereby, submit same to you for your review and appropriate action.
>
> Upon your review of the facts, it will be apparent that Mr. Ralph L. Smouse, Jr., Assistant Superintendent for Vocational, Technical and Adult Education, Hillsborough County Public Schools, 901 E. Kennedy Boulevard, Tampa, Florida 33601, has made on several occasions attempts to discredit me by clearly violating the Code of Ethics and the Principles of Professional Conduct for the Education Profession in Florida.
>
> In support of this, I have prepared a summary, making reference to documentation that I have compiled in book form. The book contains a chronological log of such conduct which includes the dates, facts and witnesses who will be willing to testify in an investigation.
>
> I respectfully request that you consider this matter by reviewing the summary, carefully reviewing the facts in the document book, and take all steps required by and to adhere to the Code of Ethics and the Principles of Professional Practice in the Education Profession in Florida.

Since my documentation book, The Big Black Book, was so large, and because this filing of a complaint was most critical to my future success in education, I decided to deliver it to Tallahassee in person. I took one of my "personal days" on Friday October 9, 1987, flew to Tallahassee and took a taxi to Karen B. Wilde's office. I had made no appointment in advance. When I submitted my letter to her, she told me that the filing of complaints is done with the Professional Practices Services Division. They are the ones that do the investigation and then it is presented to the Professional Practices Commission. She drew a map instructing how to get there. I met with Catherine L. Birdsong, a Consultant with the Professional Practices Services. I gave her my letter and my documentation. She stamped my letter "received" and gave me a copy. She was very courteous and helpful.

I asked for her to explain the procedure that filing a complaint entails. She said that the Commissioner of Education decides if there is a "go or no go" for a legal case. She usually consults with the attorney for this. Then, if there are legal grounds for a case, a case number is established and notification by letter is sent to the one who made the alleged violation. Also, a letter would be sent to Hillsborough County Schools, specifically to Dr. Binnie in Personnel, she said, and a copy to me to acknowledge the opening of a case. Then, an on-site investigation would be made by a local consultant to do fact finding. She believed that the consultant would be Kathleen Richards. After the fact finding, the consultant would write a report and submit it to the Commissioner of Education. The Commissioner would then review the report and decide to either dismiss the case or to file formal charges. If formal charges are filed, then the alleged violator could surrender his teaching certificate or ask for a hearing with the Professional Practices Commission.

I informed Dr. Cammaratta about my filing in Tallahassee. We had several meetings with the Professor. We met at different restaurants. We told the Professor about the filing of the complaint with the Professional Practices Commission. The Professor told us about talking with the Commissioner's office on the phone. The Professor apparently had a direct line of communication with Tallahassee and the Commissioner. The Professor found out that the Commissioner wasn't sure what she was going to do about my complaint, but that she said she would surely do something before April 1st. We asked the Professor why. The Professor said that April 1 was a significant date because the Florida Legislature begins its session then. Then the Professor suggested to Cammaratta that he write a letter to Betty Castor to thank her for the nice letter that she wrote and to encourage her to run for Governor. There were rumors that she was looking at that possibility. Cammaratta had recently received an award, with national recognition, for his contributions to private vocational schools. This award was supported by a letter from Commissioner Castor which highly complimented Cammaratta for his dedication and promotion of private vocational-technical schools. It must have been an insult to Smouse that Cammaratta received this recognition and not Smouse. Why didn't the Commissioner write a letter of recommendation for Smouse?

A few weeks later, the Professor, Cammaratta and I had lunch at a different restaurant and he told us something very startling. The Professor often talked about an inside contact that would provide information from the superintendent's office. The Professor had information that superintendent Shelton had said that "Wieser has gotta go!" The Professor asked me if there was any time that I embarrassed or did something highly unusual to the Superintendent. I said that I couldn't think of anything other than going to him with my concern about Smouse. I did go to a School Board member first (Rampello), but I didn't think *that* informal meeting was anything radical.

I hypothesized. Was Shelton concerned that I was too close to information about the Textbook Scam? Was he concerned that, if I uncovered damaging information, even by mistake, that I would stand-up and point it out? Because of my position in the vocational division, was I a risk to the "welfare" of other administrators—past and present?

Since I filed my complaint in Tallahassee, I was on the edge of my chair waiting to hear from the Commissioner to see if she determined that I had a case against Smouse. I knew the state attorney was going through all of my documentation (The Big Black Book) and it would take awhile to do that. When I developed the complaint, my attorney, Jack Craparo, and I agreed that we would not list the individual rules that we felt that Smouse had broken because we didn't want to restrict any rule that we would not identify. We felt it would be better if we presented all the facts and then let the Commissioner interpret the rule infractions because she was more experienced with that. The rules for educators that we thought might be applicable to our situation were as follows:

Shall maintain honesty in all professional dealings.

Shall not intentionally distort or misrepresent facts concerning an educational matter in direct or indirect public expression.

Shall not intentionally make false or malicious statements about a colleague.

Shall not use coercive means or promise special treatment to influence professional judgement of colleagues.

While I was waiting to hear of any progress from the Commissioner, A. Leon Lowry, Sr. was stepping down from the Commission because his term had ended. Another educator from Hillsborough County Schools, Chamberlain High School principal James Gatlin, was nominated by Commissioner Castor to fill the vacancy. I consider Gatlin to be a good guy and know he will be a credit to the Commission. Both Lowry and Gatlin were black. I guess it was a way to keep the Commission's representation reflective of the population. I had worked directly with principal James Gatlin and highly respect him for the job that I saw he was doing. I even sent James Gatlin a note of congratulations on his appointment. He would soon be one of my witnesses to testify at my hearing; he too had a couple of "run-ins" with Smouse.

I sat on the edge of my chair until January 11, 1988. On that day I received a letter from Martin B. Schaap, Administrator, Professional Practices Services. The one paragraph letter addressed to me read this way:

> This letter is to acknowledge receipt of your complaint against the above named individual (Ralph L. Smouse, Jr.). This file has been assigned to Ms. Kathleen Richards, Consultant, Professional Practices Services. Ms. Richards will contact you in the near future regarding your complaint against Mr. Smouse.

I didn't expect it to take over three months to acknowledge receipt of my complaint and to determine that there are legal grounds for a case, but it did. To say the least, I had a relieved outlook that the Commissioner was going ahead with the complaint against Smouse. This letter told me that the Commissioner indeed had found "reason to believe."

State Consultant Kathleen Richards called me in January to make an appointment for a fact-finding interview. Cammaratta told me that she had called him and made an appointment for the same day. I told him that I would answer any question that she asked and provide her with additional documentation. Hopefully, I could tell her about the things that happened to the grievance that I filed.

I met with her in the supervisor's conference room so that I would be away from my secretary and coordinator. She said that they found reason to believe that a rule was violated during the alleged coercion of Cammaratta by Smouse to change my evaluation. She asked me about that and I told her about the statements that Cammaratta made immediately after he had met with Smouse on that day. (These statements and my comments were already reviewed in Chapter 13—"Power Hour.") Ms. Richards requested of me to write an affidavit specifically about the facts that took place concerning the attempts to coerce my immediate supervisor in lowering my yearly evaluation. It had to be notarized and mailed directly to her.

I managed to answer some of her questions by telling her about the outcome of my grievance here in Hillsborough County Schools. She took extensive notes during my interview. When I told her about the grievance happenings, I said I could go and get her some documentation, but she said it wasn't necessary. I guess that it didn't have direct influence on the violated rule that she was investigating. However, I did feel that it had related significance about the manner in which I was being treated in this school system.

At the end of my interview, she reminded me to send the affidavit and then told me "not to talk to anyone about this." She also said that if I needed to contact her, to call her on the number on her card. The interview lasted about forty minutes.

I mailed my five-page affidavit, which summarized the interview, on January 26, 1988. Included with the affidavit were six letters of appreciation from principals and teachers, and other assorted evaluation memos and evaluations that were already in The Big Black Book that was in the Commissioner's possession.

Later in the day, I saw Cammaratta and told him that I had interviewed with Kathleen Richards and that she said not to talk about the case. He said that she had instructed him to do the same. We really didn't need to talk about it because we kept in touch with other things that were going on right here in the school system.

Now it was time to sit and wait again for the red tape to be processed in Tallahassee; It was late January, the Professor said I would hear something before April 1st. I just wished it would be sooner. Hurry up and wait.

On February 19, 1988, I wrote a letter to Kathleen Richards to inform her that I had felt unnecessary pressure and continued harassment in doing my job since she was there. Smouse had directed me to meet with him every other week to review my performance. He said that if he didn't see significant improvement in six weeks that he would request another year of probation. If I refused the probation, he would be forced to consider not recommending me for renomination next year. I indicated to her that it was not his position to make that recommendation because he was not my immediate supervisor. Plus, how could he make that recommendation when all my evaluations have "exceeded the standards?"

I also noted that Smouse was down-grading my immediate supervisor, Cammaratta, citing the following reasons: Preparing a written statement for a subordinate, William Wieser, to use in a grievance; Providing information to William Wieser from private conversations between yourself, Dr. Shelton, and me; Assisting William Wieser in the use of school system resources to prepare a complaint against your immediate superior; and, in reference to Teamwork; Not working well with your immediate superior regarding resolving problems with the Supervisor of Industrial Arts and Industrial Education.

In reference to these accusations by Smouse, I point out that school board policy states that "The Board and all parties in interest agree to make available all pertinent information not privileged under law or Board policy, in their possession or control, and which is relevant to the issues raised by the grievance." Was Smouse trying to over-ride Board policy and was Cammaratta suffering from it on his evaluation?

In one of my six attachments to my letter, Cammaratta responded to Smouse's concern of lack of Teamwork. Cammaratta stated the following to Smouse:

> I have responded quickly and accurately to each one of your memoranda related to this concern. I attempted to resolve this issue early at the inception of this problem. You did not seem concerned. As I have told you on many occasions, and my record speaks for itself, I completely support the concept of teamwork. I have conscientiously throughout this issue worked as an intermediary, seeking resolutions. I still am working toward this end.

At the end of my letter I stated to Ms. Richards: "Any assistance that you could give me to have Smouse cease and desist would be most appreciated."

My confidence in the Code of Ethics of the teaching profession in Florida was staunch and faithful. I later became aware that my ignorance was a "trial by fire" education in educational politics.

20
PROTECT THYSELF

Florida has one of the highest crime rates in the nation. The crime rate in Florida is caused primarily by crack cocaine. Florida is seventh nationwide in spending for police protection. A crime occurs every 29 seconds and a violent crime occurs every three minutes and 29 seconds.

During 1986–88 I would frequently go into work early before anyone else and often I would stay late or return to the office at night to catch up on work. In the evening, I would park in the reserved supervisors lot adjacent to the entrance for the supervisors' offices in the Vo-Tech Center. This was on the side of the main building and was toward the back. At night the back gate was locked and only the front gate could be used. There was no light on the outer side, and it was rather dark at that end of the parking lot. It was like a cave. There was a security fence around the reserved lot and building. A night security officer made his rounds but mostly stayed in the front of the building. My parking space was only ten steps from the building, but I was concerned about my safety late at night when I went to my car. I would say that the Vo-Tech Center was not located in the best part of town. There was a bar on one corner and another across the street. Also, there were several pawn shops down the street, if you know what I mean. I heard a story about a person that was shot while stopped at a red light down the street. An illegal alien had tried to steal his wallet at gunpoint when he stopped for the light.

In 1987, I kept hearing more and more about crime and an increase in incidents in which students brought weapons to school in the Tampa Bay area. Considering these facts and the crime rate in Florida, I decided I needed some type of lawful self-defense.

I made the decision to purchase a handgun. I had no firearms at home because I had sold my hunting rifles. It was several years since I hunted, so I enrolled in a firearm safety course at the community college. There was great interest at that time in Florida to obtain a concealed weapons license. To be sure that I stayed within the law, I too applied for a license. You had to complete a training course like I was taking at the community college, a fingerprint card and an application. I received my license several months later.

I purchased a Smith & Wesson 9MM automatic pistol. It was small, light weight and easy to conceal if I wanted to carry it on my person. I put it in a special place at home.

While I was taking the training course at the community college, a Crime Prevention and Awareness program was presented at the Erwin Vo-Tech Center where my office was housed. It seems others had similar protection concerns as I did. All of the staff from the supervisor's office were invited to attend. The class was presented for the benefit of both men and women. A consultant from the Citizens Against Crime spoke to the class about learning what to do to protect yourself against crime. The program content included crime prevention in the home, in the car and on the street. It was an informative crime awareness program. I highly recommend it to everyone.

Several months after I purchased my handgun, several people were shot at a school in neighboring Pinellas County. An assistant principal who was shot died several days later.

Why is all this happening in our great country? Are these the precautions we must take to insure quality education for our students? They never taught about this in graduate school.

21

TAP TAP TAP

In earlier chapters, I spoke about the discord between Smouse and Cammaratta going back about ten years ago when Smouse was appointed to the position that Cammaratta had as Assistant Superintendent. Additionally, my confrontations with Smouse began before I was appointed as supervisor in 1985. These trails of friction came to a head in May of 1987, when Smouse didn't want to accept Cammaratta's evaluation of my performance. Then, on September 18, 1987, when my attorney and I sought the assistance of the Superintendent for a resolution to the actions of Smouse, our hopes were crushed when Dr. Shelton refused to handle the issue himself.

I was well aware of the possible repercussions from this unsuccessful attempt to resolve a problem quickly and quietly. It was true that we went into the Superintendent's office on the offense and came out on the defense. I always heard talk about the strategy of defense. You protect yourself on all sides, from all angles.

One area that I became more mindful of was the telephone in my office. I remember my first attorney, Fritz Grey, saying not to talk about any of my personal life while on the job because the school board could look for something to use against me as leverage. I put a greater emphasis on his advice now because of the gut feeling I had after the meeting with Dr. Shelton. My intuition told me I was perceived as a hazard or risk that could cause professional harm or embarrassment to him as Superintendent. I don't remember Dr. Shelton thanking me for coming to him. Did he feel grateful, threatened or something else? I was there in conference with him twice, and only I can say what my gut feelings were in reference to his perceived reaction. It would be wise to consider what each of us had to lose from the consequences of my request. I could eventually lose my job, and possibly so could he. Which one had more to lose?

My office telephone was something I always respected. I always spoke as though someone was listening, even if it was my own conscience. It helped me do a better job. I developed this uncertain belief that my office phone was tapped. I told my immediate supervisor, Cammaratta. He said he had a similar hunch about his phone because he received a new and additional private phone line that was hooked directly to the downtown administration office. Only he and his secretary could access this private line. He told me the strange part of this was he didn't ask for it. They just came in and installed it. It was supposed to give him quick access to the school administrative center downtown where Smouse and Dr. Shelton were located. He said you usually have to fight like hell to get an extra phone line, especially when the vocational supervisor's offices already had about seven lines.

On September 21, 1987, three days after my meeting with the Superintendent, I purchased a cellular telephone from Radio Shack. It was the expensive unit that was small enough to put in your coat pocket. If I had to make a private or personal call, I would wait until I was in my car on the way to a school, a meeting or lunch. The mobile phone also gave me greater contact with my office when I was "on the road." I did not tell my secretary about my mobile phone. I'm sure she realized it when I would check in from the interstate and there would be static from some overhead wires or road noise from trucks. As you remember, my confidence in my secretary's dedication remained low.

I never realized how easy and convenient it was to have a mobile phone. It sure helped me in doing my job. I didn't want to brag about the phone. I tried to keep it confidential. I knew of no other administrator in the system that had one. I gave my mobile number to Cammaratta. I wanted him to be able to reach me whenever I was out of the office. I also offered that he use the convenience of the phone to check in with his secretary if we car pooled to a meeting or lunch. He liked the phone and he often checked in with his secretary, although she knew where he was.

A funny thing happened a few weeks later at lunch. Cammaratta and I met with the Professor. The three of us had met several times before. The professor told me he had some information for me. He found out my office phone conversations were being "monitored." He wasn't sure if my phone was tapped or if my secretary or someone was writing down whom I called. Nevertheless, he said again, my calls were being monitored. Cammaratta and I looked at each other as if to confirm the hunch we suspected earlier. He then told the Professor about the private line he got without asking for it.

I told Cammaratta I found out from a friend that a company doesn't have to get a court order to do a wire tap within their own system. The Professor indicated that he believed this to be correct. I also said I wasn't surprised if my phone was tapped because it didn't matter to me. I was doing a good job and would continue to do so.

If this were true, if my phone calls were being monitored, what did they think when they found out I bought a private mobile phone? I'm sure they weren't pleased with my promenade. Was this perceived as another indication that I was "standing up" against the system or did I just beat them at their own game? Touché.

22

GRIEVANCE LEVEL I

The purpose of the Grievance policy is to secure equitable solutions to the problems which may, from time to time, arise affecting the rights, welfare, or working conditions of all persons connected with or seeking employment with the Hillsborough County School System. The grievance procedure is divided into three levels.

In general terms, the Level I procedure starts with the filing of a form with the Affirmative Action Supervisor with the objective of resolving a grievance. The supervisor named in the grievance will give a written decision within ten working days to the person making the claim. If the aggrieved person is not satisfied with the disposition of his grievance at Level I, he may file the grievance on a Level II form within ten work days. Proceedings shall be kept confidential at all levels of the procedure.

The Office of Affirmative Action shall have fifteen work days, after receipt of the Level II grievance, in which to prepare the formal case, schedule and hold a hearing before the Superintendent's Review Board. The Review Board, consisting of three members, will be composed of persons appointed by the Superintendent of Schools. The Superintendent's Review Board shall submit its findings to the Superintendent. Within ten working days, the Superintendent shall provide the grievant with a written explanation either accepting or rejecting the grievant's position and detailing the reasons for his actions. All hearings at Level II shall be in closed sessions and no news releases shall be made concerning the progress of the hearings. If the grievant is not satisfied with the Level II decision, he may appeal for a Level III School Board hearing within ten working days from the time that said decision was rendered.

Upon receiving a Level III appeal request, the Supervisor of Affirmative Action will have five days to inform the School Board. The Level III appeal shall not be a retrial of the grievance and no evidence will be taken. Instead, the Board will review the record of the case as presented at the Level I and II and shall affirm the decision of the Superintendent provided it is supported by substantial competent evidence and is in accord with applicable law. The Board shall render its decision within fifteen working days of receipt of the Level III appeal. The grievance shall have reached final resolution within the school system at Level III, upon a decision rendered by the School Board.

Miscellaneous procedures also include that documents and records dealing with the grievance will not be placed in the permanent personnel files of the participants. Also, the Board and all parties in interest agree to make available all pertinent information not privileged under law or Board policy, in their possession or control, and which is relevant to the issues raised by the grievance.

Before the final decision was made to file a grievance, I met separately with Cammaratta, John Miliziano, previous supervisor of Affirmative Action, and Kenny Allen the present supervisor of Affirmative Action. I asked John Miliziano about general information concerning the grievance policy and specific questions about due process, unfair treatment and violation of School Board policies. I asked Kenny Allen, who was relatively new to the job, about details in the process of a grievance and I picked up an SB60801 Grievance form. These conferences assisted me in understanding the grievance process. Then, I met with my immediate supervisor, Cammaratta, and told him about the probability of me filing a grievance against Smouse and why. I had already told him about the recommendation to file a grievance from the Superintendent. Then finally, I met with my attorney, Jack Craparo, and he advised me to file a Level I grievance with the school system.

On October 5, 1987, I filed a Level I Grievance against Smouse. On the grievance form, I circled the grounds for which my grievance was based. These grounds were Violation of Due Process, Unfair Treatment and Violation of School Board Policies. Then, I added another violation of the Code of Ethics and the Principles of Professional Conduct of the Education Profession. Kenny Allen had told me to attach a page or more listing the reasons for filing the grievance and my suggested recommendations for a resolution.

My attached page of reasons included several things that I was ordered to do, things that other supervisors were not required to do. I had to form a "Steering Committee" for my office and I had to keep a daily log of activities, while others didn't. I stated that due process was avoided in several matters. The Steve Cannella memo (Chapter 7), had statements about me and this memo was never produced when it was requested. Also, I questioned Smouse's procedures in reaching his conclusions of my job performance. And last, Smouse had intimidated my immediate supervisor to change my year-end evaluation.

Some of my suggested recommendations for a resolution included the following:

Require that all future statements of job performance be based upon factual data and not on hear-say information, stories, opinions, bias, personal preference, and/or rumors.

Remove all defamatory correspondence from William F. Wieser's personnel file. Immediate transfer of the Coordinator and Secretary in the Industrial Education office.

A letter of apology be sent from Mr. Smouse to William F. Wieser for his unprofessional actions.

Consider the work overload of the Supervisor of Industrial Arts and Industrial Education and to relieve the situation by adding an additional coordinator.

Recognition of William F. Wieser's achievements by the Assistant Superintendent for Vocational, Technical and Adult Education.

I then attached fourteen additional pages of supporting documentation, right out of The Big Black Book, to sanction the listed reasons why I filed the grievance. The complete package of seventeen pages was hand-carried by me to the Office of Affirmative Action. I asked for and got a receipt of delivery.

The day after I delivered the grievance, October 6, 1987, Kenny Allen notified Smouse, by memo, that I had filed a grievance against him. Kenny stated the ten-day response rule and gave him other instructions and information about the grievance procedure.

On October 16, 1987, Smouse wrote a letter to me at my home address officially responding to my filing of the grievance. His letter included the following:

> I have reviewed the information you provided with regard to the grievance procedure form which you filed with the Affirmative Action Supervisor. I have also reviewed correspondence and documentation of my actions going back to September, 1986.
> I find that the handling of the items being grieved is within the responsibilities that I have as Assistant Superintendent for the Division of Vocational, Technical and Adult Education to assure that personnel carry out their

responsibilities in an appropriate, effective and timely manner. I have found no instance of unfair treatment, violation of due process, violation of School Board policies and regulations, nor violations of the Education Standards Commission's Code of Ethics of the Education Profession in Florida.

I would be pleased to discuss this matter further with you if you should so desire.

First of all, the Code of Ethics belongs to the State Board of Education not to the Education Standards Commission.

Secondly, I would have been surprised if I had received any other type of reply. Essentially, he said he was just doing his job and he did nothing wrong. That means that I would have to prove my case. And that is why there is a Level II in the grievance procedure, which includes a hearing with witnesses. The handwriting was on the wall.

I met with my attorney and showed him the letter. Jack Craparo agreed with my conclusion about the content and he said the obvious next step was to file the Level II grievance, but first I should check with Kenny Allen to see if there was a possibility of a compromise between Smouse and myself. In Smouse's letter, he had stated he would discuss this matter if I desired. I met with Kenny Allen again and asked him if there was a possibility that Smouse would work out a compromise. He said that he would go talk to Smouse and get back to me. When I next met with him, he said that he believed that Smouse and I were too far apart to compromise. He said that if Smouse had his way, he would fire me, and if I had my way, I would fire Smouse.

I shared this information with Craparo.

My weight remains to be a problem to me. As a bachelor, I don't cook often, thus, I go out to eat or I order out and bring it home. I remember that I used to order a medium pepperoni pizza for dinner. I would eat half of it and keep the second half for another dinner later in the week. Things have changed. The competition between pizza places has made two-for-one pizza specials common. Presently, I order two large pizzas and a quart of free coke and I eat one whole pizza and half of the other, drink the coke and save the rest of the second pizza for a lunch snack later in the week.

I see food as my friend. It is one of the few things that makes me feel good and doesn't argue back.

Secretly, I know I'm gorging myself and this must be some type of disorder.

23

GRIEVANCE LEVEL II

On October 28, 1987, and on the advice of attorney Craparo, I filed a formal Level II grievance against Smouse and hand carried it to the Affirmative Action Office.

Again, I was to submit all documentation and a list of witnesses to the Office of Affirmative Action long before the hearing. No additional documents or witnesses were to have been introduced on the day of the hearing. In addition to stating the grounds for the grievance, the grievant must state what resolution is being sought. I restated the same violations as in Level I and basically the same recommendations for a resolution except I added several more resolutions. Based upon Smouse's written denial of any wrong doing, I recommended the following; the disclosure of the letter from Steve Cannella to Smouse concerning my alleged actions (noted in Chapter 7—"The Cryptic Memo"); and, Smouse's immediate resignation from the school system.

It is important to stress that school board regulations assert that no new information can be presented after a Level II; any documents or testimony for the case must be presented at that time.

I listed twenty-two specific violations against Smouse as a basis for my grievance. My documentation was based upon The Big Black Book (Chapter 14) which was submitted in its entirety. My documentation totaled 403 pages.

A list of eligible witnesses had to be submitted with the documentation. My stated violations centered around Smouse's actions of putting things into writing and into my personnel file without my due process rights. I took each one of these major actions and listed specific witnesses that could speak to his performance and mine in each event. Therefore, my list comprised 51 eligible witnesses. It was a cross-section of administrators, principals (senior and junior high), teachers, clerical workers, and several people from outside of the school system.

Smouse submitted 49 pages of documentation and a list of 9 witnesses. His documentation consisted of the letters he had sent to me which already happened to be in The Big Black Book. There wasn't anything new.

The office of Affirmative Action distributed a case file to all parties of interest and a hearing date of November 19 was set by Kenneth R. Allen, supervisor.

After being notified of the date, I suddenly found out that my attorney, Jack Craparo, would be on a big game hunt out west on that date and would not be able to make the hearing. I requested a postponement of the hearing and all parties agreed to a new date of December 10.

In the meantime, the three-member Review Board that would hear my grievance and recommend their findings to the superintendent was changed. Originally, James Randall, Don Taylor and Harold Clark comprised the Review Board. Randall was assistant superintendent for administration and Taylor was director of comprehensive educational planning. They were replaced with David Binnie, director of instructional personnel and Jack Pilsbury, director of transportation. Harold Clark was assistant superintendent for supportive services. All were high-level administrators (above me) within the school system. Two had positions below that of Smouse and one had the same level position as Smouse. There were six assistant superintendents in the school system's matrix.

I received a call from James Randall's office and was told he wanted me to meet with him, but not what it was about. When I arrived at his office, Kenneth Allen was there too. Allen wanted to remove Superintendent Shelton's name from my list of witnesses. I said I listed him first because he had been involved in my case from the very start when Smouse wanted to chose someone else for my job. Shelton would have been my best witness. Allen argued that the superintendent could not make a non-biased final ruling on my Level II grievance if he was involved in the process. I saw the handwriting on the wall and I gave in to Allen. I knew long ago that things like this might happen when Shelton suggested that I go through the grievance process rather than he solve my (his) problem when I originally met with him.

Things continued to go down-hill. Randall, who was considered to be Shelton's right-hand-man, asked me why so many principals were on my witness list. I indicated that because of the inordinate amount of documentation Smouse did on me, I listed fourteen principals who could speak to the many specific issues and events addressed by Smouse. He wanted to restrict my witnesses because he couldn't see how all these witnesses could be gone from the schools at one time. I said they were from different schools. Randall suggested that instead of my four high school principals, that I send only one. I didn't like his suggestion because I felt there was strength in numbers; besides, how could I guarantee that all four would show up? How could he guarantee that the one principal would show up? All these principals had already agreed to come, and I felt their attendance would be a way to emphasize to the Review Board my positive working relationship with the schools, contrary to the image that Smouse was painting of me. I saw Randall's approach as a tampering with the legal process of the formal grievance. I felt like I was being manipulated and intimidated by his position of authority. This meeting should not even have taken place. I could tell that since Kenny Allen was new to this job, Randall was putting a power play on me.

Randall said that because he had no subpoena power, the administrators' appearances were strictly voluntary. It would be up to them if they came or not. I thought to myself that the system should have some responsibility to see that my witnesses show up at a formal grievance. This was not a come-if-you-have-nothing-better-to-do party.

Additionally, Randall told me that there was "no budget" for providing substitutes so my teacher witnesses could miss half of the school day. It seemed that it was going to be my responsibility to get my witnesses there, not the school system's. This didn't seem right.

My number-one priority turned to getting my witnesses to the grievance. I drafted a form letter to my witnesses and requested their attendance at my hearing on December 10, 1987, at 1:30 PM in the Library Conference room in the School Administrative Center downtown. I sent it to about 45 people on my list. I had Cammaratta's secretary type the letter because my secretary had already been identified as one of Smouse's witnesses. My secretary never told me Smouse had called her along with Richard Hair.

Several witnesses couldn't make it to the hearing; they wrote letters concerning my job performance to take their place. I must share three of these. Janelle L. Wade, Principal of Greco Junior High, said "I have always found him to be informed, willing, professionally responsive, and cooperative. I appreciate his attention with my concerns...."

William I. Troutman, the Principal of Dorothy Thomas School, a special center for severely emotionally disturbed students, wrote:

> In 1971, Dorothy Thomas School had an industrial arts program in name only—for there was no building, no designated shop space, etc.—until we hired a young man from Wisconsin named Bill Wieser. As our first official Industrial Arts teacher, Mr. Wieser taught his classes out of the trunk of his

car under the roof of the campus barbecue shed. It was there that we first became aware of the genius of Bill Wieser. With some of the most difficult students in Hillsborough County, he captivated the curiosity and imagination of these students and involved them in a variety of innovative and stimulating activities.

Now, 16 years later, Bill Wieser, continues to make a wonderful contribution to our program....

The best letter was really an affidavit from a teacher. Joseph M. Mandracchia was department head at Mann Junior High. Shortly after he received my form letter to attend the hearing, he had to go to New York for a funeral. Later he told me since he didn't want to miss out on this one, he saw an attorney, composed an affidavit, signed, notarized and sent it special delivery. In addition to saying I was doing a fine job, he said "There are many other teachers, including myself, who welcome this 'new blood' with new ideas."

That was the good news. Then the not-so-good news came. About seven of my teacher witnesses said their principals would not let them off to attend the hearing. When I talked with them, four said not to worry because they were going to take "personal leave" from their sick time to get out of class and attend my hearing. This was encouraging to me because it told me of the dedicated support that I had in the system. I didn't want to over-look the other three who had release problems. To show my respect to them for agreeing to come to the hearing, I decided to pay for a substitute for the half-day they would be out of the classroom.

I called downtown and asked for the cost of a half-day sub which was $25.00. I wrote a letter to Accounts Receivable, Hillsborough County Schools, and indicated that I was paying for half-day subs for three teachers to attend my hearing. Copies went to the teachers and their principals. I was almost sure the school system wouldn't cash my check, but send it back to me because I now would have documented proof that it denied witness release time to a formal grievance hearing, a hearing recommended by the superintendent. To my surprise my $75.00 personal check was cashed.

In the meantime, I was told (by an administrator who wishes to remain anonymous) about a meeting that took place between Smouse's nine witnesses and Walter Sickles, assistant superintendent. Kenny Allen told me that Smouse and I had the right to be represented by a consultant at the hearing. Allen said Sickles was going to represent Smouse because Shelton couldn't.

This anonymous administrator told me that all nine of Smouse's witnesses met in Sickles' office and they talked about my case and Sickles' secretary took notes. I was offended. Hey, I never saw Perry Mason do this. I didn't think the truth needed a dress rehearsal.

Then Cammaratta told me that he too had a meeting with Sickles in a few days. I called Kenny Allen and inquired about the first meeting and he said it was okay to meet with grievance witnesses before a hearing to be sure their facts are correct. I told him that I disagreed. I also mentioned Cammaratta's up-coming meeting. He said he would check on it. A day later, Cammaratta told me his meeting was canceled. I'm sure they were going to pressure him about what he was going to say at my grievance. Some damage had already been done.

The Professor told Cammaratta and me he heard that Charlie Harris, principal of Bloomingdale High, was called and discouraged from attending my hearing. We told the Professor that we heard that another principal, Vince Thompson, East Bay High School, was also called by an administrator downtown and discouraged from attending my hearing. We compared notes and concluded that it was Pete Davidsen, General Director—Area III, who works under James Randall that called Thompson. The General Directors supervise the principals at the schools. Our information said that Davidsen told several principals "to use their heads" because I was asking that Smouse resign. Davidsen reportedly told principals that it was their option if they wanted to attend the hearing or not. I came away from this meeting with the professional feeling that the system was trying to torpedo my attempts to correct the wrongs that Smouse had done to me.

Later, I had heard that at least one other principal, Ed Ballas from Jefferson High, was called from downtown and discouraged to attend. How many others were called that I didn't know of?

I met with my attorney, Jack Craparo, and confirmed that he would be my counsel during the Level II hearing. I told him I would prepare my presentation against Smouse. I also said that I invited Don Gillette, Executive Director of Hillsborough Association of School Administrators (HASA), to attend the hearing. He was the "union" representative for administrators in the county. It was his role to act as a liaison between the school system and administrators when any problems arose. Plus, Cammaratta would already be there because he was called as a witness by Smouse and me.

The day of the hearing came. I was there about an hour early because I had to make two trips from my car with boxes of documentation to use in my presentation. I had my opening statement, charges against Smouse, order of witness presentation, supporting reference documentation, and a closing statement all ready and set to go. My "day in court" was finally here.

My witnesses started to arrive. There was a small reception area outside of the Library Conference room. Soon it became crowded. I didn't keep a head count, but it seemed like all forty-something witnesses showed up except for about two or three principals. It was magic and it was noisy; people filled the small reception area and spilled over into the hallway. About forty feet down the hall was Smouse's office and reception area. My witnesses could look down the hall and see Smouse's witnesses peeking around the corner to see what all the noise was about. I saw my secretary, Cathy Lakes, and my office assistant (coordinator) Richard Hair down there, along with a few others. Smouse had no principals as witnesses. One of Smouse's witnesses, a teacher, was embarrassed to be with Smouse's group, I was told, so he came to wait with my group and his fellow teachers from Tampa Bay Vo-Tech.

I greeted everyone and thanked them for coming.

Vince Thompson and Charlie Harris didn't show. I wonder if the phone calls had anything to do with it. Ed Ballas did show up. He had previously told me that he didn't care for Smouse when Smouse was promoted to assistant superintendent in the first place and still didn't care for his leadership now in the vocational division. This was a perfect time for him to speak out about just that. Later, however, Vince Thompson did write a nice letter to Cammaratta complimenting my job performance by saying "consistently acting in a professional manner;" nothing came from Harris.

Then I witnessed something disgusting. While my witnesses were waiting for the hearing to start, Shelton walked through the group. Wearing his kelly green blazer, he mingled and talked with the principals and others witnesses. His presence alone was a power-play in front of my witnesses, especially the teachers. What was he doing there in the first place? He wasn't just walking through because I saw him there for ten minutes or more. His office was down on the first floor. If he was removed from my witness list by Allen because of a conflict of interest, then why was he here now intimidating my witnesses and me? I also saw members of Shelton's Review Board mingling with my witnesses just before the hearing started. Flagrant. I could see that my day in court was starting to fade, even before sunrise.

The hearing began behind closed doors. Everyone could hear my witnesses talking out in the hall and they knew I had the upper hand simply because of

GRIEVANCE LEVEL II

their sheer numbers and the variety of their positions. Some of these principals had substantial clout.

Kenny Allen started the meeting by giving some hearing guidelines and stating that he was tape recording the hearing. (Copies could be obtained from him later.) He said I would have one hour to present my case. One of his rules shocked me: he said I would not be permitted to ask Smouse any questions. My presentation was based upon the facts that Smouse wrote about me and my witnesses were here to counter Smouse's allegations of my poor performance. Why were we here if we couldn't ask each other any questions. I immediately changed my presentation plan to simply present my facts and have the witnesses back them up. Then it would be up to the Review Board to submit their findings to the superintendent.

Allen asked me to make my opening comments. I read my three page statement and summarized what Smouse had done to me over the last two years. It was blunt, direct and it had impact. I was playing hard-ball now!

Then Allen began, saying that after Level I, he saw that Smouse and I were too far apart to talk this out and that brought us to this Level II hearing. The Review Board, upon hearing this statement, interjected and asked for clarification. The Review Board discussed the reasons why Smouse and I couldn't get together on the side and try to resolve this matter. A half hour later, and after much debate, the Review Board made a proposal to me: Would I be willing to meet with Smouse on the side and try to work this out? They told me that I could not have any attorney there, but would have an informal mediation conference with Smouse, our representatives, and Allen. There would be no documentation presented or witnesses testifying at the mediation conference. I looked at Craparo and he was nodding his head yes. I leaned over and said *no*, I want to go on with this now because all my witnesses were here, raring to testify. Again Craparo nodded yes to me. I thought he saw something that I didn't. I was set on getting it over here and now; I had the upper hand. Reluctantly I took my attorney's advice and said I would meet with Smouse and Allen in mediation. The conference was set for the following Monday.

Later I thought to myself, why was the superintendent's Review Board so adamant about Smouse and me meeting on the side? Why didn't they want this Level II hearing to go forth? It wasn't their job to maneuver things like this; it was their position to observe and report a finding. Was it their job to stop the Level II grievance if they could? The influence of power was coming from all directions.

Reluctantly, I went out in the hall after about a one-hour hearing that got nowhere and told my witnesses that things were postponed. I'm not sure they understood. I was exhausted and they could tell. I thanked them again for coming. I felt that I had let them down, but I was still trying to work within the system for a resolution.

I also sent thank you letters to every witness who showed up. I told them that their concern for vocational education and support for me was appreciated. Then I said they may not need to appear as a witness in the future if current activities succeeded in a resolution.

Cammaratta later told me that one of my most important witnesses was called back to his school while he was waiting to testify. James Gatlin was principal at Chamberlain High. Cammaratta said Gatlin was called back to school because a student was busted for drugs. Surely, one of his four assistant principals could have handled the arrest of a student. Gatlin said to Cammaratta "I know what they are doing to me; I'll be back!"

I originally met with Gatlin and told him I had filed a grievance against Smouse and asked him to be one of my witnesses. He confided in me and told me about several heavy confrontations he had with Smouse at his school. He said the situation was so bad that he was forced to write to the superintendent to prevent Smouse from acting unprofessional again. He said he would be glad to be a witness for me. The superintendent knew of this letter and how Gatlin would speak out against Smouse. Gatlin was a prime witness to silence. I speculated about who pulled my best witness out of my hearing. This effort to silence my witnesses gave me more encouragement that I was right in what I was doing because they were trying so hard to sabotage my efforts for a remedy.

I was told, not asked, that the mediation conference for Monday was moved to Tuesday. I wondered what maneuvering they were doing now. The conference was to be held in Randall's conference room on the second floor of SAC.

I asked Cammaratta to join me as my representative. We arrived at the conference room early. Then Smouse, Allen and Randall entered. Randall sat at the head of his conference room table and began the conference by stating he was in charge of the meeting; he instructed that Kenny Allen wasn't allowed to make any comments, nor were we allowed to ask him any questions. I wondered why he was even there. He was supposed to chair this meeting, not Randall. I asked Randall why he was there. He said the superintendent asked him to be there. That told me the superintendent was worried about this case and he wanted his right-hand-man there. The superintendent had his hand in the cookie jar. Was Randall removed as one of the original Review Board members because he could better be used to pull the strings "outside" of the case?

Randall said that some people grieve to solve a problem and some to air their problems. Was he referring to me specifically? Why did he make that statement? Was he playing dirty pool? He didn't scare me; I know right from wrong.

Randall asked me to review the requested remedies that I proposed in the grievance.

Over the next two and a half hours, I reviewed the ten suggested remedies. Randall was able to get me to "give-in" on four of the remedies. Smouse stood-fast and gave in on none. He wouldn't budge. I was beginning to see that this "mediation" conference was going to be one-sided.

Smouse came up with some interesting responses. For example, one of my remedies requested the disclosure of the memo from Cannella which alleged improper actions on my behalf (Chapter 7—"The Cryptic Memo"). When I questioned Smouse about this memo and the one he wrote to Cammaratta concerning my performance, I simply asked for a copy of the memo that was sent to him by Cannella. He explained that he didn't have it. When I asked why, he said that two hours after he received the letter, he sent it back to Cannella. I didn't want to laugh out loud, but then again, I was insulted. Was I supposed to believe this explanation? Did they think I was that stupid? What management technique says one should receive a memo, write a response to it, and then get rid of it by returning it to the sender? Randall said that I should get the memo from Cannella or from Richard Roland, Director of Vocational Student Services, who is Cannella's boss and had a copy. His office was located next to Smouse's.

In the middle of our conference, Crosby Few, the school board attorney, arrived. He didn't knock; he just opened the door, walked in, and sat down. Randall started talking to him about some grievance that was going before the school board that evening. What was this all about? Was it a plan to interrupt my conference, just another show of power by the administration? I thought that Few's unannounced interruption was in poor taste. Was he just ruffling feathers? He stayed about four minutes.

The conference was running late. Randall said we should resolve this matter on a Level I. He said we should continue this conference two days later at 8:30

in the morning. We were adjourned. Then Randall came over to Cammaratta and me and told us that we should calculate the cost of developing The Big Black Book and I should pay back the school system.

As Cammaratta and I walked out to our car, I told him I wasn't going to calculate the cost of The Big Black Book because it was all school business and I owed the system nothing for its development. Besides, Shelton wouldn't return the book to me. That told me that Shelton was claiming ownership. I also confided to Cammaratta that if Smouse didn't make an effort to compromise in the continuation meeting, I was going to continue the Level II grievance.

In the meantime, I visited Roland and asked for a copy of the Cannella memo. He was sorry, but he couldn't find it. I also asked Cannella and he became very upset and indicated that he destroyed the letter long ago and it was all over and that was the end of it. That letter must have been rather juicy because Smouse returned it, Roland lost it, and Cannella destroyed it. Doesn't anyone keep copies anymore? This letter was obviously a dead-end road. But the damage had already been done. Ouch. Zap. (Holy disappearing acts, Batman, no paper trail here!)

Two days later, same time, same channel. Randall tried to cut apart more of my suggested remedies. He said four of my remedy items, in addition to the four I already gave in on, were (school board) "policy matter" and were not related to a grievance. Randall asked me what I thought. I told him I wanted to know which of my suggested remedies Smouse considered to be appropriate for us to reach a resolution. Smouse said none. I then looked at Randall and said "I wanted to continue with the Level II hearing" and I requested that Allen schedule a hearing date. Randall clarified that we would continue the grievance less the four remedies that I was willing to give up. I said *no*; we would continue as I originally filed the case. Allen set a date then and suggested a hearing time of 2:00 PM on January 12, 1988. Randall again commented that he thought some of my witnesses may not show up because of the time. I was confident.

I kept Craparo informed about the lack of a resolution at the mediation conference with Smouse. I told him about the new date for the continued hearing. I informed him of my frustration with the administration and their handling of the grievance so far.

Again I sent request letters to my witnesses to attend the new hearing. I assured them that things would go more smoothly this time.

I happened to find out more information about release time for witnesses. The Guide Book of Policies and Procedures, section G-48.16, states that all parties "agree to make available all pertinent information" which is in their possession and relevant to a grievance. I interpreted this policy as meaning that if witnesses had information, either they sent it or presented it orally. Moreover, a communication from the negotiated teacher contracts in 1985, and in force until 1988, refers to the grievance procedure. Section 20.4.6 states the following:

> When it is necessary at Level II or III for a teacher to attend a meeting or hearing during the school day, the Superintendent's office shall so notify the principal of such teacher, and he shall be released without loss of pay and with a substitute provided for such time as his attendance is required as such meetings or hearings.

Did Randall lie to me when he said there was no budget for release time for my witnesses? Hey, shouldn't I receive a $75.00 refund? What about those teachers who took personal leave time? Should they be reimbursed too?

To be sure that there was no slip-up this time, I wrote a letter to the superintendent requesting release time for my list of eligible witnesses. My letter said I was requesting release time of my witnesses "to speak about my job performance and specific issues." To my astonishment, the superintendent sent me a memo on December 31, that said:

> I cannot grant your request for release from duty the personnel you listed in the memo of December 29, 1987.
> This grievance is not about your job performance. You brought the grievance about Mr. Smouse's actions.
> Please coordinate with Mr. Ken Allen relative to a few witnesses.

The superintendent forgot to wish me a Happy New Year.

When I saw Allen, he said I was permitted to bring only ten witnesses to the hearing. When I told him he was wrong, he replied that the superintendent informed him about the limit.

I lost just about all the respect I could have for Shelton. He suggested the grievance to me and now he cuts my legs from under me. Educational politics at their best!

Cammaratta and I met with the Professor. The Professor was surprised at

Shelton's response; he was perhaps even more surprised that it was put in writing. He said this was the last straw. The superintendent just hanged himself. Was this a conspiracy to obstruct justice?

The only thing I could do now was to continue with a list of my best ten witnesses and try to think of some way to get this information to the Board if the hearing turned out to be "incomplete." I didn't start the new year in the best frame of mind. I wondered if the superintendent was going to cut back the nine witnesses that Smouse requested.

Then, several principals started sending me notes regretting that they couldn't attend my hearing because of a variety of nonsensical reasons. I think the administration was finally getting to them.

On January 6, 1988, I sent a revised list of ten witnesses, five principals and five teachers to Allen, and requested release time for them.

Out of frustration, I went to see Craparo to get some legal advice. We reviewed my status in the case. Craparo recommended that I drop the Level II grievance, citing these reasons: Shelton and the Review Board mingled with my witnesses just before the hearing; the Review Board was biased because they were from within the school system and they had connections to Smouse; I only would have one hour to present my case and I needed more time; I was unable to get Cannella's memo from Smouse; my witnesses were restricted from appearing; the Superintendent was disqualified as my witness; Smouse didn't make a reasonable effort to resolve this dispute in the mediation conference; principals were called and discouraged from attending the hearing; one principal (Gatlin) was called back to his school during the hearing that never was; and there was no progress with my case filed in Tallahassee. Therefore, he concluded, I could not present my facts in the grievance with all this outside interference.

Craparo said drop the grievance because things weren't fair and we could still fight this in Tallahassee. Out of disillusionment, I agreed.

The day before the scheduled hearing I wrote a letter to Allen canceling my Level II. I said I couldn't get a fair hearing and I was taking my grievance to the Education Practices Commission in Tallahassee. I came the grievance route because it was recommended by the Superintendent. Now it had been torn apart under his administration.

Some time later I ran into Don Gillette at a school board meeting. He had told me back then that instead of him getting involved, that I should follow the advice of my attorney. He asked about what came out of my grievance. I explained about the mediation meetings, the witnesses and other significant details. He said it sure sounded like it was a kangaroo court. I was sorry that he didn't help more and put in his two cents as the HASA administrators representative. HASA was affiliated with FASA, the Florida Association of School Administrators which was affiliated with AASA, the American Association of School Administrators. I guess he just didn't want to take a chance and spoil the good job he had.

I was depending on Tallahassee and Betty Castor, the Commissioner of Education, for closure on this dispute with Ralph Smouse. I tried to wait patiently for word from her.

I was starting to think about The Bill of Rights. Now what?

24

OKAY...
DON'T ANYBODY MOVE

Were you ever in a bar and the cops came in and yelled "Okay...don't anybody move!" Well I never was, but I have seen it on television often and it was easy to imagine the surprised and fearful feeling those people had. It was the same feeling that I had when I received a phone call from School Security stating that a couple of detectives were investigating me and wanted to interview me in my office.

I was professionally humiliated and insulted that I was being investigated. I knew it had to do with the grievance that I filed against Smouse. I felt like an innocent fugitive. I felt that now I would be labeled as the supervisor who was investigated by School Security. No one would know all the facts, but my reputation would become tarnished and questionable. However, I wasn't afraid to be investigated because I believed that I didn't do anything wrong. My faith in truth and justice remained high. Little did I know.

Using the privacy of my mobile phone, I called my attorney, Jack Craparo, and told him of the call from School Security. I said they wanted to meet at my office but I preferred not to because I wanted to keep this investigation confidential from others in my office complex, especially my own secretary and coordinator. I knew that people would "gossip" if they heard that a supervisor was investigated by school security. Jack Craparo suggested that I have the meeting at his office and he would do all the talking. He double checked with me about the comment made to me by Kathleen Richards, State Investigator for the Professional Practices Services, which was "not to talk to anyone about this case."

The meeting at Jack Craparo's office took place on February 3, 1988. The two School Security Detectives introduced themselves as Wayne Dasinger and

Renee Escobio. Jack knew Renee and greeted him by saying something in Italian. It appeared that they were old friends. The four of us were in Jack's office with the door closed. Jack started with a question to them. "Who sent you?" he asked. "Dr. Binnie," [Director of Instructional Personnel], they replied. Then Jack asked, "Who triggered Binnie?" They said they could not tell us.

It is interesting to note that Binnie was one of the three members of the Superintendent's Review Board that was appointed to hear my Level II grievance. Why would Binnie want to do this? As a Review Board member, he was given a full copy of my document to read before the grievance hearing. Did he read it? If he did, then he would know the full story about the conflict between Smouse and me. Furthermore, it is interesting to note that five months had passed since I originally presented The Big Black Book to the superintendent to seek his remedy. At that time, his emphasis of concern was not Smouse's actions, but my time in the development of the document. The emphasis should have been on the problem with Smouse. Did this indicate a weakness on the School Board's part? And you may remember that the superintendent would not return the book to me when I asked for it. Now, five months later, and three weeks after I canceled my Level II grievance, why is an investigation about the preparation of this grievance document being done? Why wasn't it initiated back in September when the superintendent first received it?

When Jack informed Dasinger and Escobio that I was instructed by the State Investigator "not to talk to anyone about this case" and that I would make no statement today, they asked for the investigator's name. He told them "Kathleen Richards." Jack did all the talking.

I believe that it was Detective Dasinger who then said they were investigating only one thing: how much county time, equipment and personnel was directed toward the preparation of the grievance document (The Big Black Book). Dasinger responded that Binnie said it was reasonable that fifteen to twenty pages be used to prepare a document for a grievance. But Dasinger then said that we are dealing with a document of 450 pages. I would think that Binnie would realize that the bigger the grievance, the bigger the grievance document.

Here is a point of interest. Smouse submitted a response to my grievance document that consisted of fifty-nine pages. This obviously was in excess of the so-called twenty-page reasonable limit. Dr. Binnie received a copy of Smouse's document because he was on the grievance Review Board. Did Binnie request School Security to do an investigation on Smouse for developing a document in excess of twenty pages for a grievance? Did Smouse use county personnel (his secretary), school board supplies and equipment in the preparation of this document? In addition, did Smouse consult with the School Board attorney in the preparation of his response document? If no investigation was done, was Binnie biased in his decision to investigate me and not Smouse? Is this a double standard?

Let me go one more step further back. When I first produced this document (a.k.a. The Big Black Book) it was not meant for the purpose of filing a grievance. The purpose was to solve a problem that I felt existed and was growing. I first took it to Sam Rampello, School Board member. I told him I perceived a problem and asked for direction as what to do (Chapter 15—"Now What?"). He told me to meet with the superintendent (Chapter 18—"CEO and ME"). The superintendent said to go the route of the grievance process. I followed his suggestion and then was forced to cancel the Level II grievance because I felt I couldn't get a fair hearing. Then, I am investigated by security because I produced a document and presented it to the superintendent. The Big Black Book was not a "grievance document" until the superintendent suggested that I file a grievance. Did the superintendent set a trap for me, a trap I fell right into?

As the interview continued, one of the detectives, I can't remember which one, said that I "attempted to have practically every administrator in Hillsborough County called as a witness." This is not true. There are several hundred administrators in Hillsborough County Schools. I placed nineteen administrators on my list to be *eligible* to be called as a witness at my grievance hearing. I did not ask all of them to testify at the hearing. The point is that the investigating detectives came in with a biased demeanor. Where did they get this information? And besides, what does the number of witnesses I call have to do with the purpose of the investigation which they said was the use of county time, equipment and personnel in the preparation of a grievance document? My faith in the honesty of the investigation process was slackening.

They said another question they had to clean up concerned the "problems" in my office. I had no idea what "problems" they were talking about. Were they referring to the conflict between Smouse and me? I already went to the superintendent to try to solve those problems. If these were the problems they were trying to investigate, were they qualified? Did they have degrees in education? Were they certified and experienced in administration and supervision in a large school system? They did say that they interviewed about five or six people in this case. Specifically, who else did they get information from? My concern now was what would be done with this information. My confidence in the investigation process was withering.

When Jack heard them say they were looking into the problems in my office, he jumped in and stated that he felt that Shelton didn't read the book (The Big Black Book); if he had, all this would not have happened. Jack said that Shelton could have solved this case the day we went to him last September. Then, he said he felt this was a witch hunt. He warned them that, no matter how many members are recruited to participate in this case, it would never- the-less be finally revealed as a witch hunt. The investigators said they would put it in their report.

After the meeting, when Jack and I were alone, he told me that he didn't do liable and slander suits and if I were going to file a suit against the School Board, it would *not* be out of his office. Did I miss something here? It was so abrupt and out of the blue—what was he actually telling me? I took his advice to cancel the grievance and now his office says no to filing a suit. My remedies were starting to thin-out.

Later, Cammaratta told me that his interview with security was short, lasting about five minutes. They asked about his secretary, Mary Ann Dunn, doing some of the typing on the grievance document. He told them that he believed she did the work after hours. He said school supplies were used and he felt that the document was school and job related and not for personal gain. He asked them who initiated the security investigation. They said that Superintendent Shelton did. That's funny because they told my attorney that Binnie did. I sure hope they get their facts right when they write their report. I asked him if they asked about the "problems" in my office and he said no. If that was part of their investigation, then why didn't they ask my immediate supervisor, Cammaratta? My confidence in this investigation was now out the window.

Over the next few weeks and then months I kept waiting to hear from Binnie on the results of his security investigation of me. I heard nothing, no letter, no phone call, no memo in my file, and no bill to pay for the school resources that I used in the preparation of the grievance document. I had hoped that I would be sent a letter stating that the investigation turned up no improper actions on my behalf. But I got nothing, not even a copy of the investigation report. I knew that I had done nothing wrong. I assumed that the report came out "negative" and I did not have to worry about it. I also thought it was a technique to put pressure on me, but I remained strong because of my belief that I had done nothing wrong.

Sixteen months after the security check, in June of 1989, my curiosity overcame me and I called Binnie to see if I could obtain a copy of the School Security investigation report. He mailed it to me on June 27.

The Offense Report Form from the Security Department had CONFIDENTIAL stamped across it in big letters. The date of the report was February 3, 1988, the same day as my interview. The type of incident was listed as Information Report—Employee Grievance Document—William Wieser. There was a four page summary report and a twelve page supplement report of the transcripts from the tape recordings of the interviews with my Coordinator, Richard Hair and Cammaratta's secretary, Mary Ann Dunn. A total of seven people were interviewed and quoted in the report.

The report starts with the two detectives meeting with Binnie. He stated that I had filed a grievance procedure and requested that they investigate the preparation of the grievance document which consisted of approximately 478 pages. He said there was concern whether it was appropriate for a document of this size and scope to be prepared during working hours with Hillsborough County School System Personnel and school materials. He requested that the detectives interview personnel in the office to see if they participated in the preparation.

Binnie was overlooking a fact that he knew damn well. The largest section in The Big Black Book was a copy of my daily logs that Smouse directed me to maintain over a ten month period. A job task that I obviously prepared during working hours. Why was Binnie so blind to the contents and purpose of The Big Black Book?

I believe the easiest way to give an overall perspective of the report is to summarize the summary and to quote selected questions and responses from the transcript. During the transcript quoting, I'll make comments where necessary, identifying it as "My Comment" to be sure to separate it from the official transcript.

The first person interviewed was my secretary Cathy Lakes. The summary report says that she didn't want to be taped during the interview. Therefore, there is no transcript in the supplement report. She said that she was aware of the grievance preparation. She stated that she personally typed thank you letters to witnesses, received numerous phone calls and overheard phone calls being made in reference to the grievance procedure. The report noted that there was apparently not a good relationship between Ms. Lakes and me. Lakes stated that her observation is that there is a lot of time when I was apparently not doing productive work. She had observed that I spent a lot of time in Cammaratta's office. She stated that, in her opinion, Hair who is the Coordinator for Industrial Arts does the bulk of the work in the office.

My Comment: I need to remind the reader that as a suggested remedy in the grievance with Smouse, it was my request to transfer my secretary and coordinator from my office. This request was also presented to the superintendent the previous September. She told me that she became aware of this. It is also important to note that in the previous year's evaluation, I evaluated her very low and suggested most directly to her to look for another position because I was not pleased with her work. I wonder if this security investigation interview was a vehicle for her to strike back at me? She was listed as a witness for Smouse to testify at my grievance hearing against me. Where do you think her allegiance was, to me or Smouse?

It is also important to comment that it is School Board policy to keep grievance procedures confidential. It was none of my secretary's business to know what I was doing in reference to the grievance unless I specifically requested her assistance. I felt that if I included her in the preparation of this document, that before I could confidentially meet with a School Board member or the superintendent, the information would be passed on to Hair or Smouse. It is difficult to do daily work with a secretary with whom you have no trust, let alone prepare a confidential grievance.

The next interview was with Hair my coordinator. The interview was taped and the transcript consisted of six single-spaced typed pages. The report summary says that Hair reiterated Lake's statement that there is an adversarial relationship [between us] and that he (Hair) does the bulk of the work in the office. The report noted that Hair was a competitor with Wieser for the job of Supervisor. Hair stated that he feels that a large amount of county time and county materials were devoted to the preparation and distribution of the document.

My Comment: Just who was it that broke Board policy and showed my confidential grievance documents to Hair for him to draw his conclusion about the large amount of time and materials allegedly used to prepare the document?

I wondered why it was such a lengthy interview, since Hair had absolutely nothing to do with the preparation of the grievance document. Again, I kept the grievance as confidential from him as I could. There was no professional reason to share my personal activities with him. Plus, School Board policy says to keep it confidential.

This was part of the summary report. I now will select several questions and responses from the six page transcript to give you an overall tone and perspective of the interview.

DASINGER: Mr. Hair as we discussed earlier we have been assigned to investigate a set of circumstances behind this grievance preparation that Mr. Wieser prepared, I believe down in your office, he is your direct immediate supervisor? And we want to talk about that and any other problems that you have that you might think we need to address. You can just talk and I may interrupt with questions or something or when you get finished I'll probably have a few questions. Basically let's get started with the work situation down there, what is your view of that?

HAIR: Well the work situation has been very low, the morale is very low, and it got to the point where I even called and went to Dr. [name omitted] with the Human Resource, I think that the center of the county did have, because I was getting to the point where I was I guess getting an ulcer because of the strain and the tension that we were always under there and you never knew what to expect when you came into the office and it was just working under constant pressure and tension that keeps you all upset and you go home and start yelling at the family and things like that where I got to the point where I just had to try to block it out.

My Comment: Binnie assigned this investigation to look into the preparation of a grievance document. Why is Detective Dasinger wanting to "talk about any other problems you might need to address?" Hair was correct that we were working under pressure, but it was put there by Smouse, not me.

DASINGER: Would you say there is some sort of adversary relationship between you and your supervisor down there or what?

HAIR: Well what is there is that there is really no communication other than he, you know, gives you work to do, things that he should be doing, he never, well the teachers call him and want to know about things and he never follows up with any of this, it is always turned over to me to do....

My Comment: Again, I thought the purpose of this interview was for the investigation of the grievance document, not for Hair's to exemplify his viewpoint of the working relationship between him and his immediate supervisor. Could Detective Dasinger's question about "some sort of adversary relationship" be considered a leading question away from the assignment of the investigation?

DASINGER: Would you say, in your opinion, you carry the bulk of the work load in there?

HAIR: Oh I carry, I would say, about 75% or better.

My Comment: Dasinger's question has nothing to do with the assignment of the investigation. I obviously disagree with Hair claiming to be doing all the work. A simple perusal of the daily work logs that I was required to keep by Smouse would easily show my extensive work load.

DASINGER: How does Mr. Wieser spend his time?

HAIR: Well to be honest with you most of his time he spends in Dr. Cammaratta's office, he spends better than 50% of it in there, either that in the office or they are on the road going somewhere and I have some documentation here where I have kept track of times that they have gone.

My Comment: Dasinger comments that he will go through that in a few minutes and begins to ask questions about the grievance document.

DASINGER: How much would you estimate of his time or Dr. Cammaratta's secretary's time or what percentage of this was done on county time with county equipment?

HAIR: Well looking at that I would estimate oh Lord it would be hard to, typing, I would say there is probably a good two or three weeks worth of typing and then reproduction, I'd say probably a good month's time or more.

My Comment: It was not Hair's business to know what Cammaratta's secretary was doing. Plus, how could Hair estimate the amount of county time and equipment if he did not work on it himself.

DASINGER: In your opinion was the majority of this stuff done during regular working hours?

HAIR: Well, I cannot say for sure but I know, from what I could see around there because Mrs. Dunn never came in early, to work on it, or stayed late to my knowledge.

My Comment: "To my knowledge" is the key phrase there. Hair's working hours start at 8:30 AM until 4:30 PM. I know for sure that Hair would leave at 4:30 sharp! Dunn's hours are from 8:00 AM until 4:45 PM. She came in before and left after he did on a daily basis. So, how could Hair have any "knowledge" of Dunn's work schedule? One additional comment here. When Hair says something like this and it is placed in a security report, it casts doubt on the testimonies of others.

DASINGER: The relationship between Dr. Cammaratta and Mr. Wieser, are they like personal friends or is that why he spends so much time in his office?

HAIR: Well I can't say that I do know that they are very good friends and they do spend an awful lot of time together.

My Comment: What does the topic of "friends" have to do with the investigation of the document? Why was Detective Dasinger going in this direction?

DASINGER: O.K. You were talking about some documents you had.

HAIR: Yes, Oh one other thing I know that they, you know, they do meet every morning, specifically, or have been, and have breakfast together before they come to work and then generally they go to lunch together and take quite a bit of time. All right what I have here are things that I started, well I didn't keep up with it back in 1986 about personal things that he did in the office which I guess at one time or another we all you know make personal calls, you know, starting then, well here is one for instance where he left the office at 11:34 AM and he was going to Webb (Junior High School) and then lunch and returned at 2:10 p.m; left at 8:30, he was going to the bank and Credit Union and returned at 9:33 and came dressed in blue jeans.... And he left the office on 12/11/86, left the office with Dr. Cammaratta, did not tell any of us in the office where he was going, he left at 3 and he came back at 3:55 PM.... Here's another on 1/5/87, left at 8:50 to go to a budget meeting, returned at 1:05 and left again for Dr. Horton's meeting and returned at 3:30 and here is another one in January, left at 3 o'clock with Dr. Cammaratta, returned at 3:30, he did leave the building, they left at 3:55 again to go to the SAC (School Administration Center) Building, did not return. It goes on, you know.

My Comment: Why was Hair "documenting" my activities? Did he decide to do this because he didn't get the job as supervisor or did someone else tell him to do this? Who would benefit from this questionable information? From the above statements, it shows that he was documenting Cammaratta and myself at least as far back as 1986, two years before the security interview. I really never felt that Hair was totally dedicated to my office. Hair spoke about me making personal phone calls. I remember the Professor cautioning me that my office phone calls were being monitored. Was Hair "monitoring" my office calls? The Professor's information has been reliable.

Often, Cammaratta and I did have breakfast together at 7 AM before we came into work as stated by Hair. But how was Hair able to document this? Was he following Cammaratta's and my movements while we were on our own time, before our jobs started at 8 AM? Or was the school security department following us? *Was* there a "pipeline" to Hair about my personal activities, which was speculated upon by Grey, attorney number one? Conspiracy? Aren't things going beyond the normal call of duty?

How would you like to work with someone who was your "right-hand-man" and was secretly documenting your movements? Was he vengeful because he didn't get my job? I believe I was justified to request that the superintendent transfer him from my office. Again and again, what does all this have to do with the Security Department's investigation of the grievance document?

Hair's actions were not a part of his job description. Who authorized Hair to (obviously) use county time and materials to document my activities?

Also, where was my opportunity to defend myself against Hair's bold statements in his two year "documentation" campaign?

DASINGER: ...I gather from my scanning of this grievance is that Mr. Wieser's position is that he is overworked and doesn't have time to get everything done that he needs to do and that, well he just doesn't have time for all of this stuff, but in your opinion, you work there and you see it on a daily basis, would you say that he has a fair amount of free time to do as he pleases?

HAIR: Yes, he does as he pleases.

My Comment: I'm not sure what Hair meant in his answer. I do know that I put in long hours; I regularly arrived long before he did and stayed later on a daily basis. The investigation questioning sure was getting off of its assignment.

DASINGER: He might have a tendency to procrastinate a little about work.
HAIR: Yes.

My Comment: The question has no relationship to the investigation and sounds like it is a "leading" question. It is like asking someone, what color is the sky...blue? There wasn't time to procrastinate, because there was too much work to be done.

DASINGER: Would you say that you all's office is not very efficient at this point?
HAIR: Well, I'd say, well I guess I would have to say yes.

My Comment: I would say yes too, because of all of this extra work load that was placed upon me and my office by Smouse's actions. I had the feeling that Smouse's reputation was more important to him than the vocational programs and the students in the classrooms.

DASINGER: ...Would it be a fair statement to end this thing with that you feel that a considerable amount of time from office staff and county equipment was dedicated to the preparing of this document?
HAIR: Yes, I would have to say so.

My Comment: It seemed obvious to me that from the interview facts, Hair was no authority to answer a question of this type. Unless they were just looking for opinions or lies and not the facts?

DASINGER: You personally observed the copies and stuff going on that they didn't want you to see what it was and that kind of thing?
HAIR: Right.

My Comment: I believe that all School Board policies should be followed and that includes the confidential aspects of a grievance. Hair should not put his nose into other people's business.

DASINGER: Is there anything else that you want to get on the record before we turn the tape off?

HAIR: I believe I've said about all.

My Comment: I believe he said it all too. Now his "ulcer" can go away?

The next person that was interviewed was Marilyn Baker who is the receptionist in the vocational office. Her statement was short. She said she was not aware of any work that she did on the preparation of a grievance document. In her opinion, she did observe me spending more time in Cammaratta's office than the other supervisors. Her interview was not taped.

The fourth person interviewed was Cammaratta's executive secretary, Mary Ann Dunn. The summary of the report indicates that she was *asked* by Cammaratta to assist me in the preparation of my grievance document. She estimated approximately 40 hours spent in the preparation. She stated that she stayed after work to do about 30 hours of work and did approximately 10 hours of work on school time. She stated that I paid her out of my own pocket. The reason she did the work was because I felt more comfortable with her doing the work rather than my secretary.

I will again select several quotes from the transcript to give the tone of the recorded interview with Dunn.

DASINGER: O.K. As I explained to you we are investigating or trying to determine to the best of our ability how much time, county time, and county materials were directed towards the preparation of this document of this grievance that was filed by Mr. Wieser. Do you know who he is?

DUNN: Yes.

DASINGER: As I told you the grievance is not the issue, the grievance is being addressed by whatever agency is supposed to do that. My job is strictly to try to determine how much of your time or anybody else's time in that office was spent in the compiling, copying, and distribution of this document for the grievance because as I said there is a feeling that the documentation is excessive, do you understand what I am talking about?

DUNN: Yes.

My Comment: Take specific note at Dasinger's statement about what his job was, "My job is strictly to try to determine how much time..." Did Detective Dasinger forget this when he interviewed Hair the day before?

DASINGER: Did, was there any conversation or were you instructed to not tell anybody about doing this? or hide it from other people or anything like that?

DUNN: Well, you mean, well it is not something that you would broadcast anyway, and....

My Comment: It was no one else's business. Board policy said to keep it confidential.

DASINGER: Did you, did it occur to you at anytime that maybe you might be spending too much time on this rather than your own job?

DUNN: Well usually when I did it I stayed after work a lot, so you know they asked if I could do that, so most of that was done after hours, after my regular....

My Comment: Cammaratta had *asked* Dunn if she would do it on a voluntary basis because she was going to get paid by me. Note that she said she stayed after work, after Hair had already left the office.

DASINGER: Well I'm not going to keep you very long, I'm sure you are in a hurry to get back to work. Let me ask you some general things about the office situation down there. From what I could gather there seems to be a definite division of people down there for some reason, specifically speaking, Mr. Hair and Ms. Lakes seem to be on one side of the fence and then we have other people on the other side, can you enlighten me on that, is it professional or personalities or what's the problem as you see it?

DUNN: I feel the main problem was when Mr. Hair didn't get the position, that's my own feeling, I don't know enough about this.

My Comment: Detective Dasinger's question is drifting from the purpose of his investigation.

DASINGER: He was up for the position that Mr. Wieser got?

DUNN: Yes they both applied.

DASINGER: So in effect Mr. Hair is a subordinate to Mr. Wieser now, is that right? Would you say that there is anything besides that, do you think that there is any basis to Mr. Hair's contention that he does the majority of the work in there, have you observed anything like that?

DUNN: I don't know if anybody is doing any work.

My Comment: I'm surprised at her answer, she knew of all the work that I was doing.

DASINGER: Well our only interest is you know to get the work done that the school system needs and if it is not getting done then we need to know that too because I think that was part of the original concerns that were brought up and then this whole deal with Mr. Smouse and all of them and I think their main interest is trying to get an efficient office down there and then people took offense of maybe criticism that they got or whatever, I mean I must have read one hundred memos where they dashed memos back and forth to each other.

DUNN: It has been a paper war.

My Comment: Dasinger's question could have been answered if he read The Big Black Book. The problem wasn't in my office, but in Smouse's.

DASINGER: That's what it looks like to me exactly, they, one of them will write a memo and the other one will dash one back off, you know, and I don't think that is exactly conducive to a smooth operation.

DUNN: No, when it starts you don't have much of a chance.

My Comment: Smouse's memos usually directed some type of response. If not, then I responded simply for my own defense. It *was* a paper war. Smouse usually sent his many memos about me to Cammaratta and directed him to inform me. This directive did require frequent office visits with Cammaratta.

DASINGER: Would you categorize his (Cammaratta) relationship with Mr. Wieser as good friends or, cause frankly speaking I have been told that Mr. Wieser spends an extraordinary amount of time in Dr. Cammaratta's office more so than the other supervisors, for whatever reason, is that in your observations?

DUNN: Yes, I would agree with that.

My Comment: I'm not sure which of the two questions she is answering. Personally, I would say that Dr. Cammaratta and I became professional friends because Mr. Smouse's directives caused us to work closely together.

DASINGER: Do you think most of that time is spent talking about business....

DUNN: I'm sure a lot of it is, but I wouldn't know whether it is or not.

My Comment: What do these questions have to do with the investigation of the preparation of the document?

DASINGER: Let me ask you this, do you know where these notebooks came from?

DUNN: I know that he told me that he bought them himself, he did tell me that, at one of the office supply stores on the other side of town, I know which one it is, but I can't remember the name of it right now.

DASINGER: Well that is alright, it's not that big of a deal, I was just wondering because some mention was made that there were six of these ordered and paid for out of the school funds.

My Comment: What does he mean it's not a big deal! That is part of what the investigation was supposed to be all about! Where did the factual information come from that six notebooks were paid for out of county funds, or was this just rumor?

DASINGER: How many copies of this did you all make?

DUNN: I've only made about three, I made one during work one time, and then one day I stayed after and made two more, but that is the only time I know for sure.

DASINGER: Do you know how many pages are in this?

DUNN: No, how many?

DASINGER: There is 404 or something like that....

DUNN: See I really had nothing to do with putting it together.

DASINGER: You just typed specific parts or made copies for specific parts?

DUNN: O.K.

The fifth investigation interview was with my immediate supervisor Cammaratta on February 3, 1988, the same day as my interview. Apparently, contrary to the procedures followed for Hair's and Dunn's interviews, detective Dasinger did not ask to tape Cammaratta's interview and there was no submitted transcript. Why was there an inconsistency? Why didn't detective Dasinger ask to tape it like like he did with the other interviews?

The summary report states that Cammaratta oversees the operation of my office and Hair. The report continues to say that Cammaratta states that his secretary did do some work on the grievance document; it was done after work and it was paid for by me. Cammaratta did acknowledge that there had been a clash of personalities in the department and that there had been a problem between Smouse and me. He stated that the reason he felt that the grievance was filed was that Smouse had placed certain documents in the personnel file of Mr. Wieser and that Mr. Wieser's concern was that he had several years left to work with the Hillsborough County School System and he felt that those documents may be damaging to his career.

Cammaratta originally told me that his interview was very short. I thought it seemed strange that Cammaratta had the most information about the development of the grievance document and his interview was the shortest one. The summary report of Cammaratta's interview was twelve lines in length, about one fourth of a page. However, Hair's interview transcript stretched to five and one half pages not including the summary report. Why did the interview questions drift from the assignment of looking into the preparation of a grievance document to "any other problems that you might have?" Why weren't the same questions asked of each person interviewed?

Why weren't all the interviews taped? There was too much inconsistency in the investigation.

The next interview was mine. I summarized this meeting with my attorney and the two detectives at the beginning of this chapter. I feel it is significant to review some statements made in the summary report. The detectives did not ask to tape the interview and there was no transcript of my interview in the supplement report. Again, why did they ask to tape the others and not ask to tape my interview. Was it because they wanted proof of what negative comments that they expected would be made about me from my secretary and coordinator? But how would they know what they were going to be told? Was it a setup?

The summary report stated that they attempted to interview me but my attorney, Craparo, advised them that state consultant, Ms. Kathleen Richards, directed me not to talk about this case; therefore, I would make no statement. Craparo "feels his client is the victim of a large scale conspiracy among the administrators of the Hillsborough County School System," the summary noted. Craparo further stated that more people are becoming involved and he will pursue this matter to whatever level necessary up to and including the court system or going to various news media and campaigning against school board members if necessary. Craparo stated that I was originally willing to resolve the matter in house, but that Shelton pushed me into taking the action with the Professional Practices Council. Detective Dasinger stated that he advised Craparo that the focus of their investigation was to determine how much school system time and money had been used in the preparation of the grievance document and not the grievance itself. Craparo stated that he felt that our investigation was merely a part of the conspiracy against his client and a continuation of the whole process.

The summary report ended with a meeting on February 3rd, between Detectives Dasinger and Escobio and Binnie. They advised him of the results of the investigation thus far.

This is their summary in full:

> Based on the interviews and results of this investigation it is apparent that there is a personality conflict in the Vocational Supervisory Office. As to the preparation of the document the most specific witness we could find was Ms. Dunn who stated that she did, in her opinion, spend approximately 10 hours of school board time and materials in the preparation of the document. She stated that all copies which she made even when she stayed after work were

made on school board copy machines and used school board paper and materials.

It should be further noted that I am going to contact Ms. Kathleen Richards, the Investigator for the Professional Practices Council to ascertain if she had advised Mr. Wieser not to consent to an interview with the Security Department. A supplement will be forthcoming relevant to that information.

No further information at this time.

On the last page of the supplement report, there is an update on Detective Dasinger's contact with Kathleen Richards, on February 17th, in reference to remarks made by Attorney Craparo.

The supplement report states that Ms. Richards advised him (Dasinger) that she had personally never met Mr. Craparo and that she did not advise me not to talk to School Security. She stated that she did tell me that it was not a good idea to discuss the details of this investigation with outside parties; however, she never intended to advise me not to speak to School Security.

Ms. Richards stated that she did not know the reason for Mr. Craparo attributing these remarks to her. She further stated that she was in the process of closing her investigation as far as Mr. Smouse having a conspiracy against Mr. Wieser. She did not know what the final conclusions of that investigation were at that time.

And now my overall summary to this extensive chapter. I was professionally insulted when this investigation was initiated because I believed that I had done nothing wrong. Also, why was the investigation delayed until five months after the superintendent received this document and eight months after a School Board member received it? I could see no purpose for this investigation other than to label and harass me. Why did the investigation stray from its original objective of the preparation of a grievance document to opinions of office and working relationships and "friendships?" What was the real purpose of this investigation? Was there a hidden agenda? Who had the authority to assign school security to do an investigation? Look at the overall security report and ask yourself, who was harmed by this report, if anyone, and who would benefit from this report being done in the manner that it was done? How was this information going to be used? Was there an underlying purpose for this investigation? Consider the timing in reference to other things that were happening.

I know one fact for sure. The security investigation drove a wedge further between my office staff and myself (if that was possible). Office continuity was curtailed which put additional strain on my ability to provide efficient and effective services to county programs, principals, teachers and students.

My faith in truth and justice remains high. Be that as it may, I am finding that justice is not automatic, but you have to stand-up and fight for it. Place my accusers in front of me and allow me to defend myself.

One final comment: state investigator Kathleen Richards stated she was in the process of closing her investigation in reference to my filing of a complaint with the State Commissioner of Education concerning Smouse. Nevertheless, the state case was not closed before a copy of this School Security Investigation Report, sent with Smouse's documentation, was completed, sent to Tallahassee, processed, and secured, no doubt, in my file.

Okay...don't anybody move, I just felt a hellish quake shake my footing. I think it originated from deep down, within the center of the earth.

25
WHISTLEBLOWER PROTECTION PROGRAM

The topic of whistleblowing, as addressed in the American Association of School Administrators' (AASA) book titled *Ethics*, begins as follows:

> Exposing to public view people who are guilty of wrongful behavior—gross waste of resources, violation of laws, disregard for rules and regulations—is painful but essential. Unfortunately, too many people view whistle blowing as an act of disloyalty. That is, an employee who exposes or "rats on" a dishonest boss quite often runs a risk of public scorn, loss of trustworthiness, and the wrath of colleagues.
>
> This is unfortunate because it is an attitude based on the idea that organizational loyalty is restricted to loyalty to people. Loyalty to the ideals of an organization is of paramount significance. Therefore, the person who, in deference to cherished ideals of ethics, exposes a crooked boss is loyal to the organization but not to the boss....

I heard about the new federal whistleblower protection program on TV and then saw an article in the newspaper. Most of the news was about the corruption in the defense industry and their contracts with the government. Some company employees had come forward to expose the truth about fixed bidding or exorbitant pricing on replacement parts or hardware.

I thought about the concept of the program and wondered what different types of assistance were available for someone like myself. I didn't like the term whistleblower; it had a negative connotation. Regardless, by definition, I guess I was one. I was proud of what I was doing because the problem I wanted to solve was hurting the system I worked for. Plus, I didn't think that Smouse was providing the ethical leadership that we deserved in the Vocational

Division. If the leaders don't lead, then the managers can't manage, then the supervisors can't supervise, then the teachers can't teach, then the students can't learn. Hence, we all die a little bit. It's called the "trickle-down" theory. Verifiable sad.

The U. S. Department of Labor had an office in Tampa and I inquired about the Federal Protection Act of 1988. When I revealed that I worked for the public school system and wanted to know if I was eligible for any assistance, I was told that it was only for federal employees who blow the whistle on government wrongdoings.

My quest for protection or assistance of any kind, such as legal advice in a law suit, was short-lived. I still wonder today if the Whistleblower Act could have assisted me in some way. I guess it was just too new.

I, too, was naïve.

The Textbook Scam drew some closure. The textbook supervisor pleaded guilty and was sentenced to nine years in prison. There was no trial. It has been said that a trial would have implicated others. And it has been speculated that textbook supervisor Martinez went to jail to protect others. What was the real story behind the Textbook Scam? Was there a bigger picture?

26
ATTORNEY NUMBER 3

Hindsight told me that Jack Craparo's (attorney number 2) recommendation to cancel the Level II grievance was not the best advice; without it, the grievance would never get to the Level III and the School Board. Foresight told me that the filing of a suit would not come from the office of Jack Craparo. These two observations led me to the conclusion that I must seek another council with the potential of filing suit against the School Board if and when necessary.

A friend told me of a renown Tampa labor attorney that he had just heard speak at a local meeting. I called this attorney on my car phone. I told him of the recommendation and he was honored, but he said that he only handled corporate work and he recommended that I call Mark Kelly. I thanked him for his advice and called Mark Kelly.

I briefly told Kelly of my case concerns and he recommended his law firm associate Robert McKee. Using my private car phone again, I called to make an initial consultation and the secretary said there would be a fifty-dollar fee. I had never paid for the initial meeting before, so I said would consider it and call back. I checked the yellow pages of the Tampa phone book under Attorneys-Labor Law. Eighteen attorneys listed represent Management and four attorneys listed represent Employees. Three of the four attorneys listing Employee representation were with the law firm of Kelly and McKee. I thought this must be the place.

Again I called Robert McKee's office to set up a consultation and I asked the secretary one final question. I asked her what was Mr. McKee's political affiliation? The secretary said she had never been asked that before, but did check and said she believed that it was Democratic. I felt this was acceptable since my case had already reached the State Commissioner's office, an elected position, and I did expect my case to go to the elected members of the School

Board. Considering all persons involved, I had the premonition that politics would play a part in my case.

In February of 1988, I had my first meeting with attorney number three, Robert McKee. I asked Cammaratta to come with me to assist me in providing the facts of my case. In the hour meeting, I told McKee all about my appointment as supervisor, Smouse's documentation of my performance, The Big Black Book, my meeting with the Superintendent, the Grievance Levels I and II, the Code of Ethics filing with the Commissioner, and the meetings now with Smouse in his office. Cammaratta told him about the year-end evaluation confrontation with Smouse.

McKee said that he had worked with the educational system in Pinellas County. He knew some of the names from Tallahassee that I mentioned. He said he had seen the type of documentation that Smouse was doing and he said it was called "papering my file." He asked several questions about the political climate in the school system. He said he would look into statutes on tenure, retaliation regulations and renewal of supervisor's continued contracts.

I gave him a copy of The Big Black Book and a handful of significant documents that were generated since The Big Black Book was assembled. He had plenty to review to grasp the situation that I was in with Smouse and to anticipate future occurrences.

I left the meeting feeling good because I had found an attorney who had experience with the school system. McKee seemed bright and confident to me. I considered him young and new and certainly on the way up. I viewed his partner, Mark Kelly, the same way. I knew they would consult each other.

At a future meeting, McKee said that he had heard that some people in the community didn't regard Smouse very highly. He also said that a relative of his knows one of the industrial arts teachers that I work with. This teacher said that "he knows that Wieser is doing a good job, and Wieser is getting f----ed!" These comments from Bob McKee told me that he was checking up on the story that Cammaratta and I told him. It also told me that his outside source of information was confirming my story as "truth."

27

YES...AH...NO!

In 1981, Joe D. Mills, Director of Vocational Education, State of Florida, disseminated to Vocational Administrators a written philosophy of Vocational Education. He stipulated the function of the Division of Vocational Education in a list of fifteen statements. Two of those functions were the following.

8. Work cooperatively and maintain effective communication with other divisions of the Department of Education, governmental agencies, institutions, professional and civic organizations, business, industry, and all other agencies.

13. Make provisions for special short courses and training programs to meet the immediate needs of business, industry, and the community.

Betty Castor was elected Commissioner of Education in 1986. One of the major emphasis she has promoted is developing more "partnerships" with the community. This coincides with the number 8 function, stated by Joe D. Mills, about working cooperatively.

Joel DeVolentine, Director of the Hillsborough Alternative Residential Program, requested that I become a member of an Advisory Council for the Hillsborough Halfway House in Tampa. They were building a new residential facility and they wanted to incorporate a vocational training program. He wanted my expertise on the council because he applauded my ability when I was involved in designing the vocational building at his detention center. (I had training and experience in facility design. I considered the time that I spent designing the new building was a part of my regular job. I received no payment for this designing role.) I was honored and I accepted his request. I became the council's representative to the Hillsborough County School System.

The Hillsborough Halfway House is State operated, under the Department of Health and Rehabilitative Services (HRS), for court-committed delinquent males between the ages of 14 to 18. It is a short-term residential treatment center with a capacity for 28 boys. Residents attend the alternative education programs at the facility and, when appropriate, may maintain employment in the community. The primary philosophy is to assist in the re-entry of delinquents into the community by developing their talents and abilities to function in a socially acceptable manner and diminish their dependence on delinquent behavior.

Eighteen Advisory Council members, from diverse community backgrounds, provide advice and direction to the Halfway House Administration. The membership comprises representation from positions such as Tampa Fire Department, Hillsborough County Sheriff's Office, University of South Florida, HRS, Tampa Police Department, MacDill Air Force Base, General Telephone of Florida, Tampa Electric Company, The Salvation Army, Sun Bank, Gatlin's Body Shop and Hillsborough County Schools.

The Advisory Council strongly advocated the funding for a two-year pilot project to operate a short and intense vocational training program. This request through HRS was supported by State Senator John A. Grant, Jr. and State Representative Helen Gordon Davis. The state funding request was granted. The teaching unit for the training program was then sought through the Hillsborough County School System. This is where my experience helped.

The public school system had different types of alternative programs around the county. The school system already had a teaching unit at the Halfway House for academic assessment and instruction. It was my recommendation that the council request a teaching unit for the Halfway House vocational training program.

In July of 1987, after approval from the Advisory Council, I wrote a memo to my boss, Cammaratta, requesting a teaching unit for the Halfway House. I enclosed a draft copy of a contract they were considering. Several more memos of questions and information were exchanged between myself, Cammaratta and Smouse. Then on October 19, 1987, Smouse sent a memo to Cammaratta. The memo said the following:

> I have presented to Superintendent's staff the request for a 12-month teaching unit at Hillsborough Halfway House on the campus of the W. T. Edwards complex. Staff has given approval for us to proceed, with an anticipated starting date of the first day of the second semester of the 1987–88 school year. The only modification in approving your request was that the

teacher be placed on the payroll of the Tampa Bay Evening Vocational School in order not to establish another teacher payroll work location.

I was pleased that the teaching unit was approved. At the next Advisory Council meeting, I gave my report and passed out copies of Smouse's memo. The first day of the second semester was January 26, 1988. An existing building was being converted to house the program. It was planned that the vocational facility would be ready by then.

I also read in the "School Board Digest" of October 20, 1987, that the School Board took positive action on specific agenda items. One item was the Approved cooperative agreements with DACCO, Hillsborough Regional Juvenile Detention Center, *Hillsborough Halfway House*, Hillsborough County Health Department and The Spring, for alternative education programs. This Board approval confirmed Smouse's memo giving the go ahead with the teaching unit at the Halfway House.

On January 12, 1988, Smouse sent a memo to Cammaratta stating a decision was made not to offer the teaching unit at the Halfway House. He said this decision was made last week at a staff meeting. He emphasized that no school system support would be provided for this program. Some of his reasons included the length of the program at the Halfway House. He said the 240 hours of instruction would not qualify a person to work as an entry-level employee in the auto body trade. That is true if you compare it to the 1100 hour program for full-time students. However, 240 hours of instruction is a lot more than the zero hours of training the Halfway House youth had now. Any training would be helpful for them to enter an occupation rather than just try to walk in off the street and get employment. Another reason given by Smouse was that there would be no guarantee of the students transferring to our Tampa Bay Vo-Tech Center to complete the additional hours of instruction and complete the full program. True, there is no guarantee, but the option is there for each student to gain additional training. Plus, the student who moves back to his home city in Florida could also enroll in the same auto body repair program at that local Vo-Tech Center and complete the program there, full-time days or part-time nights. There were many options for further training of these youths. But we must get them started. Then, Smouse said it would not be cost effective to operate a program which would never have any completers. This is false because programs are evaluated upon the placement of completers, not just those that don't complete the program. Where is the flexibility in the State philosophy of Vocational Education, mentioned earlier, about making provisions for short courses for community needs? Lastly, Smouse stated that we would only have an FTE maximum of 13 students enrolled in the program. He said this would not produce sufficient funding to support the program. Well, there are other programs that already have "low" FTE enrollment in the county. Why can't this alternative education program be like the others. One more counterpoint: why then was approval previously given for a brand new Bowling Maintenance and Repair program to start in this same month of January, at the Brewster Technical Center, when it only had two students enrolled to start and only an average of 6 student FTE for the next several years. Smouse is showing an inconsistency in his reasons to turn down my program requests when others are approved. Why am I treated this way and others are not?

The reasons he gave for turning the unit down were debatable, but that is not the point here. The point is, the unit was given the go ahead and plans at the Halfway House were made accordingly, then an unexpected reversal and no unit. As the Hillsborough School System representative, on the Halfway House Advisory Council, I was professionally embarrassed and personally insulted in front of all the other prominent council members. Public humiliation. What was I to say to them? Where was the School System's commitment to delinquent community youth in need of alternative education, when Florida ranks as number one in the nation in crime? Was Smouse neglecting the needs of delinquent teenagers? Was this a ploy by Smouse to make me look bad in the eyes of the community?

During the Summer of 1988, I recommended that Mr. Ron Johnson, chairman of the advisory council, meet directly with Smouse to again request the support of the school system for the teaching unit. The request was denied. Then, in September of 1988, I recommended that another request for a teaching unit be made. This time a letter was sent directly to the Superintendent, from Don Lewis, Program Administrator with the Department of Health and Rehabilitative Services. The request again was turned down.

It is interesting to note, my original request for the teaching unit came in July, 1987. Smouse's approval came on October 19, 1987, fourteen days after I filed a Level I Grievance against him. Then on January 11, 1988, upon the advice of my attorney, I dropped the Level II grievance against Smouse. And then, one day later, on January 12, 1988, Smouse sent a memo canceling the unit. No further comment needed.

Despite the reluctance of the school system, budgets within HRS were rearranged and a teacher was finally hired part-time in April, paid by HRS. Finally, on June 14, 1988, the Vocational Training Facility and program had its dedication and ribbon cutting. It was time to celebrate with a beautiful ceremony. State Representative Helen Gordon Davis was the guest speaker. I was a speaker on the program too. We had TV coverage and a newspaper article, with a picture, that appeared in *The Tampa Tribune.*

The crime rate in Florida is one of the highest in the nation. I wonder why? Do you think it has anything to do with people who just don't care about the education of troubled kids?

Author's note: Later, the teaching unit at the halfway house was approved under the new supervisor, Mike Grego and is still in full swing as of 1992. However, in August of 1992, the Bowling Maintenance and Repair program at the Brewster Technical Center, a program approved by Smouse at the same time that he reneged on the halfway house program, was disbanded because of a lack of interest according to a report in *The Tampa Tribune.*

28
WHO'S THE BOSS

For this chapter to have meaning, we have to look back at some the established rules under which we should be functioning in education. I favor to point out some ethics and some rules of supervision in the evaluation of an employee.

The Florida State Board of Education has a set of Administrative Ethics and Rules. The rules are called the Principles of Professional Conduct for the Education Profession in Florida. Section 5, rule "m" is quoted below:

(5) Obligation to the profession of education requires that the individual:
   (m) Shall seek no reprisals against any individual who has reported a violation of Florida School Code or State Board of Education Rules as defined in Section 321.28(1), Florida Statutes.

Next, the rules of the assessment procedures, or evaluation, in Hillsborough County Schools start with the superintendent establishing procedures for assessing the performance of duties and responsibilities of all instructional employees. Such assessment shall be based upon sound educational principles and contemporary research in effective educational practices.

Florida Statute 231.29 (5) states: The individual responsible for the supervision of the employee shall make the assessment of the employee and forward such assessment to the superintendent for the purpose of reviewing the employee's contract. The Hillsborough County School System's Guidebook of Policies and Procedures states in policy B-45.5 that: The County Superintendent or the person directly responsible for the supervision of the individual shall make the assessment. And policy B-46.1 states: The *immediate* supervisor shall formally evaluate each administrator or supervisor one time each year. Finally, policy A-31.1, Responsibilities of the General Director of Vocational-Technical Education, states: The General Director of Vocational-Technical Education shall be responsible to the Assistant Superintendent for Vocational, Technical and Adult Education. This position (General Director) shall direct the activities of vocational-technical supervisors and coordinators in the planning, implementation and operation of vocational-technical programs.

For the last twelve years, Cammaratta, as General Director, has been assessing the vocational supervisors and coordinators. His signature appears on these formal yearly evaluations.

I'm sure that we can conclude that by State Statute, County School Board Policy and traditional practice, Smouse assesses Cammaratta and Cammaratta assesses me. It is clear to see who is the boss at each level according to the policy book.

You may recall that on January 11, 1988, upon the advice of my attorney, I canceled my Level II grievance. I'm sure this was a great relief to Smouse and the Superintendent. Then on January 28, 1988, Smouse wrote me a letter about his concerns with my performance on the job. Late January was approximately the time that Kathleen Richards had interviewed me about my filing of a complaint with the Commissioner of Education against Smouse. I can expect that she interviewed Smouse and others around that time. It is interesting to note, although I am getting ahead of my story, that this letter of January 28, 1988, was submitted and became a part of the state Investigative Summary Report submitted by Kathleen Richards (as depicted in the upcoming Chapter 31—"The Commissioner's Ethics").

Back to the letter from Smouse on January 28, 1988. He states in this letter that he is directing me to meet with him to address my deficiencies. The letter is sent directly to me and not through my immediate supervisor, Cammaratta, as he usually has done in the past. Smouse is breaking the "chain of command" by excluding my immediate supervisor.

The letter was addressed to me from Smouse. Again he has circumnavigated the chain of command and avoided processing this through my immediate boss, Cammaratta. Copies went to Shelton, Shields, Binnie and Cammaratta. The letter was dated January 28, 1988, on the first page and January 25, on the second page, which was rather peculiar. The letter read as follows:

> After a review of the activities of your position since September, 1986, I have become very concerned with respect to your performance of the duties associated with your position. Specifically, numerous deficiencies exist which lead to my concern. These deficiencies can be described as follows:

1. Your apparent inability to consistently follow Hillsborough County School Board policies and procedures.

2. Poor organizational skills as evidenced in the attached information.

3. Failure to follow directives from my office.

4. Lack of proper attention to detail with respect to documents produced by your office.

5. Numerous occasions wherein you exhibited what I perceive to be poor judgement.

Specific instances wherein these deficiencies are exemplified are described in the attached summary.

I am very concerned that you address these deficiencies immediately. To this end I am directing you to make appointments to meet with me every other week to review your performance and to give me the opportunity to provide direct help and assistance with respect to these deficiencies. Further be advised that I will direct other members of my staff to work with you as is necessary to help you rectify these problems. If upon review of this letter you feel there are other types of support that I might give you that you feel might be helpful, please let me know.

It is imperative that you take appropriate steps to address these deficiencies. If I do not see significant improvement between now and the end of March, 1988, I will request that you accept a fourth year of probationary status. If you do not wish to accept the fourth year of probationary status, I will be forced to consider the possibility of not recommending you for renomination.

It is my desire that you succeed and that you satisfactorily correct all these deficiencies. If you have any questions or concerns relative to any of the thoughts expressed herein, please contact me immediately.

Sincerely yours,

R. L. Smouse, Jr.

I showed this letter to my attorney Robert "Bob" McKee. I also told him about the chain of command in the school system. I said that Smouse asked, in his letter, if I had any questions about what he was doing. The only question I had was should I challenge Smouse's authority in what he was trying to do or follow his directives? He said go ahead and let Smouse meet with me and "do his thing." If we didn't, it could be considered an act of insubordination. My question was answered. What was important, he said, was what Smouse would do with this information. We had to wait and see what that might be.

Smouse's letter told me that he was going to take the role of a college professor and teach me how to do my job. To my knowledge, Smouse had no university experience in teaching graduate courses in supervision. It would be interesting to see what curriculum he develops for me.

There was a three page attachment to Smouse's letter which was a summary of his concerns and recommendations for me. The list of fifteen items was a summary of the documentation on which he was basing his decision to terminate me. It may take some time, but I feel I should itemize his list now and comment on each of his points. Don't forget that several of these items have already been addressed and I responded in writing to most of the items at the time Smouse pointed them out. However, you must also remember that my written responses to Smouse must have fallen on deaf ears because he still holds each item as a "fault" of mine, regardless of my response and explanations. Where were my due process rights to defend myself in these matters?

A Summary of Smouse's List of Fifteen Concerns

I'll summarize each of his fifteen items listed by number and then I'll make a comment on each.

1. *Lack of textbooks at two schools.*
   Smouse faulted me because two schools didn't have all the books they said they needed. The request for needed textbooks was sent out by Dr. Horton's office from the School Administration Center and then forwarded to my office. My office ordered what was requested on the list. How was I to know their list wasn't complete. When I found out about the "shortage," I quickly remedied the situation. One principal said his automotive instructor wanted some supplemental books in addition to the required classroom textbook. So, there was a lack of "supplemental" books, not required ones. It is interesting to note that the textbook responsibilities in my office were assigned to my assistant, Richard Hair, Smouse's choice for my position as supervisor.

2. *Construction of a partial boat cover by me using school facilities.*
   At first Smouse implied that I had arranged to have a boat cover made at the expense of the school system, which is quite different from the above statement. I did admit to him that I personally made a small cover for the console of my fishing boat. I purchased maroon colored marine material

and the matching colored thread, brought them to the school and then used one of the school system sewing machines to sew it together with the permission of the upholstery instructor. Although, I was taught that this was an acceptable practice, I do admit it could be considered improper. I didn't do anything like it again.

3. *Field purchase order returned after two month's elapse time.*
This was the situation where my secretary "lost" this purchase order for two months on her desk. Then she mailed it to Smouse without notifying me. I got the blame. I never thought she was loyal to me, but to Hair. Why didn't the superintendent transfer her out of my office as I had originally requested?

4. *Information for Frank Zeitler travel form received 37 days after requested.*
This was addressed earlier in this book. It wasn't easy to get information from a teacher who was on vacation during the summer months. Zeitler was in no rush to be reimbursed for his travel. What was Smouse's rush? This travel information is routinely gathered by my secretary as it is with the other supervisor's secretaries. For some reason, my secretary had trouble getting this completed and I had to take over. I had to do her job. The blame for not submitting information in a timely manner was given to me.

5. *Similar to number 4.*
This time it was information about Jack Campbell's travel form. It was submitted 15 days after it was requested. Again Campbell had difficulty finding his motel receipt after I had requested it. He said he was in no hurry to be paid. This too was the job of my secretary. I had to take over again. This matter ended up with a letter in my personnel file, not hers. However, I did evaluate her accordingly on her yearly evaluation.

6. *Non-expenditure of $20,000 in funds for equipment.*
Due to a bookkeeping oversight in my office, I did not spend all of my equipment budget by February. The remaining funds would be returned to the district office and be made available for other supervisors to spend before the end of June, four months later. I still can't understand why this was a problem. Had I over spent my budget, then I think I should have been called on the carpet for it, but I had made sure that didn't happen. It is interesting to note that I assigned the responsibility of equipment to Hair. However, I had the responsibility to overwatch him. I believe my total equipment budget that year was around $160,000.

7. *Requesting a walk-through purchase order for bus rental.*
   I had checked with the finance office and they had told me that this request was "no problem at all, and that Smouse's office makes walk-through purchase orders all the time." Smouse was making something out of nothing. I did not frequently ask for walk-through purchase orders.

8. *Incomplete travel form submitted for Mike Grego.*
   I explained over and over again to Smouse that my office was not sending Grego to the conference, his principal was. Grego brought the travel form to my office by mistake. My office did not originate the travel form, nor was it paying for him to go. I forwarded it to Smouse because of the time factor of the teacher leaving on the trip. Smouse still blamed me even after his office was notified by Grego that his principal was sending him.

9. *Late travel request for Rodney Norris.*
   Just like the Grego affair, he was being sent by his principal and not by my office. By mistake, he brought the travel form to my office. I sent it to Smouse. I got the blame even though it was a matter between the teacher and his principal, not me.

10. *The misspelling of one word in a letter.*
    The one word was spelled "metal" and should have been spelled "medal." I honestly misspelled this one word. I told Smouse that all of us do make these errors from time to time. Nobody is perfect. By the way, how did he know that it wasn't just a "typo" error? Did he call my dedicated (?) secretary and ask her?

11. *Did not show up in time to give remarks at a banquet.*
    I was fifteen minutes late to our end of the year Co-op banquet on a Saturday night. I went home sick from work the day before and was sick all day Saturday. Shortly before the banquet, I felt well enough to go. It was across town, lots of traffic; I arrived late and another person was making some remarks in my place. I was one of three people asked to make remarks. I asked if I could give my remarks then and was told no. Why couldn't I explain to the audience why I was late and give my remarks then? I guess it would have been better not show up at all. My philosophy is not to give up.

12. *A memorandum that had a misspelled word, a word used incorrectly and a grammatical mistake.*
    Smouse was right; I did make those errors. I must have been in a rush and didn't review it as carefully as I should have when I signed it. *It was not a*

continuing problem. It was the only letter in three years that was pointed out to have a grammatical mistake or a misused word. I have accumulated a pile of communication from within the school system in which misspelled words and grammatical mistakes exist from other administrators. It was an example to show that all of us do make these minor mistakes *including* the superintendent of schools, Ralph Smouse and a host of other school administrators.

13. *Request for approval of Vernon Wynn to be VICA district advisor when he did not meet the standards.*
Four people applied for this teacher-supplemented position. I recommended the person I thought best suited for the district position. There was one standard that Wynn didn't meet. However, these established standards were used as guidelines only; they were not School Board policy. I didn't break any rules; I just made a recommendation based upon the information I had and Smouse disagreed with that recommendation.

14. *Request to send Vernon Wynn to a VICA advisors training workshop in Miami, including a cruise to the Bahamas.*
Wynn had no VICA chapter responsibilities. The Florida Department of Education financially sponsors a yearly training workshop for both new and experienced VICA student club advisors. This year the workshop was being coordinated through a grant at the University of South Florida. It was a week-long seminar, with college credit, to be held in Miami this year. One of the days was to include a day trip on the SeaEscape cruise ship to the Bahamas. A meeting room was reserved on the ship to continue the workshop. I thought this was unusual for a state-sponsored workshop, but I knew the teacher needed the training. In previous years, I have sent several teachers to attend these state-sponsored training workshops. That year I had recommended Wynn. Smouse disagreed, saying Wynn had no student chapter responsibilities. Because of Smouse's ignorance that the workshop was for new student advisors too, he blamed me for making an improper "request." Incidentally, I had heard later that the state workshop was canceled.

15. *Inappropriate use of school personnel, equipment, and materials in the preparation of a book used for a complaint to the Superintendent and to plead a grievance.*
This is the most ridiculous charge Smouse could have listed. It really wasn't only ridiculous, but resentful. The main purpose of The Big Black

Book was to stop something that I perceived to be wrong. The book was made for the Superintendent. It was information for him to use in resolving a problem under his administration that he may or may not have been aware of. After all, the Superintendent—who had a copy of the book in his possision—was the one who originally suggested I file a grievance against Smouse. All of the documentation used in the grievance had already been given to the Superintendent by way of this book, to ward off the possibility of a formal grievance. But no, the grievance procedure was recommended. Again Smouse blames me for filing grievance documentation against him. Sour grapes?

Furthermore, someone authorized the School System's Security Department to do an in-depth investigation about me and the alleged misuse of school personnel, equipment and materials in the development of a book for filing a grievance. I was found innocent. The security report never concluded or suggested any "inappropriate use" (as stated by Smouse) by me in the development of The Big Black Book. It was all school board business and none of it was for personal gain. I was never asked to pay for any supplies, equipment or personnel usage; neither was I given any type of reprimand, verbally or in writing. Smouse was using this "wild goose chase" by the administration to try to show improper behavior on my account. It was all poppycock. This was the criteria that Smouse enumerated to support the claims in his letter of January 28, 1988, the letter in which he stated that, if he didn't see significant improvement, he would request that I accept a fourth year of probation. If I didn't accept the fourth year of probationary status, he would be forced to consider recommending non-renomination.

Of course, each of the above-mentioned complaints was addressed in separate letters which I had to sign indicating that I had received and viewed them. Naturally, all were filed in my ever-growing personnel file. Considering all of the responsibilities that I had as supervisor on my job description and the extra assignments that were given to me, this list from Smouse seemed to be lacking any significant elements to show that my job responsibilities weren't being met.

The time now was January of 1988, three and one half months after I had filed my complaint with the Commissioner of Education. It is interesting to note that there was little if any documentation by Smouse of me during this period from October to January. Why was there a "slack" in his activity?

Shortly after I had received his letter of January 28, I received a call from Smouse's secretary. She wanted to confirm a meeting date on February 16, between Smouse and me. She told me to bring my appointment calendar because he would be setting up other meeting dates. At the first meeting on the 16th, Smouse set future meeting dates that were open on my calendar. They included March 1, March 11, March 18, and April 1, 1988, a total of five meetings.

I will summarize all five meetings because there are some relative and interesting happenings in each. Don't forget that Smouse said he would review my performance and "provide direct help." He would also be making a decision about my job status if he didn't see "significant improvement."

I had thought to myself that this seems like a kangaroo court because it was going to be such a short time for him to evaluate me. He wouldn't have time to provide direct help and see significant improvements. February 16 to April 1 is only a month and a half. I was skeptical as to what this was really all about. This whole thing smelled like three day old catfish.

All meetings were conducted in his office. Each time he sat behind his desk and I was seated in front.

MEETING ON FEBRUARY 16, 1988

After he set the meeting dates, he told me that he would provide a written summary after each of our meetings. I knew right away that I would be requested to sign these summaries and they would be placed in my personnel file. I was beginning to understand why we were having these meetings after all.

According to my notes, he then told me directly that he was the one to recommend me for renomination and tenure and that the Superintendent was the final authority. I knew this was contrary to Board policy, but McKee said to let Smouse "do his thing" so we could see where this was leading.

He wanted me to tell what I had been doing on my job. I told him about my activities with program review, vocational student clubs, unit allocations and my serving on the state committee to plan our state industrial arts conference.

He discussed his letter of January 28 that was detailed earlier in this chapter. He emphasized that he had three options in relation to me: First, to give me tenure, which would be very difficult; second, to give another year of probation if he saw significant improvements; and third, (he said "we don't want to talk about it"), to fail to renominate, therefore resulting in termination on June 30 of that year. He made it very clear what his three options were.

He said it was important to work together and keep in touch. In closing, he indicated that it was his "sincere desire" that I improve and succeed and he looked forward to a "cordial working relationship."

He took notes during the entire meeting. It lasted about thirty minutes. A copy of his written summary went to Cammaratta.

MEETING ON MARCH 1, 1988

Same setting as before. All meetings were the same. I told about my activities in planning the state conference, working on program review, planning regional vocational student contests and working on unit allocations.

Things went routinely until he asked me if I knew of any programs that needed special attention. I knew this sounded like a loaded question. What did he mean by "special attention?" I said I didn't know of any. He told me he knew of two.

The first one was a single teacher wood shop program at Blake Junior High. Smouse told me that the dust exhaust system wasn't working and had been broken several months. He also said it had broken down several times before. Smouse blamed me for this. He said "all the responsibility goes on my shoulders."

But he was incorrect. The dust exhaust system is considered to be a permanent part of the facility. It is a rather large unit, about the size of a refrigerator, and has a four to six inch duct going to each wood cutting machine in the shop.

There is a very clear line of authority on who has responsibility over this type of equipment. Since it is a permanent part of the building, the principal had the responsibility, not the county supervisor.

Nonetheless, Smouse directed me to go out to the school and take charge. When I got to the school and told the teacher why I was there, the teacher, Wayne Canady, told me it wasn't my responsibility; it was the principal's. I knew I could talk to Wayne, so I explained to him what Smouse said to me. Wayne commented that I was getting "screwed." He said it was the principal's job to fix it by submitting a repair order request to the county maintenance department. Wayne said the county fixed it eight times in the last seven years. And when I spoke to the principal, Mr. Bexley, that same day, he said not to worry; he had already called maintenance to repair it.

I knew this was the procedure. Smouse just made me look like a fool by trying to have me step on the toes of the principal whose responsibility it was. Plus, this gave Smouse more "fodder" for my personnel file.

The second program was also a single teacher "orientation" class at Oak Grove Junior High. Smouse told me that the program was "seriously hampered" in carrying out the competencies of the course frameworks because many of the equipment items necessary for the program had been inoperable for a year or more. Smouse then directed me to contact Dr. Orlan Briant, Area General Director—he supervises the principal at Oak Grove and other schools—and "enlist his assistance" in having our maintenance electricians provide the plugs, receptacles and switches to resolve the problems of the inoperable equipment. He also gave me a list of *"Equipment inoperable due to need for electrical work"* with twelve items listed.

The list had a note at the bottom that said Smouse hadn't personally observed the last three items on the list but indicated these items still needed attention according to the principal, Mrs. Mary Padgett.

Smouse also said in his summary letter of this meeting that he mentioned that Oak Grove had a serious roof leak problem and the water from this roof leak could pose a safety hazard where the operation of electrical equipment is involved.

This meeting too lasted about thirty minutes. A copy of his written summary went to Cammaratta.

The first thing I did after the meeting was to go over that afternoon to Oak Grove with Smouse's list. (I had also checked on Blake Junior High too, as I mentioned above.)

The wood shop teacher was Jacquelyn Rozman and she had been there a number of years. I showed her the list from Smouse and said I wanted to check on these items because of Smouse's concern. She looked at the list and said "this isn't your job!" I told her that I agreed, but I had to check them anyway.

Jackie knew that it was not the responsibility of the county supervisor to contact the school maintenance department to connect equipment; nor was it my responsibility to repair the school building.

You see, there is a fine line between the school principal and the county program supervisor's responsibilities. For example, I have a budget to purchase new equipment for programs throughout the county. When the equipment is delivered to each school from the manufacturer, like a table saw, then it is the responsibility of the school administrator to process a "request for maintenance" form through the school's maintenance department to hook it to the electrical box. The following example may seem a bit trivial, but it indicates that Smouse appears to be unaware of my job duties. As county program supervisor, I can purchase yellow safety paint to paint yellow safety lines on the floor of the shop around each power machine. These yellow safety lines are considered part of the "safety program." However, I can't purchase gray paint to paint the floor itself, if it has worn off, because the floor is considered part of the building and that comes under the responsibility of the school administrator. The school administrator has a budget for that. This also refers to the dust exhaust system at Blake Junior High too. The dust exhaust system is considered to be a permanent part of the facility like the air conditioner or sink.

I need to make an important point before I go any further. I'm trying to show these lines of authority only because I'm responding to specific documentation that was generated by Smouse. The point I want to make is that I have worked very hard to develop sound working relationships between principals, teachers and myself. If there is a problem in a program, I do want to solve it. I have always told teachers that if their principal can't get something accomplished and it is affecting the program, then call me and I will see whether I can assist the principal.

But, when Smouse places specific allegations in writing, makes me sign them denoting that I have seen them and then places them in my permanent personnel file, I have to draw back to the traditional rules of operation and specific job responsibilities.

Finally, let's look at the specifics of Smouse's list. The twelve items *all* had to do with the building or with the county maintenance department. The list included items such as: replacement of plugs on two machines, three machines in need of minor electrical maintenance, a 4-inch hole in the cement wall, roof leaking, dust collection system not working properly, and a light switch, light and exhaust fan that weren't working.

The last three items had already been repaired, contrary to the principal's knowledge. I must say that the principal was new to the school and had been there for less than one year. (Although, a number of years later, she was transferred to the position of county-wide middle school supervisor.) The two plugs were on a belt sander and a scroll saw. Work could be done on the other belt sander; there were two. And the scroll saw work could be done on the other two band saws that were in the shop, also working. The radial arm saw needed a switch, but these cuts could be done on the table saw. The program wasn't in an extreme emergency as Smouse portrayed it to be. Nonetheless, this list of a dozen items did make it into my personnel file. How come Smouse became aware of these items, but no one sought my assistance? Who was communicating to Smouse?

If Smouse had worked closer with me, he would have seen just what my supervisory responsibilities were and these incidents would never have been put down on paper. He made a fool out of himself in my eyes and a fool out of me in the eyes of others.

MEETING OF MARCH 11, 1988

This meeting went like the others. Smouse did a follow-up on the items at Blake and Oak Grove from the last meeting. We also talked about industrial arts program review, VICA regional contests and a teacher placement memorandum that I was asked to look into.

I told Smouse that I needed equipment repair monies to handle repairs for the remainder of the year. He said to give him a specific amount at our next meeting.

Smouse questioned me about the wheel alignment system at Tampa Bay Vo-Tech High School. He asked if they could do four wheel alignment and I said no, only two wheel alignment. I also said it was the same for most auto programs in the county. He instructed me to begin utilizing equipment funds to purchase four wheel alignment systems in order that programs can teach the competencies associated with current automobiles.

The meeting was relatively short. Copies of his written summary now went to Shelton, Shields, Binnie, Cammaratta and Sickles. This was a change in pattern. What was up? There was an awful lot of paper work with my name on it being shipped throughout the school system's top administrators. What would your thoughts be?

MEETING OF MARCH 18, 1988

This meeting went routinely except for one amusing incident at the end.

Again there was follow-up on Blake and Oak Grove and now on Van Buren where they had some ceiling fans that needed repair. A similar situation to the other schools at Oak Grove and Blake: it was the principal's responsibility.

Smouse cited an incorrect date in his summary. In his opening paragraph, he said the Oak Grove issue was brought up at our February 16th meeting. That was an incorrect date; it was initiated at our second meeting on March 1st. I hope Smouse understands that we all make minor mistakes.

I spoke about an automobile used for training at one school that was no longer needed. I recommended it be transferred to the HRS program at the

Hillsborough Halfway House that was talked about in the last chapter. Smouse said he would request Board approval.

I indicated to Smouse that I estimated that I needed $3,500 in repairs for the rest of this year. He said he would check into it with Shelton. I should have reminded him to explain to Shelton that I had $50,000 in my repair budget last year and had requested an increase to $60,000 for this year. However, due to budget cut-backs at the highest levels, I only ended up with $17,000 this year and that was why I needed some emergency equipment repair monies now. This sure caused a lot of flack from the teachers. I'm sure some teachers and programs had to go without repairs. Safety?

Now comes that amusing part.

Smouse said he would be preparing a letter for me next Tuesday, March 22, indicating his decision with regard to either renomination, a fourth year of probation, or non-renomination for my school contract for 1988-89. He said I was to meet with him. I said that I would be unable to meet with him on that day because I would be out of town. He looked startled and asked why. I told him that, as current President of the Florida Technology Education Association, the state association for teachers, I was going to the national conference for Industrial Arts Educators in Norfolk, Virginia. He should have already known this; he signed my travel form and authorized me to go, eleven days before, on March 7. Since he was keeping this relentless scrutiny of my activities, why didn't he remember I was going to be out of the state? How soon he forgets. Didn't he know he was going to make this decision?

He seemed puzzled for a moment and then said I should *call* him, from Virginia, at his office on March 22, in the afternoon. He would then read his letter of decision, which turned out to be two pages, as to his three choices of my employment status for next year, over the phone to me. I could answer him at that time or think it over and call back long distance two days later on March 24 with my response. Then he told me to wait just a moment, he wanted to double check with Dr. Binnie in Personnel if this plan was okay.

As I waited for him to return, I thought this was the most impersonal, ridiculous and asinine proposal that I had ever encountered. I laughed to myself. I thought that I must be working in a zoo or a circus; I wasn't sure which it was, perhaps both. Now let me see, Mr. Ralph L. Smouse, Jr., said I was to call him from Virginia and he would read his letter to me over the phone and I could decide then or two days later? He seemed to be set on his agenda and could care less about mine. Picture this: I would be 800 miles from home, all alone in my hotel room, at a national conference, trying to enjoy myself, calling long distance, listening to him read his (two page) letter of decision to me over the phone and I was to make a decision then which had to do with the future of my career and life? Didn't he think that I might want to talk it over with my family, friends and/or attorney? He obviously had no compassion. And why was the date of March 22 or the 24 so important, that it couldn't wait until the next week when I returned? This was absurd.

He came back into his office after spending a few minutes with Binnie. He said that Binnie said it would be okay to call. The meeting was over; I got up to leave and he shook his head up and down and said Binnie also said "to call collect." Of course, I sure would hate to have to pay for a call if it was going to be bad news. At least Binnie showed a little pity for me and my situation, a real consolation prize. And you thought the winter headquarters for the circus was in Sarasota, Florida? Send in the clowns, . . . nevermind.

I couldn't wait to get to attorney McKee's office. I told McKee what Smouse just told me about calling collect from Virginia. McKee thought this was a ridiculous way to proceed (McKee's specific reactions are described in the following Chapter 29—"Probation Equation").

The meeting lasted about thirty minutes. Copies of his written summary went to Shelton, Shields, Binnie, Cammaratta and Sickles again.

So tell me, were things being maneuvered around me? How can you stand up for your rights with something so complex as this? There were so many details to my case, where do I go and with whom?

I was very skeptical about what Smouse was going to do. He had told Cammaratta to work closely with me. Now Smouse was going to evaluate me from his distant office downtown. Smouse was not able to see or experience my total performance; nor did it appear that he tried to. Nonetheless, he was going to make the final decision. I saw this activity as a part of the continued harassment of me by Smouse because I filed a grievance against him.

Smouse's original stated intent of these meetings was to review my performance and "provide direct help and assistance with respect to these deficiencies." In other words, he was going to be my college professor and teach me how to do my job. And according to his time-line, he was going to re-educate me in one and a half months, in thirty minute meetings, every other week. During the sequence of these meetings, Smouse was unable to point out anything that I did contrary to my job description. As a matter of fact, he never referred to my Board-approved job description. He didn't teach me how to do anything, he just asked me what I was doing. He put in a lot of script about building maintenance at several schools, but these were not my responsibilities, they were the building administrators'. Smouse's attempt to be a college professor was lacking; his curriculum was ill-founded. The only "direct help and assistance" that Smouse gave me were facts that lead me to the conclusion that this was a witch-hunt for the purpose of besmirching my reputation and for providing misleading documentation for the purpose of supporting his recommendation to terminate me.

It looked like he was going to be the police, judge, jury, prosecutor, executioner and undertaker, a package deal.

"Might does not make right."

29

PROBATION EQUATION

In the series of meetings between us, Smouse told me of the three choices that he had in reference to my employment status for next year: give me tenure; offer me probation; or recommend non-renomination.

Immediately after Smouse's meeting, on March 18, I went to speak to McKee and informed him of Smouse's directive that I should call the school board next week from Norfolk and ask Smouse to read his decision on my status of employment for next year over the phone, and then give him my response.

McKee said Smouse's procedure was no way to conduct business. McKee decided that he would pick up the memo from Smouse and submit a response within the time limit. He told me not to worry about it, that he would handle it and I should plan to enjoy my national conference in Norfolk. He then drafted a letter to Smouse and his secretary typed it immediately. He wanted me to hand deliver it that day and get approval from Smouse. The letter was addressed to Smouse, Re: William Wieser, dated March 18, 1988, copy to me, and read as follows:

> I have been retained to represent William Wieser regarding his employment with the School Board. Mr. Wieser advises me that a written decision will be forthcoming from you on Tuesday, March 22, 1988, regarding his future employment with the School Board. In view of the fact that Mr. Wieser will be out of town on that day on School Board business, he has authorized me to receive the letter on his behalf and to submit a response thereto within the prescribed time. If there is any problem with this arrangement, I shall appreciate your communicating with me prior to March 22. If I do not hear from you before that day, I will send someone from my office to pick up the letter.
>
> Your cooperation is appreciated.

I took the letter right down to Smouse. I gave him the letter and as soon as he looked at the letter, a surprised look came over his face. He shook his head and queried inquisitively "this is from a different attorney?" In a quiet voice, I said...yes? I wondered what he meant by that? Then Smouse quietly read the rest of the letter and said that it was alright.

Again, Smouse's immediate and surprised reaction to attorney McKee's name on my letter made me contemplate his concern. Why should he be worried at all what attorney was representing me? Smouse had the protection of his superiors in the system and they had the protection of the school board attorney. This made me think if attorney Craparo's abrupt decision not to file suit from his office had anything to do with Smouse's reaction. Why did Smouse react so dubiously?

I returned to tell McKee that Smouse accepted the letter. He said good, told me not to worry and to have a good time at my conference and he would see me when I returned. Two days later, I left on my trip to Norfolk.

Don't forget that I was still waiting to hear from State Commissioner Castor about the decision on the complaint that I filed against Smouse. Remember that the Professor said she would make her decision before April 1st. Time was getting close.

After I returned, I met with McKee to learn of the outcome of Smouse's decision and McKee's response. As I had guessed, Smouse decided to recommend that I accept a fourth year of probation. Smouse's letter to me, dated March 22, 1988, had copies to Shelton, Shields, Binnie and Cammaratta. His letter, in part, stated the following:

> This letter is in regard to my indication to you in my letter of January 28, 1988 (copy attached) that I would be making a recommendation to the Superintendent as to your employment status for the 1988–89 year.
>
> We have met four times from February 16, 1988 to March 18, 1988, to discuss, review, and give you direction and assistance with regard to your responsibilities and activities as Supervisor....In my judgement, your performance is still deficient in each of these five areas as listed below:
> 1. Your apparent inability to consistently follow School Board policies and procedures.
> 2. Poor organizational skills as evidenced in the attached information.
> 3. Failure to follow directives from my office.
> 4. Lack of proper attention to detail with respect to documents produced by your office.

> 5. Numerous occasions wherein you exhibited what I perceive to be poor judgement....

In view of your performance and deficiencies, your inadequate follow-up, and your failure to keep me informed, I have decided to recommend that you accept a fourth year of probation in order to give you a further opportunity to improve your performance....

The letter also included a summary about our March 18th meeting. Smouse recapped his statement where he told me to telephone him on March 22 from Virginia to have him read this letter to me. He also summarized that later that day, I came in with the letter from Attorney McKee in which he would pick up my letter.

McKee told me that if I accepted probation, I would be saying that I perceived my job performance to be substandard. I would also be in a position next year for them to fire me. He said this situation needs to come to a head *now*.

In response to Smouse's letter of March 22, McKee sent the following two-paragraph letter to Smouse on March 24, copy to me.

> I am in receipt of your letter of March 22, 1988, to William Wieser regarding your recommendation to the superintendent that he be required to serve a fourth year of probation to insure that he corrects numerous alleged deficiencies in his performance. You are advised that Mr. Wieser strenuously objects to your recommendation. It is inconceivable that you expect Mr. Wieser to perform yet another year under your relentless and unwarranted scrutiny. Indeed, it is most unusual for an Assistant Superintendent to have so immersed himself in the day-to-day performance of a supervisor and to have by-passed the General Director regarding the recommendation for continued employment, as you have done in this case.
>
> Based upon the foregoing, Mr. Wieser would prefer that you either recommend unfettered continued employment or recommend that he not be re-employed. If the latter recommendation is made, Mr. Wieser intends to avail himself of all administrative and judicial remedies.

Robert McKee was new to me and my case, but from the above action, it sure was evident to me that he knew his stuff and he was doing just what I wanted and expected him to do. When Smouse bypassed the General Director and made the recommendation himself, he went around Board policy. It had been previously documented that Cammaratta had this responsibility and had made the recommendations for reappointment over the last ten years.

Meanwhile, back at my office, I had received a memo from Smouse dated March 22, 1988. The memo stated the following:

> The original letter to you dated March 22, 1988 was personally picked up at my office on March 22, 1988 by Carol Sierra of the office of Robert McKee, Attorney at Law.
>
> Attached are two copies of the letter. Please sign and return one copy to acknowledge your receipt.
>
> Thank you for your assistance.

It is significant that I mention that frequently Smouse would send confidential documentation to me at my office through the school mail. He would ask me to sign and return it because he was placing it in my personnel file. However, then unannounced, he would send my copies of these signed letters in one package, which was not marked personal or confidential. It was opened by my secretary with the other mail and placed on my desk. This package included his recommendation to the superintendent that I not be renominated and other documentation that he had previously sent confidential. Did he want my secretary and my coordinator, Hair, to have the opportunity of knowing what he was doing to me?

This memo was date stamped March 23, 1988, by my secretary when my office received it. This piece of school mail, from Smouse to me, was *not* marked "Confidential," meaning that my secretary automatically opened it when it was received. And of course it was available to her to read. I don't know if she did read it or not, but she was given the opportunity by Smouse's office when it was not sent "Confidential." Did Hair also have had the opportunity to read it while it sat on my desk that week when they knew I was 800 miles away? Was this Smouse's way of communicating to them on what he was doing to me? Naturally, because of the office working relationships, these questions did pass through my mind.

MEETING OF APRIL 1, 1988

The last meeting between Smouse and me (Chapter 28—"Who's The Boss?") was held on April 1st—April Fool's Day. I'm not superstitious, but I did remain alert.

Smouse started this meeting with discussing my decision not to accept a fourth year of probation. He then said, according to his summary letter, my not accepting probation would result in him "recommending to the Superintendent either renomination with tenure or non-renomination for the 1988-89 school year." He went on to say it would be "highly unlikely" that I would be renominated. He said the decision would be made in the next few days, probably after the Easter vacation break. (I wished myself a nice vacation and peace of mind. I knew this issue would haunt me all during the "vacation." It did.)

He continued the meeting by talking about my planning for the state VICA contest, my repair budget, the number of first, second and third place VICA winners at our regional contest, my attendance on a certificate program committee and a letter from a masonry instructor asking to continue the program.

Twenty-six VICA students became eligible to go on to the state contests. I believe this was a reflection of my office, but no compliments came from Smouse which had come in previous years to me and other supervisors when this would happen. I guess this was not a time that he would be handing out compliments, especially to me. Was he one-sided?

Then he brought up the topic of automotive wheel alignment equipment. I told him that three schools had the four wheel alignment system and eight did not. He directed me to give priority number one to the Tampa Bay Vo-Tech automotive program and then to prioritize the rest of the schools.

It is interesting to note that Smouse is blaming me for the lack of these alignment systems in the programs, but he failed to point out that budget cutbacks by the Superintendent prevented me from getting equipment money to put all needed pieces in the schools. The memo went into my personnel file, not the Superintendent's. It's misleading.

Another interesting note is a comment Smouse made about the two-wheel alignment system at the Erwin Vo-Tech Center. He told me to consider a "trade-in" of the old two-wheel system on a new four-wheel system like they did at Erwin. I wasn't informed that Erwin even did this. Traditionally, all equipment, purchased new or disposed of, had been routinely passed through my office as county program supervisor. That way I can make appropriate decisions as to county program needs and transfer used equipment to other schools if necessary. Traditionally, all equipment that was disposed of went through my office and then on to our warehouse to be auctioned off during an announced public sale. You see, the monies received from these sales then would revert back to the "downtown" general fund for use by those administrators there. Now, it is acceptable for the Erwin Center to trade-in some equipment and to save some of their allocated funding, allowing them to purchase more equipment. Previously, I wasn't allowed to do this. Now, after the fact that the Erwin Center did it, Smouse suggests that I do it.

The Erwin Center administrators knew they didn't have to inform me or seek my approval of their actions because what ever they did would be approved by Smouse. Besides, the Erwin Center always got a larger share of the equipment funding than the other schools. They didn't need my authority to do what they wanted; they had the money. Again, it was undermining my supervisory authority.

This next part becomes a bit provocative. Smouse brought up the topic of the upholstery program at the Erwin Vo-Tech Center. He said that the program would be closed when the teacher retires at the end of this school year and it would be replaced by another program, a Business Education one.

The upholstery program is under the supervision of Home Economics and not my area of Industrial Education. So what does it have to do with me, especially if it is going to be changed to a Business Education program? Was Smouse confused? Why did Smouse add this as another item in his meeting and detail it in his written summary which ended up in my file. Was he just looking for more "hamburger helper" again?

This is another clear example that Smouse didn't know my job responsibilities nor what programs my job encompassed. How could he, with any level of impartiality or proficiency, evaluate my performance and take the authority to make a recommendation as to my future with the school system?

This was the last meeting and it lasted the usual thirty minutes and copies of his written summary went to Shelton, Sickles, Shields, Binnie and Cammaratta.

I feel the job stress. One of my ways to relax was to watch the "Bob Newhart Show." I enjoy his type of humor. I immediately would relax when his theme song would come on in the Vermont setting. You saw the boat out on the lake and then the car would come around the corner; I knew I was in for a short time of instant relaxation, no stress, just humor. During some shows, I would even laugh out loud. Thanks Bob.

P.S. Handyman "George," played by Tom Poston, used to buy flowers in my mom's flower shop on his visits to Pine's Lake, New Jersey. He rode a motorcycle. Hi Tom.

30

A RARE HAPPENING

I always have respected the School Board as our top management officials who are elected by the people to educate the youth and adults of the community. They were a political entity, but I really didn't look at them that way. I saw them not as typical politicians, but as people who are politically "neutral," because the elections are nonpartisan. I saw them as leaders, people caring about kids and concerned with the strength of our community, state and nation through education and knowledge.

I also saw them as the ultimate body to go to when an ultimate problem exists. What I mean is you go through all the other steps in the "chain of command" before you take a problem to Thee Board. With all that has happened to me, I thought that I had reached that ultimate time.

The Hillsborough County School Board members during 1988 were as follows:

Rev. A. Leon Lowry, Sr., Chairman

Sam Rampello, Vice Chairman

Cecile W. Essrig

Roland Lewis

Joe E. Newsome

R. Sonny Palomino

Marion S. Rodgers

Because I had confidence in Cammaratta, I told him I would like to present my concerns to the individual School Board members rather than presenting my case to them at a public Board meeting. I still wanted to keep this problem with Smouse "in-house" and confidential. I informed Cammaratta, in February of 1988, that I wanted to talk directly to each Board member or get information to them about my case because I wasn't satisfied with the events that took place concerning the grievance process. I asked him if he had a line of communication with them to set up a meeting for me. I then added that I wanted him to come along with me to these meetings and give support information about my case.

The first Board member that I wanted to see was the Chairman, Reverend Lowry. Cammaratta set up the first meeting and we met with him at his church. I told him about events of the last year, including the grievance. He said that he didn't like it when things like this happen. He said it wasn't right when my witnesses were restricted. I gave him a copy of The Big Black Book and asked him to review it for a couple of weeks.

A few weeks passed and we made another appointment. During this meeting, I asked for The Big Black Book back. He said he wasn't finished with it yet, so I asked him to keep it longer. During our conversation, we talked about what Smouse said about possibly not recommending me for reappointment for next year. Rev. Lowry then stated that, earlier that week, he was in a meeting with several top administrators and a Board member, Sam Rampello. He said that they specifically discussed my situation about reappointment and that "everything was on hold." This put me at ease because there was time to stop any action against me. Little did I know that it didn't remain on hold long. Later, I wondered if it was really on hold at all. About two weeks later, Reverend Lowry had finished with The Big Black Book and I picked it up from his secretary at his church. Reverend Lowry had been a Board member for twelve years and was up for re-election.

The next Board member I wanted to contact was Marion Rodgers. Again I asked Cammaratta to contact her and set up a meeting. We met at her house. I explained about my concerns about the grievance process including Smouse and the things that he was doing to Cammaratta. Sometime before our meeting, I had Cammaratta drop off the copy of The Big Black Book to her at her house for her perusal. She didn't ask me any specific questions about the book. She just asked me to start from the beginning. When I told her about Smouse requiring me to keep a daily log of activities, she commented that it was usually done as a form of punishment. In talking about the grievance, she said that the superintendent should have selected an "outside" Review Board from the community to hear my Level II grievance. I agreed with her because the Review Board was too close to Smouse. The visit lasted for one hour. She said that I should contact the other School Board members. I thanked her for her time and concern.

I decided to contact Cecile Essrig myself. I called her at home one evening, told her who I was and asked to meet with her. She asked if we could meet over the phone now and I said that I'd rather meet and speak with her in person. She said that she was very busy and asked again to talk with her now about my problem. During our twenty minute phone call, I capsulized my problems and concerns. Since I had some experience telling my story to the other Board members, I could streamline my story with just the nitty gritty when necessary. When I told her about all the road blocks during my grievance, she commented that they (the administration) always do that. They try to suppress the problem rather than try to solve it. At the end of our conversation, she said that I should be nice to Mr. Richard Hair, be pleasant to Mr. Smouse until he can't stand it, and that I should do the best job that I ever did. She also told me to visit with the rest of the Board members and keep her posted.

Since we talked on the phone, I didn't have a chance to show her The Big Black Book. For some reason I had the feeling that she already knew about it and didn't want to see it. It was one of those gut level feelings that tells you something that you didn't hear. She had been on the School Board for twenty-one years and just had a new school named after her. Considering all the things that have happened to the school system recently, I felt that she was ready to retire since this was an election year and her district seat was up for election. I expect that she would at least tell me that my problem was serious and she would check into it with the administration and other Board members. But instead, she said to be nice to Hair, pleasant to Smouse and contact the other Board members.

I honestly felt that I should only have had to contact one Board member with the problems I presented. I saw my job as getting the ball rolling and the elected Board members would do the rest. To cover myself, it was my intention to contact most of the Board members to be sure that my problem couldn't be ignored or disregarded. Now I can laugh at an ignorant statement like that.

Board member Sam Rampello was the first one to receive The Big Black Book (last year). He and Cammaratta talk every now and then so I didn't need to meet directly with him again since he did know about my problems with Smouse.

The next meeting was with Joe Newsome. Again I asked Cammaratta to call him and ask for a meeting for the three of us. Joe suggested that we meet early for breakfast at the Holiday Inn in Plant City because he was busy with work in his orange groves. Again I repeated my story, problems with Smouse and my concerns about my job for next year. Joe seemed very shocked and had a hard time believing what we told him. He said he was disturbed about what was happening to me, but then he said he was *really* upset at what they were doing to Cammaratta. He reassured Cammaratta by reminding him of their long working relationship and then said he would check into this to see if it was really all true. He asked if I had talked to other Board members and I told him that I did. I then gave him the well-used copy of The Big Black Book and asked him to read it because it would back up most of what we told him concerning last year's incidents. He bought our breakfast and seemed genuinely concerned. I felt that he was really going to help us. Several weeks later I picked up the book at his pharmacy in Plant City. I was sure that he had read at least part of it, if not all.

Following the visit with Joe Newsome, my next contact was with Sonny Palomino. I apprised Cammaratta that, since Sonny was a practicing attorney, I thought it would be best to let him review the copy of the book. If necessary we would meet with him. He was a Board member for eight years and was also up for re-election. Cammaratta took the book to him and picked it up several weeks later. Palomino viewed The Big Black Book as an attorney;...politically, however, he seemed to remain noncommittal.

The final Board member to contact was Roland Lewis. He was a Board member for over twenty years and recently had a new school named after him. There were loud rumors that he was planning to retire this year instead of running for re-election. I was getting worn out talking to all the Board members while trying to do my job, keep up with Smouse's directives, and keep my head screwed on right. I decided not to contact Roland Lewis because I felt he might not do anything because he was planning to leave. Besides, the other Board members should have contacted him.

That was it; I went the route of the School Board. Of all the approaches for a remedy that I have sought so far, there were only two ways left if it didn't work out with the Board. The next two steps would be through the courts and then to the people in the community. Then if none of these worked, my career was as good as dead.

I mean death by education, a rare happening?

31

THE COMMISSIONER'S ETHICS

For the benefit of review, I filed an ethics complaint against Smouse with Betty Castor, State Commissioner of Education, in Tallahassee on October 7, 1987. Earlier, it was shown that Betty Castor had some roots in Tampa when she served as a Hillsborough County Commissioner from 1972 to 1978 and then served as Directional of Governmental Relations for the University of South Florida from 1979 to 1981. I restlessly waited until January 11, 1988, at which time I received an acknowledged receipt of the filing of my complaint and the assignment of a case File number: 88004-R. Then again, I vigilantly waited for a decision of action before the "predetermined" deadline of April 1st that was forecast by the Professor through contact with the Commissioner's office.

I had hoped and prayed that the Commissioner would take some kind of action against Smouse which then would stop the harassment that he was aiming at me, even if it were the least penalizing action—a reprimand by the Education Practices Commission. I looked through a copy of the Education Practices Commission's Annual Report, 1985-86, and saw that different people had received a reprimand, probation or a restricted scope of practice as a result of actions taken by the Commission. I wasn't convinced that the Commissioner would go as far as to revoke the teaching certificate of Smouse, but I knew it was very possible. Nevertheless, several types of a lesser action were available and have been applied by the Commission in the past.

And then...POW, BAM! Holy Decisions, Batman! Who's Robin who? I received a copy of a letter from Commissioner Betty Castor that was dated March 29, 1988. The letter was addressed to Mr. Ralph Smouse, Re: File Number 88004-R, and was from Commissioner Castor. The two paragraph letter was as follows:

Pursuant to the provisions of Sections 231.262 and 231.28, Florida Statutes, and Rule 6A-4.37, Florida Administrative Code (Rules of the State Board of Education), I have determined to find no probable cause to suspend or revoke your teacher's certificate at this time.

Therefore, I am directing Mr. Martin B. Schaap, Administrator, Professional Practices Services, to prepare and make all required notices of this decision.

First of all, because of her ruling, the case was now closed. I was devastated that no action whatsoever was taken, not even a slap on the wrist. Why wasn't there a hearing before the Professional Practices Commission so that my witnesses and I could testify? Secondly, I believe that somehow this decision immediately made me stronger in my belief that I was right in what I was pursuing and that I must prevail. Still, my story had not come into the observable domain of public accountability. Thirdly, the Professor hit the nail right on the head when he indicated that a decision would be made by the Commissioner before April 1st. The Professor's prediction several months earlier was exactly correct. The Professor's credibility continued to be solid.

Did Commissioner Castor's decision to throw out my complaint have anything to do with the fact that she had received the highest award possible from the Florida Association of School Administrators (FASA), an affiliate of the American Association of School Administrators (AASA) of which Superintendent Shelton was the national president?

The next day, I showed the letter to Cammaratta. He was more devastated and disappointed than I, because this directly involved him in the coercion issue. I also showed it to my attorney, Bob McKee. He was not my attorney at the time that I filed the complaint, so he didn't know of all the details of my filing. He saw my disappointment in the decision and indicated that I could request a copy of all available information about the case under the Florida Public Records Act, Chapter 119, if I wanted. At the time, I didn't see any benefit to look through the paperwork of this case since the final decision was already made. I had too many other important things to concentrate on at work.

Meanwhile, back at the job, I had just refused Smouse's offer of probation and I was still waiting for him to decide if he was going to recommend that I receive tenure for next year or recommend that I be non-renominated.

Cammaratta and I met the Professor for lunch at one of our usual secure restaurants. I had already told the Professor about the Commissioner's decision. The Professor spoke softly and told us an earful. The rumor was that a Board member from Hillsborough County Schools called the Commissioner and made a deal. In my opinion, maybe a deal was made to possibly support the Commissioner in her run for governor, but there was no conclusive proof. This sure was a surprise to us. We never heard anything this heavy from the Professor before. Although, it did have our concern because we thought the Commissioner did let Smouse off lightly. All of the past information from the Professor had been credible. There was no way to prove this rumor, but it put us in a precarious posture of seriousness. The Professor emphasized again that the local administrators were "ruthless!" It scared me. The situation was real and big. Why was all this happening? Why?

To add credibility to the statements by the Professor about the Board member supporting the Commissioner in her possible run for Governor, I will refer to an article printed in *The Tampa Tribune* a bit later that year, August 15, 1988. The article, written by Elizabeth Skewes, and titled: "Castor's high profile sends mixed signals." It discusses the Commissioner joining school officials statewide via satellite to get their input on the two-year budget that will take the schools through 1990. The article reports that, "Castor says such high-profile speeches and meetings, including recent trips to Denver, Atlanta and Boston, focus a spotlight on Florida's educational needs." Later, it asserts that "Castor, 47, denies any aspirations to the governor's job in 1990." I would speculate, from that article, that there may have been some earlier considerations behind the scenes about the Commissioner running for Governor. Who knows?

A while later, Cammaratta was talking to a high level administrator who should have known about my complaint in Tallahassee with the Commissioner. To the best of our knowledge, this person did not know the Professor. This administrator asked Cammaratta how I was doing. Cammaratta told the administrator about the Commissioner's decision and said that I was disappointed. The administrator leaned over to Cammaratta as they walked down the hall, and said, "It was fixed!" Cammaratta didn't ask any more questions. Now suddenly, there was a second and separate source that supported the things that the Professor said about my case being allegedly overlooked by the Commissioner.

Additionally, one year later on April 21, 1989, Cammaratta was attending a national job training conference in Albuquerque, New Mexico and he saw an administrator he knew from the Department of Education in Tallahassee. They talked about several things and then the conversation turned to Smouse. The administrator said to Cammaratta, "They (administrators in Tallahassee) knew that he (Smouse) was asked to leave." When Cammaratta shared this comment with me, I responded by saying that this was a third source that points to the concept of my case allegedly being overlooked by the Commissioner. He agreed with me and said there are more parts to this puzzle than we know. Although this rumor about Smouse being asked to leave the system was persistent, we were never able to confirm whether, in fact, it actually happened. If so, who suggested it? Would Smouse be asked to leave if he did nothing wrong? Was a "deal" struck in Tallahassee which essentially said that the complaint would be overlooked if Smouse retires?

I became inquisitive and my curiosity overcame me. I remembered what Bob McKee said about the Florida Public Records Act, so I called the Professional Practices Services to see if I could get some copies of the information on my complaint. I just wanted to see who said what.

I called Martin Schaap, Administrator PPS, and asked if I could get a copy of the case that I filed. He said sure and he asked what my name was. When I told him, he responded by saying " Oh. . . that was the one with that administrator down there in Hillsborough County." I said yes, the administrators name was Smouse. He said that he was just ready to send this file over to the archives, but he would send me a copy right away.

The information came in the mail on June 23, 1989. As I read through the Investigation Report, I noticed that the physical evidence consisted of Notebook A, from me, (The Big Black Book), with Sections 1-17:, which was located in the Master File. Also there was another notebook, Notebook B, submitted by Ralph L. Smouse, Jr., Sections 1-12, pages 1-87, which was also located in the Master File. I double checked the information that I had received and found that I only had pages 1 to 71 of Smouse's 87 page "notebook."

I called Martin Schaap again and asked if I could have access to the rest of Smouse's notebook. He said sure. Then he said that originally he wasn't sure if I wanted it all when I first called. He said he would send it right out.

A funny coincidence, a kind of deja vu, occurred. My curiosity extended back to about a year ago when the School Security did an investigation on me about the development of a document for a grievance. I never heard anything about the results and I now wanted to know. So, I called the security department and talked to Detective Dasinger. He said I would need approval from Dr. Binnie to get a copy of the report. When I called Binnie and asked for a copy, he said he would send it right out. I was glad that it could be released to me. I wanted to see if any conclusions were made about the investigation. Wouldn't you be curious if you were investigated by your employer's security department?

Now, I was waiting for the "missing" pages from Smouse's notebook in Tallahassee and for the school system's security report from Binnie. On June 29, I walked over to get my mail and I received a manila envelope from Betty

Castor's office. I opened it and inside was the security report from Binnie. I did a double take and looked at the envelope again. It wasn't from Binnie; it was from Martin Schaap and it was the missing pages from Smouse's notebook.

As you may remember in Chapter 24—"Okay—Don't Anybody Move," this security report investigated my development of a grievance document and the report appeared to go beyond the purpose of the investigation. Why didn't Martin Schaap send these missing pages in the first place? Was he trying to cover up something like the confidential security report? Or was it just an oversight on his part? I did receive the same security report from Binnie a few days later. I'll never cease to be amazed by the coincidences that occur in life.

I began to study the total amount of 152 pages of information that I received from Tallahassee. A lot of the documentation wasn't new; I had seen it before, but there were a few new meaty parts. The Investigative Report consisted of 65 pages and Smouse's notebook contained 87 pages.

The Investigative Report had a five-page summary, an index and then fifty seven pages of assembled documentation from my notebook, Smouse's notebook and the administrative procedures of the case.

The documentation in Smouse's notebook included his two-page response, a three page synopsis of events regarding the performance of William F. Wieser, approximately fifty pages of his documentation and the sixteen-page school security report.

I had wondered if Smouse, upon seeing Hair's two-year "documentation" of my office and personal activities in the security department's report while he was on county time, wrote a letter to be placed in Hair's personnel file. If so, was it a letter of wrong doing or one of compliment?

The documentation in my notebook was described in Chapter 14—"The Big Black Book" and then in further detail in Chapter 19—"The Commissioner's Code of Ethics." A cover letter and my notebook, in its entirety, were presented to the Commissioner.

For me to give an understanding of the crux of the case, I'll basically concentrate on new documentation from the Investigation Report, Smouse's notebook and from my notebook.

Each case starts with the "Legal Sufficiency" of a violation. As you may remember, when I filed my complaint, I didn't specify the violations but provided all the documentation of the actions of Smouse. The Commissioner had to review the documents and identify if they constituted any violations.

In the Investigative Report, there was a memorandum from Charles S. Ruberg, Assistant General Counsel, Department of Education, to Kathleen M. Richards, dated January 8, 1988, and the topic was Legal Sufficiency of

Complaint By William F. Wieser Against Ralph L. Smouse, Jr. It was apparent that Ruberg was requested to give advice if there was legal sufficiency which contained grounds for revocation, suspension or other penalty in the complaint. Ruberg stated that a complaint is legally sufficient if it contains the ultimate facts which show a violation has occurred as provided in Florida Statute 231.28.

In a part of Charles Ruberg's Comments and Summary of Conclusions, he stated the following:

> The materials submitted by Mr. Wieser do include allegations of one episode which appear to me to be legally sufficient within the meaning of 231.262, F. S. I am referring to the allegation that Mr. Smouse sought to coerce Dr. Cammaratta to modify Dr. Cammaratta's annual performance evaluation of Mr. Wieser. If such conduct occurred, it would violate the prohibition against using coercive means to influence the professional judgement of colleagues.
>
> As the second-level supervisor, Mr. Smouse is entitled to a different opinion than the immediate supervisor regarding the evaluation of a subordinate's performance. He is also entitled to express such differences in writing as part of the personal file documentation. However, he is not entitled to coercively influence the judgement of the immediate supervisor. Since Mr. Smouse would be responsible for evaluating Dr. Cammaratta's performance, he is in a position to exercise a coercive influence. The issues for investigation is whether he did so.
>
> My recommendation is that any investigation made pursuant to Mr. Wieser's complaint be limited to the issue of whether Mr. Smouse attempted by coercive means to influence Dr. Cammaratta to give Mr. Wieser a more adverse performance evaluation than would be reflected by Dr. Cammaratta's unimpeded exercise of his own judgment.

The case was opened on January 11, 1988.

The affidavit that I submitted was quoted under Victim Testimony in the Investigative Report. The quote included the following:

> On April 28, 1987, Dr. Cammaratta completed and signed my year-end summary evaluation....His summary evaluation of me was 2.9...Cammaratta told me...that Mr. Smouse would not accept my evaluation and that Mr. Smouse directed him in writing to evaluate me with an average of 1.
>
> Dr. Cammaratta told me Mr. Smouse said "his (Dr. Cammaratta's) evaluation was not done yet" when Dr. Cammaratta refused to change his evaluation of me. Then Mr. Smouse said he would take him to an "administrative

hearing" if he didn't change the evaluation....Mr. Smouse said to Dr. Cammaratta that "his job was on the line" because he would not change his evaluation....

The affidavit that Cammaratta sent in was quoted under Witness Testimony in the Investigative Report. The quote included the following:

>...Since Mr. Smouse had made allegations early in the school year (September 22, 1986) relative to Mr. Wieser's inefficiency and ineffectiveness, I was asked to monitor Mr. Wieser's performance....During my discussion with Mr. Smouse, he told me that he rated Mr. Wieser...(improvement needed)...Mr. Smouse...said to me "Cam, I have not done your evaluation yet."...I again reiterated saying in good conscience I could not rate him as directed. At this point Mr. Smouse told me that "he would have me before an administrative hearing."...he stated "Your job is on the line...."

Smouse responded in writing to the allegations. He was quoted under the Mitigation section of the Investigative Report. Smouse's informal conference was scheduled for March 3, 1988. He submitted a written response to the allegations and also provided a notebook of documentation. The Investigative Report included the following:

>On Monday, May 4, 1987, I met with Dr. Domenic P. Cammaratta...to review with him preliminary copies of performance evaluations he prepared....Dr. Cammaratta indicated that he felt that Mr. Wieser should be rated as exceeding the standard. ...I indicated to Dr. Cammaratta that I could not agree that Mr. Wieser was exceeding the standard...in view of the difficulties Mr. Wieser had been having since early in his appointment to the supervisor position....
>
>I indicated to Dr. Cammaratta that I felt his judgement was less than adequate with regard to his evaluation of Mr. Wieser and that I would have to take this into consideration in carrying out my responsibility to evaluate Dr. Cammaratta. I also stated that it may be necessary for me to ask Dr. Shelton to meet with us to review this difference in judgement.
>
>Dr. Cammaratta became very upset and stated that he felt that I was threatening his job. I replied that, to the contrary, I was carrying out my responsibility as his immediate supervisor....
>
>At no time did I attempt to threaten or coerce Dr. Cammaratta to change Mr. Wieser's evaluation....

I have a question on some of these statements by Smouse. One particular one is stated in his response, but wasn't quoted in the Investigative Report.

Concerning my evaluation, Smouse stated "We later met with Dr. Shelton and Dr. Shelton stated to Dr. Cammaratta that he agreed with me on the judgement issue but realized that neither of us could require Dr. Cammaratta to change his evaluation." My concerns and comments are about the fact that it took Smouse three weeks longer to accept Cammaratta's evaluation of me than it did to accept all the other supervisor's evaluations. If the statements by Smouse are true, then he should have told Cammaratta that he disagreed with my evaluation at that time, but then accepted it with the others and then gone on to concentrate on the evaluation of Cammaratta's performance as he said it was his responsibility. Why was I, and my evaluation, held hostage for three weeks longer than the others? It seems to me that they were putting the pressure on Cammaratta and hoped that he would change my evaluation during the delayed time that they met with Smouse and Shelton. The purpose of going to see the superintendent should have been to discuss Cammaratta's evaluation, not mine. Could the meeting alone be considered an act of collusion or intimidation?

Don't forget that in Chapter 13—"Power Hour," in my evaluation process by Cammaratta, Cammaratta included documented input from my supervisor colleagues, principals, teachers and others that I work with on a weekly basis to support his evaluation. However, the *only* documentation of a negative nature was solely from one individual...Smouse. Remember to look at the total picture and see who was doing what and why.

To continue the review of the case, I want to quote Raymond Shelton who was quoted in the Witness Testimony section of the Investigative Report. His quote in the Report was short, and it is included below in its entirety. The letter, on School Board stationary, was dated February 5, 1988, and addressed to Kathleen Richards, and was from Raymond O. Shelton, Superintendent of Schools.

> This is to confirm in writing our conversation of last week relative to a suggested intimidation of Dr. Domenic Cammaratta relative to an evaluation he made of Mr. William Wieser. I was involved in the selection of Mr. Wieser, along with Dr. Cammaratta and Mr. Smouse, and was well informed of everything that developed relative to the evaluation of this individual and the attempts to insure that he was doing his duties properly as a supervisor in Hillsborough County. It was our collective judgement at the time of employment that Mr. Wieser was weak, but was the only candidate available at that time, and that he would need very close supervision in the performance of his work in Hillsborough County. Mr. Ralph Smouse provided such supervision and Dr. Cammaratta was supposed to be doing the same. It appears, however, that Dr. Cammaratta and Mr. Wieser became friends; Dr. Cammaratta

changed his opinion relative to his abilities and assessed him much higher than would have either Mr. Smouse or myself. This led to Mr. Smouse's discussion with Dr. Cammaratta that he would be evaluated according to the manner in which he discharged his duties in evaluating his subordinates.

I talked with both individually after the situation involving the evaluation and also with them together. It is my opinion that Mr. Smouse at this point is the better judge of the capabilities of Mr. Wieser than is Dr. Cammaratta.

I support Mr. Smouse completely in his efforts to see that both Dr. Cammaratta and Mr. Wieser discharge their duties in accordance with their job descriptions and in a satisfactory manner.

I wouldn't want to call the Superintendent a liar, but he should know that I was not the only candidate available at the time. Four applications were accepted for the position of Supervisor. These four people went through the screening process (interview) before a screening committee of seven people consisting of administrators and teachers. Smouse was one of the interviewers and chaired the meetings. Three of the four people passed the screening by exceeding the minimum score of thirty points out of a perfect forty. There were three candidates, certified and qualified, and available for the job of supervisor at that time. School Board policies B-4.1.1 and B-4.1.2 state, in reference to the screening and selection process of supervisors, that the objective of the screening committee shall be to ensure that only the "best" and "qualified" candidates are considered for vacancies. These facts appear to challenge the statement by the superintendent that I was the only able candidate available.

Furthermore, the superintendent said that it was "our collective judgement...that Mr. Wieser was weak...and that he would need very close supervision...." First of all I wasn't weak; I was strong. I had previously worked in Hillsborough County in the office of the supervisor, as the coordinator, for five years, and all my evaluations were satisfactory or above. I interviewed before the screening committee of seven people including Smouse. This committee questioned me for one half hour as they did the other candidates. Most of the committee members were familiar with my work from before as they were with the credentials of the other candidates. If I were weak, why did I receive a passing score from the committee, including Smouse's score, and why did they score me the *highest*? Because I was the best one for the job.

Let me play the devil's advocate for a moment. Lets assume, by some form of judgement, that I *was* "weak" and the only candidate available for the job. If you were the twelfth largest school system in the nation, would you hire me knowing that I was weak? Or would you re-advertise the position based upon insufficient applications and re-interview for a quality candidate for the position? Or even easier and quicker, why not do an internal lateral transfer from another department to this position of supervisor? School Board policy B-4.2.9 states that personnel presently serving in an administrative or supervisory level shall be eligible for transfer without appearing before the screening committee. These options, which are normal personnel operating procedures, give questionable status to the claim of "weak" and "only one available" status of my candidacy. I was strong and the Board hired me. You don't hire weak people.

One further point, where was the documentation that I was weak? Why wasn't I told that I was weak at the time of my employment and that I would need close supervision? Why does this information only come out in the open after I file a complaint with the Commissioner against Smouse. And one final item. When I was identified as being selected as the choice for the job as supervisor, Smouse sent me a letter to me at my home before I started work. The October 2, 1985 letter, started by saying the following:

> I want to take this opportunity to welcome you back into the vocational family of Hillsborough County Schools. *I feel sure you will do an excellent job in the position of Supervisor of Industrial Arts and Industrial Education.*

Please allow that I took the liberty in the above quote to italicize the second sentence for emphasis in reference to the remarks earlier by Shelton that I was weak. Here, at the beginning of my job, Smouse told me that he was sure that I would do an excellent job. That is far from being "weak." If anyone thought that I would need close supervision, then that was sure kept a secret from me.

Another point, the superintendent said that I needed close supervision and that Smouse provided such supervision. I would expect that close supervision would include all aspects of my job. Furthermore, the superintendent said that in his opinion Smouse was a "better judge" of my capabilities than Cammaratta. Smouse *never* visited me while I worked in my office; he *never* accompanied me when I visited schools and worked with principals or teachers; he *never* attended any of my monthly department head meetings; he *never* attended and observed any of my teacher inservice meetings at the beginning and middle of the school year. I personally conducted these day-long inservice meetings for 150 teachers twice a year. Where was Smouse? How can Smouse adequately provide "very close supervision" of me from his distant office? From Smouse's own letters and memorandums, he has shown that he *did not* know the general or specific details or limits of my job responsibilities. How could the superintendent say that Smouse *did* provide very close supervision? How could the superintendent say that Smouse was the better judge of the capabilities of me than was Cammaratta? Hooey! Hogwash! Rubbish! Bunk!

Shelton also mentioned that it appears that Cammaratta and I became friends and therefore Cammaratta assessed me higher than he would have. This is difficult to understand because I don't know what Shelton's meaning of "friends" is. There are professional friends, personal friends, neighborhood friends and others. I disagree with Shelton that the professional association between Cammaratta and myself caused an improper evaluation. To justify his evaluation, you may remember in Chapter 13—"Power Hour," Cammaratta included many others in the evaluation process to draw the accurate conclusion of my evaluation rating.

I wonder if the School Security Investigation Report that was supposed to investigate the development of a grievance document had anything to do with the superintendent stating that Cammaratta and I became "friends." In Chapter 24—"Okay—Don't Anybody Move," you saw that the investigator asking the questions, Detective Dasinger, asked a leading question, in my opinion, to Hair and Ms. Dunn if Cammaratta and I were "friends." Why did the Detective initiate this type of question? What did it have to do with the investigation of the development of a grievance document? The School Security report was filed on February 3, 1988 and the Superintendent wrote his letter on February 5, 1988. Was there any coincidence in this timing?

When the detectives interviewed Cammaratta, he asked who sent them. They replied Shelton. However, when they were asked by my attorney (Jack Craparo), they said it was Binnie. When asked "who triggered Dr. Binnie," they said that they could not tell us. Did Shelton indeed initiate the investigation or approve it *five months* after I had already presented the grievance document (The Big Black Book) to him? I emphasize again, what was the purpose of the investigation, the *real* purpose of the investigation?

The part of Shelton's letter about Cammaratta and I becoming "friends" did make it into the summary of the Investigative Report by Kathleen Richards. The part about them judging me as being "weak" was quoted. Of course, I was never made aware of these comments and I did not have the chance to respond.

To continue about the Investigative Report by Kathleen Richards, I'll quote the last witness who was summarized in the summary report. Dr. Walter L. Sickles, Assistant Superintendent for Instruction, submitted a one-page sworn statement on January 28, 1988. Rather than use the summary quote, I'll quote the entire letter so that I can make comments on specific parts.

The statement was on allegations by me against Smouse. The letter read as follows:

During a portion of the time when Mr. Smouse was attempting to modify the behavior of Mr. Wieser, one of his supervisors, he consulted with me in my role as Assistant Superintendent for Personnel. I urged Mr. Smouse to document the process according to district policy and procedure. In my judgement, he followed district procedures. During the process, Mr. Wieser filed a grievance against Mr. Smouse. I moved from the personnel position to my present position in instruction in January, 1987.

It is very important in Hillsborough County to make sure that an annual contract administrator or supervisor perform in an acceptable manner since individuals up through the supervisory level achieve tenure under a local Tenure Act. In my judgement, Mr. Smouse attempted to modify a supervisor's behavior and perform in an appropriate manner with a person who was performing in a less than satisfactory manner.

Because of my involvement in conducting hearings in the Personnel Division over a number of years, Mr. Smouse requested that I be his advocate at the Level II hearing. In that hearing, each party in a dispute may select an advocate. Mr. Wieser selected an attorney as his representative. Normally, in these very informal hearings, individuals select from three to five witnesses to support their case. Mr. Wieser had thirty-five witnesses including teachers, principals, supervisors, and directors. I do not know of any person who was discouraged from testifying at the hearing. Though I did not count to see if all were there, there was a large group of people milling about in the hall outside the hearing room.

I have known Mr. Smouse for almost twenty years. During that period, I have never heard of a single incident where he was either rude or abusive in dealing with employees in his division. He is a strong advocate for vocational education and is aggressive in defending his programs. I perceive that as appropriate and necessary in this time where all of us must compete for scarce resources.

I can understand Sickles standing up for another Assistant Superintendent, Smouse, but I think that it should be remembered that Sickles was Smouse's counsel during the Level II grievance. In other words, wasn't Sickles defending the actions of Smouse in his role of counsel? After all, the School Board's term for having a hearing representative is "counsel," much different from Sickles' self-declared "advocacy."

Sickles said that he was requested to be Smouse's "advocate" at the Level II hearing. And then he stated that I "selected an attorney" as my representative. Why did he say this? What was the meaning of his statement? Was he trying to make it look like I was resorting to excessive means? I did file a grievance; I knew the severity of my filing and, because I'm no dummy, I did hire an attorney as my "counsel." I knew that Smouse and Sickles had access to the "in house" School Board attorney, Crosby W. Few, and I was certain that they would avail themselves to this proximate legal source. I just wanted to be sure to keep the odds even.

Then Sickles said "in these very informal hearings, individuals select from three to five witnesses to support their case. Mr. Wieser had selected thirty-five witnesses...." What was he trying to say with this statement? Was he implying that I went overboard? I filed my grievance because I saw my career in jeopardy. Smouse had accumulated a lot of documentation and I had the appropriate number of witnesses to speak specifically to the documented statements that he had already placed in my file. This was a big case. I have never heard of a supervisor ever filing a grievance against an Assistant Superintendent; it was something new to Hillsborough County Schools. Why was Sickles making such a big issue about the number of my witnesses?

It may be true that, typically, individuals select from "three to five witnesses" to support their case; however, this was by no means a typical case. I tried numerous ways to resolve this conflict with Smouse before I reached the point of filing a grievance. Hence, at that time, and because of Smouse's extensive documentation, my case was larger and at a higher level than what Hillsborough County had typically seen in the past. My number of witnesses accurately reflected the size of my case and the specific documentation generated by Smouse.

Let me go back and comment on his statement about a "very informal hearing." A handout given to me by Kenny Allen, Supervisor of Affirmative Action, states that grievances can be formal or informal. An informal grievance does not have disputed issues; therefore, documentation and witnesses are not required. A formal grievance exists when there are disputed issues of material fact. At the Level II hearing of a formal grievance, both parties may submit documentation, call and cross-examine witnesses, and be represented by counsel. I must say to Sickles, that to the contrary, my grievance was not "very informal," but was *formal* (School Board policy I-3.7.4). I ask again why was he emphasizing very informal rather than formal? What was the point? Whatever it was, it was an *inaccurate* statement by Sickles. A Level II grievance against an assistant superintendent is a very serious matter.

One final point on Sickles' statements. A substantial part of his letter was about the grievance I filed against Smouse concerning the alleged coercion of my immediate supervisor in May of 1987. The grievance was filed in October of 1987. Why did Sickles keep referring to the grievance issue when it had nothing to do with the issue of whether or not Smouse attempted to coerce my immediate supervisor five months before I filed the grievance? According to the "Legal Sufficiency" memo, it was recommended that the investigation be limited to the issue of whether Smouse attempted to coerce Cammaratta.

I just recalled a comment that Cammaratta made to me. He had talked to Sickles about Smouse and his documentation of my performance. Cammaratta told me that Sickles told him, that in Sickles' opinion, Smouse "may have gone too far" in reference to me. Cammaratta said that Sickles repeated this same statement again during a formal interview session. If Sickles felt that Smouse "may have gone too far" concerning me, then why did he act as counsel for Smouse during the grievance? Why didn't Sickles ethically or morally react to Smouse going too far and put a stop to his actions?

I think I can explain why the grievance issue was brought up in Sickles' statement. When Kathleen Richards interviewed me about the coercion issue, she also asked how was I being treated by other administrators in the school system. I immediately recalled the happenings earlier that month of January, 1988, about my grievance. I told her that I felt that the grievance process was not fair and pointed out the fact that my request for release time of my witnesses to testify was denied by the Superintendent. How could I have a fair hearing if my witnesses did not have access to the hearing?

I told her that I could go to my office, down the hall, and get some documentation on that from the Superintendent and others. She said that wasn't necessary. It makes me wonder if she followed up with questions about the grievance procedures to the others that she interviewed later. If she did, I never heard anything about it again. I didn't have a chance to respond to the others she interviewed about the grievance. Why didn't she want to see my documentation?

At the end of the interview with her, she told me to write a statement detailing my knowledge about the alleged coercion issue. I did that and restricted it to only the coercion issue. If I had known that others would write about the grievance issue and have it appear in the Investigative Report, then I too would have made statements and provided documentation such as the one letter where my witnesses were denied access to the grievance hearing. I wish I knew this was all happening at the time.

The Investigative Report contained two items of physical evidence, a notebook from me and one from Smouse. Smouse's notebook contained twelve sections and had eighty-seven pages. There were thirty pages of documentation related to my grievance filed in Hillsborough County Schools against Smouse. All this paperwork begs the question: why was there so much documentation presented about the grievance issue, an issue which happened five months after the alleged coercion issue? Remember, I had submitted no documentation on the Hillsborough grievance issue. Why wasn't the state investigation restricted to only the issue of alleged coercion? Did Smouse attempt to coerce my immediate supervisor or not? That was the only issue that should have been investigated according to the Commissioner's attorney.

Most of the other documentation in Smouse's notebook had already been submitted in my notebook or it was talked about earlier in this book. However, there is one section, a synopsis, that I would like to spend some time on because it contains new conflicting information.

The title of the paper was "A SYNOPSIS OF EVENTS REGARDING THE PERFORMANCE OF WILLIAM F. WIESER, SUPERVISOR OF INDUSTRIAL ARTS AND INDUSTRIAL EDUCATION." The paper was not dated or signed. It does appear that it was written by Smouse.

For me to review this paper, I think it best to quote one paragraph at a time and then make comments. The "synopsis" paper began as follows:

William F. Wieser was employed as a Coordinator of Industrial Arts and Industrial Education from July 30, 1979 to February 3, 1984. During this period of time, Mr. Wieser performed his duties with some concern on my part for his lack of efficiency and effectiveness. Mr. Wieser resigned February 3, 1984 to accept a position in another county.

My Comment: Smouse made it appear that I couldn't perform my job as coordinator and therefore, resigned and left the county. Smouse may have had "some concern" but he didn't produce any documentation with the synopsis to back it up. However, I can say that during my tenure as coordinator I performed my job in a satisfactory manner according to my evaluations and according to Smouse, who sent me several letters of compliment on my performance as coordinator, which have since disappeared from my personnel file. There was *no* negative documentation. Besides, if his allegations were true, why would he allow me to return to Hillsborough County in a higher position than when I left?

Synopsis quote continued:

In July, 1985 the Supervisor of Industrial Arts and Industrial Education for Hillsborough County schools retired, creating a vacancy. The vacant supervisor position was advertised and screening of applicants was conducted. There were four applicants for the position, including William F. Wieser. One applicant did not obtain a sufficient screening score to be further considered; another applicant had a relatively low screening score; and William F. Wieser and Richard Hair (who was the Coordinator of Industrial Arts and Industrial Education at that time) had relatively high scores that were separated by only a fraction of a point.

My Comment: There seems to be a conflict of facts between Smouse and Shelton. Shelton said in his statement that I "was the only candidate available at that time." That information is in conflict with the information Smouse offered here, where he said that there were "four applicants" and only one didn't receive a high enough score to be considered. Therefore there were three qualified candidates at that time. Then Smouse states that Hair and my screening scores were separated "by only a fraction of a point." The information that I have is that Hair received a score of 33 and I received a score of 36 out of forty points. I did receive the highest score as evaluated by the committee. The calculation is made by eliminating the highest and lowest scores and then averaging the five remaining scores.

Smouse's statement of available applicants contradicts Shelton's. This generates suspicion as to the veracity of their other statements. Couldn't the Commissioner notice this?

Synopsis quote continued:

Dr. Don P. Cammaratta, General Director of the Department of Vocational-Technical Education, and I discussed the qualifications of the applicants and agreed that either Richard Hair or William F. Wieser should be given serious consideration for appointment to the position of Supervisor of Industrial Arts and Industrial Education. I expressed to Dr. Cammaratta my reservations about Mr. Wieser's ability to satisfactorily perform the responsibilities of the position and indicated that my feeling would be to select Mr. Hair. At this point, Dr. Cammaratta stated to me that Mr. Hair had been involved in some improprieties with regard to Mr. Hair placing his arm around the shoulder of some of the female employees in the office when he was talking to them and Mr. Hair having invited one or more of the female employees to join him for a drink after work. Dr. Cammaratta further stated that several of these female employees had indicated to him that it would seem that he was condoning this type of behavior if Mr. Hair was selected for the supervisor position. I asked Dr. Cammaratta if he had discussed this with Mr. Hair and he indicated that he had not but that if I felt it was appropriate, he would do so. I requested Dr. Cammaratta to meet with Mr. Hair and discuss this matter with him and impress upon Mr. Hair the seriousness of the situation and that this behavior should cease immediately.

My Comment: Smouse mentioned some "improprieties" of Hair. I'm not sure whether his details were as complete as they could have been. Plus, I was told by others that there were other "personal and professional" problems concerning Hair that Smouse didn't cite, including one that happened in the classroom while Hair was a teacher. If Smouse is going to point out the "improprieties" of Hair, then he should cite the complete story for all parties involved to see and judge.

According to Cammaratta, Smouse also forgot to mention another important item. Before Smouse had talked to Cammaratta about the selection, he (Smouse) placed the name of Richard Hair on the recommended approval list for the School Board meeting agenda for next week. In the middle of the meeting between Smouse and Cammaratta, Smouse had to call in his secretary to have her immediately take Hair's name off the Board agenda until he could check on Cammaratta's concerns about Hair. It appears that Smouse had already decided and took action on the selection of the new supervisor before Cammaratta had a chance to give input. Was Smouse trying to pull the wool over Cammaratta's eyes?

Synopsis quote continued:

A few days later, Dr. Cammaratta and I met with Dr. Raymond O. Shelton, Superintendent of Schools for Hillsborough County, and discussed with him the two applicants we were considering, Mr. Hair and Mr. Wieser. The three of us agreed that, considering the foregoing described situation, it would be inappropriate to place Mr. Hair in the supervisor position.

My Comment: For it to be inappropriate to consider Hair for the promotion, then he must have done some serious things. Would it have been appropriate for the superintendent to request a school security investigation into the activities of Hair in the office? The superintendent thought it was appropriate to do an investigation of me because of the development of a grievance document. Why wasn't some action taken against Hair when these "concerns" became known to Smouse and the superintendent?

Synopsis quote continued:

Dr. Shelton and I both had reservations with regard to appointing Mr. Wieser to the position, considering Mr. Wieser's previous experience. However, Dr. Cammaratta strongly supported the selection of Mr. Wieser, and Dr. Shelton and I agreed to the appointment with the understanding that Dr. Cammaratta and I would provide close supervision and assistance to assure that Mr. Wieser would have every opportunity to succeed. Mr. Wieser was appointed to the position of Supervisor of Industrial Arts and Industrial Education effective October 14, 1985.

My Comment: Smouse says that he agreed that he and Cammaratta would provide close supervision. I think that I have already shown that Smouse didn't provide *any* close supervision of me during the first eleven months of my employment nor did he indicate to me that he was going to do this. However, do you remember the school security report when the detective interviewed Hair, and Hair said that he had documented the activities of Cammaratta and me. He kept notes and gave them to the security detective. Smouse didn't keep close supervision, but Hair, who didn't get the job, did. Was the wrong person keeping close supervision? They, Shelton and Smouse, had reservations with regard to my previous experience. No documentation was presented about this previous experience deficiency. Present the fact and let me defend myself.

Synopsis quote continued:

On October 2, 1985, Mr. Wieser, Dr. Cammaratta, and I met in my office and discussed the responsibilities of the supervisor's position and I followed with a letter welcoming Mr. Wieser and outlining some of the things we had discussed (See Enclosure #1).

My Comment: Yes, Smouse did welcome me back in a letter, but he forgot to specify that in the exact same letter he also said "I feel sure you will do an excellent job in the position of Supervisor...."

In the next page of the paper, Smouse speaks about specific problems that he "documented" about my performance. (These problems were discussed in Chapters, 9 and 28.)

Smouse concluded his three-page paper with the last paragraph as follows:

Synopsis final quote:

In late September, 1987, Mr. Wieser and his attorney met with Dr. Raymond O. Shelton, Superintendent of Schools, and presented him with a document of some 400 pages addressing his complaints against me. The Superintendent reviewed the document and in a meeting a few days later, informed Mr. Wieser that he felt that I had been carrying out my responsibilities in an appropriate manner and that Mr. Wieser should try to improve and carry out his responsibilities effectively. During these two meetings, Dr. Shelton asked of Mr. Wieser if this over-400-page document was prepared on school system time utilizing school system personnel, equipment, and materials. Mr. Wieser indicated to Dr. Shelton that school system time, personnel, equipment, and materials were used in the preparation of the approximate 400-page complaint document. Dr. Shelton told Mr. Wieser that such utilization of school system resources was entirely inappropriate to his job responsibilities. Dr. Shelton discussed with me these foregoing conversations with Mr. Wieser in order that I, as Mr. Wieser's supervisor, would be fully aware of these circumstances. In late January, 1988, Dr. Shelton requested the school system's security department to conduct an investigation of Mr. Wieser"s use of school system resources in the preparation of his complaint (See Enclosure #12).

My Final Comment: In the first sentence, Smouse states that I met with the Superintendent and presented him with a document addressing my complaint against him (Smouse). Totally true. Smouse should have also said that I was told to meet with the Superintendent by a School Board member, Sam Rampello. Then Smouse says that the Superintendent told him that he told me that Smouse was carrying out his responsibilities in an appropriate manner and I should try to improve. According to my notes, I don't remember either of these comments being made about Smouse or my performance. The Superintendent seemed noncommittal on anyone's performance and therefore recommended that we go the route of the Grievance. You may remember in Chapter

18—"CEO and ME," I was so surprised that the Superintendent didn't talk at all about Smouse, but did comment about The Big Black Book. My attorney (and witness), Jack Craparo was at the first meeting when Shelton suggested I go the grievance route.

Also, I don't remember the Superintendent asking if I used school system personnel, equipment, and materials to prepare the book. I *do* remember the Superintendent specifically asking "how long did it take me to do this?" as he referred to the book. I told him that it took one year.

Finally, Smouse states that he (Shelton) requested the school system's security department to investigate my use of school system resources in the preparation of the book. (I told this story about the security investigation in Chapter 24—"Okay—Don't Anybody Move," and I have the same observations.) If the Superintendent was so concerned about my use of school system resources in the development of the book, then why did he wait five months after he received the book to request an investigation? Again, why did the Superintendent wait until after the results of my grievance, the end of January, 1988, to file the request for an investigation? How come only days after the security report was available, did Smouse obtain it, include it and submit it to Tallahassee as a part of his documentation in his defence against my complaint? Was this security report available as public information when it was sent to Tallahassee by Smouse? It was stamped "Confidential." One more time, what was the real purpose of the security investigation report?

Allow me to look at my filing of a complaint against Smouse in another manner. As a resident of the state of Florida, I filed a complaint against a private individual who possessed a Florida teaching certificate. He owned that teaching certificate, not the school system. In the defense of his personal teaching certificate was he authorized to use school system personnel, equipment and materials? Were his letters of communication to Tallahassee typed by School Board personnel, on School Board typewriters, with School Board materials? Would Shelton say that this "was entirely inappropriate to his job responsibilities?"

As an example, let's say that indeed it was judged appropriate for Smouse to do this. Then we would need to shift to the length of the response document of eighty-seven pages. A security investigation was done on me concerning the development and the size of a grievance document. The detectives said that Binnie indicated that fifteen to twenty pages was acceptable. Consider this, Smouse's response report to my complaint in Tallahassee was eighty-seven pages, well beyond the acceptable limits suggested by Binnie. The question arises, did Smouse use school system resources? If so, did anyone request that a security department investigation be done on him? I don't know, but it seems that there should have for the same reasons they investigated me.

During the ongoing investigation, I never saw a copy of this "synopsis," I never was asked to verify it nor did I know of its existence. If I had, I would have responded with like "comments" as stated above along with the appropriate documentation.

And so this chapter on filing a complaint against Ralph L. Smouse, Jr. with the Commissioner of Education concludes.

In summary of this chapter, the basic facts in this case included a signed affidavit by me stating the alleged attempt of coercion. You remember that I was the first person to talk to Cammaratta after his "coercion" meeting with Smouse. Included in my documentation is a statement by Cammaratta that was written a few days after the alleged coercion attempt occurred in May, 1987, which was also included in The Big Black Book in July of 1987. Also included in this case was a signed affidavit from Cammaratta stating the facts about the coercion meeting: that Smouse repeatedly tried to coerce him in lowering my evaluation. Then there is a signed "response" by Smouse, that was written about eight months after the coercion meeting, where he said he didn't threaten or coerce Cammaratta. This response is signed, but not dated. Also, it was not an affidavit. It was on plain letterhead.

Two additional items are of importance to Smouse's position, a letter from Shelton and a statement by Sickles. First, the signed letter from Shelton, on School Board letterhead, was not an affidavit and was not notarized. Nowhere in the letter did Shelton say that Smouse did not attempt to coerce Cammaratta nor did he say that in his opinion the coercion attempt did not happen. In Sickles statement, he didn't address the coercion issue either. He didn't say that Smouse did not attempt to coerce Cammaratta nor did he give any opinion about it. Sickles "statement" was on plain letterhead and notarized by a Notary Public on January 28, 1988.

(**A note of Interest:** The February, 1989, issue of the *Communicator*, a newsletter of the Florida Association of School Administrators, reports that Dr. Walter L. Sickles, deputy superintendent for instruction in Hillsborough County, has been elected the new chairman of the Education Practices Commission. He has been a member of the Commission since its inception.)

Therefore the main facts in the case were the affidavits from Cammaratta and me stating that the attempted coercion took place. In addition, there was a "response" by Smouse saying that he didn't try to coerce Cammaratta, plus the letter from Shelton and the "statement" from Sickles which do not even address the attempted coercion meeting. With these facts in the case, why wasn't a hearing held so that I could present my witnesses and documentation in reference to the other documentation submitted by Smouse?

I believe there was incomplete, conflicting and confusing information submitted in the investigation on Smouse's behalf. I have difficulty understanding how a decision, by state Commissioner Betty Castor, of "no probable cause," could have been made on the single issue of whether Ralph L. Smouse, Jr. did or did not attempt to coerce my immediate supervisor in lowering my yearly evaluation.

And what was the role of the Governor of Florida during this investigation by a member of his Cabinet? Well, I have no specific information as to what Gov. Bob Martinez's role was, but I do know the Governor serves as chairman of the state Board of Education. Bob Martinez was born in Tampa, graduated from Jefferson High School and the University of Tampa. He became a teacher in the Hillsborough County public school system before becoming executive director of the Hillsborough County Teachers Association and then Mayor of Tampa. He was a featured speaker at the 1984 Republican National Convention, having switched party affiliation in 1983. After being defeated in his gubernatorial reelection bid in 1991, he was appointed as the nation's drug czar by George Bush, the "education" President.

I share a quote from the Code of Ethics of the Education Profession in Florida, part (3) with *all* persons connected with this investigation including the Governor, Commissioner, Superintendent, administrators and myself.

> Aware of the importance of maintaining the respect and confidence of one's colleagues, of students, of parents, and of other members of the community, the educator strives to achieve and sustain the highest degree of ethical conduct.

32

POWER PLAY

I received a call from Dr. Walt Sickles' office and I was told that Dr. Sickles, Deputy Superintendent for Instruction, wanted to see me. The appointment was set for Monday, April 11, 1988, at Sickles' office downtown.

I was not told what the meeting was about and I didn't know who would be there. It didn't matter; I'll talk to my superiors whenever they ask. I didn't know what to prepare to take to the meeting, so I just took a yellow note pad in case I needed to write down some information.

As you may remember, Sickles' position title was Assistant Superintendent, but he was promoted up to Deputy Superintendent, along with James Randall, because of additional responsibilities that were given to them when Shelton was going to be gone about 50% of the time. Superintendent Shelton was elected as President of the American Association of School Administrators and this association paid the School Board half of Shelton's approximate $108,000 annual salary because he had speaking and association duties to fulfill during his tenure as President of the national association.

The organizational chart for the administrators would now show the Superintendent at the top, next the two new Deputy Superintendents (Sickles—Instruction and Randall—Administration), and then the other four Assistant Superintendents (Beth Shields—Personnel, Ralph Smouse—Vocational, Harold Clark—Support Services, and Michael Bookman—Business). The other administrators that followed on the chart remained the same.

(Before I get to the meeting, I need to recap on Sickles' role in my case thus far. Remember in Chapter 8—"Equal Pay Please," that it was Sickles who said no to salary credit for my previous years of experience as an administrator. Plus, in my grievance Level II hearing, Sickles was Smouse's consultant. And he wrote a letter, in support of Smouse, that was part of Smouse's defense in reference to my ethics complaint with the Commissioner and the Code of Ethics.)

Now back to the meeting. I went to meet with Sickles. The meeting was just between him and me. Board policy B-49.3 states that "The employee shall have the right to have a representative present at a conference related to employee dismissal." I had no idea of what this meeting was going to be about. To begin the meeting, he urged me to accept a fourth year probation. He said that he felt this was the best thing to do. He told me that in the past, that if someone did not take probation, then the Superintendent *did not* renominate that person. I considered that to be a threat! What he was saying was take probation or you're out on the street. And then he indicated that non-renomination is not a termination. I wasn't sure that I agreed with that terminology. I can remember when my Dad talked to me about the concept of being fired. He said when a company tells you not to return to work, then you are fired no matter what word they use to identify it. There was no reason to get into a debate over termination language.

Then, Sickles said that maybe he and I should "sit and talk" with Cammaratta. I didn't know why and he didn't say why, but being defensive now, I thought to myself that Dr. Shelton should "sit and talk" with Smouse. It sounded to me as though they were trying to throw water on the wrong fire.

Sickles appeared humble, but repeated himself again and said that he urged me to accept probation. The threat was emphasized. I told him that question had already been addressed; a decision was made and I was taking the advice of my attorney, Robert McKee.

He then asked about McKee's background. He bluntly asked if I knew whether or not McKee was experienced in this kind of matter. I told him that I didn't know. I was impressed with what McKee had done thus far. Also, I wasn't going to tell the administration that I had the greatest attorney in the world, because of the way they were treating me; I didn't owe them any favors. He who has the best attorney wins; haven't you seen that bumper sticker? This question now gave me better insight into the reaction that Smouse had when I took him the letter from McKee about picking up Smouse's decision about my job status when I was out of town, and he said "this is a different attorney?" Why was Deputy Superintendent Sickles so concerned about my new attorney? I was forced to play their game in educational politics; but now I changed the rules; I got a new attorney. They never asked me any questions about attorney Craparo. Several weeks after Smouse reacted to my new attorney, Sickles reacted and gave me the third-degree about McKee. I can understand Sickles' curiosity about McKee, but why did he go to the extreme to call me into his office—one-on-one? There is something to this; I can't figure it out yet.

Sickles then asked me why I thought all this happened. I answered by saying that I didn't know; it would be better to ask Smouse. But if he was looking for speculation, I told him I thought that it was because Smouse didn't get his way in the selection of the supervisor which was the job I got. Sickles didn't make any comment. His conversation seemed one-sided. Was that why this all happened or was there another reason, a reason bigger than the both of us. It made me theorize if his inquisitive approach had anything to do with the Textbook Scam and the unrecovered $700,000.00. Was he probing to see what I discovered since phony industrial book orders allegedly came from my industrial office and because I testified in the investigation?

He then asked me what I wanted to come out of all this. I wasn't sure exactly what he was looking for, so I responded with saying that I didn't want another year like the last two years. In reference to specific remedies to this overall problem, I had already listed suggested remedies in my filing of the grievance Level II. I'm sure that he saw them. What was he searching for? Did he have a hidden agenda?

And then he asked me if I "had been looking for jobs." I indubitably said "no!" I'm sure that told him I was ready to make a stand. Besides, any job search by me wasn't any of his business. He wished me the best of luck. I thanked him and the meeting was over. It had lasted about fifteen minutes.

The best that I can surmise is that the purpose of this meeting was to try to get me to change my mind, by the use of a threat, and accept probation. A power play from the top. It would have been the easy way out for them. I saw that my refusal to accept probation could now put them into a bind. Now, Smouse had to recommend either tenure or non-renomination. If non-renomination was recommended and the superintendent agreed, then I would be given the opportunity to appeal to the School Board and have a public hearing within fifteen days from the date that I received notice. I don't think they wanted this case to reach the public. Did that mean they had to recommend tenure?

The ball was in their court. Another power play?

33

UMBILICAL DISCORD

Ralph Smouse asked me to attend the School Board meeting on Tuesday, April 12, because my arrangement for a used car from an auto shop to be given to the Hillsborough Halfway House for training purposes was up for approval by the Board. I was there in case there were any questions from the Board. As I sat in the School Board meeting that night, I noticed that the approval of the reappointment of administrators and supervisors for next year was also on the agenda. As this agenda item came up, I listened very carefully. I kept seeing Smouse looking around in the audience; I wasn't sure what he was looking for. I think he was looking to see whether I was there.

The Board discussion on the reappointments was relatively short; they approved the list of administrators and supervisors that was given to them. The question that I had was how do I find out if my name was on the list or not? The list was not passed out to the audience and I had received no official notice as to my reappointment status from the Superintendent. It made me wonder if my efforts in speaking to numerous Board members (Chapter 30—A Rare Happening) did any good. I never did receive any feedback from any of them.

The next day I met with Cammaratta and told him about the Board meeting. I told him that, since no names were mentioned concerning the reappointments for the next year, I was apprehensive about my name being on the list or not. I asked him if he could find out. He made a few phone calls and found out that my name was not on the list to be reappointed. He also asked whether there was another list of those *not* reappointed. His contact in Personnel said no. He double checked at the same time to see if his name was on the list to be reappointed and it was. This was all still unofficial information that we were getting. Could my appointment be on hold until the Superintendent made a decision and notified me?

I presented an update of this information to my attorney Bob McKee. He had completed some research on Florida law in reference to reappointments of supervisors. Basically, he found in Section 230.33(7) (a), of the Florida Statutes, that the Superintendent is responsible for recommending to the School Board the names of persons to fill positions necessary to make possible the development of an adequate school program in the district. Such recommendations regarding principles and supervisors must be made no later than 8 weeks before the close of the post-school conference period. The post-school period in Hillsborough County ends on June 14, 1988. That would place the recommendation to the Board and me at approximately the middle of April. I had not been notified yet. Could I have caught the Superintendent on a "technicality" if he didn't notify me according to Florida Statutes?

As I stated in Chapter 28—"Who's the Boss," it is School Board policy (A-31.1 and B-46.1) that the General Director evaluates the vocational supervisors. Dr. Cammaratta had been the General Director for the last ten years and had done the yearly evaluations and recommendations for reappointment for the upcoming year for the vocational supervisors. For some strange reason, the responsibility of reappointment recommendations was taken away from him in 1988 without any notice. However, he did all the usual yearly evaluations. The recommendations for reappointment were done by someone else. Why was there a change in procedure? Did it break any Board policies?

On Thursday April 14, 1988, I received, via school mail, a piece of mail marked "Confidential." In it were two letters, one addressed to me from Smouse and a copy of one to Superintendent Shelton from Smouse.

The first letter, to me from Smouse, was dated April 12, 1988, which was a Tuesday. His letter started off by stating "Please be advised that I am not recommending you for reappointment for the 1988-89 school year. The reasons that you are not being renominated are as follows: inability to follow policies and procedures, poor organizational skills, failure to follow directives, lack of attention to details, and poor judgement" (the same ones listed for his probation recommendation in Chapter 29—"Probation Equation"). In the second and last paragraph, he goes on to say ". . . Your performance, in my judgement, is too deficient to warrant my recommending that you receive tenure so I have no alternative other than to recommend to the Superintendent that you not be renominated for the 1988-89 school year." Copies of the letter were sent to Shelton, Sickles, Shields, Binnie and Cammaratta.

The second letter was really a memo to Shelton from Smouse. It too was dated April 12, 1988. The subject was "NON-RENOMINATION - William F. Wieser." The memo started with the sentence: "Please be advised that I am not recommending William F. Wieser, Supervisor of Industrial Arts and Industrial

Education, for reappointment for the 1988-89 school year." The rest of the memo is essentially the same as the letter to me. Copies went to the same people plus me. Again these were sent "Confidential." Confidential was highlighted with a red marker on the envelope.

So there I was on Thursday with a letter from Smouse and a copy of a memo to Shelton not recommending me for reappointment. Let's see now, Smouse's letter was dated Tuesday, April 12, the same day as the School Board meeting. I didn't receive the letter until two days later, two days after the Board meeting where reappointments were made for the next year. The common procedure deadline for submitting information for the School Board agenda had traditionally/always been the Thursday before the next Tuesday's meeting. This gives time for Board members to go over the agenda before the next meeting on the following Tuesday. Did Smouse's letter, dated April 12, have any significance or timing in the reappointment list submitted to the School Board for approval? If so, then it sure was a last-minute action. Was this all a "set up" to recommend and receive Board approval before I had even received a communication of a "recommendation of non-renomination?" These are questions that I can't answer. But these are real questions.

Then on Friday, April 15, I received a memo from Smouse that was dated April 14: "Verification of Correspondence." He wanted me to sign the letters of April 12 so that he could place them in my personnel file. This memo, with copies of his recommendation for non-renomination letter to me and the Superintendent's memo attached, was *not* sent "Confidential." It was naturally opened by my secretary and date stamped. I don't know if she read it or made a copy of it, but the point was that she had the opportunity. Why would Smouse send this letter confidential on Tuesday and then on Thursday send copies of it without confidential status? Again I ask the question: was this a way to get the information across to others about what he was doing to me, especially those subordinates in my office? I considered this letter of non-renomination most private and sensitive to me and to the effective operation of my office to which I had the responsibility!

The only thing I had in writing was the letter of recommendation from Smouse to Shelton. McKee and I knew that it was Cammaratta's responsibility to do that according to Board policy, but that didn't matter as much as what the Superintendent would do with that information. The ball was in Shelton's court. We would wait for him to take the next step.

According to School Board policy B - 50.1, employees who are not renominated shall be entitled to an administrative hearing before a committee. Upon receiving the non-renomination notice, the employee shall have fifteen days to file an appeal on the action. Parties to the appeal shall have the right to be represented by an attorney.

My lawyer and I considered that the "letter of recommendation" for non-renomination from Smouse was clearly not a "letter of notice" of non-renomination. According to state statute, the Superintendent, not Smouse, was to "notify" me.

I looked back at what had happened over the last year. I went to Board member Rampello for direction last summer. He recommended that I see the Superintendent. The Superintendent recommended the Grievance process. That process failed. My attorney (Craparo) recommended the Code of Ethics and the State Commissioner. There was no success in resolving my problems there either. I took my problem to six of the seven School Board members; it fell on deaf ears. Now I would wait for the decision of the Superintendent. It was already decided that, if Shelton recommended non-renomination, I would file for an appeal and the whole story would then be told in public before the Board. I kept wondering if Dr. Sickles threat was right (Chapter 32—"Power Play"): that the Superintendent usually did not reappoint someone if that person did not accept the offer of probation. We were waiting for the Superintendent to do something.

Here I was just waiting for the next move that may affect my career and future in the field of Education. Each day I was sitting on the edge of my chair; I felt like I was on the razor's edge waiting for my lifeline to be cut. It didn't make it easy on my mental workload or my job workload either. My stomach hurt.

34

READ MY LIPS...NOT MY MEMOS

One month after I received a copy of Smouse's letter of recommendation concerning my non-renomination, I received notice to attend a meeting for the dissemination of information with regard to implementing a pilot project for vocational students. The meeting was planned for May 16, 1988, at Leto Comprehensive High School in the Media Center.

Many of the top administrators were there including Smouse. We were outside of our meeting area a few minutes before the meeting began and I went over to ask Smouse a question. I asked him about my VICA advisor recommendation for next year and he responded with "It doesn't really matter, since you will not be here next year." I asked him "Why do you say that?" He said "Because I wrote you that letter that you signed and returned to me." My response was "So you are saying, based upon that letter from you, I will not be back next year?" He said "Yes." Then I stated "I thought the Superintendent would notify me." He said "No."

The meeting lasted all day. My mind kept returning to the statements by Smouse. I couldn't wait to get to my car phone and make a private call to my attorney Bob McKee and give him this critical news.

When I contacted him, he said that we need to confirm what Smouse said. Essentially, Smouse was saying, read my lips . . . not my memos. His memo of April 12 was clearly a letter of recommendation, not a notification. McKee said usually a termination letter clearly spells out the employee's right to an appeal and specifically states the time limit and procedures in an appeal. Smouse's letter said nothing of this. McKee then suggested that I meet with the Assistant Superintendent for Personnel, Beth Shields, to confirm Smouse's verbal information.

I set up an appointment with Shields for May 17, 1988. I walked into her office, sat down and told her what had happened the day before. I told her about what Smouse said about me not returning next year. The purpose of me coming to her was to see whether it was true or not. She indicated that I was on an annual contract, and when Smouse didn't renominate me, I wasn't renominated. She asked if I understood it that way. I told her that I did not, because I viewed Smouse's letter as a "recommendation" not to reappoint, *not* as a "notice" of non-renomination. My understanding was that Superintendent Shelton was going to notify me. Then she asked whether Sickles told me that I was not renominated during our meeting (Chapter 32—"Power Play"). I said "No;" that's why I was waiting to hear from the Superintendent.

She then pulled out a red policy book. She indicated that supervisors are given a letter that indicates non-renomination. I told her that the letter Smouse sent me said he was recommending that I not be reappointed. She said that she couldn't believe I would understand it that way; she felt that my thinking was so wrong. She couldn't believe that I didn't know that letter from Smouse was the notice of non-renomination. She then went to get my file.

When she returned, I asked if I was going to be getting a letter from the Superintendent or not. Her response was that since no action was necessary not to renominate me, it didn't take any action on the part of the Superintendent. It was Smouse's obligation to tell me I was not renominated, she stated.

The little light went on in my head and said I would not be getting a letter from the Superintendent. Well deja vu, I saw one more time someone saying read my lips. . . not my memos. Rather, read my interpretation of Smouse's memo.

The next phase in the process was to file for an appeal to Smouse's decision. Therefore, I asked if I still had the right to an appeal hearing. She said, "not according to policy." The letter from Smouse was dated on April 12, and therefore the fifteen days to file an appeal were gone.

I sure felt that I was losing ground in this meeting. It was now apparent that I wasn't going to get a letter of notification from the Superintendent and it was too late to file an appeal with the School Board on Smouse's letter of "notification."

I decided to try to salvage some type of progress from this meeting. I asked Shields if she felt Smouse was non-biased in making the decision not to renominate me. She said, "Well, he was the one to make that decision." That answer didn't really tell me anything.

I had the feeling that my attorney and I were playing by the rules of the game and that the school system administration was not. The playing field wasn't level. So who said it was going to be fair. Boy oh boy, am I getting an education? They didn't teach me about this in graduate school. You learn all that book stuff, but nothing about on-the-job politics in education and the "power and turf" issue.

I reported this information about the Shields meeting to attorney McKee. We concluded that I would not receive the expected letter from Shelton as required by state statute. All the information available told us that there was only one way left to get the attention of the School Board and the Superintendent: legal action must be taken.

Subsequently, two days later on May 19, 1988, Smouse wrote a memo to Cammaratta with the subject of "Vacancy for Supervisor of Industrial Arts and Industrial Education." The memo started with the sentence stating "As a result of Mr. William F. Wieser not being renominated as Supervisor...we will have a vacancy in that position effective July 1, 1988." Copies went to Shelton and Sickles.

It is interesting that Smouse wrote me his "recommendation for non-renomination" memo on April 12 and then remained silent, until after the fifteen day period had expired for me to file an appeal, when on May 19 he notified Cammaratta by memo that there was a vacancy for my supervisory position. Why didn't Smouse notify Cammaratta immediately after his April 12th decision? Why did he wait over a month?

This was the first time that I saw anything in writing indicating that I was to be terminated. Where was the notification from the Superintendent? McKee commented to me that he never heard of any assistant superintendent in the state of Florida that had the authority to terminate personnel. I said if the superintendent recommended me to the Board to be hired, he should be the one to recommend me to be fired.

You can read *my* lips on this one: no new terminators.

35

SEE YOU IN COURT

My ship was sinking, I was going to the bottom quickly. I had to take some remedial measures now. It was apparent that no "pink slip" was coming from the Superintendent and it was too late to file an appeal against Smouse's "decision" to non-renominate me.

Attorney McKee and I were in concert. There was only one way to get the attention of the School System and that was to file suit in court. Then we would be operating under a new neutral set of rules.

I told McKee that I believed my professional integrity had been besmirched and directed him to present my case in a way that my colleagues would know the true facts of the matter. I wanted to be sure that my name and reputation were cleared.

The Florida court system consists of the Supreme Court at Tallahassee with five district courts of appeal which have appellate jurisdiction for most cases. They are located in Tallahassee, Daytona Beach, Miami, West Palm Beach and Lakeland (with a branch in Tampa). There are county courts in each of Florida's counties and 20 circuit courts have jurisdiction over one or more counties. All circuit and county court judges are chosen by the people in nonpartisan judicial elections. Justices of the Supreme Court and judges of the district courts of appeal are appointed by the Governor after their names have been submitted to him by a nominating commission.

The Circuit Court of the 13th Judicial District of Hillsborough County is the court of general jurisdiction. The Circuit Court has 28 judges in the county. The Circuit Court is comprised of six divisions: criminal, civil, probate, traffic, juvenile and family cases. The Civil Division handles matters of professional malpractice, product liability, auto negligence, eminent domain, contract, indebtedness and other civil matters.

During the third week of May, 1988, McKee filed a COMPLAINT FOR WRIT OF MANDAMUS in the Circuit Court of the Thirteenth Judicial Circuit in and for Hillsborough County, Florida. Civil Division. William F. Wieser, Plaintiff, vs. Raymond O. Shelton, as Superintendent of Schools and The School Board of Hillsborough County, Defendants. Case number 88-9921 was assigned to Judge Vernon W. Evans, Jr.

It is my understanding that basically a Writ of Mandamus is a request of the court to require an employer to enforce any rights or perform certain duties that accrue to an employee. Essentially, the Writ centered around the Hillsborough County Teacher Tenure Act, enacted by the Legislature of the State of Florida, 1975 Revision. Section 1(5) of the Tenure Act establishes the probationary period for teachers in Hillsborough County to be three consecutive years. However, if any teacher had previously held tenure in any county in Florida, that teacher—deemed to apply to teachers, principals, assistant principals, supervisors and other instructional personnel, according to Section 1(1)—shall only serve a two-year probationary period.

This Tenure Act fit me perfectly. I previously had tenure in a county in Florida. As a matter of fact, I had Tenure in Hillsborough County when I was a county-level Coordinator (1979–1984). I then left for two years and went to another county. I returned to Hillsborough County in the position of county-level Supervisor.

In the Writ of Mandamus, I asked that the court take jurisdiction over the actions taken by the school system and enter an Order directing the School Board to grant me, the Plaintiff, a continuing contract of employment.

The attorney representing the Superintendent and the School Board was Thomas M. Gonzalez, Esquire, of Thompson, Sizemore & Gonzalez in Tampa. I wondered why the School Board didn't use its regular attorney, W. Crosby Few, of Few and Ayala, who participates at all the School Board meetings.

On June 3, 1988, McKee wrote a letter to Thomas Gonzalez which, in part, stated:

> ...I shall appreciate your discussing with your client the possibility of keeping Mr. Wieser on the payroll pending the outcome of the litigation. By doing so, the School Board would avoid complicating this matter inasmuch as we would otherwise be required either to seek injunctive relief before June 30, or to amend the Complaint to seek an award of back pay and attorney's fees.

The request fell on deaf ears.

One June 7, 1988, R. L. Smouse, Jr. sent a memo to Raymond O. Shelton about Vacant Positions. He said that due to budget restraints in the past year, vacancies had occurred. He continued to say "it is imperative" that we consider filling the vacant positions. My position was listed in the memo, indicating the position would be vacant 6/30/88. He concluded his memo by stating that the vacancies need to be filled "as soon as possible" to assure continuance of programs. Copies went to Sickles, Cammaratta and others. Cammaratta showed me a copy of this memo and I, of course took it to McKee.

On June 9, 1988, W. Crosby Few and Thomas M. Gonzalez further responded on behalf of their client with a MOTION TO DISMISS ALTERNATIVE WRIT OF MANDAMUS. They claimed that I was not entitled to tenure as a matter of law arguing that I should have served a three-year probationary period since I was promoted to a higher position, and therefore I had no right to continued employment. Their Motion also included a NOTICE OF HEARING on July 18, to hear the Motion to Dismiss before Judge Evans.

My first impression when McKee gave me copies of these transactions was personal insult. When you put all of yourself into a job, especially teaching *people*, you normally react personally; it comes with the territory. I soon got over the fact that they wanted to throw my request out the window. I saw it as normal legal shuffling, but it still annoyed me. Why couldn't their attorneys read the law and see that I had the right to file?

On June 16, 1988, Cammaratta and I both signed Affidavits at the request of my attorney which attested that the facts stated in the Writ were true and correct. Cammaratta's was a bit more detailed. His affidavit stated that he had direct supervisory authority over my position of Supervisor. It also indicated he was never consulted about Smouse's decision not to renominate me; nor was he (Cammaratta) given an opportunity to perform an evaluation of me in context of my eligibility for tenure. Had he been, he stated that he would have given me a highly favorable evaluation and recommended me for tenure.

Because of the memo from Smouse on June 7 about vacancies, I told McKee that it looked like the school system was not going to back down and was going ahead with advertising and filling my position. A decision was made to enter a MOTION FOR TEMPORARY INJUNCTION. The Motion, filed on June 23, asked to restrain the Defendants from terminating me or taking final action on the appointment of a successor, pending the outcome of this case. The Motion went on to explain that my loss of a tenured position could not be remedied with money. Moreover, for the Court to order the Defendant to remove my successor, should I prevail, would be dubious. Plus, it would be contrary to public interest if I won my case and the school system had to pay two of us to do the same job. The Motion asked to restrain the School Board from issuing a contract to my successor. However, they could advertise, interview and evaluate potential candidates. Our prediction on the estimated length of my case was two or three months. We felt it would take this long to go through the advertising, interviewing and appointing of my successor. Past experience told us that much.

My first hearing was requested before Judge Evans to hear the Motion for Temporary Injunction. Coincidentally, it was granted for Friday, July 1, 1988, the day after I was "officially" to end my job.

Although I wasn't keen on the School Board and the Superintendent's response, filing of the law suit did get their attention. They did listen to me and they made their response. At last, I am on an even keel with them by appearing before a balanced authority. I trust the courts.

I finally will get my day in court. A long journey ends and a long one begins. Godspeed.

There was no news coverage, print or electronic, to inform the community that any of the legal actions (writ of mandamus, motion to dismiss or motion for temporary injunction) were filed in the circuit court.

36
A.C.L.U....HELP?

In May, 1988, during a conversation with a professor friend of mine from the University of South Florida, the topic of the American Civil Liberties Union (ACLU) came up. He asked me if I had seen a recently-published letter-to-the-editor about the ACLU; when I told him I had, he suggested that I contact them about my case. Since I knew this professor fairly well—I had worked with him for two years in the seventies and I knew that he had experience with the inside workings of the school system—I decided to take his advice to heart.

The Letter that he referred to was titled "ACLU Is Against Harassment." I did feel that I was being harassed on the job; therefore, I thought they might be a good source of information. The Letter explained the views of the ACLU on certain matters and was from the Tampa Chapter.

I didn't know that much about the ACLU but I thought it wouldn't hurt to ask for some assistance. I heard they didn't charge their clients for their services so I wondered if they would provide assistance in paying for my upcoming attorney's fees or give advice on a specific law that related to my particular situation in the area of due process rights.

I wasn't sure how to contact the ACLU, so I looked in the Tampa phone book. There were two listings for the ACLU, but they were both in Miami. I called the first one and the line had been disconnected. I called the second one and spoke to the receptionist. She explained that the Tampa Chapter was not active. I asked how things work when you request assistance. She explained that a group of local attorneys volunteer their time and meet once a month and review the cases that are submitted. I would have to write a letter and explain my case and submit some documentation along with it. They would review it and let me know of their decision.

I wanted to find out more about the ACLU. I asked them to send me some literature about their role and purpose while I prepared a summary letter of my case. Their brochure, Guardian of Freedom, states that the purpose for which the ACLU was founded in 1920 was to maintain the rights of free speech, free press, free assemblage and other civil rights. I felt that my due process rights were violated and, hence, my case generally fell within the ACLU's stated purpose for existing. However, it would be up to them to decide. Of course, I would appreciate any feedback or assistance they would give me about my situation.

The ACLU brochure included a list of paperback books for sale. One caught my eye titled *The Rights of Teachers*. I purchased it and read through it after I sent in my request for assistance in my employment situation. It contained seven chapters and one was about The Right to Due Process of Law. The 141 pages about this topic alone were quite informative. I learned a lot. I showed the book to my Tampa attorney and he was already familiar with it. He said it would be good for me to read it. I did: there were a lot of boring parts and some highly technical, but it was educational.

My request for assistance to the ACLU was written on May 23, 1988. It was sent to the Chapter in Miami with a copy and attachments to the National Office in New York. My cover letter opened with "As a citizen of the United States, I write to you for any assistance that you can provide to me in my current employment situation." I went on to say that I felt that my due process rights had been denied and that my employment was scheduled to be terminated at the end of the next month. I asked them to please review the enclosed material to see if they could provide any assistance.

My enclosed attachments included a two-page summary of events, four pages about the alleged coercion attempt of Cammaratta by Smouse, my request for assistance to the Superintendent of Schools (September 18, 1987), the Executive Summary and my recommendations for a solution from The Big Black Book, a copy of the Code of Ethics and Principles of Professional Conduct of the Education Profession in Florida, copy of the memo from the Superintendent denying release time for my grievance witnesses and a copy of the letter from Smouse recommending non-renomination.

The two-page summary highlighted the events in my three years as supervisor, and finally, the verbal notice that my job would end on June 30, 1988. A part of my summary letter is quoted to give you the disposition of my request for assistance:

> The Superintendent, when presented with all my documentation, did nothing except to suggest that I go through the grievance procedure. To this

date the Superintendent has still done nothing in reference to my original request of concern and action.

While going through the grievance process, I was denied substitute time for teachers to appear at my Level II hearing. Teachers had to claim sick time to show up to testify. I also paid for, out of my own pocket, substitutes for three teachers to come to my grievance hearing. I was told that several of my principals were called and encouraged not to show up at my hearing to testify in my behalf. One of several principals that did show up was called back to his school because of a drug bust. He was another who was not available to testify in my behalf as he said he would.

After a side meeting to try to settle this grievance, the Level II grievance hearing continued. This time I requested in writing to the Superintendent, for release time for fifty-one of my witnesses. The Superintendent responded and said "only a few" witnesses could appear. When I received his memo, I went outside of my school building, walked toward the road, stopped, turned around and looked atop of the flag pole. To my surprise, there *was* an American flag flying there. But, I felt that I was in Russia because I was not allowed to present my facts and witnesses to defend my rights.

I waited and waited for some answer from the monthly meeting of lawyers. I called the Miami office in June and the receptionist told me that I had just sent it in, please wait longer. Then on July 15, 1988, I received a large brown envelope from the ACLU in Miami. The postmark showed that it was mailed from Pompano Beach, Florida, on July 12, 1988.

Inside the envelope was my original cover letter and my attached documents. There was no letter, no note or any information that my request was reviewed or rejected. I received no other communication from the Miami or New York office.

I was disappointed and gave up any further contact with the ACLU. I put all my energy and time into my local attorney, McKee.

Later in August, 1988, I briefly met a person in Tampa who said he was associated with the ACLU. He confirmed that the Tampa Chapter was inactive. When I told him about my letter to the Miami office, he said that he was familiar with my request. Our brief meeting didn't allow me the chance to follow up. This generated more questions about the ACLU's silent response.

If you ask me about the ACLU, I'll say, *"No comment!"*

37

GOING PUBLIC

When you file a law suit in Circuit Court, the information becomes a matter of public record. Up to this point, I pride myself with the fact that I tried repeatedly to keep this situation inside the educational system and solve it from within. In spite of repeated correspondence to Smouse, an initial meeting with School Board member Sam Rampello, a meeting with the Superintendent, the filing of a grievance with the school system at Level I and then Level II, the filing of a complaint with the Commissioner of Education, consulting with several attorneys, personally contacting most of the School Board members, all this while doing a good job as Supervisor, the problem did not get solved. When I filed the law suit, it automatically put me in the visible public domain. If this was the way it was going to be, then I wanted to be sure that the public, who vote, have children in the schools and pay taxes would know my full story. I wanted to get this whole thing over with so that I could get back to doing the job I was hired to do.

I knew it would be better for me to go directly to the news media rather than having them calling me on the phone with different reporters just getting bits and pieces. To go one step further, I decided to go to one news source and give them a complete and exclusive story. I chose a television station, WFLA Channel 8, a local NBC affiliate.

WFLA happens to be located directly across the street from the downtown main school administration center. But that was not the main reason why I chose this station. Veda Martin, Executive Producer of Special Programs, was an employee of WFLA and had worked closely with the school system. I remember her winning an award at our yearly vocational awards banquet for her work with the vocational programs.

I told Cammaratta that I planned to contact Channel 8. He said that he had worked with Veda Martin on several committees. I asked him to please come with me to ensure some creditability to my story.

We met with her when I knew my suit was forthcoming and told her the significant details. To say the least, she appeared most concerned and interested. I told her that, when I was ready to break the story, I would come to her for an exclusive presentation. She said they would be ready when I was and she would have a reporter ready. At this first meeting, I gave no documents to her.

When I was ready to file suit, we met with her again to give her the exclusive story. We met in her office at Channel 8 and she brought in Ava Thompson, a reporter. I started at the beginning and gave an overview of my story to Ava Thompson because Veda said she would be handling it. Cammaratta didn't say much at all. I guess he didn't need to. I also presented Ava with about ten pages of documentation which included a summary of my case from The Big Black Book, the Superintendent's letter denying my witnesses access to my grievance and information about the filing of the Writ of Mandamus in the Circuit Court. The meeting lasted about thirty minutes. On the way out I told Cammaratta that it seemed like they were interested. We will see what happens. I had mixed feelings about what I just had done.

About a week later, Cammaratta and I met with the Professor for lunch. I told the Professor that I had talked to Channel 8 about a week or more ago and still hadn't seen anything on TV yet. The Professor suggested that I call and find out what's up. So, I called on my mobile phone and spoke to Ava Thompson. She said that "the higher ups are going to wait until my case goes to a higher court before they do anything." I knew that was a bunch of baloney. There must have been some other reason why. Don't you think the voting and tax-paying public would like to know why a supervisor was fired and about my suit against the School System? Isn't this newsworthy? The Professor said that I'd just have to go to another news source.

Some time later, one of Channel 8's advertisement in the newspaper, with a picture of the news team, said "If you think the news should leave you well informed and give you an in-depth look at the issues, your news team is NewsWatch 8. The people in touch with Tampa Bay." Yeah, sure.

My next plan to "go public" was to contact the other television stations in the Tampa Bay area. I called Channel 10, WTSP TV, a local ABC affiliate, and spoke to reporter Jim Larson. I briefly told him what happened and his only question was "is this thing political?" I said I wasn't sure and then he asked again if it was political. I then said that I guess it could be. He said that he would check into it. I never heard from him again.

I had remembered that Channel 10 also had an "I team" that would do special investigative reports and would try to solve unsolved crimes in the Bay area. Channel 10 advertised that viewers could "Count on 10." So, I was counting on them. I hand-delivered a packet of papers to investigative reporter Kevin Kalwary. In my short conference with him, Kevin asked me what I wanted him to do with this information. I thought that was a dumb question, since *he* was the news reporter, but I said I would like him to determine if it was newsworthy. I didn't come there to demand that they air my story. I don't own Channel 10, so I didn't think I could tell them what to do. At the end of our conversation, Kalwary said this story will probably "just end up as a pissing match between you and Smouse." I thought he had reached a premature conclusion, but I gave him the papers anyway. I said again it was up to him to decide whether it was newsworthy. I thanked him for his time and left. I never heard from him again. No story came out.

There were more stations. I called Channel 13, WTVT a local CBS affiliate, and I spoke with assistant news director Mike Shapiro. I briefly told him about my story and asked if I could drop off a packet of papers. Later that day, I did hand-deliver the packet to Channel 13. Mike wasn't in at the time, so I left it at the front desk with his name on it. I didn't hear from him again. Channel 13's local self-promotional advertisements stressed the topic of Leadership in news media. Their advertisement said in part, "Leadership means innovative technology and community commitment."

I was starting to lose my confidence in the electronic news media. I called one more station, Channel 44, WTOG. I spoke to Kathryn Bursch. I always asked to speak to someone who reports on the school system. I talked for about three to four minutes about my story. She seemed more than surprised, but less than shocked about what had happened to me. Then she said she would have to check on all this to see if it were true. I was already past the point of truth, and was hoping that the news media would pick it up from there and try to determine whether it was right or wrong, not whether it was true or not. I decided not to give her any documentation because I felt it wouldn't do any good. I never heard from her again. I wonder who she checked with?

That was as far as I went with electronic media. Next up were the newspapers. The Tampa Bay area has two dailies, *The Tampa Tribune*, here in Hillsborough County, and *The St. Petersburg Times*, in Pinellas County. I was a bit leery about the *Tribune*, so I chose the *Times*. I would estimate that the *Times* had about a 15% share of the market in the Tampa area. I can remember hearing about it as an award winning newspaper, said to be one of the top-ten in the nation, therefore, I considered it to be an up-and-coming paper on this side of the Bay. I thought the *Times* would jump at a story like mine. Hey, so don't you wanna sell newspapers?

The *Times* ' "Tampa Edition" had a school reporter by the name of Wendy Weyen. I called her and asked to meet with her about a story with the school system. We met at T.G.I. Friday's restaurant in Tampa in the late afternoon. I told her my story and gave her several documents similar to the packet I gave to the others. I had told my story so many times by now, I had it down pat. For some reason, I was a bit nervous. I guess all of this "going public" stuff was starting to wear on me.

I ordered something to eat and had an iced tea to drink. She only had iced tea. During our fifty-minute meeting, I had a feeling, a gut level feeling, that she was more concerned in analyzing me rather than the story I was telling. I had the impression that she was thinking, "Okay, go ahead and tell me your story; I'll pretend to listen." It wasn't anything she said; it was just how she appeared. Toward the end of our meeting, she said she needed to run to the school board meeting which was that evening. I thanked her for meeting with me. She didn't write an article about my story.

Did you ever start to lose confidence in your own thinking? I thought my story and law suit would be newsworthy.

Mike Shapiro from Channel 13 later moved over to Channel 10 as the assistant news director. In February, 1989, he was arrested for stealing newsroom information from Channel 13 by way of the computer system he designed there. Shapiro and another employee were fired by Channel 10. According to *The St. Petersburg Times*, both employees were sentenced to five years of probation.

Some time later, I received information from a friend who said one of the executives at Channel 8, Doug Duperrault, Director of Local Programs and Public Relations, had a wife who worked for the school system at that time as a Coordinator. The friend wondered if there was an unspoken influential relationship; Channel 8 wouldn't air anything that would directly embarrass the Superintendent or the School Board, consequently ensuring no retaliation against a wife. You scratch my back . . . . It sounds possible, but I have no information that it is true. It just makes you think.

I can't help but to return to the topic of ethics. This time instead of administrative ethics, it's news media ethics. So, what is the difference? It all has to do with trust.

And then I was told this all sounds like a suppression of the news. I was told it was analogous to a "conspiracy of silence" since there was a variety of media involved. If this were true, who was the "conspiracy" protecting? It sure made you put on your thinking cap.

I still had the strongest feelings that the community would like to know about my story. Plus, I needed to clear my name and reputation. There were continuous questions and concerns that came from my school system colleagues, neighbors and friends during the years of aggression by Smouse. That told me that the non-educational community would also be interested and concerned. It wasn't just "my" story.

So far, my experience of going public was comparable to having a party and no one showing up. That's Okay with me; I'm strong, I will follow my course in the court system.

I remember asking Bob McKee about the news media calling me at home. I decided, with his approval, that I would tell any news media to contact my attorney for any facts since the case was then in litigation. I guess I didn't need the media now, like I thought. I have reset my priorities. By the way, no one from the media ever called McKee to my knowledge.

In the Winter 1990 issue of *USF* magazine, from the University of South Florida, there was an article about a new Chair in Media Ethics. The article said in part:

> USF's St. Petersburg campus is the recipient of the University's first endowed chair in media ethics, a welcome boost to the growing graduate program in journalism.
>
> This gift is part of a business agreement between the Times Publishing Company and Poynter-Jamison Limited Ventures Partnership to operate as joint owners of the *St. Petersburg Times.*
>
> "The establishment of this chair will allow the St. Petersburg campus to hire an eminent scholar for the 1991-92 academic year," said Dean Winston Bridges. This individual will join the two faculty members currently in mass communications.
>
> Bridges added that the Poynter gift will compliment the University's integration of ethics into other courses as well.

I'm glad to read of the support for this ethics chair and I compliment the donors for making it possible and the University of South Florida for its emphasis in the area of ethics in mass communications.

May it enhance our trust in those that we depend on in this age of public information and public disinformation.

38

MONEY MEANS POWER

This chapter is easy to understand. It simply says that the authority someone has in making decisions is directly correlated to the amount of money in that person's yearly operating budget. In my position as a county program supervisor, I was one of six vocational program supervisors. Our total yearly budget was allocated by our supervisor, Cammaratta. He was one of four directors who divided up a yearly budget from their immediate supervisor, Smouse. Therefore, Smouse allocated money to the four directors, who allocated it to their subordinates. In Cammaratta's case, he allocated it to the six vocational program supervisors and then we would allocate it to the teachers at the schools around the entire county.

Back in the fall of 1979, when I was promoted out of the classroom and to a coordinator's position, I observed that when the new equipment money was divided up among the six vocational supervisors; the ones with the loudest or most demanding voices ended up with the largest amounts. Often, big bucks went to the industrial programs with little left over for the smaller programs. Being a fair shooter, I saw a great need for some equity here. Since I was new, I thought I might be able to present an unbiased plan.

I developed what I called the Equipment Funding Formula guide. Since I was a coordinator, I presented it to my boss who was one of the six vocational supervisors. He liked it and said we should present it to his boss, Cammaratta. Cammaratta thought it was great and suggested that I present it to the supervisors and allow them to decide if they want to apply it.

At the next department meeting, Cammaratta introduced the topic and I made my presentation. All the supervisors liked it and they voted to use it starting with the 1980 budget. It worked.

The Equipment Funding Formula is based upon four different statistics to arrive at one average percentage factor among the six vocational programs.

These four criteria included: the number of students in the programs, the number of teachers, Full Time Equivalency (FTE) amounts, and program cost categories from the state department. A percentage was calculated in each of the four categories and then an overall percentage was arrived at. I believed that if I used four areas it would allow for little variation in the calculation and consistency over the coming year. This all was explained during my presentation.

Then the formula made a direct allocation to each supervisor which totaled 75% of the yearly budget with 5% set aside for contingency. Then, the remaining 20% was up for grabs depending on any special needs for the coming school year. This is where the "big voices" could still have their day, and it wouldn't knock anyone out cold.

I was proud of my formula and the reception it received. I was new to the county office staff, but I was glad to show them I was a team player. No programs would go without now. I knew the teachers and students would benefit in the long run, too.

Each year when the supervisors divided up the equipment money, Cammaratta would then send a letter to Smouse indicating the allocations to each program. Since my formula was new, Cammaratta informed him about the formula and sent him a copy of it.

On January 20, 1981, Smouse wrote a letter to Cammaratta that had one short paragraph. It read:

> I have received your equipment funding formula and feel you and your staff have done an excellent job in its development. I encourage you to continue using this approach to budgeting and allocation of funds.

Cammaratta showed me a copy of Smouse's letter, noting that Smouse believed that the staff developed the formula. He said Smouse didn't know I had done it single-handedly. I told Cammaratta that was fine with me because it didn't matter who got the credit as long as it was being used. We left it at that.

Then, much later in 1986, after I had returned to Hillsborough County as a supervisor, things started to change. After Smouse started to "paper my file," he changed the way we were to allocate the equipment funds.

For example, in 1987, the total amount of just categorical equipment funds was $841,223.21. The formula's 5% contingency amount was raised to 10% and it would be kept by Smouse rather than by Cammaratta. Plus, Smouse made a direct allocation of $227,000.00 to Boyd Wilborn who was the Director over the three vo-tech centers. Then the remainder of $530,000.00 was allocated to Cammaratta and the supervisors. The major change confused all of the supervisors. Traditionally, we, the supervisors, would decide how much money the vo-tech centers received along with the other vocational programs across the county. Now, 27% of the total budget went to one person who was over three schools, and we had to spread the remainder over some forty odd other schools throughout the county. These other schools obviously weren't getting their fair share. Some schools went without any equipment funds some years. This is a disgrace to the teachers and the students. How could I explain it to the principals or parents? Some schools had to continue to use older machinery that often needed repairs and maintenance. What if the teachers didn't do the repairs because machinery was old or repeatedly broke down? Could this situation become a safety problem because of no money to purchase new machinery? What about the quality of the program if the students had to work with obsolete equipment?

Oh yes, I almost forgot to mention that we still had to allocate some of our left-over monies to the three vo-tech centers even after they already got their direct share. I call this double dipping and it was put in motion by Smouse. It wasn't fair to the teachers and their students. There wasn't anything I could do but to follow the boss's directives. No one of the other supervisors spoke out either.

Maybe Smouse didn't know it, but he was undermining the authority of the supervisors. Our money was cut; and so were our decision-making responsibilities. The vo-tech director didn't need us any more because he had his money and our voices were meaningless.

I have to say that I speculated that somehow Smouse found out that I developed the funding formula and this would be a good way of intimidating me by making the formula a laughing stock. He took the equity out of the formula that I worked so hard to put in. It's possible he was attempting to countermand my own authority in the industrial programs. You see, the industrial programs usually had the largest part of the equipment budget; therefore any cuts would hurt me the most and affect the working relationships that I had built up with school principals and teachers. They counted upon me for quality programs. If you cut my money, you cut my power. And he had the power to do it. Could it be that students aren't the central issue in the school system? Was Smouse's administration of the budget shortchanging some students?

In the following year, 1988, Smouse allocated 28% of the funds to Wilborn and the vo-tech centers. In 1989, I heard it was business as usual. It's not fair to the students.

Here is another prime example of how money means power. In April of 1988, Smouse directed me to meet with him. We discussed several things including the status of the four-wheel alignment machines in the automotive mechanics programs that I supervised. I reported to him that three schools had the new four-wheel alignment while eight had the old two-wheel alignment. He was upset that all the schools didn't have the new equipment especially Tampa Bay Vo-Tech (TBVT). He blamed me. However, Tampa Bay Vo-Tech is one of the three centers under Wilborn's direction. You remember how much money he got for his schools. But nooooo. . . , it's my fault because I didn't spend my budget for this (Wilborn's) school.

Then, in a letter on April 15, 1988, Smouse directed me to give Tampa Bay Vo-Tech priority for the purchase of a four-wheel alignment system for the next year and then prioritize the others. It was my job responsibility to make this decision as a supervisor, but if he wants the money there, then okay. I'll do it because he's my boss's boss.

This must have been a major concern to him because only one month later, in May of 1988, Smouse found some $110,000 in equipment monies and gave it to Cammaratta. He said to Cammaratta that $19,000 of that was to be spent on a four-wheel alignment system for Tampa Bay Vo-Tech. Smouse's letter to Cammaratta, of May 10, 1988, said at the bottom: "Please proceed as rapidly as possible to expend these funds for necessary equipment." And that was done.

I still couldn't understand why Smouse prioritized Tampa Bay Vo-Tech as the most needy school of the eight without the equipment. They already were given so much more money than the other schools. This made that imbalance even worse.

Well, shut my mouth. You won't believe what occurred during the following month of June. I happened to be fishing for drum with the two automotive mechanics teachers from Tampa Bay Vo-Tech. We were in a boat, in Tampa Bay under the bridge and they told me a story about Smouse's daughter. You see, one of his daughters works at their school as a secretary. They both told the story about Smouse's daughter bringing her car into their auto shop for some work. She needed a rear wheel alignment on her small car. They both started laughing, but I didn't know what was so funny. They asked me if I knew how much she weighed and I nodded yes. Well, they said they couldn't align her left rear wheel because they didn't have a rear-wheel or four-wheel alignment system. They continued to point out that the car leaned to the left because she was so fat that the rear spring was ruined and had thrown off the alignment.

I gave a so-so laugh, but my brain immediately went into gear and thought about why, two months ago, Smouse blamed me and then directed me to place an alignment system at Tampa Bay Vo-Tech. Was he insulting me on purpose, because his daughter's car couldn't be aligned at TBVT? And did he prioritize equipment for TBVT because his daughter's car needed the work? I have drawn my own conclusion.

Money means power. If you ask me, it sure doesn't necessarily mean equity or safety in vocational programs.

I'm still feeling the stress from the job. I can't help but to take it home with me. There are days when I get home from work, eat dinner, watch the 6:00 news and immediately fall asleep on the couch from exhaustion. I roll over in the middle of the night and then crawl into my bed. The next morning my alarm tells me to be ready for another day at the office. I sleep so deep that I sometimes don't even hear the phone ring. That scares me a little.

39

I DID MY BEST

The image and function of the vocational-industrial program and its responsibilities cannot be fully appreciated unless the viewer is on the front line where the action is. The School Board's job description for the Supervisor of Industrial Arts and Industrial Education lists 20 job functions. It is incumbent upon the supervisor to discharge these responsibilities in an effective and efficient manner. An exceptional supervisor is one that exceeds these expected standards and requirements. I have shown through my last three yearly evaluations that I "meet" or "exceed" the job performance standards.

Because my reputation has suffered a few blows and shows some signs of bruises, I feel compelled to toot my own horn for only a moment. Following is a brief list of accomplishments during my "non-tenured tenure" as supervisor (October 1985 to June 1988) with the school system:

1. Guest Speaker–University of South Florida, Department of Adult and Vocational Education. 1985 and 87.
2. Member–Pinsetter Mechanic Program Advisory Committee. Brewster Campus, Erwin Vo-Tech Center. 1985 to 88.
3. Member–Florida Beginning Teacher Team at junior high, senior high and vo-tech levels. 1985 to 88.
4. Selected by Ohio State University, the National Center for Research in Vocational Education, as a member of a DACUM panel to develop a national listing of competencies for vocational administrators. 1986.
5. Established a County Industrial Steering Committee. 1986.
6. Vocational Student Organization activities were increased. Vocational Industrial Clubs of America student membership increased from 250 to

480 in 1986–87. There also was an increase in regional, state and national contest winners.

7. Host–School Board Exhibit, State Fair. 1986 and 1987.
8. Judge–American Industrial Arts Student Association, Florida State Conference, student/school competition. 1986 to 88.
9. Member–Vending Machine Repair Program Advisory Committee. Brewster Campus, Erwin Vo-Tech Center. 1986 to 88.
10. Establish an Industry Partnership with Tampa Electric Company to produce electrical safety curriculum. 1986.
11. TV Interview–WFLA Channel 8, an NBC local affiliate. Promotion of special industrial programs at Brewster, 15 minutes. 1986.
12. Member of a team to develop a new list of professional knowledge and skills of beginning teachers in Florida. Selected by Ralph Turlington, Commissioner of Education. 1986.
13. Member–Vocational Advisory Committee, LaVoy Exceptional Center. 1986 to 88.
14. Judge–Craft displays at the Plant City Strawberry Festival and Hillsborough County Fair. 1986 and 87.
15. Guest Speaker–Tampa Electric Company. Presentation on electrical safety awareness program. 1986.
16. Member–Hillsborough Halfway House Advisory Committee. HRS. 1986 to 88.
17. Coordinator–State Fair Technology Education Exhibit. 1987 and 88.
18. Member–American Industrial Arts Student Association (FL-AIASA) State Advisory Committee. Recommended by Bill Wargo, State Program Director. 1987 and 88.
19. Judge–Hillsborough Regional Science Fair. 1987 to 89.
20. President of the Florida Technology Education Association. 1987 to 88.
21. Planning Committee–Vocational, Technical and Adult Education State Conference. Industrial Arts Division. 1987.
22. Member–State Industrial Arts Technical Advisory Committee. 1987 and 88.
23. Florida Vocational Association Board of Directors. 1988.

During the school year 1986-87, I decided to encourage more teachers to participate in and emphasize youth clubs (VICA and TSA) as a part of their regular vocational class. These clubs are nationally chartered and promote leadership through various club activities including vocational competition among individual students, schools and states. I was pleased to see that we had a record number of teachers and students participating that year and the next.

Then, in the school year 1987-88, I placed an emphasis on safety in the industrial shops. I emphasized that teachers should teach and practice safety as well as keep their equipment in safe working condition. I received copies of all student accident reports, form SB383, from Fred Dudney, county supervisor of risk management. I'm proud to say that there was a noticeable reduction in shop accidents. The following compares the last two years:

	1986–87	1987–88
Accidents Reported	56	13
Different Teachers Reporting	39	10
Different Schools Reporting	22	8

Furthermore, I pride myself on the continuing effort to establish and mold cooperative and professional relationships with teachers, individual school administrators, district personnel and the business community.

I was also a member of the Hillsborough, Florida and the American Vocational Associations among a variety of other state and national organizations.

My most rewarding work, as a supervisor, was in my direct contact in working with students in the Vocational Student Organizations during their officer training sessions and through their regional, state and national competition. Providing leadership and support to these students and their teachers was the pinnacle of my career.

I knew I could make a difference and I did my best. I cared about students.
"Every man's work is a portrait of himself."
Samual Butler, 1903

40

LAST DAY ON THE JOB

The School Board hired me and I felt that the School Board should fire me, not someone else. When I was hired, I received written and verbal notice of my starting date of employment. I had only received notice from Assistant Superintendent Ralph Smouse saying he was not recommending me for reappointment. I had no "official" written or verbal notice of termination from the body that hired me, the School Board, via the Superintendent.

Dateline: Tampa, Florida, Thursday, June 30, 1988.

Since I was not satisfied to leave my employment with the "sketchy" information that I had on June 30, I decided that I would show up for work on Friday, July 1, to see what would happen.

I was also concerned that if I didn't show up, the Board might be able to say that I "abandoned" my job. I wasn't going to take any chances. My decision was based upon the fact that I had no paper work instructing me that I was terminated. Nothing from the Board said that my job would end on June 30, 1988.

Dateline: Tampa, Florida, Friday, July 1, 1988.

This was the day of my first court hearing in my suit against the School Board and the Superintendent. But first, it was off to work. It was 7:30 A.M. sharp. I came into my office as I usually did. Regular working hours for everyone started at 8:00 A.M. I was the second one into the office; Cammaratta had already arrived as usual. I had told him the day before that I was coming in and I told him why. He said that he, my immediate supervisor, didn't have any paper work that indicated that my job ended on June 30, 1988.

In addition, I cleared my actions with my attorney, McKee. He too was inquisitive to see what they would do because he felt the same way about the lack of "official" notice of my termination. He said he never heard of an Assistant Superintendent in Florida with the authority to fire someone. Where was the notification from the Superintendent?

The morning was routine until 10:52 A.M. when Cammaratta spoke to Smouse on the phone. Smouse called Cammaratta about a travel form for Guenter Steffan, a teacher. For some reason, Smouse asked if I was there. Dr. Cammaratta said yes and then Smouse asked him to tell me to call Smouse. He told Cammaratta that I should not be there.

At 11:03 A.M., I went to an empty supervisor's office down the hall to make my private call to Smouse. I had a pen and pad ready to make notes about the conversation; I had a hunch it would be interesting. Smouse asked what I was doing there. I told him that I was working at my job because I had nothing in writing that told me not to be there. He responded, quite intensely and briskly, that anybody with a grain of sense would know I should not be there. He asked sarcastically, "You have no contract, do you?" I said "No, I don't." Because contracts normally don't come to supervisors and administrators until November or December, or even later anyway, technically, no one "had a contract."

After my answer of "No, I don't," he told me to "Pack up my personal belongings and get out of there." I told him that it would be impossible for me to pack up all my personal things that day because my office was full of my antique office decorations. I had decorated my office with old industrial tools. It set a comfortable atmosphere for the industrial teachers and industrial vendors that would visit. I did get many positive comments from people about my unique, interesting and appropriate office decor.

Smouse and I agreed that I would leave the building immediately and return on the first work day of the next week (Tuesday, July 5) to remove all my personal belongings from my office. So here it was...the day I left my job, Smouse and I had agreed on something! I left my office at 11:30 A.M.

Over the weekend, I found out from Cammaratta that Smouse and Sickles came through the office together during the lunch hour on Friday. I wonder if they were there to be sure I left the building. It seems to me this should have been a Personnel Department matter with Beth Shields, Assistant Superintendent for Personnel. But I guess that Smouse had to see this through to the end.

I returned to my office on the following Tuesday at 8 A.M. with Frank Zeitler, an Industrial Arts teacher. He brought his pickup truck and I had my Chevy station wagon. We loaded my personal belongings in the two vehicles and were out of the office in 1½ hours. Cammaratta was out of town and he put Dr. June Saltzgaver, Supervisor of Health Occupations, in charge. There were no formal or informal good-byes from anyone. I'm sure all people in the office complex knew what was happening.

Cammaratta later told me that Smouse asked Saltzgaver if I had taken anything that I shouldn't have. Cammaratta said her response was that she didn't know.

Even after I was gone, my professional character was being challenged. I'm told that I do take these things personally. I care what people think; that's why I'm a teacher.

The Professor didn't call much anymore since I hired McKee, attorney number 3, and went into litigation. I remember calling the Professor on my mobile phone and telling him that I changed counsel to file suit because I didn't think the school system was afraid of Craparo, attorney number 2. He agreed, and then brushed it off. The Professor would call me at home occasionally; I returned some of his calls. Our relationship started to wane after I was terminated.

According to the newspapers, the Textbook Scam was expected to reach a settlement. Money and condominium properties would be given up by the suspended textbook supervisor. The school system was expected to recover between $70,000 and $200,000 according to W. Crosby Few, school board attorney. Some of the cash was in 12 accounts across the state. The tentative settlement would place the school system in a position of owning resort condominiums.

41

HEARING NUMBER ONE:
MOTION FOR TEMPORARY INJUNCTION

Hearing number one was held on July, 1, 1988, in the chambers of the Honorable Vernon W. Evans, Jr., in the Hillsborough County Courthouse in downtown Tampa. I met attorney McKee at his office and we drove over to the courthouse in his car. We arrived early in the judges' chambers before anyone else.

As we waited, to my surprise in came Superintendent Shelton, Assistant Superintendents Sickles and Smouse. I looked at them and they made no eye contact with me whatsoever and of course there were no hellos or handshakes. They asked the secretary if they could wait in an adjoining conference room. McKee asked me who they were and I told him. Neither of us expected them to be there. Shortly, the school board counsel, Thomas M. Gonzalez, came in and then soon after the secretary announced that Judge Evans was ready.

The issue to be heard that day was my Motion for Temporary Injunction. Basically, this motion asked the court to keep me on the job until my case was resolved.

It is essential to note here that, apparently, no court reporter was called by either side to record the hearing. Therefore, no transcript was created for future reference. Remember this.

Being new to this type of hearing, I observed that each attorney gave his opening statement; a discussion followed with questions coming from Judge Evans. Attorney McKee started with the proposal to keep me on the job until this was settled. Judge Evans said he wasn't sure that he could encumber the school system like that. He then said that even if I were to win my case, the school system may want to appeal. I looked at Shelton and Sickles just then; they sat in the back near me and they remained silent, nodding in unison like two trained horses, to show agreement with the Judge that they may appeal a decision against them. Evans then said he could not require them to keep me on the job. Motion denied. McKee then looked for some help from the court. He asked Judge Evans to restrict the Board from actually finding my replacement, but allowing them to advertise, interview and select the person. Again, Evans denied this motion. I do remember Judge Evans saying that he could make me whole. I specifically do remember him going on to say that the school system should inform the new supervisor that litigation is in progress and the new supervisor must move over if I win my case. I wished for more; nonetheless that seemed fair.

I believe that McKee hit the nail right on the head to ask for the injunction. What he was saying is that it would save the public a lot of money in the long run by allowing me to work for my pay during the litigation rather than having to pay me back-pay for sitting at home (meanwhile paying someone else to do my job). The affidavits that he had Cammaratta and me submit helped to support what he was saying to the court. I think McKee had a good feeling that we were going to win this one, even though we lost the Motion for Injunction.

The hearing lasted about thirty minutes. They all left first. I asked McKee to review what just happened while we drove back to the office. And he did.

Still, there was no local news coverage by the newspapers or TV stations as to my filing suit against the School Board.

BEGINNING OF SCHOOL YEAR 1988-89

42

DON'T BEAT A DEAD HORSE

Since I was unemployed, I decided to apply for unemployment compensation with the Florida Department of Labor and Employment Security. Right after the July 4th, 1988 holiday, I filed a claim for benefits under the compensation law.

It was a busy day. I had already cleaned out my office at work for the last time and now in the afternoon, I was at the unemployment office. I filled out the form, took a number and then waited and waited and waited. It was a gloomy and dejected atmosphere in the unemployment office. It was like a funeral and we were the ones that died. We all were reaching out for resurrectional support because we knew life must go on.

My turn came and ended routinely. I was to report once a week and I was required to make three contacts per week with prospective employers. Sending or submitting a resumé did qualify as a contact. Because you don't receive benefits for the first week after filing, I would get my first check in three to four weeks.

Things were moving along on schedule. On July 14, the Department sent me a Notice about my claim. It said, under Determination in Section II, "Benefits are payable." A copy was sent to the School Board. I looked forward to my first check as a consolation gift because I believed I really should not have been terminated.

Then, things came to an abrupt stop. I really hit the skids on this one. On July 25, the Department sent me another Notice about my claim. It said, under Determination/Redetermination in Section II, "Benefits are not payable because: The reason for quitting was not attributable to the employer. The law requires disqualification from 6/26/88 and until you earn $3400." A copy was sent to the School Board.

I said to myself,..."self, what the hell is going on here?" I didn't quit; I was fired. Who said I quit? Somebody, please, show me a copy of my resignation letter. I can't believe this. Did I fall asleep and miss part of this movie? First they say "Yes," now "No." What turned this around? This circumstance reminds me of a game little kids play where yes means no and no means yes. Then one kid would ask the other if he wanted to get pinched. He would say "yes," (meaning no), and he would get pinched. Damned if you do and damned if you don't. What game is the school system playing with the Bureau of Unemployment Compensation and me? Is the school system a totally believable institution because it is so big and powerful and I'm only perceived as the disgruntled employee? Did somebody know somebody? Was a phone call made? Was there an air of fraud and collusion here?

Under Section IV of the Notice, claimants have appeal rights. I had 20 days to file an appeal. No doubt about it, I filed an appeal right after I came out of professional shock on July 29. A "Notice of Hearing" was sent to me and the Board. The hearing was set for August 16, at 10:00 a.m. in Tampa. The Notice said the issue in my appeal was "Separation." It said they must determine whether claimant voluntarily left employment without good cause. It also said exhibits and evidence could be brought as long as I provided the original and two photo copies. An Appeal Information pamphlet was also enclosed. Remember, copies of all of this were sent to the Board, too.

There is an Appeal Referee in charge of the Hearing. Entry number 14 in the Appeal pamphlet describes the Impartiality of the Referee: it says "The Referee is charged with conducting a fair and impartial hearing. In so doing, it is the Referee's responsibility to protect the rights of all parties." The Referee will render a decision and mail it within one week after the Hearing.

I brought this news and information to attorney McKee. I asked that he attend the Hearing with me, which was permitted, because I didn't know who the Board might bring. I have learned to prepare to fight fire with fire. Their attorney is "free" to them; the Board just says go and he'll be there. I had to pay for McKee's appearance because this was a separate issue from my law suit. I couldn't get over the fact that I had to hire an attorney to fight a ruling that was so contrary to the truth. Was all this happening just to cause me grief, frustration and more money? I was getting worn down.

McKee and I arrived early at the Hearing location in Tampa. No one from the School Board was there yet. When we were called into the Hearing room, we knew no one showed up from the Board. My first impression was that the

Board's non-representation was tantamount to an admission of guilt and that I would win the appeal. The Referee put me under oath and asked me questions for about thirty minutes. The questions were easy to answer. At the conclusion of the questioning, McKee made a closing statement which said in no uncertain terms, that I was discharged and I didn't quit. He also stated there is current litigation in the courts over my wrongful termination. We left feeling rather good, especially because we thought the Board "threw in the towel."

The Notice of Decision came from the Unemployment Compensation Appeals Bureau on August 24. The Conclusions of Law Section stated the following: "...The evidence clearly revealed that the claimant voluntarily left his employment when he refused to accept continuing employment on a probationary status...." The Decision Section said the determination of the claims adjudicator was affirmed. Other copies were sent to McKee and the Board.

The decision was a frustrating one to say the least. I went back through the rules of the hearing. Under the topic of Importance of the Hearing, is written the following:

> Each party should be prepared to present evidence under oath on all issues at this hearing. The appeal will be dismissed if the party who filed the appeal (appellant) fails to appear. If the other party (appellee) fails to appear, the Referee will proceed with the hearing and will render a decision based on the evidence presented at the hearing.

This has got to be a bunch of baloney. There is a contradiction of equitable processes here. If I don't show up, the Hearing is dismissed. If no Board representatives show up, the Hearing proceeds. It sounds like I'm guilty until I prove myself innocent and the employer is innocent until I prove them guilty. Is there a due process rights violation here? What was the referee's decision based on? Papers the Board submitted? Hey, I don't remember seeing any papers taking an oath to tell the truth. How can I cross-examine a folder anyway?

If the "Referee will render a decision based on the evidence presented at the hearing," then how could the Board come out the winner if they weren't there to present anything?

It seemed that the Board placed all its case on the fact I didn't accept the offer of probation. However, it appears the Board didn't inform the claims office that there were two other options that Smouse had to choose from after I made my decision. My denial of probation was not an automatic termination. Smouse decided to chose to terminate with the approval of the Superintendent. Why didn't the Board send this letter of information to the claims office? Was this a misrepresentation of the facts? Was this the whole truth, or only half? Fraud is a felony.

I saw McKee again. He had already received his copy of the decision. I told him I would appeal to the Unemployment Appeals Commission in Tallahassee. He said fine. I filed on August 29.

The State Appeals Commission consists of three people, a chairman and two members. They review the matters contained within the official record which was before the appeal referee. They would determine if the decision was supported by competent substantial evidence in the record and if the legal conclusions were in accord with the essential requirements of the law. A written Order was sent to each party.

The Commission sent the Order on November 2, 1988. I picked up the mail and saw the letter from the Commission. I waited to get inside my condo before I opened it. This is one of the self discipline games I play. I sat down and opened it slowly. The Order said the Commission "Affirmed" the decision of the appeals referee. It was like playing the Florida Lottery. You expect to win while you know you really won't.

I visited with McKee one more time on this matter. He explained my option to file a judicial review. He indicated that the appeals up to this point had been "free." If I decided to go with a judicial review in the District Court of Appeal, it would start costing me some serious money. He said I already had a suit asking for back wages from the Board. If I collect any unemployment compensation, it would be subtracted from any back wages. Filing a judicial review for unemployment compensation would be a duplication of effort. I agreed, but expressed the hardship the School Board had created for me; however, I didn't mention my frustration concerning truth and justice. Nevertheless, I believe he understood because he did not require me to pay his monthly bill of his services until this was settled. He was understanding of my non-income status.

I wanted to continue and prove the Board wrong in the denial of my unemployment compensation. It seemed like an easy case to win if I could only get in front of the District Court of Appeals and on the public record. Nevertheless, money always seems to get in the way between my principles and someone else's.

It remains a matter of public record with the Florida Department of Labor and Employment Security that I quit my job because of poor performance. I sure hope this record doesn't come back to haunt me someday.

In spite of the decisions of the Division of Unemployment Compensation, I kept sending three resumés to prospective employers each week. And I'll still seek back wages from the School System if I can't find similar work elsewhere. This dead horse has nine lives.

My weight continues to increase. Much too much. I heard of a medical study which showed a lesser chance of a heart attack if you take one aspirin per day. I began to participate even thought I'm only in my forties. I think this job situation has subtracted ten years or more from my life. There is that "stress factor" you know. Be that as it may, God walks with me.

43

THIS SOAPBOX DIDN'T REMOVE THE STAINS

It was July, 1988 and the School Board campaigns were well under way. Four of the seven school board positions were up for grabs. Two board members retired and two were seeking re-election.

I was out of work, needed an income and was sending out three resumés per week to school districts around Florida asking for employment. I still wanted to work in education. I thought if I couldn't work in education as an employee, why not work in education as school board member. I was sure I could contribute to education in this leadership position. Even when I was promoted out of the classroom, my major concern was still the student. I had seen the inside of the election process before, since I worked on some campaigns in another school district. I saw this as an exciting and honorable opportunity for me.

I remember there was a letter from Ramona M. Updegraff, mayor of Redington Beach, in the *St. Petersburg Times* about catching the American spirit by running for public office. It reminded us about the spirit that our forefathers, who were eager to have a government that would work for them, had 200 years ago. Updegraff said, "I have observed that it is extremely easy for elected officials to forget whom they represent and choose to use their position for personal gain, for social contacts, and for their own personal agenda rather than to serve for the good of the public.... You must care about the long-range future of your town, city and state and be a visionary." Finally, she said the rewards of public service are many.

On July 20, 1988, I paid the approximate $600.00 filing fee and signed the loyalty oath to support the Constitution of the United States and the State of Florida. I was an official School Board candidate. It was a non-partisan race

THIS SOAPBOX DIDN'T REMOVE THE STAINS

with an unprecedented seven candidates in my district alone. There were a total of twenty candidates county-wide. The election was scheduled for September 6. Education was one of the hottest issues of the decade.

Roland Lewis, a twenty-year veteran, was stepping down in District 1. Cecile Essrig, also a twenty-year veteran, was retiring from District 7. Current Board Chairman, Rev. A. Leon Lowry, Sr., was seeking a forth term in District 5 and R. Sonny Palomino, a Tampa attorney, was seeking a third term in my District 3. Palomino moved his candidacy from District 3 to the county "at-large" District 7 race, which only had one other candidate, a homemaker.

My motto was "We Can Do Better." I stressed my background in education and my civic involvement. Specifically, my civic resumé included: Advisory Council—Salvation Army Spouse Abuse Center; Judge—Hillsborough Regional Science Fair; Advisory Council—Hillsborough Halfway House; Judge—Florida Strawberry Festival Crafts and State Advisory Council—Florida—American Industrial Arts Student Association.

I was putting my campaign schedule together and starting to write my speeches. To get a quick jump in the on-going schedule, Pete LaBruzzo, a school administrator and president of the downtown Tampa Lion's Club, suggested that I talk to fellow club member Glenn Barrington. Barrington was a school board candidate in District 1. I too had known Glenn and worked with him in the school system when he was an assistant principal. We had a good working relationship. We met and he gave me a number of vital and useful suggestions.

The Hillsborough Association of School Administrators (HASA) sent a letter to all candidates asking for a statement to be included in its newsletter. Don Gillette was the Executive Director. I prepared the statement with the usual introduction and background of professional and civic experience. Then I started to add a few lines about my concerns with my due process rights, the grievance procedure and the Superintendent. In conclusion, I stated, "Your (Administrators) involvement *is* essential *before* and *after* the election to maintain our professional dignity."

The Hillsborough Classroom Teachers Association (CTA) sent a similar letter, but was asking for an interview before the political committee. Speaking before that group, I told the teachers that I supported a major pay raise to bring teacher's salaries up to the national average. I stated that the school system was unfair because it used authoritative measures to deny me my job. I said I wanted to know how I could help them and that I needed their input.

Early on, *The Tampa Tribune* published the customary introductory article about my declared candidacy. The interview was conducted by Lindsey Peterson, a staff writer, who later wrote in the article that I quit my job to run for this Board seat. She never even asked about this topic in the interview. The next day I went to see her and explain the inaccuracy. She was busy and didn't have much of a comment. I started to speculate about this "misprint." This was the first article about me that was seen by the voting community since I had filed suit against the Board, and it says I quit. It should have said that I was fired and I filed suit. *That* was the story.

I had speculated before I decided to run as to how to handle my story of corruption in the school system. I didn't want to be perceived as a "sour grapes" candidate. But, I didn't want to ignore the first-hand experiences I had which would give me the intestinal fortitude to provide the leadership that was needed to turn around our failing educational system. I felt obligated; however, I was uncertain how to disclose the facts in my case about the performance of the administration and the Board. I decided to wing it.

As part of a joint project between the League of Women Voters of Hillsborough County and *The St. Petersburg Times*, a questionnaire was sent to all candidates. It would be too lengthy to compare the published answers of all seven candidates in my District 3 race; therefore, I'll quote some of my answers to give the reader an overview of my stance.

QUESTION: What three issues do you consider of top priority for your constituents and Why?

MY ANSWER: (1) The Superintendent: I am not pleased with his leadership style in administering School Board policies. (2) Budget: Make wise expenditures with current resources and strive for more equalization of state funding. (3) Teachers: Increased support through appropriate salaries and classroom assistance. More inservice training for a changing curriculum.

QUESTION: Do you feel changes need to be made in the educational curriculum? What changes do you propose to help students function in today's society?

MY ANSWER: Increased input from teachers, parents and the business and industry community to reflect on today's world society and tomorrow's career needs. Closer academic, vocational and guidance interaction at the appropriate levels. Educate for living in a high-tech world society. Consider career options, which will include: high-tech, medium-tech, low-tech and no-tech. Ensure that every student has the minimum basic skills, then provide options for each student to become all they are capable of being.

During the speaking circuit, I stuck to the regular issues such as: budget; drop-out rate; teacher's salaries; sex education; discipline. I added a topic of my own about the need to review the performance of the superintendent. No one else would touch this "untouchable" subject. I made as many public addresses as I could—both to small groups (I once spoke in a church basement to a group of eight), and to large (a public gathering of several hundred people at a community college auditorium: the local public access channel broadcast this one). All the other candidates also spoke at community centers, club houses, the CTA office, picnics, association luncheons, community forums at public schools and outside of a football game. This doesn't count the times I spoke while in the grocery line, at the movie theater, out to dinner and visiting with friends and neighbors. I quickly became a full-time politician. I was proud.

I specifically remember a savory moment with a minority voter, dressed in a white shirt and tie, at the televised community college forum. After we (District 3 candidates) had responded to questions from a neighborhood panel, he spoke with me about the issues. He said "You are a fighter" and he liked my style. He said he was going to vote for me and tell his friends to. I was elated, since I was a political novice. This response symbolizes that my message was clearly getting through, but how far, I didn't know.

I had limited campaign funds, therefore I decided to place an emphasis on road-side signs rather than expensive newspaper ads. TV advertisement was out of the question; this was just a school board race, not the state Senate. I had made 200 "stake" signs that were two sided, 12 x 20 inches, with red and blue color on a white background. I also had fifty 4 x 4 foot posters made that would fit on a 4 x 8 piece of plywood that was cut in half.

Frank Zeitler was most helpful in assisting me put out my campaign signs. He was an industrial arts teacher and we had worked together for several years, especially with the vocational youth clubs. Along with his students, we traveled to regional, state, and national student competitions. He had been a navigator aboard the B-52's during the Vietnam war. Teaching became his second career. He had generally been aware of my ordeal with Smouse and the Superintendent and he apparently did support my philosophy for education.

I was registered in District 3, but voting was county-wide; therefore campaigning was county-wide too. Frank lived in Brandon on the east side of the county, while I lived in the northwest. We usually put up the stake signs on our own, but it took two of us to handle the 4 x 4 posters. These posters were on quarter-inch plywood nailed to two ten foot long 2 x 4's. We needed a post-hole digger to place these posts two feet into the ground. The signs really looked good. I was the only candidate to paint all the exposed wood on the sign. In other words, the red/white/blue signs had red colored stakes and/or posts. It was an extra mess to paint on the side of the road, but it was a class act. I put my best foot forward.

Sadly, Frank reported to me that most of the stake signs that he put up over the weekend were down. He saw tire marks in the grass where someone would drive off the road and knock down my signs without even getting out of the car. He said he put back up what signs he could, if they weren't broken. I also told him that several poster signs over here on the West side had the paper poster ripped off the plywood. I replaced them too.

Once, I was notified by the county elections office that I had a stake sign in violation within the City of Tampa limits, and I was instructed to pay a fine. Someone placed one of my stake signs on Nebraska Avenue. It was ruled to be too close to the street; it was placed in between the sidewalk and the street. The city was correct; my sign was in the wrong place, but I didn't put it there. This particular section of Nebraska Avenue was well known for prostitutes working the sidewalks. The county always takes a picture of illegal signs. I never saw the picture, but wondered if a hooker was in the background. Not the tone I wanted to project in my campaign.

I had concentrated placing the big poster signs on heavily traveled roads in the county. I put one up in the backyard of a house which bordered Interstate Highway 275 in north Tampa because it is noted for its rush hour traffic. I *always* had asked permission to put up a sign and gave the landowners some of my campaign literature so they could contact me if necessary. During the next rainy weekend, I drove by and my sign was down and in the mud. I took pictures of the four foot chain link fence bordering the interstate, showing that someone had probably pulled off to the side of the exit ramp at Fletcher Avenue, jumped the fence and broke one 2 x 4 in half and then pulled the other one out of the ground. I didn't replace this one. I started to take this personally.

Augie Martines, industrial arts teacher at Gaither High, helped assemble some of the poster signs. He suggested that I put one up on his uncle's property facing the north side of Interstate 4 in the Ybor City area. A week after he and I put up the sign it was down. We went to check and saw the tire rubber marks on the posts and the plywood was ripped to shreds. We put up another big sign, and a few days later, it was gone. Not down,...*gone!*

In the middle of all this chaos, Augie and I had a big laugh. After we had put up the sign on the north side of Interstate 4, I wanted to place one on the south side because of the extreme rush hour traffic jams this section is noted for. It was getting late in the day and I drove over to the other side. Basically, this section of town, near downtown Tampa, was a poor district and it would be best not to be there at night. There was a small vacant grassy lot between two houses that looked perfect for a sign to face the Interstate traffic.

I knocked on the door of the adjacent house and asked the older lady if I could put up my sign next to her house in the vacant lot. She said yes and I gave her the usual literature. Augie and I quickly assembled the poster on the 2 x 4's and started digging the holes for the post. It just got dark and I said we need to be careful that we don't dig up any dead bodies. Just then, we hit something hard with the fence post digger. Augie threw the shovel full onto the grass and white "bones" clearly fell on top of the dark soil. We never worked so fast to get out of there. Once back in the car, we laughed and speculated that we really dug up some old oyster shells that had a shiny white inside. Who knows? I needed a good laugh.

During one of the times Frank and I were putting up signs in the Plant City area, there was a radio call-in talk show sponsored by the League of Women Voters of Hillsborough County. School Board candidates were to call in and would be given an opportunity to answer a question about a campaign issue. Frank pulled his truck over to a phone booth and I called in while he listened to the radio. I was the third candidate to call in. The question given to me was "Would you enforce the concept of requiring parents to attend one day of school per year with their child?" I was sure this was a no-win question. If I said yes, I was forcing parents to do something they might not want to. If I said no, I looked if though I didn't care about parent involvement. Hey, why did I get this question? The other candidates were given much more "easy-answer" questions. Besides, this was not even a campaign issue, no one ever talked about it before or after the radio interview. The other candidates got questions about school funding and the curriculum, but not me. In my answer, I walked the fence, stating the benefits of increased parental involvement, but also pointed out the pitfalls of a requirement that may conflict with a parent's work schedule. Nonetheless, I thanked the League for allowing me to call in.

When I returned to the truck, I asked Frank how I sounded, he said they had cut me off. He reiterated, in an insulted way, "They cut you off!" My respect for the League of Women Voters of Hillsborough County took a turn downhill. I also saw in future debates among other candidates that the League had some "questionable" procedures. In one debate, questions on 3 x 5 cards were collected from the audience. However, the monitor could select which question was given to the next candidate. I lost even more respect for the League because of its sloppy political procedures.

Frank suggested that we place a big poster sign in the east side of the county on state Highway 60, the main thoroughfare in bustling Brandon. Frank got permission from the owners of Topper King, a business that sold a variety of canopies for pick-up truck beds. Frank and I placed the sign in the grass about five feet from the business's eight foot chain-link fence surrounding the topper models on display. A few days later, he told me that my sign was gone.

Frank contacted Topper King and found out that someone had torn the 4 x 4 foot plywood poster off the 2 x 4 posts and threw it over the eight foot fence; nails were sticking out of the plywood, but the wood luckily missed the topper display models and did no damage. The posts, painted red, were gone. A couple of days later, we went to the topper dealer to get the 4 x 4 sign and ensure that no damage was done. I spoke to the wife of the owner and she said "I can understand this type of behavior if it were a state race, but...for the local school board...come onnn?" I agreed with her and apologized for any inconvenience that my candidacy may have caused for her or the business. I was embarrassed for acts that were not within my control. Things were getting serious. These just weren't pranks anymore. Damage to my other signs continued.

In the darkest night, bright stars do shine. Frank and I were purchasing wood for signs at the Home Depot store in Brandon. While rolling our stock of wood out of the store, we passed a crew of young men who were getting out of a lawn maintenance truck, towing a trailer of riding mowers. It was late in the afternoon and the crew, typical long hair and cut-off jeans, looked like they had worked a long and dirty day. I happened to catch the eye of the driver of the truck and he looked back at me. He said "Aren't you Mr. Wieser?" And I said yes as I recognized him. He introduced himself and asked if I remembered him. I said "Yes, Brandon High School, 1978. Didn't I suspend you for fighting?" He responded elatedly with "Yeah...Yeah!" He told me he was in business for himself and was doing well. I could see that by the investment he had in equipment alone. Then he asked me "Aren't you runnin' for something?" I said yes, the School Board. He wished me luck in the race and I wished him continued success in his business. I shook his hand, no matter how dirty it was, because teachers live for moments like this, a successful student. I smiled all the way back to the car.

As Frank and I were pulling out, he put the icing on the cake for that meeting. He said there are two kinds of students. I asked what he meant by that? He said, the first kind is one who hates your guts because you suspended *him*. The second kind, respects you fully because *you* suspended him. Frank said he could easily tell that this student was a number two. Now that made my day, if not my campaign.

During the middle of my campaign, Tracey Hymes, a reporter from *The Tampa Tribune*, called me and wanted an interview. I saw this as my chance to tell my story to the *Tribune*. Although, the *Tribune* wasn't my first choice; *The St. Petersburg Times* already turned a deaf ear to my story, along with four local television stations (Chapter 37—"Going Public"). She asked me to visit at the *Tribune's* regional office on Fowler Avenue. I brought a suitcase full of documentation, just in case. Hymes was a young women in her early twenties, and I had the impression that she had recently finished college and that this may have been her first job in her career field.

We met in the conference room and of course she took notes. She started asking me the usual questions about my reason for running, background and experience and my major issues concerning education. I told her that we needed to return the professional pride to Hillsborough County Schools. My statement of the issues was a pivotal point; it brought us to my story about Smouse and then on to the Superintendent and the Board. My answers to her questions spurred more questions about the same topic. I could tell of her interest and some initial disbelief about my facts. She was writing and listening so intensely that she stopped asking questions. I often paused because of her extensive writing. The documentation I offered gave her confidence about my inside story of the school system.

The interview lasted two hours and we needed to leave the conference room because it was previously scheduled. I asked several times if she wanted copies of my documentation. She said she didn't need it.

A week later Hymes called me again and asked to continue our interview, same place. Again in the conference room, she asked a number of review questions and then we expanded on my story details. I was armed with more documentation and was ready for any question she had. At the end of this one hour and forty-five minute session, we were moved out of the room again because of another meeting. We went into another office. She asked for a copy of several key documents and I obliged. On the bulletin board in the office we were visiting was a copy of "The Journalist's Creed." Since she was making copies, I asked her to make me a copy of the creed.

A few days later, Hymes called me at home and did a fifteen minute follow-up interview over the phone. I never liked to do phone interviews, but since we had already spent almost four hours together, I agreed. Her questions centered around the Superintendent. I had previously and publicly announced that I was not pleased with Shelton's performance. She asked, if I were elected, what I would do. I said I would need to see improvement in his performance. "Then what?" she inquired. I said that remedial measures would be taken. Again she quizzed me, "Then what?" If improvement wasn't satisfactory, then steps would be taken to remove him from office.

Her questioning was obviously different from the hours of interviewing we had already completed. It seemed that her questions, and line of questioning, were scripted. I also had a feeling that someone else may have been listening to our conversation. She didn't announce it as a conference call, and I have no proof that it was; I just had that gut level hum. No one, during the entire campaign, ever asked questions about the superintendent's performance or possible termination. No candidate spoke about his questionable performance, except me.

An article about my extensive interview with reporter Hymes appeared later in the *Tribune*. It scratched the surface of my story, but didn't give the documented details that Hymes and I spoke about for over four hours. My friends said the article developed more of a "cloud" over my termination rather than clarify my documented charges of unethical and wrongful actions by the Superintendent and the Board. Again, I believe the media botched my chances to tell my story to the voting community.

Later, in 1991 the *Tribune* ran a promotion about their community support. Large print decried "WE CARE" with the following message:

> Your daily newspaper is not only a reflection of your community, but also an integral part of it. That's why *The Tampa Tribune* involves itself in numerous community projects and events each month, lending support to the people and agencies who help make Tampa Bay a better place to live and work. . . .

The promotion listed charities to whom the *Tribune* donated advertising. It ended its promotion with: "THE TAMPA TRIBUNE—Cornerstone Of A Caring Community."

"The Journalist Creed" from an office in the *Tribune* was written by Walter Williams, Dean, School of Journalism, University of Missouri. Excerpts from the creed are as follows:

> I believe that the public journalism is a public trust; that all connected with it are, to the full measure of their responsibility, trustees for the public; that acceptance of a lesser service than the public service is betrayal of this trust.
> ...I believe that suppression of the news, for any consideration other than the welfare of society, is indefensible.

The St. Petersburg Times, Tampa Edition, sent a letter to all political candidates, congratulating us on qualifying as candidates. We were invited to a workshop which would assist us in getting our messages to the voters through the newspaper. The letter said "Your goal is to get elected. Our goal is to give the readers of *The St. Petersburg Times* the information they need to make informed choices on election day." The letter was written by John Costa, Editor.

For the most part, I had lost my faith in the *Times* because of my previous interview with reporter Wendy Weynan (Chapter 37—"Going Public"), with no follow-up article about my story or law suit in the news. Editor Costa's letter invited all candidates for an interview with the Editors. He stated they "would like to hear your views on the issues."

In the Editor's interview with the *Times*, I touched upon my concerns with the superintendent, but they didn't respond with any follow-up questions.

It was the same setting with the *Tribune* Editors' interview with candidates. I stressed the fact that I had first-hand experience and full documentation of the Superintendent's less-than-acceptable performance. And I mentioned my law suit which I was sure they were already aware of.

My thoughts drifted back to the concept that a "conspiracy of silence" existed around my story, a secret agreement to keep silent about an occurrence to protect or promote selfish interests. I still had no proof of a conspiracy, but all of the ingredients for the recipe were there. Was there a chef who put the recipe on the front burner?

On September 7, the primary election results were in. Homemaker Faye Culp toppled Palomino. She was the first to upset an incumbent Board member in the last twenty years. We became friends during the campaign and exchanged ideas about the race. I received an invitation to her home to celebrate her win. There was plenty of food and political issues were still discussed among the guests. I appreciated the invite.

In District 1, Glenn Barrington and Jo Jetter would be in the runoff on October 4.

I lost the race in District 3. I had spent the least amount of money among the candidates; nonetheless, I came in fourth out of seven candidates, with just over 6,000 votes (9%). My name was at the bottom of the ballot because candidates were listed alphabetically. Since I had the least amount of campaign funds, I feel I got the most "bang" out of my buck, dollar for dollar, compared to the other six candidates. I publicly thank all 6,000 voters who went out of their way to support my philosophy of education. I continued to hold my head high; I performed well. Yvonne McKitrick and George Mayer, first and second place, were now in a runoff.

McKitrick had raised the largest amount of contributions. One of her biggest contributors was local resident George Steinbrenner. She ran a good race and had started her well-planned campaign early on.

In District 5, Rev. Lowry was in a runoff with Carole Henning, a homemaker and mother of three. She pulled in more votes than Lowry.

With experience in the political arena, and in spite of "losing," I saw that I had an opportunity, if not an obligation to my profession, to support several of the remaining candidates in the district races. Some of these candidates were going to win, and they would be the ones providing leadership to the system that I was trying to rejoin after I had been dismissed.

I had observed and interacted with most candidates during the intensive campaign schedule. Selecting to support Barrington was a natural because of our previously established communication and working relationship. I knew he could do a good job.

I supported McKitrick because she was the best candidate. She was a retired supervisor in early childhood education and we knew each other briefly. We had both been members of the Hillsborough County Supervisor's Council.

My disappointment in Rev. Lowry's performance in my non-renomination process caused me to drift away from supporting him. He mislead me when I had asked him if my name was on the list to be terminated in the spring of 1988. He told about a meeting he had with other Board members and top administrators, and said that a decision about my renomination "was on hold" when, in fact, my name was on the termination list. It was a matter of crucial timing in preventing me from filing an appeal. I also heard a rumor that he wanted to step down, but the Superintendent asked him to stay on for one more term. He announced that this would be his last term. I didn't think his heart was in the job. Lately, he had the reputation for falling asleep during the long Board meetings.

I told Yvonne McKitrick that I wanted to pledge my support to her campaign. I remember her saying and quoting how important "my 6,000 votes" would be to her runoff election. I brought five people to her fund-raising spaghetti dinner. She thanked me again for my support and said "when this is all over, we'll get together and we can talk all about your situation with the school system." I didn't ask for any favors, but politically I wasn't so stupid to turn down this offer from a front-running candidate to look into my conflict with the system, should she win. I was eager to show my support for new blood on the school board.

My shiny $22,000 jet black full size Chevy Blazer, 4-wheel drive, with gold mag wheels, was one year old. I mounted four foot campaign poster signs from the candidates on my small flatbed trailer and towed it behind the Blazer which had smaller signs on each side of the cab. It was a first class act when we rode up, down and around Tampa Stadium for several hours before the weekend NFL home football games in plain sight of the 70,000-plus local ticket holders who were "tailgate" partying or entering the stadium. While I did this, the candidates strolled the sidewalks carrying campaign signs and greeting voters first hand. I did this for all three candidates (Barrington, McKitrick, Henning) on different game days. On one weekend, I had two vehicles circling the stadium.

I remember a complementary moment while I was driving around the stadium in my Blazer. The big poster I had mounted on my trailer for McKitrick was a two-color screen print, green and black lettering on a white background. Her symbol on the poster was a four foot long pencil, outlined in black with no coloring. My artistic genes from my school teacher mother told me to color in the plain pencil with a yellow hi-lite felt marker. Now McKitrick had a three color campaign poster for the price of a two. The big yellow pencil gave an aesthetic "zing" to the poster's appearance. When I drove slowly by McKitrick, she noticed the pencil emphasis, pointed to it and looked at me with a big smile. I smiled back and waved. It made my day.

When I pledged my support to Carole Henning, she commented on how well she liked my campaign signs. She asked me to design a new sign for her runoff campaign. I sketched a rendering and she approved it. I recommended that they all be the 4 x 4 foot posters, mounted on quarter inch plywood, supported by ten foot high 2 x 4's. She agreed. I put up her signs at strategic locations around the county. They did look good.

Henning included me in her regional campaign planning in using computer precinct printouts purchased from the supervisor of elections. She also involved me in some of her other campaign strategies. I was impressed. She introduced me to three state legislative candidates and I briefly worked on their election campaigns and received letters of appreciation from them.

Of course, while I was giving my support to the runoff candidates, I attended the debates and speaking forums. Several people, recognizing me and knowing I was out of the campaign, asked "why are you here?" I explained that although I was out of the election race, I still had an interest in education. They said "That's good."

October 5, the elections were over, sort of.

Glenn Barrington won. He invited me to his home for the celebration. It was nice, food in every room, many familiar faces and a good line of communication with Glenn. I gave him a 5 x 7 inch framed color photo of his campaign signs on my Blazer in front of Tampa Stadium. He thanked me for my support.

Yvonne McKitrick walked away with her race. She invited me to her celebration at a downtown Tampa law firm. The first thing I remember were the hors d'oeuvres, but that didn't overlook the appreciation she paid to me by saying how important my support was. Again she said "when this is all over, we'll get together and we can talk all about your situation with the school system." I was glad that she was the type of person who would at least listen to my side of the story. I also gave her a 5 x 7 inch framed color photo of her campaign signs on my Blazer in front of Tampa Stadium. It would act as a graphic reminder of my committment to her in the position of a new School Board member. She was a bit surprised, but most grateful.

I waited for McKitrick to call me for the discussion she said we should have about my situation with the system. She never did.

The Lowry and Henning race was a cliff-hanger. With 96 percent of the votes counted, Henning was ahead by 256 votes. With 100 percent of the precincts reporting Lowry was ahead by 105 votes. There was an automatic re-count the next day and Lowry won by 125 votes out of the 55,000 cast. Henning did have a get together for those who worked on her campaign. It was a sad atmosphere that she lost, but much of the talk was upbeat and bright about future possibilities. For her records, I presented her with a notebook picture collage of her campaign sign locations. She was most appreciative.

The Hillsborough County School Board members as of 1989 were:

Glenn Barrington
Fay Culp
A. Leon Lowry, Sr.
Yvonne McKitrick
Marion Rodgers
Joe E. Newsome
Sam Rampello

To show the newly-elected School Board members, including re-elected Lowry, the depth of my ability to support someone, I sent congratulatory rose corsages to McKitrick and Culp, and rose boutonnieres to Barrington and Lowry. I wanted to surprise them and set the tone for their installation. These were delivered to them on the evening of the school board meeting when they would take the oath of office. My card wished them "The Best" in their term of office. McKitrick was the only member to send me a thank you note for the corsage and for "the many things I did to support her campaign."

It was my overall intention to take an active part in selecting who will fill the vacancies on the School Board. That was accomplished. It was my intention to show selected candidates my willingness to support them. I believe that was accomplished. It was my intention to show the community that I caught the American spirit and continued to display it after my election race ended. I believe I accomplished this. It was my intention to be proud of my community involvement and myself. I know I accomplished this. I now waited to see what the "new blood" on the school board would accomplish. Time will tell and so will I.

During the campaign, the message on my phone recorder had announced that "you have reached Bill Wieser, candidate for school board, District 3..." and such. After the pressures of the campaign were over, I decided to lighten up a little. With all of the problems I had with Smouse's aggression, I changed my phone message to "You have reached the Center for the prevention of Smouse abuse, please leave a message at the beep." It was one way to air some of my frustrations. And it was the truth. I did get some humorous comments from my friends about it.

Election rules state that candidates have thirty days to remove their signs after the election. I had planned to donate what signs I had left to another candidate in a run-off election. Consequently, my poster signs started to disappear the day after the election. A week later, my signs started popping up around the county, sporting a blue cover-over paint job and promoting another candidate I didn't even know. The Republican candidate was running for a very prestigious county-level office. Frank and I picked up a couple of these signs and I brought them to my home and disassembled them, showing my red paint. I took some pictures to act as a record, should I ever need to defend my actions of rescuing "my" signs.

My quest for a job as a school board member failed and so did my continued desire to uncloak my story to the community. I had a slight feeling that if the media had opened my complete story to the voting public, I would have had a good chance to be elected. The community was hungry for someone new to stand up and fight for what was right for them and their children. I had already proven my allegiance to stand up for what was right by putting my job on-the-line during my interchange with Smouse. And now, as a political candidate, I've shown that I have caught the American spirit and will perpetually step forward to fight for it.

However, in any event, the stains remain on me.

44

ONE DOWN, ONE TO GO

On December 31, 1988, Mr. Ralph L. Smouse, Jr. retired from the Hillsborough County Public School System. He had begun his career thirty years ago as a business education teacher in this county. He left the county for two years to work in the Orange County School System (Orlando) and then returned to Hillsborough.

They had a nice retirement reception for him and as usual all school personnel were invited. I didn't go because first of all, I wasn't invited and "second of all" doesn't count because first of all supersedes it. I was told that most of the top administrators were there including School Board members. Of course, Superintendent Shelton made a complimentary speech about Smouse and his service to vocational education. I'm glad I wasn't there.

Although my case was still tied up in court, I was glad that Smouse was gone because I sensed that his power of authority in his position had been unlimited, unrestricted, unrestrained and almost omnipotent. He said he sought and received direction from his colleagues and superiors. The latter is what scared me the most. I felt so strongly that he continued to violate my due process rights time after time. I continuously look back at his handling of my due process rights in his attack on me and I view him as a "jack of all trades." In reference to my performance evaluation, Smouse was a one man show. I perceived him as the arresting officer, prosecutor, judge, jury and executioner. No one else even had to get involved for Smouse to fire me. How could one person have so much control or should I say have so much *out of control*.

I was glad that Smouse was getting out, glad for me and glad for the vocational teachers and their students. However, I was still depressed during the Christmas season since my case was taking so long. My emotions kept going down hill. I would bump into friends in the community and I always found myself in a defensive conversation to explain my situation. It got to the point where I didn't want to be seen in public. I would choose my travel wisely. I kept saying to myself "Smouse retires in fame and I'm fired in shame." That is how everyone must have viewed it. Those were the facts. It was eating away at me every day. Happy Holidays!

It is intriguing to note that Cammaratta told me that Smouse, coincidentally, first announced his intentions to retire the week following my public registration as a candidate for the School Board election in July, 1988. Cammaratta said Smouse announced his upcoming December retirement in a staff meeting. We thought it was unexpected, even unusual, for an assistant superintendent to announce six months ahead of the time he was going to step down. Why announce in the middle of the summer when the regular school session is out? Later, we speculated about whether his retirement announcement had anything to do with the news media avoiding the details of my story now that I was a "public figure" running for elected office. Was someone protecting Smouse's image? The Superintendent's? The School Board's? Hmmm....

Immediately after Smouse's retirement, he took a position as Executive Director with NCLA, the National Council of Local Administrators of Vocational, Technical and Practical Arts Education. I believe it is a position that allows him to work out of his home.

One last point to make in this chapter. During my last month of employment in June, I was scheduled to participate with my teachers and their students at the national competition as I had done for the last two years. I had worked closely all year with these teachers and students in preparation for this year-end competition. I had already attended officer training sessions, and regional and state competition with them. Plus, when they received a Proclamation from the Governor, in the presence of the Commissioner of Education in Tallahassee, I was there supporting them. I even helped one student review the speech that she gave to the Governor. We were a close-knit group by the end of the year.

All of the teachers and even some students commented about how nice it was for them that a supervisor cared enough to work so closely with them in this competition. Hardly any other supervisor in the state was as active as I was in these student activities. It was most important for me to have this student contact because that is why I was an educator. I like kids. I care.

Of course Smouse rejected my approval to attend this national competition with our teachers and students even though money was already approved by him and I had been working toward this all year long. He said he saw no benefit to the school system if I went. And that was that. The King had spoken.

He sure appeared totally unreasonable and distant from the student's needs and support.

It was only a few days before I was scheduled to leave that Smouse said no go. And I had to inform the teachers and students that I wouldn't be attending. The flight was scheduled to leave at 6:30 a.m. on a Saturday morning. I showed up early wearing the same jacket that they all were wearing. One of our clubs, Van Buren Junior High School, had won first place overall in state competition. To celebrate, they had jackets made with their championship displayed on the back. The county clubs jointly awarded one to me because of my continued support. I wore it proudly and still do. Anyway, I told the teachers I was not going. They laughed because they knew I often joked around. Then I said it was because Smouse decided I would not go. They still didn't believe me because it was so ridiculous. They asked me why I showed up at all. I said I was here to send them off and wish them the best at nationals. It was the next best thing to going along. They still didn't believe me; plus they were so excited about winning state and going to nationals that my jokes weren't funny right now. When they boarded the plane and I didn't get on, then and only then did they believe me. I felt extremely sorry for them and for me. This wasn't fair to our students. They deserved my continued support and presence, especially during nationals. I thought Smouse had lost all rationale in reference to my position as a professional and as a person. Humiliation is one word that I do not have to look up in the dictionary. Were vocational students receiving the support they deserved under Smouse's administration?

Let me not forget the point that I was trying to make. Three weeks before Smouse retired from the school system, *he* went on a trip, on School Board time and funds, to the American Vocational Association national convention in St. Louis, Missouri. Now, how come he could see no benefit to the school system for me to go on a planned trip in my last month of employment, yet he sees no problem with himself going to a national convention three weeks before his retirement? Did the school system benefit from him going? Is there a double standard here? Did Smouse go because he had personal business to discuss with officials from the NCLA at the convention which employed him immediately after his retirement?

Maybe I spoke too soon, perhaps the school system *did* benefit when he went away for a week!

45

NO FURY

During August of 1988, when I was campaigning for a seat on the School Board, I would receive a handful of messages on my phone recorder each day. One message said "Hi Bill, this is Donna. Give me a call." The message had no phone number and I didn't recall meeting a "Donna" lately on the campaign trail even though I had met a lot of people in the last month. There was something about this voice that sounded familiar. I played the tape several times, but no recollection was sparked by the sound of the voice. I forgot about it and went on with my campaign.

Then, a few months later, after my campaign was over, I was working in the garage and the phone rang and the voice said "Hello Bill, it's Donna...Donna LaBarbera."

Donna was the wife of a good friend of mine, Larry LaBarbera. He and I were colleagues in the school system. We knew each other about eight years and we both worked in vocational education. He was the Center Coordinator at the Brewster Technical Center in Tampa and our jobs often brought us together. At the yearly state conferences in Orlando, we would often see each other at the vendor parties or out dancing at one of the local lounges. We each had boats and went fishing several times with his two boys. One year Larry and I took a one week vacation and went to Hawaii after a convention in California. Donna had stayed home.

When she called, she asked me how was I doing. Fine. She said she hadn't seen me in a long time. I asked how she was doing; she had just gotten divorced. I told her I was sorry to hear it; any divorce of a friend reminds me of my sad divorce. Then she said "Let's go out and get drunk!" Since I wasn't dating anyone, I said Okay, I'd be glad to. She said she wanted to be "friends."

Our first "date" was to take place at my condo because she thought I might feel uncomfortable at her house because I knew Larry. I was pleasantly surprised when she arrived at my door. Donna was about ten years younger than I. Slim, tall, and beautiful, she had long, straight, chestnut brown hair. She didn't wear a lot of makeup—she didn't have to—and her easy-going, almost hippy-ish demeanor was perfectly captured in her dress: tight, low-slung jeans and a simple top. She was the quintessential "earth mother." She cradled a cold six pack of Rolling Rock beer in her arms. I had bought a couple bottles of wine; I didn't know she preferred beer. She greeted me with a big hug. We talked and talked about old times at the state conferences when we would go out to dinner and dancing in a big group and everyone would have a fun time. She said the reason she called me was that she always remembered I was able to have a good time and sometimes I was the life of the party. She said she needed someone who could make her laugh and show her a good time. She talked about being thrown back in the dating world which wasn't easy.

I was flattered with her compliments. And I needed some compliments, since I was feeling down because of all the problems with the school system. I told her generally what had happened to me. We talked about the problems she was having in her insurance job. I enjoyed her company because she laughed at all of my jokes. I'm one who needs humor as a part of my life.

A few weeks later she called me again and said she wanted to talk about her car. We went out to dinner, Mexican, and then came back to my place. She got the car in the divorce but it was a lease vehicle and the lease was almost up. Reviewing her policy, I calculated it would be far better to purchase the car from the leasing company than to buy a similar car elsewhere.

She had more questions about my job and seemed sincerely concerned about me. Then, she asked questions about Cammaratta too. She said that she understood Cammaratta and I were very good "friends." This statement made me recall a similar statement made by Superintendent Shelton when he gave information to the state ethics investigator in support of Smouse. Shelton stated that Cammaratta and I had became "friends." I explained to her that we were forced to work closely together because of Smouse's actions. I explained to her that we did have a close professional working relationship and that I respected Cammaratta very much. We had a few beers and somehow, I really don't remember how, we ended up on the living room floor. I was giving her a message because she was feeling so depressed. Then, she suddenly jumped up and looked out my back sliding glass door toward the apartments across the street. I live in a second floor condo. She asked me if anyone could see us from over there. I didn't know who could be looking. I had already lived there for five years. I said I didn't think anyone could see us because I had hung some hanging plants from the porch and it was difficult to see in. Plus, there was a reclining chair in front of the sliding window. Cautiously, a gut reaction told me something just wasn't kosher here. Why was she so concerned about someone seeing us?

I became extremely cautious concerning her sexual advances. We continued to talked, this time more about me than her. She was really concerned about how I was able to live and survive without a job. Her questions about my well-being became more specific. She would ask a question about the school system; I would answer; then she would probe deeper about what the school system did: "how do you feel about that" or "what are you going to do about that?" These and other questions were not the questions I would expect from her. If I went somewhere for a weekend and she called and got no answer, she would call again and ask where I went. If I said the beach, she would ask "which beach?" I was beginning to have the feeling she wanted to be more than the "friends" we were supposed to be.

We saw each other several more times. Each time *she called me*. I didn't call her because this was all initiated by her. She would fade away for a few months and then suddenly she'd call. She said she was dating someone steady over the last several months but it didn't work out. I gave her a man's point of view of what went wrong in her relationship. Once or twice I saw some tears. Soon thereafter we got back to the specific questions about me and the progress or loss I made with the school system. I kept thinking that the information she was acquiring was information that I'm sure the school system would love to know. This information exchange included my very personal thoughts, planned legal undertakings, my mental, physical and financial status which would be useful to the school system (and attorney) in making their decisions or planning their strategy.

As time went on, I became more general in my answers to her questions to the point that I could answer them without answering them at all. I didn't respond to any of her sexual advances; I wasn't going to chance getting myself into a compromising position, figurative or literal.

After the long gaps when we didn't get together, I analyzed what possible reasons she could have to want to be so inquisitive about me. Her step-father was Dick Roland who was the Director of Vocational Student Services for Hillsborough County Schools. His boss was Ralph Smouse. Roland's office was two doors from Smouse's office in the downtown School Administrative Center. Roland had once received a copy of a derogatory memo about me from his subordinate, Steve Cannella. When I asked Roland for a copy, he said he was sorry, but he couldn't find it. I didn't think he was being truthful. Could her step-father's position in the school system have any influence on the need to gather information about me? I didn't know.

I thought some more and remembered that, about four years ago, Donna interviewed for an Occupational Specialist position with the school system. She didn't pass the screening. She had worked with a local insurance company, then transferred to a large industrial parts company. If she had received the Occupational Specialists position, which is in the guidance department, she would be on the same pay scale as teachers. I contemplated if she was considering seeking an Occupational Specialist position again. I'm sure this would be a significant raise in salary and benefits for her, most meaningful now that she was single.

Back in 1989, she called and wanted me to fix some things around her house like the dishwasher and the lawn water pump. I could foresee this wasn't a good thing to get involved with at her house. I told her what work needed to be done, gave an estimate of how much it would cost and who she should call. I kept my distance.

In May of 1990, she called and we talked for a while on the phone. She asked me a question about an action the Board was going to take, only I didn't know about it yet. Specifically, she wanted to know if I was going to file suit against the Board at the end of this school year. Was it just coincidental she asked about that issue or did she know more than I did? She did seem to be getting rather assertive. She must have taken one of those courses.

Again, on June 30, 1990, I had been out sick for seven days and she called. She asked if I was feeling alright and how things were going. Did she know I was sick before she called or was this coincidental too?

She called about six times in the fall and I decided not to return any of her calls. When she would leave a message, she always used a very sexy voice and told me to call her at home or work. I kept our relationship as "friends." She never spoke about making a serious commitment.

I just thought of another possible reason why Donna might want to know so much detail about me. She had told me about her unexpected divorce filed by Larry. She told me that apparently Larry had a girlfriend before his divorce was final, because he got married shortly thereafter. Soon, the new couple bought a house and was doing a major remodeling job, while Donna got to live in her present house. I detected a bit of jealousy there. Her two boys would spend every other weekend with Larry. Donna would tell me the stories the boys would bring back home to her. There definitely was jealousy in the "who got what" divorce syndrome.

NO FURY

The girl that Larry married probably weighed about 30 pounds more than Donna, and all the excess heft rested above the waist and in front. Donna kind of made a point about this. Larry's new wife also became an Occupational Specialist at one of the junior high schools. More jealousy? By the way, Larry's new wife was a divorced daughter of Dr. Cammaratta. I now saw the connection as to why she asked so much about Cammaratta. It made me wonder if she had ill feelings towards Cammaratta and his family because his daughter married her ex-husband? Then, I wondered why she originally sought me out and meddled so much in my personal and professional affairs. Was she a friend like she said or a foe? Could, some how, personal information about me and my rivaling plans with the School Board have any impact on Cammaratta and his position with the school system? Could it have impact in my legal standing with my suit against the Board? Who knows? Are the parts of this puzzle too small to see the whole picture?

Nonetheless, there is nothing like a women scorned...something, something,...how does that saying go?

46

HEARING NUMBER TWO:
MOTION TO DISMISS

My second hearing was held on July 18, 1988, in the chambers of the Honorable Vernon W. Evans, Jr., in the Hillsborough County Courthouse in Tampa. My attorney, Bob McKee, was ill that day, so his law partner, Mark Kelly, was my counsel. I knew that he had been kept abreast of all my legal matters, so my perception of him was very positive. This time School Board attorney W. Crosby Few presented the Board's Motion. I was the only other witness attending this time. McKee had arranged for a court reporter; her name was Marie D. Elliot.

Attorney Few started the proceedings with a Motion To Dismiss the Writ of Mandamus; in other words, he wanted to drop the whole thing.

To quickly review, I was a teacher in Hillsborough County and then was promoted out of the classroom into the position of county coordinator. Three years later, I received tenure as a coordinator. I left Hillsborough County and went to work in Pasco County, in Florida. I then returned to Hillsborough in the position as a supervisor. Three years later I was fired. The Board claimed I did not have tenure; I claimed I did. Hence, the legal interpretation of the Hillsborough Schools Tenure Law was up to the court.

Board attorney Few argued that when I was hired by the school system, I was "promoted" to the higher position of supervisor because I had left Hillsborough County as a tenured coordinator two years earlier. Therefore, to again be eligible for tenure or to be tenured, I must serve three years of probationary employment according to the tenure law.

Kelly argued, on my behalf, that I was a "rehire" and could not be "promoted" since I was not presently working for the Hillsborough County school system. Kelly gave an example of a teacher who already earned tenure and was promoted to a supervisor's position. The teacher would have three probationary years to prove himself in the new position. If he couldn't perform satisfactorily, he would then fall back to the original tenured position as teacher. Whereas an outside person hired as supervisor would have two probationary years to prove himself. If he could not perform, then he would be out on the street with no back-up position. Kelly said the two and three year rule was a trade-off.

After about thirty minutes of arguments, Judge Evans said he would take it under advisement.

I thought Kelly did a good job in presenting and arguing my case. The next time I saw McKee, I told him about Kelly's performance.

On the next day, July 19, 1988, Judge Evans signed the Order denying the Board's Motion To Dismiss. Copies were sent to Few, Gonzalez and McKee.

Six days later, on July 25, 1988, McKee sent a letter to Tom Gonzalez. The letter, in full, said:

> In view of Judge Evan's denial of your motion to dismiss, it appears that it would be in everyone's best interest to expedite this matter at the Circuit Court level so that we can move on to the appellate level. Since the School Board's back-pay and attorney's fee exposure increases as this thing drags on, and since, by your client's admission, Wieser's replacement would be subject to being displaced by the Court should Wieser ultimately prevail, I will entertain any suggestions you might have to help move this matter to a conclusion.

This letter helps to substantiate some of the proceedings that took place in hearing number one, when we asked for a temporary injunction to keep me on the job. More specifically, it confirms that Judge Evans ruled, and the School Board agreed, that the new supervisor should be removed from his position if I win my case. Remember, there was no transcript for that hearing.

47

HEARING NUMBER THREE:
SUMMARY JUDGEMENT

Hearing number three was held on September 20, 1988, in the chambers of the Honorable Vernon W. Evans, Jr., in the Hillsborough County Courthouse in Tampa. Again I met my attorney, Bob McKee, at his office and we drove over to the courthouse in his car.

The others in attendance included attorney Thomas M. Gonzalez, hired by the School Board and Alexander Ferrara the court reporter requested by McKee.

This hearing was set by my Motion on August 22, 1988, to request Summary Judgement. McKee had me complete another Affidavit in which I again attested that I was employed by the school system and did not agree to serve a fourth year of probation. Apparently, this document would substitute for me having to testify during the hearing, although, I told McKee I was willing to testify at any time on any issue. He said Evans might call on me since I was there, but he didn't think so. Of course I did attend all hearings, but never was called to speak.

Since we filed the Motion, McKee started off the proceedings. He said we were here on the Plaintiff's Motion for a Summary Judgement. He summarized issues that had previously been mentioned and then said that if the Board wanted to terminate my employment, it must afford me all procedural and substantive rights of the Tenure Act, and not terminate me (or, in the Board's double-speak, non-renew my contract) as it had done in 1988.

Attorney Gonzalez argued that McKee's point didn't fulfill the *intent* of the law, and then continued to say that he didn't think I was entitled to anything. He said I was offered a job, with probation, and a guarantee of employment throughout the year. He then said Wieser "didn't lose out of any money on account of any act by anyone other than himself. So, we don't think there is any remedy that is available to him."

Just then, McKee asked to respond briefly and said "I think the Court is obligated to give this statute its principal meaning." He spoke about the "trade off" of the two and three year probationary period that his law partner, Mark Kelly, spoke about at the last hearing.

Right after McKee gave that argument, Judge Evans said "I'll grant the Plaintiff's Motion." These were words of relief to me. However, I remained motionless. We weren't finished yet.

Another battle began on the topic of back-pay. Gonzalez seemed bitter that he had just lost the major issue, and like a cornered animal came out fighting against back-pay. He argued that, since I was offered a job (regardless of the probation that came with it), I could have worked and earned all my salary and therefore I didn't have a right to back-pay. Somehow, I think some school officials were upset that I had been a candidate for the School Board and now I was going to collect back-pay for that time. I felt that running for School Board was simply another attempt—albeit futile—to find employment.

As I sat there, I couldn't help to feel the emotions that were taunting me. I win reinstatement and then a big fight starts over my back-pay. It was hard to separate the two. Nonetheless, Gonzalez was fighting so hard against it. I imagined I could hear in his voice each one of the School Board members talking against me, even those that I had helped in their recent elections. Why weren't they there in court to go through these emotional upsets like I had to. It was McKee's turn. He said that my back-pay was "part and parcel" to this statute concerning lost wages. McKee went further and said that I was not just suing for reinstatement, but also for what I should have been paid had I not been unlawfully discharged. Gonzalez, arguing that I had to mitigate my damages, said again that he thought I "had an obligation to go out and find work elsewhere."

Then Judge Evans ruled that I was entitled to back-pay. The amount would be worked out between McKee and Gonzalez. If they couldn't work it out, then we would have an evidentiary hearing on the issue of mitigation.

As McKee and I drove back, I asked him how things proceeded from here. He said that Gonzalez talked to him in the hall after the hearing and Gonzalez said he would write up the Final Summary Judgement and then pass it by McKee before it went to the Judge to sign. McKee said that was alright with him. I personally didn't like that approach because I didn't like Gonzalez's attitude; plus he had just lost a case.

Further, Gonzalez asked McKee if I was considered an employee of the School Board. McKee responded, according to Judge Evans' ruling, yes. Then Gonzalez continued by saying that if it was true, if I was legally re-employed, that I would be fired under the procedures set forth in the Tenure Act. I was shocked, but I knew it was unofficial chit-chat outside of the courtroom. McKee comforted me by reminding me that this talk came from an attorney who just lost a big case. I calmed down a bit, but I knew I just had a peek at the strategy they had planned against me if I won. The words that came to my mind were vindictive, viscous, unethical, unprofessional, immoral, the list goes on and on. I didn't feel good about the things to come.

The Final Summary Judgement was finished by Gonzalez and ready for our review. I read it and said to McKee that it looked good to me. And it was good to see it in writing, specifically, the statement "Therefore, the Court hereby enters Final Judgement in favor of the Plaintiff, orders him reinstated to the position of Supervisor of Industrial Arts and Industrial Education until such time as he is removed for cause as defined in the Tenure Law and in accordance with the procedures set forth therein...." I'd get back-pay and attorney's fees. Judge Evans signed the Order on October 14, 1988.

Being a neophyte to the legal system, I was a bit disappointed that this suit took four months rather than the two estimated by McKee. I couldn't remember the last time I was out of work or school for such a long time. Little did I know this delay was going to be just a drop in the bucket.

48

TWO DOWN, A PYRRHIC VICTORY ?

Doctor Raymond O. Shelton was hired as the Superintendent of Schools of Hillsborough County in the summer of 1967 and resigned on June 30, 1989 making his 22-year tenure a record for the longest term in the nation for a superintendent of schools in a large school system.

Several newspaper articles will give us an overall look at his later years with the school system.

On October 13, 1988, *The Tampa Tribune* published an editorial about Shelton's recently announced retirement. The following is an excerpt:

> The announcement was welcomed by many segments of the community, not because he served this county poorly but because his contributions to the school system have waned in the recent years.
>
> Shelton accomplished what he was hired to do: overhaul a school system plagued by double sessions, poor student performance, and the indictment of the previous superintendent on charges of embezzling school property.
>
> To Shelton's immense credit, double sessions are a thing of the past. Hillsborough students now score at or above the national norm on standardized tests rather than below that norm, as they did when he arrived in 1967. And only recently—in 1986—were there any hints of scandal in the school system. That's when the textbook supervisor was convicted of embezzling $875,000 from the schools. A state audit concluded the school system's laxness in keeping tabs on purchases contributed to the problem.
>
> Shelton also steered Hillsborough public schools through two very tough crises—the teachers' strike of 1968 and school desegregation in the early 1970's. He helped write a state education-funding formula that was more equitable to poorer counties. He established a strong summer-school program.

And he strived to provide good vocational and technical programs for students not bound for college....

Even in 1984, when he made what many board members considered his greatest mistake, Shelton survived unscathed. He proposed 284 teacher cuts in the middle of the school year and then, after the board voted on the issue in front of an angry crowd of parents, later revealed that the budget could still be balanced without those cuts. Several board members were infuriated, but not long afterward he was awarded a new three-year contract.

The story is different in 1988. Shelton's support has eroded—most particularly among teachers, school employees and parents, but also among some school board members, the community at large and a growing number of influential people around the state.

The 1986 textbook scandal, budget problems of the last two years, and Shelton's escalating arrogance turned the tide. Teachers en masse called for his resignation last year. Voters this year elected new board members who seem more willing to demand changes from Shelton. And numerous lawmakers and school leaders around the state are saying his public comments may be doing education more harm than good....

Back on September 14, 1987, *The Tampa Tribune* had published an editorial entitled "Why Is Hillsborough Neglecting Its Teachers?" The following excerpts summarize the point of the editorial comment.

First of all, Hillsborough County teachers continue to lose ground to teachers in neighboring counties.

Hillsborough's pay scale has lagged behind Pinellas' for years. But *every* nearby county offered a higher pay raise than Hillsborough this year. And with those raises, starting salaries in Hernando, Polk, Highlands and Manatee counties would be larger than in Hillsborough. So too would pay at the top of the scale in most of those counties. Hillsborough would no longer have an edge over any nearby county in beginning teacher pay—an important tool for attracting the best college graduates....

The School Board must step into this quagmire and sort out the facts—specifically, why Hillsborough is slipping in teacher pay while others counties, even "poorer" ones by Shelton's standards, are moving ahead.

Without competitive salaries, Hillsborough schools won't attract the best teachers. And without that, children here won't receive the quality of education that we think Hillsborough parents want, deserve—and should demand.

On January 4, 1988, staff writer Lindsey Peterson, of *The Tampa Tribune,* encapsulated Shelton's experiences over the last twenty years. Shelton had just

TWO DOWN, A PYRRHIC VICTORY?

been elected as president of the American Association of School Administrators. The article was titled "Shelton Still Enigma After Two Decades" and continued on an inside page with the title "Some say Shelton lost control of well-oiled machine he made." The following selections are meaningful:

> It was a year of accolades and acrimony for Hillsborough County Superintendent Raymond Shelton.
> ...To his supporters, he's caring, intelligent, precise, even humorous. To his adversaries, he's aloof, unbending, and out of touch.
>
> He's known for his direct, unequivocal way of expressing himself. But, in the words of one school employee, he's an enigma—a cool-tempered man who has outraged hundreds of employees.
>
> The only statement about Shelton that even he wouldn't dispute comes from former Hillsborough NAACP head Bob Gilder: "He's not God; he's a man."
>
> ...But critics say the school system has grown beyond Shelton's control and money problems have diverted his attention from the instructional program.
>
> ..."He's always been known as an outspoken superintendent," said state Rep. Carl Carpenter, D-Plant City, who was on the School Board when Shelton was hired. "Most of the time he said whatever he wanted. Sometimes it was effective, sometimes it was ineffective."
>
> Co-workers say he's not a back-slapper or a hand-shaker and that he's never cared much about his public image. But he's skilled at working with his own board.
>
> "He's very astute and very low-key," said administrative assistant Bob Queirolo.
>
> Shelton rarely has problems persuading the board to see things his way, he said.
>
> He's serenely self-confident, Queirolo said.
>
> "He knows what's important and what's not. And he has an amazing sense of timing."
>
> "They'll be going along, he'll bring up something and the next thing you know, it's passed."

He also arrives at meetings loaded with information.

"He knows everything," Queirolo said.

Sometimes too much, said Guilder, ex-head of the National Association for the Advancement of Colored People, who attended School Board meetings to keep up with busing decisions.

"There were times I felt that, for the most part, he overpowered the board," Guilder said, "not with brute strength, but with knowledge.... He's a man that would kill a mosquito with a tank."

But not everyone always was persuaded.

State Sen. Pat Frank, D-Tampa, said she frequently collided with Shelton when she was on the School Board, from 1972 to 1976.

"He didn't care for the fact that I didn't necessarily accept the things he said without questioning it," Frank said. "He treated me like a little old lady in tennis shoes. His attitude was: 'Would you please be quiet.'"

..."He's loyal to his administrators, and he expects the same loyalty in return," Frank said.

...Shelton speaks of his critics with the casual manner of someone lifting lint from his sleeve. But the discord gets to him, Assistant Superintendent Sickles said.

Publicly he was unflappable when a teachers union vote showed that 3,000 of 6,800 members wanted to give him the boot. He announced that he would change nothing about the way he did his job. Nearly all the School Board members also pledged their support for Shelton, whose contract expires in June.

But privately, the union vote pained Shelton, Sickles said.

"It hurt him because he and his wife and his family know how much effort he's put into his job," Sickles said.

The challenge was especially troubling to Shelton because he deplores controversy, Sickles said. He believes it hurts the system.

That attitude bothered Frank.

"I think sometimes problems weren't aired as openly as they should have been," she said. "There needs to be a feeling that if you air problems you aren't going to be condemned for revealing the problem....They just didn't surface."

Something else that observers say has angered school employees is a belief that some administrators were promoted more for their loyalty than their competency.

...Employees speak privately of a "good ol' boy network" operated by trusted men who don't have a lot of accountability.

... Rumblings began soon after the start of salary negotiations last summer when Shelton told negotiators that there was little money for raises.

The board finally gave the teachers a 5 percent increase, but it was followed by recommendations for wide-ranging budget cuts. It was these cuts that prompted the call for Shelton's resignation.

Meanwhile, Shelton and the School Board insisted Hillsborough's problems were in Tallahassee....

I look back at Shelton's role as superintendent and question why he made the decisions he did concerning the AASA. In early 1988, he was installed in the prestigious position of president of the American Association of School Administrators (AASA). With 17,000 dues-paying members, this is *the* national association to join if you are a school administrator. Why did Shelton decide to put half his time and energy into this association? Why didn't he invest all his needed efforts back at home with the problems with budget, teacher morale, et cetera? Was it self-serving to accept the presidency as a crowning event to his forty-one years in education, no matter the cost to students and others in Hillsborough County?

Did he view my case involving Smouse and himself as an embarrassing and threatening situation that he just didn't want to happen at that time? Was my case going to rain on his parade? Were Smouse's actions concerning me an embarrassment to Shelton, and to save face, I would be fired to make it look as if Smouse and Shelton were right? My friends have asked me some of these same questions. I couldn't answer their questions for sure, but their inquisition made me ponder the facts a lot...every day and every night, over and over again, over and over again. Why me?

To fulfill the responsibilities as president of the AASA, the superintendent was to spend half of his time on the road at meetings and speaking engagements. Consequently, in March of 1988, the superintendent proposed an interim administrative reorganization to the board. He suggested that instead of adding staff in his absence, Dr. Walter Sickles and Mr. Jim Randall be promoted to the positions of Deputy Superintendent for Instruction and Administration, respectively. The AASA had agreed to compensate the board for half of Shelton's salary, and, therefore, that money would be used, in part, for these two men's raises. In Shelton's absences, Sickles and Randall would both be in charge in the general administration of the system and would alternate at board meetings. You may remember their roles in my Level II grievance hearing.

I predicted that, when Shelton returned, Sickles and Randall wouldn't be demoted back to their previous positions; nor would their salaries be reduced.

Pete Davidsen, General Director - Area III, was promoted into Randall's vacant position of Assistant Superintendent for Administration & Operations. You may remember he was the one that I was told made phone calls to principals which may have discouraged them from attending my Level II grievance hearing.

Due to these promotions, another opening occurred and David Binnie was promoted to the position of Assistant Superintendent of Personnel. Binnie was one of three on the Level II grievance review panel.

I still have mixed emotions about the superintendent leaving for half of his time and insuring the promotion of Sickles and Randall. I still don't approve of how Randall and Sickles acted during my grievance procedures. I think it would have been better if the superintendent retired and then took on national association responsibilities on his own time.

Moving up to the School Board meeting of October 11, 1988, it was not a routine meeting; it was standing-room-only because the board would address the issue of pay raises and benefit cuts for clerical workers and teacher aides. Outside with the overflow crowd, pickets in front of the administration building had drawn TV coverage. Many expected the superintendent to make his retirement announcement. After several hours of presentations by employees, the board approved a salary package that required them to spend several million dollars more than they had budgeted. Business as usual? Late that evening Shelton did announce his resignation effective in June of 1989.

A few week before Shelton announced his retirement, the School Board attorney must have informed him of the final summary judgement decision by circuit judge Vernon W. Evans, Jr. The court had ruled in my favor, and I was to be reinstated. I'm sure this information was immediately given to Shelton and the board. I would love to say that this decision was the "straw that broke the camel's back" and led to the timing of Shelton's announcement, but I don't know that it was.

In June, 1989, a reception was held for retiring Superintendent Shelton at a local first-class hotel. Over 2,000 people attended. Somehow, I had received an invitation to attend. I believe the occasion fee was $25.00. I decided not to attend, mainly because of my lack of respect for the man, not the position. Also, I doubted anyone would want to be seen talking to me if I made an appearance since my litigation was still pending against Shelton and the board. It would have been awkward for both of us. However, deep down it did hurt me that I had apprehension about being seen with my colleagues.

A newspaper report of the event indicated that several proclamations on behalf of the school system and the community were made. Shelton and his wife received his-and-her golf bags to go along with a ten-day golf trip to Hawaii.

The county School Administrative Center built during Shelton's tenure would now carry the Superintendent's name.

The only thing the school system named after me was an investigative security file. Again, as with Smouse's retirement, my family, my friends, and I had the feeling: another administrator retires in fame and I remain fired in shame. The facts are the facts. It hurts me that my name carries this connotation.

The school board's search for a new superintendent had begun when Shelton announced his intentions in October, 1988. In December, the board hired an executive search firm to comb the country for qualified candidates. The board's guidelines for the committee, which was to to search, to screen, and interview candidates, required that the number of qualified be reduced to a group of about six.

To be considered qualified, each candidate must possess a doctoral degree, at least ten years' experience as classroom teacher and principal, and experience in financial management, long-range planning, and community involvement. The search was not to exclude any local administrators who were interested. The field would be narrowed down to six candidates in April, and a final choice made by May 15, 1989, to allow for some overlap time with Superintendent Shelton who would retire on June 30, 1989.

Upon announcing his plans to retire, Superintendent Shelton was quoted in a *Tribune* article: "the good has far outweighed the bad...." This may be true, but during the last several years of his administration, I believe, the bad outweighed the good, especially in my case.

A pyrrhic victory is a victory gained at too great a cost. I still can't believe that the superintendent denied my witnesses access to my grievance hearing. My case with Smouse might well have been resolved then and all this waste of time and taxpayers' money could have been avoided. The cost to my reputation was too, too high.

49

WHAT "RIGHT TO WORK"

It was the fall of 1988, and Smouse had announced that he was planning to retire at the end of the year. His upcoming vacancy was advertised for several weeks in the Administrative Bulletin of Hillsborough County Schools. I also believe there was additional advertising on the national scene.

It had been my desire for many years to continue my professional growth by advancing within the school system. I knew I was qualified for Smouse's position of Assistant Superintendent and I felt that I had good experiences inside and outside of Hillsborough County Schools. I was further encouraged because both Smouse and Shelton were retiring and I could possibly start anew.

On October 13, I submitted my application for Assistant Superintendent for Vocational, Technical and Adult Education. It was the standard four-page application (which included a recent picture). I exceeded the minimum job requirements of a Master's degree because I held Education Specialist certification. It also required certification as "Director of Vocational Education or Adult Education." I had *both* of these which is unusual. The job also required experience in teaching a minimum of three years in vocational or adult education. My teaching experiences exceeded three years and were in the public school, community college and university levels of education. Moreover, many people within the school system were aware that I had excellent interviewing skills. In my opinion, on paper, I was a prime candidate. However, I was aware of the politics of the job too.

A short time after submitting the application, I met with Dr. Cammaratta for a cup of coffee at a restaurant. We talked about the fact that we both applied for Smouse's job. I had already told him that I was going to apply. He told me he was going to take an unusual approach to his application. As you remember, he was in this same position, as Assistant Superintendent, ten years earlier.

Well, surprise, surprise, on October 17, 1988, Assistant Superintendent for Personnel, Beth Shields wrote me a letter, attached to the original application that I submitted, which said the following:

> This is to inform you that your application for Assistant for Vocational, Technical and Adult Community Education cannot be accepted. You are not eligible for reemployment in the Hillsborough County School System until the conditions for which you were not renominated change. Please call if you have any questions.

I was shocked that my application was sent back to me. I took the letter to my attorney, McKee, and asked what I should do. He said to call Beth Shields and confirm what she had said in her letter. McKee thought it was unusual and a bit ridiculous that the system would react this way to my application because McKee had just recommended that I apply to be a substitute teacher to earn some money while my case was pending.

On October 20, 1988, I was able to contact Beth Shields. I asked her questions about her letter and she said it was the standard information given to all people that are not renominated. She said that I must prove that I have changed my inadequacies since not accepting a fourth year of probation. I indicated to her that the circuit court ruled in my favor and that I was to be reinstated. Then she said that to her knowledge, there is a stay on that decision and I am not employed by the school system at this time.

I got back to McKee and told him Shields confirmed her letter over the phone. When I told him that she said the court decision had a "stay," he wasn't sure what she was referring to.

So, here I am, not permitted to apply for any kind of employment with the largest employer in the county. The school system based its decision solely upon one man's decision—Smouse's. No consideration was given to the positive evaluations I received from Cammaratta on my required yearly evaluations. Plus, Cammaratta's evaluations were supported in writing by many others and Smouse's were not. This wasn't fair nor was it ethical. Where were my due process rights?

I know there probably isn't any "right to work" law. But in reference to a public institution like Hillsborough County Public Schools I must have some type of civil rights like a kind of economic equality that allows me to apply, an economic type of equality where I would have the same chance as anyone else to apply and interview for a job in which I met all the requirements. I couldn't get to first base because I wasn't even allowed to bat. In the best judgement that I can make, I believe that somehow my rights were violated. It seems to me, that to be a successful educator in today's world, you first have to be a lawyer. What a shame.

Cammaratta finally told me what his unusual approach was in reference to his application. He said he was going to talk to School Board member Sam Rampello and make him a offer he couldn't refuse. Cammaratta suggested to Rampello that he be reinstated to his original position as Assistant Superintendent in January when Smouse leaves. Cammaratta would then agree to retire six months later in June. That would leave his current position open for a person of the Board's choosing. Cammaratta's plan would give the new Superintendent the opportunity to appoint a person of his or her choosing, when Cammaratta retires, rather than having to accept one recently promoted. Cammaratta was the only one with experience in Smouse's position. Incidentally, if the Board was upset with Cammaratta because of his stand against Smouse's actions with me, this deal would be an easy way to get him out of the system soon. It was an offer hard to refuse.

I met Cammaratta for breakfast early in the morning and he told me about his interview for the job. First he said there were about five finalists that interviewed. One was from the university; another from another county and several from within the system. He said the final interviewing committee was composed of the Superintendent and five Assistant Superintendents.

He said the questioning was going along fine and then an unusual question arose. Sickles asked him the question "What about Wieser?" Cammaratta said he was shocked that my situation came up. But, he said he responded by saying, as a matter of principle, he would have done the same thing for any member of his staff. Sickles then made a few comments about Smouse and said "Smouse may have gone too far" apparently in reference to his actions against me. Don't forget, several high-level school administrators witnessed this remark. Cammaratta told me that in an earlier conversation with Sickles in his office, that Sickles said the same thing about Smouse going too far. Cammaratta considered this to be a possible signal to him that the administration was leaning towards his side since Smouse was leaving. Time would tell...and yes, time tells all.

Soon thereafter, the individual was selected for promotion. His name was Earl Lennard, Supervisor of Agriculture here in the county. Lennard was a subordinate of Cammaratta and a colleague of mine as a vocational supervisor. Both Cammaratta and I realized then that Board member Rampello did not accept Cammaratta's offer. Cammaratta and I saw Lennard's promotion as a political one because his credentials seemed to be lacking. Both our qualifications exceeded Lennard's.

Lennard was a classroom teacher promoted to supervisor and now to assistant superintendent. These were big steps, skipping over levels in between. Lennard had no experience as an administrator. As supervisor, he never hired or had the responsibility to evaluate a subordinate except his secretary. Now he was in a position where he was responsible to evaluate Cammaratta and other divisional Directors. Of the six supervisors under Cammaratta's supervision, Agriculture, Lennard's area, was the smallest program with about forty teachers in the county compared with about 125 teachers in the industrial area that I had supervised. Why promote someone to a leadership position from an area of least emphasis? Is this one reason why our educational systems in the nation are in such poor shape because of promotions like this? Do the students deserve better accountability? Perhaps there were political reasons for this promotion as Cammaratta and I thought. Cammaratta told me he heard similar comments about Lennard's selection and qualifications from within the Tampa business community and from other administrators in the school system.

Shortly after this denial of my application, I had the opportunity to visit the Oldest Wooden School House in the U.S.A. in St. Augustine, Florida. I had never seen it before, so I took the short tour. It was built over 200 years ago out of red cedar and cypress and put together with wooden pegs and handmade nails. The schoolmaster and his wife lived upstairs. Antiques provided the decor. I had extremely mixed emotions about the education depicted by this display and the vastly different education that I had experienced over the last several years. At the end of the tour, complementary diplomas from the U. S. Department of Interior are given to all which read, in part, "...as one vitally interested in promoting the Education and Culture of our youth, has completed, in a most satisfactory manner, the regular conducted tour through The Oldest Wooden School House in the United States...." I felt proud.

The best times I ever had in my work life were in education and the worst times I ever had were in education, too. So, life goes on.

50

UNAPPEALING APPEAL

What a surprise to say the least!

I hate it when this happens.

The School Board filed a Notice of Appeal on November 1, 1988, of the Order given by Judge Evans in the Circuit Court. It reminded me of trying to get cash from a teller machine, knowing you have credit, but the machine refuses your request and says the computer is down. It's frustrating to know the money is there, but you can't use it.

My first impression was that the Board was a sore loser and that it was going to take a second chance to see if it could win. So what did the Board and Sickles care; it wasn't their money they were putting on the line; it was the taxpayers'. Even if they couldn't win, I would lose simply because of the extended wait. I had a feeling that somehow or to some degree, I would come out a loser. I hate it when things like this happen.

My second impression was that the superintendent just didn't want me back while he was still in power; did he use his influence to appeal my suit, drawing it out even longer and longer? Justice plods along slowly.

The print and electronic media remain silent to the community about my case advancing to the appellate level. WFLA Channel 8 originally told me they wanted to wait until my case went to a higher court (Chapter 37—"Going Public"). Did Channel 8 mean the Supreme Court? The community has a right to know.

From the filing on November 1, 1988 until January 10, 1989, nothing happened. I knew this was going to take awhile. Then on January 11, 1989, school board attorney W. Crosby Few filed a Motion for Extension of Time to file the Brief of Appellant. Attorney McKee did not object. The heading on the motion now reads Raymond O. Shelton and the School Board v. William F. Wieser. It used to be the other way around.

Two weeks later, on January 24, 1989, the brief was delivered. Now I know why it took so long. The "brief" was 49 pages long, quoting twenty-four other cases, eight Florida Statutes and eleven other authorities. It seemed like a big snow job to me. You have heard of the "bigger is better" theory. (Basically, the main issue here was just the Tenure Law and the two year verses the three year probation question.) I wonder how much this cost the tax payers so far. It seemed like over-kill. None of this made the TV news or newspapers. Why wasn't the public informed? It was their money, after all.

The brief pointed out the Board's objections to me being awarded a continuing contract, getting back-pay and attorney's fees. The main argument was the continuing contract or tenure issue.

The brief reviewed a lot of the history in the case in the circuit court. Some of the statements were misleading and contradictory. On page three of the brief, for example, the fourth year of probation is explained as "when required by the Board of Public Instruction and agreed to in writing by the teacher." Oh contrare', according to policy, the Board can't "require" the probation; it can "offer" it. If "required," there would would be no reason for me to "agree."

Then on page five, McKee's response to Smouse's offer of an additional year of probation is quoted as follows:

> The Appellee declined the additional year of probation and demanded that the Assistant Superintendent "either recommend unfettered continued employment or recommend that he (Appellee) not be re-employed" (ROA-19) ; (ROA-57; 16).

Again this will be misleading when the Appeal Judges read it. First of all, Attorney Gonzalez said that I "demanded" continued employment. This was wrong, wrong, wrong. My letter read "Mr. Wieser would prefer that you either recommend unfettered continued employment or recommend that he not be re-employed." The words "would prefer" are a far cry from "demanded." I wouldn't want the Judges to think I was demanding anything. But, it was too late and the brief was already sent to the Court. The "demand" connotation probably congealed already.

Another deception was the omission of the sentence that followed my "demand": He forgot to include the very next sentence which said "If the latter recommendation is made, Mr. Wieser intends to avail himself of all administrative and judicial remedies." I believe the "full" and complete quotation would have given the Judges a different view-point than the "demand" that Gonzalez quoted.

On the same page, Gonzalez said that my superior, Smouse, recommended probation. Here again it is misleading, because he didn't cite that Smouse bypassed Cammaratta, my immediate superior, in making his recommendation. Also, he didn't quote the Affidavit in which Cammaratta said that if he weren't bypassed, he would have recommended that I receive Tenure. These Judges only will know what they are told in these briefs and so the papers must be accurate and true to every detail.

The Board's appeal was filled with innuendos. It was an application of legal hamburger helper. It was all baloney; there wasn't anything new to appeal. I was most upset, dismayed and appalled when I read these above-mentioned quotes in the brief. I highlighted them in yellow and reviewed all thirty seven of them with McKee.

In addition to reviewing all these items with McKee, I asked where we stood in the case. McKee said it was the end of January, and we had until February 14 to respond. McKee said we still looked good.

Since the initial brief by attorney Gonzalez was so extensive, McKee had to file our own Motion for Extension of Time to complete our response to that brief. It took a lot of research time to reference all those cases and statutes that Gonzalez quoted. It seemed like a lot of "busy" work to me. My attorney's fees were accelerating, but there was no turning back now.

Our brief was completed within the time extension and delivered on February 28, 1989. Essentially we said that the Trial Court's interpretation and application of the Hillsborough County Teacher Tenure Act was correct and should be affirmed. Plus, the Court didn't err in awarding back-pay or attorney's fees. The brief was 15 pages long and McKee felt confident in quoting only six cases.

Okay, now it was the Board's turn again. Its attorney prepared a Reply Brief on March 30, 1989. This one was 19 pages. It quoted twelve cases, one statute and seven other authorities and stressed that I was placed in a "higher position" that therefore required a three-year probation period. It said I wasn't entitled to back-pay because I didn't mitigate my damages, and I wasn't entitled to attorney's fees because of the state statute.

I highlighted eight parts, this time in pink, of this reply brief to review with McKee. My points were no surprise to him. He was on top of things already.

Everything was in; the paper work was done and it was the end of March.

Now we had to wait for our oral argument date. Hurry up and wait. Almost two months went by. I heard of no significant activity of the appeal case. This waiting was tearing me apart. My mind was on this case all day and all night. It was a part of everything I did and part of everything I thought about. My mind was full; I needed a culmination. I kept eating excessively because it made one feel good for a brief period of time. Food was my friend. Obesity wasn't. I was embarrassed with my physical appearance.

    I needed relief. Let's get on with it, I've got to get on with my life. I was eager for any progress, even if it was unappealing. And that's a sad state of mind.

51

YOUR FRIENDLY CREDIT UNION

It was November of 1988 and I had been out of work for five months. I received no job offers from all the resumés I had been sending out. I was ineligible to collect any unemployment compensation because of a School Board snafu. Originally, when I filed suit against the Board, attorney McKee estimated it would take a couple of months for this to come to a head. But, I'm finding out the court process is slow. I predicted I could stretch my finances over several long months; however, I never dreamed there might be an appeal. So I went to my cupboard and my cupboard was bare; I was broke. I needed money to exist.

I asked McKee how long he estimated it would take to complete the appeal process. He guessed it would take four to five months if there weren't any big delays. That would put it around spring time. McKee also said that generally, and he cautioned me, the appeals court usually rules in favor of the circuit court unless there is something brand new and significant that comes up. It was enough encouragement to give me a target date for my predicted reemployment. Nevertheless, I did continue to send out my resumés.

I decided to go down and see my friendly credit union. It was the Suncoast Schools Federal Credit Union, formally the Teachers Credit Union established in 1934. I applied for an $8,000 loan with my 1987 Chevy Blazer as collateral; it was paid for. It had a $22,000 sticker price when new and in its used condition had a $13,100 wholesale value.

The next day, I received a "courtesy call" from the credit union informing me that the credit committee rejected my loan request. They encouraged me to "sell my truck and apply for unemployment." I asked for, and was granted, permission to bring down some additional paper work the next day.

The following day, I brought a copy of the Summary Judgement from the circuit court. I explained to one of the loan officers the ruling meant that I would receive my back-pay and be reinstated by the school system. She appeared a bit taken back, probably because she hadn't seen anything like it. She said they would check into this and it might take a few days. I wondered who she was going to check with, the Superintendent? I still looked at my loan request as valid, because my collateral was worth $5,000 more, at wholesale price, than I was asking for the loan. Plus, I previously had other loans that were paid off and my home was currently mortgaged with them, so I wasn't going to just leave town.

(Three months earlier, in August of 1988, Dr. Walter Sickles joined the Suncoast Schools Federal Credit Union Supervisory Committee. The committee oversees and ensures the proper operation of the credit union. In 1990, Sickles, as committee chairman, supervised the internal audit which included verification of accounting records and tested the adherence to Credit Union policies, procedures and day-to-day operations. Shortly thereafter, an external audit by an accounting firm gave approval to the credit union's operation. "No material weaknesses were noted," according to the *Credit Union Courier*, the official publication of the Credit Union. How comforting to know that the credit union works as it should and doesn't discriminate against any of its individual members.)

Meanwhile, the denial for my loan came in the mail four days later. The reasons "checked" for the denial were: Unable to verify employment; and Unable to verify income. What about my collateral? What about my years of membership in the credit union? What about the court decision; was it meaningless? So, who was it that said go see your friendly credit union? Perhaps, I should have gone to see my local S and L?

Every good teacher has a secondary lesson plan. I borrowed money from family and my close friends. Soon thereafter, I did sell the Blazer for a loss. A dealer bought it, so you know he was going to make some money on it. When you start to cash in your assets, you just never come out ahead.

As the appeal continued to drag out, there were still no job offers. I kept getting what I call junk mail. This mail included various credit cards from banks in other states. They offered instant cash. I wanted to say no, but I sent them in. I needed the money. One had an interest rate of 21.9%. I knew it wasn't a good thing to do. I dare not tell my family about these cards. I didn't need a lecture. I wanted to be independent. I kept the faith that my case would end soon in my favor.

I was bound to be tough. I have always enjoyed visiting the flea markets. This time I was a seller not a buyer. I went through the closets in the house and dug through the garage for things to sell. I had quite a collection of antique tools which I used to decorated my vocational office. I sold most of them. It was sad, but it was my choosing. Why was my case taking so long to finish?

I knew I had dug a big hole and I hoped I would be able to get out. To feel good, I would eat a big meal and then have ice cream with all the fixings. Then more ice cream late at night. Food was my friend. My weight was up to 240 pounds and still rising. Too much.

>My weight was up, my energy was down,
>My blood pressure was up, my esteem was down,
>My attorney's fees were up, my bank account was down.
>Strike three, I'm just about out,...down and out in Tampa.

52

THE NEW SUPERINTENDENT

The search for the new Superintendent of Schools of the nation's 12th largest school district continued. It was the beginning of March of 1989 and the applications were in with a total of 67 candidates. They came from as far away as Alaska, California and Massachusetts, as well as some nearby school districts in Florida. Plus, there is one candidate from the Hillsborough County Public School System. Forty of the applicants have had experience as superintendents and 14 in top administration.

March 15, 1989, Wayne Blanton, a consultant hired by the School Board, recommended six finalists to the Board. In addition to two from Florida, there were candidates from South Carolina, Michigan, Nevada, and Oklahoma.

In early April, the list was narrowed to four finalists; two black and two white administrators. On April 11, a white finalist dropped out of the race by accepting a superintendent's position elsewhere in Florida.

And now there are three finalists who will be interviewed by the School Board. Consultants hired by the Board will visit each candidate at his home school district. In alphabetical order, the finalists were John Dobbs, Executive Director of the Urban Education Alliance, Ypsilanti, Michigan; James Pughsley, Associate Superintendent for Elementary Education, Las Vegas, Nevada; and Walter Sickles, Deputy Superintendent for Instruction, Tampa, Florida.

A staff writer for *The Tampa Tribune* reported on opinions in the community about the status of the search. The report opened with these two paragraphs:

> A nervous undercurrent runs beneath the smooth surface of the search for a superintendent of Hillsborough County schools.

Some community members and educators say they're concerned about leaders of the teacher's union and administrator's association endorsing Walter Sickles for the job before the other finalists even hit town.

Another report in the *Tribune*, two days later, expressed other community feelings. Some of these were as follows:

Some critics fear the nationwide search for a new Hillsborough County school superintendent ended before it began.

"Questions about the objectivity of the selection process of a new superintendent have become a matter of daily discussion in the community," according to a letter written to School Board Chairman Sam Rampello by Joanna Tokley, president of the Greater Tampa Urban League.

...Because the two out-of-state finalists are black, some board members say privately that race is necessarily an issue that could be raised. But they emphatically deny that any of the men will be chosen because he is white or black....

...The board began a nationwide search in January, paying the Florida School Boards Association $30,000 to find good candidates. Hillsborough is one of more than 15,000 school districts in America that appoints superintendents....

Incidentally, during this search for a new superintendent, the city was heatedly gripping with the issue of naming a street after Dr. Martin Luther King, Jr.; this issue polarized many segments of the community. Finally, in 1989, the city of Tampa renamed a street after Dr. King, Jr.

The Tampa Tribune printed a "Letter to the Editor" from Tampa resident Christopher Sjokvist. His letter concerned the selection process. In part his letter said:

Promoting people from within is a good idea as long as it is not the only method for recruiting new personnel for positions of leadership. Walter Sickles may already know the county system, but he will not be bringing in any fresh ideas or innovative strategies, nor will he have the guts to mount a major reorganization because he has too many friends in the system.

...It is a shame that the two promising out-of-state candidates will probably have wasted their time and effort applying for the top job. Raymond Shelton hand-picked his successor years ago.

On May 23, 1989, in a unanimous vote, the School Board of Hillsborough County promoted Walter L. Sickles to the position of superintendent.

An article in *The St. Petersburg Times* quotes Sickles as saying "I'm grateful to the board for this opportunity.... I'm excited about the prospect of providing leadership for one of the best school systems in the country and developing programs to permit each youngster to reach his potential."

On July 1, 1989, Walter Sickles took over the job of chief. Later that month, he outlined his goals for the system in the next few years. His goals were typical and expected. Talk is cheap now. His actions will tell the real story, especially when it comes to his treatment of me, should I be returned to the school system.

In August of 1989, during the pre-planning days before the students return, 10,000 teachers and school personnel attended a back-to-school assembly at the University of South Florida Sun Dome and received a rousing send-off from the new superintendent. An article in *The St. Petersburg Times* reported on the splendor of the gathering by dead-panning, "The only things missing were cheerleaders and pompoms." The get-together cost the school system about $8,200 in speaker's fees and rental costs, the article reported.

The newspapers pointed out that education plays a big part in the Sickles family. His wife, Jill, is a teacher and his daughter, Lisa, is an assistant principal, both are in elementary schools in Hillsborough County.

So then, the School Board spends $30,000 to search for the nation's best qualified candidates for the new superintendent and miraculously finds the best administrator right under its nose. Obviously, this search was a facade to the good-old-boy business-as-usual practice. The stage is set. I am anxious to see how long the honeymoon will last. Time will tell.

It has been a long year thus far since I was terminated. For this brief moment, I look at myself and how my life has changed. I used to wear dark socks with my suit, white shirt and tie every day to work and now I wear white socks because they go with my jeans, T-shirt and sneakers, which have become my daily attire. I used to shop at the mall, but now I cut out the newspaper ads for K Mart and Wal-Mart. I used to drive a new sporty Chevy Blazer to work and now I park an eleven-year-old Chevy station wagon at my home. I used to be a happy guy and now I'm sad and frustrated. I continue to send out my resumés each week, but one thing hasn't changed; I still haven't received any job offers.

Was all this worth it? The value of life really isn't gauged by the color of your socks or other tangible entities, is it? No man is a failure who has friends. Perhaps, I do have a wonderful life? Hmmm.

Donna continues to call and leave sexy sounding messages to contact her. I don't return her calls.

I happen to run into Jack Craparo (Attorney Number 2) in a Publix Supermarket. He and his wife, who was also his law office secretary, were grocery shopping and we said hello as we passed in the middle of the aisle; I'm not sure he recognized me at first; I looked different with my long hair and casual clothes. Jack came back to talk. He asked about my current status and I told him about the progress in my case and that I was in the middle of a long appeal. He was unusually concerned about just what happened to me. He asked quite a few questions and I answered them most completely. I had hoped that he would have offered some legal suggestions for me, but he didn't. Our conversation lasted about twenty minutes. He wished me luck and then joined his wife in another part of the market. His curiosity in my case intrigued me. I still wondered why he wouldn't file suit against the school board.

53

ATTORNEY NUMBER 3½

It's June of 1988 and it's almost high noon. I am getting ready to have a shootout with the Board in the OK coral. This is it; only one winner will come out of the District Court of Appeals.

All my eggs are in one basket with one attorney. I remember that during the Watergate scandal President Nixon had something like fifty attorneys working just for him. Well, my case isn't at the same level as his was, but the point was well taken. Don't leave anything uncovered. As I have said before, every good teacher has a secondary lesson plan. And I saw my plan as a second opinion just for my mental satisfaction. When you are so deep in a depression as I was, any mental satisfaction was a welcome thought.

I wanted an outside opinion that was sterile from the power structure in Hillsborough County. I asked an old-time colleague to recommend someone from the outside. He recommended attorney B. Edwin Johnson from Clearwater in Pinellas County. I was told he had ten or fifteen years of experience as the school board attorney, but now was in private practice. This sounded great to me because I could now hear from the management's side of view.

I explained why I came to him and who recommended him. He said right away that he was familiar with my attorney McKee because of dealings with the Pinellas School Board. He said that McKee was pretty sharp and then he asked why I wasn't satisfied with him. I explained that, on the contrary, I was satisfied with his work. I just didn't know if there was any little point or thing that may have been overlooked. I begged him to understand that my career, and future, depend totally on the outcome of the appeal court. He said he did understand.

I detailed the proceedings in my case up to this point. We talked about the Code of Ethics and the actions taken by Smouse. We also talked about the possibility of my case going to the State Supreme Court if I won the appeal and the Board wanted to push it even more.

In summary, we talked about possible future remedies to my case depending on how the Appeals Court rules. Some of the remedies we shuffled around were:

1. Bury the hatchet with Superintendent Sickles.
2. Get a new start in another school system by getting a letter from Sickles urging the new district to hire me.
3. File a new complaint against Smouse with the Educational Practices Commission or ask for reconsideration since the circuit court ruling favored me.
4. Consideration that Smouse interfered with my "right to contract."
5. Consider a liable suit against Smouse.
6. Ask for a public apology from Smouse about my job performance.

We had an interesting visit. I enjoy learning about the legal system, but not necessarily under these circumstances. I said I could foresee that I wasn't going anywhere in this system. I also thought to myself that my options in many other school systems were limited as well because of how many people around the state knew about my case. Attorney Johnson had a variety of nautical decorations around his office. As I was leaving, he looked at me and said that I must already know, since this has gone so far, that in Hillsborough County Schools "I'm dead in the water."

I thanked him, wrote out another check for legal fees, and left feeling good that McKee was on target. In addition, I had received options I could use against Smouse if I chose to pursue them. I didn't consult with Edwin Johnson again because there was no need to. I decided not to tell McKee that I sought an outside opinion because I didn't want to imply dissatisfaction with his performance because there really wasn't any. I was just scared about what could happen if we lost the case due to a little technical something. I could see my whole educational career going down the drain. So, I needed to know every thing was status quo. And apparently it was.

BEGINNING OF SCHOOL YEAR 1989–90

54

HEARING NUMBER FOUR:
THE APPEAL

The Appeal Hearing preparation dragged on so long, I was beginning to think it wasn't worth what I had to go through. On May 25, 1989, attorney McKee sent me a copy of the Notice of Oral Argument. The Hearing was set for July 31, 1989, in The Second District Court of Appeal of The State of Florida. We were scheduled as the first case in the first session, 9:30 a.m.

The Appeal Court consists of three judges who hear the arguments and then provide a written opinion shortly after the hearing. The three judges were the Honorable James E. Lehan, John M. Scheb and David F. Paterson. They reserve the right to limit the time for oral arguments.

My close friends reminded me of a matter of timing which might simply have a coincidental connection. They reminded me the Notice of Appeal was filed back on November 1, 1988, and the Appeal Hearing was finally set for this coming July 31, 1989. It took nine months for this to consummate. They asked if that was normal. I didn't know. They implied it was drawn out so it would take place one month after the Superintendent retired on June 30, 1989, so he could save face in case it made the news. I told them no, because I didn't think the District Court of Appeal could be manipulated. They said all those people live here right? I still disagreed. However, I gave their opinion this space, for what ever it's worth.

The proceedings were held in the Hillsborough County Courthouse Annex in Tampa. I believe McKee and I both drove and then parked together in a downtown public parking garage. We arrived at the Annex first. I sensed McKee had a bit of anxiety because this was a significant encounter, although he looked professional, was prepared, had his notes and had my confidence. I told him so.

THE APPEAL

We waited in the reception area and had some coffee. While we were waiting, a man walked in carrying a bunch of papers and a chart. McKee looked at me and said that's William Sizemore. Apparently, Thomas Gonzalez wasn't going to present today. I didn't know Sizemore, but Bob did. Sizemore is a six-year law partner with the firm of Thompson, Sizemore & Gonzalez. He had been with another Tampa law firm for 13 years. Another attorney joined Sizemore at his table but did not make any presentation. His name was not listed in the case transcript.

The court reporter was T.J. Shiralipour.

The Court Clerk announced that the next case was Raymond O. Shelton vs. William F. Wieser and we were under way.

Attorney Sizemore started the proceedings. He introduced himself and asked to reserve five minutes of his time for rebuttal. He started by saying they appeal the case wherein the Circuit Court found I was a tenured employee with the school system. He said the tenure law was a special law that was passed by the Legislature and called it the Hillsborough County Teachers Tenure Act. He claimed that it was the only law involved here. He said we are all together on the facts and this appeal is a pure question of interpreting that law. He summarized the facts about my employment with the county and then went into his argument of appeal. Again the issue of two years versus three years of probation came into center stage.

Later, Sizemore was pointing out that the Legislature builds in an ambiguity in the statute during construction, allowing for an interpretation of what people are entitled to tenure.

Judge Scheb commented in the following way:

> These acts are generally written by the School Board and given to the Legislators and so it's the School Board that creates these ambiguities, so maybe we shouldn't be that charitable in resolving in favor of them when you talk about how the Legislature has mixed it up.

Attorney Sizemore went on to discuss the definition of the term "teacher" as it relates to the Hillsborough County Teacher Tenure Act and my positions as coordinator, principal and supervisor. His presentation covered nineteen pages in the court transcript.

Attorney McKee started with a self introduction too. He said Mr. Sizemore was correct in stating that there was no dispute about the factual backdrop of this case. He said he "would like to take a moment and give the Court our dissertation on what we think the statute says and how it was correctly implied by the Circuit Court." He continued with "The Circuit Court had no trouble figuring out what the Tenure Act provides as it relates to Mr. Wieser and applying it in Mr. Wieser's situation."

McKee continued with statements about the two versus three year probation issue. He said it was very easy to figure out. He then said to the judges, if they would rule in the School Board's favor, some words would have to be added to that statute. He said it is unambiguous and it can be given its literal meaning as it is written now. McKee then reiterated a point by saying:

> The School Board is now asking you to do that which the Legislature chose not to do, and that is to add language to that statute changing the meaning of that statute. The statute is clear and unambiguous as far as how long Mr. Wieser had to serve a probationary period.

McKee followed by giving the same example given by his law partner, Mark Kelly, back in the Circuit Court. He explained that the "promoted" employee serves three years probation and if he doesn't perform at an acceptable level, he can fall back to a tenured position, while the "new-hired" employee serves two years probation and then is out on the street if things don't work out. McKee said the law made sense; it's clear, precise and had meaning.

The rebuttal argument by Sizemore began. He said words didn't have to be added to the law. He said logic tells us what they are talking about. He went on to give his reasons and examples. He presented no new information. He was hoping that the appeals court would interpret the tenure law differently from the way the circuit judge had.

Sizemore said I failed to mitigate my damages because I didn't accept the job offer under probation by the Board and then, only after that, the injunction was sought. The following is a copy of the last page of the transcript about mitigation.

JUDGE SCHEB: Did he have any duty to mitigate anyway except what the School Board offered him?
MR. SIZEMORE: Well, I think alternatively he—he could have mitigated by going out and being a brain surgeon or getting a job in Pasco County. But—but—
JUDGE SCHEB: A brain surgeon?
MR. SIZEMORE: I'm—I'm sorry—
JUDGE SCHEB: Is he qualified to be a brain surgeon?
MR. SIZEMORE: I'm sorry, I'm being facetious.
JUDGE SCHEB: Yes.

The proceedings were concluded. McKee and I left the courtroom right after Sizemore finished. We walked briskly down the hall toward the elevator without saying a word. As we got into the elevator, McKee looked at me and said two words: "we won." He said the written opinion should be out in three to four weeks. We would keep our fingers crossed. He said that the issue of payment of attorney's fees didn't come up. We would have to see how that goes.

I held my breath until August 23, 1989, when McKee called me with the good news. He was right! We won! The single page opinion came in from the District Court of Appeal with the word "Affirmed."

To celebrate this victory, I went down to Ybor City, a part of old Tampa, and bought a wooden box of expensive Arturo Fuente cigars. I then called Cammaratta and asked him to meet me in "the nick of time." This was a code name for one of our meeting spots. I got there first. I sat at the table where we usually sit with our backs to the wall. I had the waitress put one of the cigars on a dish and told her to serve it to Cammaratta when he came in. He ordered a cup of coffee as usual and received the unusual serving. He was surprised and said what's this? The waitress said nothing and then looked at me. Cammaratta knew right away what it meant. He smiled and gave a sigh of relief. We both lit up cigars. We asked one of our favorite waitress what she thought about it. She said it stinks. We both laughed because she didn't know what we were celebrating. We enjoyed our quiet little celebration in "Cigar City" (Tampa) as it is known.

The next time I had a conference at McKee's office, I gave him and Mark Kelly cigars to celebrate our win. My wooden cigar box was starting to make its rounds. A short time later, I had a laser-engraved and gold-inlaid walnut plaque made up of the one-page Opinion from the Appeals Court showing McKee's win. I presented the plaque to Bob McKee to show my appreciation for a job well done.

Shortly thereafter, the Professor called me at home and asked "what's up?" I told him about the decision of the Appeal Court and about the issue of attorney's fees. There was still time to wait and see about me going back to work as a supervisor in the County office. The Professor didn't have any news for me this time.

55

APPEAL APPEAL

On August 31, 1989, the School Board and Superintendent Shelton filed a Motion for Rehearing on the decision of the Second District Court of Appeal. They also filed a Response in Opposition to the payment of attorney fees in the Appellate Court.

They never seem to give up. When will this all end. It's driving me crazy, crazy because it doesn't make sense to me. I believe I was mistreated by Smouse and I made most Board members aware of it. Now two courts have ruled that I was wrongfully discharged. Why won't they accept this fact? Is there some other hidden agenda here that I can't see. If there is, does it have to do with saving face for the Superintendent and the elected Board members? If so, does it means they believe they are more important than me? And then, if this is true, what kind of people do we have providing leadership for our kids? I keep digging for answers I'm afraid I'll never have.

I wonder about public opinion. I wonder if the public would agree that all this taxpayer money should be spent by the Board if the public knew the whole story. This public money could be better spent in the classroom if some educators admitted that they were wrong in what they did? Is this a case of "denial?" I do believe that the system should take the law to its fullest extent if it is in the best interest of the system. My friends, family and I just didn't think it was in the best interest of the system, but that it was in the best interest of several individuals.

Three weeks after the July 31, Hearing, a full-page "profile" article, with a color picture, was run in the Business & Finance insert of *The Tampa Tribune*. The August 21, 1989, profile was titled "Lawyer specializes in loyalty" and it was about, guess who, William Sizemore of the law firm Thompson, Sizemore & Gonzalez. (As you may recently remember in the last chapter, he represented the Superintendent and the Board at the Appeal Hearing.) The profile said his resumé included the following:

Position: Labor lawyer and president of the Hillsborough County Bar Association.

Mission: To be recognized as one of the nation's best labor lawyers.

Outlook: The U.S. labor union movement will lose much more power in the next 10 years as long as corporate managers continue a progressive attitude toward employees.

The profile talked about one of his goals by saying the following:

...Though the 43-year-old lawyer contends he could never achieve the greatness of his father, he said he would be satisfied to be recognized as one of the best lawyers in the country.

To some, he has reached his goal. Sizemore was listed this year in a book titled *"The Best Lawyers in America...."*

Subsequently, one month later on September 20, 1989, the Second District Court of Appeal made its ruling on the Board's request for a Rehearing and non-payment of fees. My attorney, Bob McKee, called me at home and said he had good news and bad news. I told him to give me the bad news first. He said the Appeals Court denied my request for payment of attorney's fees for the appeal part of my case. That suddenly divulged that I would have to pay in excess of $11,000 out of my own pocket. I then asked for the good news. He said they denied the Board's Motion for a Rehearing. I thanked him for calling as soon as he got the information. He knew I was on the edge of my seat.

Even though in the original hearing the Board didn't argue the topic of attorney's fees, now the Board argues after the fact, in an appeal attempt, for the court to disallow the payment of my attorney's fees. And, shockingly, wins. No new information was submitted; we had no opportunity to challenge their request. Why did the Appeals Court over-rule Judge Evans on this issue? I feel it was unsubstantiated.

Sometimes, I believe that I was fighting an unknown force from the law firm of "Dewey, Cheetham, and Howe!"

The perception I had of winning in the Appeals Court and then losing the payment of attorney's fees was somewhat characteristic of a "hollow victory." On the outside I won, but on the inside it was going to hurt to pay the attorney's fees. The people who were making the decision to pursue this case weren't going to have to spend a penny from their own pockets; they were using other peoples' money—namely, the taxpayers'. Therefore, it was worth the gamble to appeal and take a chance I might be overruled. In the end, I won, but lost more than $11,000 out of my pocket in that one ruling.

One last thought, my close neighbor pondered the possible reasons the Superintendent and the Board chose to file a Motion for Rehearing. He asked me if it was just another step to draw this thing out and continue to wear me down to nothing until I would throw in the towel...and quit? I told him I didn't know what the Board's intent was. Although, based upon other previous decisions made by them, I said the "wear me down" theory could be true.

I have an obligation to myself and my profession to continue my mission in perpetuity!

Over the past several years, I have been invited to attend several monthly meetings of the Italian Community and Cultural Center, Inc., in Tampa. President Pete Leto had asked me to be the guest speaker at one of the meetings at Tony's Restaurant in the old Ybor City section of Tampa. He wanted me to speak and give a demonstration on my wood carving of birds. I was honored, but not as honored as I was two years later when I was asked to be president of the club.

My heritage was German/Hungarian, but it didn't stop me from working with the 100 club members, some of which I had known for years. Cammaratta was a member as were other school administrators and teachers. There were other very prominent members of the Italian community such as School Board member Sam Rampello and my physician, Dr. Frank Ciliberto.

Again, I thank the Italian club for this honor to serve.

56

DEGRADE CHARADE

On the night of October 4, 1989, I received a phone message from Bert Fernandez saying "I just heard from Augie,...Congratulations!" He had just found out that I had won my case in the appeals court. Bert and I had taught together at Brandon High back in 1979. Brandon was the fourth largest high school in the nation then. He's an auto mechanics teacher, now at Gaither High, where Augie Martinez was his department chairman.

That day I received thirteen blank messages on my phone recorder.

The following day, Augie called me. He had heard, two days before, that I was coming back to teach at Gaither in the wood shop because there weren't any supervisor positions open. Therefore, I was to teach at Gaither for a month or so until a supervisor's job opened. I asked who told him this. He would not say.

Then, on the same day, Cammaratta told me that Joy Henderson, his coordinator of Health Occupations, and Pete LaBruzzo, assistant director at Brewster Vocational Center, had heard from Lou Rodriguez, coordinator of evening industrial programs at Tampa Bay Vo-Tech, that I was going to be teaching at Gaither High.

A total of six people, from four different school sites, knew where I was to be placed before I or my attorney knew. How many more people knew? Was this a technique to discredit me because I had filed suit and won? Gossip within the school system travels fast! Could someone become a hero or a crook by way of gossip before he knew what was happening?

McKee told me to contact Dr. David Binnie, Assistant Superintendent for Personnel, in reference to my reemployment. He told me to be "conciliatory" when I met with Binnie. I wasn't going there to kiss his backside because he was demoting me into the classroom, but I would be a professional as I always have been. McKee said the main thing is to get me back on the job and getting a paycheck. I could go back under protest and then conclude it later after he had documented my activities. I called and a meeting was scheduled for 4:30 PM on October 5.

The secretary called me into Dr. Binnie's office. It was just the two of us. He handed me a letter and told me to read it. The letter was dated September 29, 1989, one week earlier. It was addressed to me from Binnie, with carbon copies to nine people. I get the idea the copies were sent before I received the letter. It began:

> I was informed this morning by Mr. Thomas Gonzalez, the School Board's Labor Attorney, that the district is to proceed with reemploying you as an instructional supervisor. Be advised that you will be reemployed as of Tuesday, October 3, 1989. Superintendent Walter L. Sickles has decided that your assignment will be that of an instructor. Consequently, as of October 3, 1989, you will be assigned to teach in a vocational position at Gaither High School. The Gaither position is a ten-month position. At some point during this year, therefore, we anticipate administratively transferring you to a twelve-month classroom instructional position once an appropriate position becomes vacant. Although your assignment is that of a classroom teacher, you will be paid as a supervisor.

Note the use of the word "consequently." Binnie noted at the bottom of the letter, in pen, that the letter was presented to me on October 5.

Needless to say, I was in "educational shock" again. I tried to control my breathing and heart beat. I put my arms at my side and wiggled my fingers to try and relax. I don't think he saw what I was doing; he was behind his big desk.

When I asked whose decision this was, he said it was the Superintendent's. Binnie said "it was done because I had a bad record as a supervisor, but I had a good record as a classroom teacher."

Several thoughts shot through my mind. First, this was done as a punitive measure just to teach me and others a lesson. Second, I had a good record as a supervisor according to Cammaratta, my fellow supervisors, principals, teachers, and others. I had a "bad" record only according to Smouse. Third, why is Sickles demoting me to the classroom when they already had offered me a contract, as a supervisor, in April of 1988, under probation. If I was good enough then to be a supervisor, why not now? Fourth, I had a good record as a coordinator for five years in Hillsborough County. Why was that position skipped over? The coordinator's position is a twelve-month position right between teacher and supervisor. Fifth, this was contrary to the order given by

Judge Evans to return me to a position as Supervisor of Industrial Arts. Sixth, what had happened to my due process rights again?

I now realize why I was in "educational shock." Shelton and Smouse were gone, and the stuff was still hitting the fan. Obviously, a great deal of "vindictive residue" has been left over here. I wonder who the kingpins are now. How big is this army I'm fighting? Well, I guess it's business as usual.

I asked Binnie to what twelve-month position would I be transferred, supervisor? He said no; it would be a twelve-month teaching position, "like Seffner is."

Seffner housed the Florida H.A.R.P. program, a 24-hour residential lockup program, operated under the auspices of HRS for 30 mentally retarded delinquent boys sentenced for crimes. It had made the papers recently because of inmate trouble there. An inmate had been raped by another on the basketball court. There were allegations of staff members using drugs. Later, in 1990, a youth supervisor would be arrested and charged with having sex with two teen-age boys in his custody. Our school system had one industrial arts teacher there. Binnie's statement was a threat. Seffner was not a desirable place to teach.

I mentioned to Binnie that information had come to me that at least six people from four different school sites knew about my demotion before this letter had reached me. He said it was the original letter. The only way it could have happened was if someone had come in and rummaged through his desk papers. I thought that answer was a cop-out. I believe the administration wanted everyone to know what it did to me. The gossip and rumor channels were apparently alive and well. The administration should have kept it under better control. Moving me back to the classroom made it look as if I had done something wrong when, in actuality, they had done the wrong. The judges had ruled against them. However, I would wear the scars for everyone to see. It was ugly.

I asked Binnie what were my chances for promotion, now that I was to be placed back into the classroom. He simply said he couldn't forecast that. I think he knew damn well that I had two chances: 1) slim; and, 2) none.

I told Binnie that I needed to review this letter with my attorney, who might need to research it. I would get back to him if I accepted this offer or not. He was a bit taken aback but asked that my attorney contact him within the next three working days. He told me that Gaither's principal was waiting to fill this position.

I took the letter to McKee. He said we should take it back to the courts. I asked him if they were in contempt of court? He said yes. The term "reinstate" from Judge Evans meant to put me back in the former position. McKee advised me to call Binnie and tell him I declined the offer and a letter would follow.

Monday morning, October 9, 1989, at 8:03 a.m., I called Binnie and spoke to his secretary Sue Radloff. I gave her the message about declining the offer. She said Dr. Binnie wasn't in yet. Was he late? Naughty. Naughty. Wouldn't he get a letter in his file?

McKee had also told me that the final judgement hearing was set for December 4, 1989. However, Judge Evans was retiring soon and other judges would take over his cases. For some reason, my gut was waving a red flag.

On Sunday evening, October 8, Ted May, an automotive instructor friend of mine at Armwood high school, called me at home. He said he had heard I was going back into the classroom at supervisor's pay. "That sounds like you won, but you lost." I said right. He told me that he thought my new situation was funny and stupid. He asked which was I, a supervisor or teacher? He couldn't understand what they were trying to do to me. Neither could I. He was going to the State Industrial Teachers Annual Workshop at Maitland and wanted to know if I was going. I said no. I didn't tell him I was too embarrassed to go because everyone would talk about my demotion. I didn't want to spend the weekend defending myself. I'm already doing that here. I was separated from my colleagues by apprehension.

Cammaratta told me that assistant superintendent Earl Lennard had spoken to him after a meeting on October 9. Lennard had asked him what was going on with me. Lennard wanted to know if I was going to accept the job at Gaither or not. Cammaratta told him he didn't know. Later Cammaratta told me that Augie Martinez, department head at Gaither, had called and asked if I had accepted the job at Gaither. Augie complained at length to Cammaratta that he didn't have a permanent teacher in the shop and it was affecting him heavily. Cammaratta wasn't able to comment. When Cammaratta told me about this conversation, he said it seemed that they believed I was causing the problems at Gaither because I hadn't accepted the job yet. Furthermore, Cammaratta had received a strong indication that Superintendent Sickles and board member Rampello were angry. They were putting the pressure on him to retire.

Every year the usual procedure in closing a class is done after the eight-day enrollment count during the first week in September. Most vocational classes are electives and are not required for graduation. If, at the beginning of the school year, enrollment is below a predetermined count, classes are combined or canceled and teacher schedules are rearranged. The School Board put a freeze on hiring any industrial arts teachers in the county. As for this job at Gaither, why did the board freeze an "open" position; why didn't the principal close a vacant position? It was now the last day of October, the last day of the nine week grading period and no certified teacher was in the Gaither program. Why was this one program put on hold for so long? Why wasn't it cancelled and the students rescheduled into other elective classes? It was a disgrace to the education of kids.

I called Binnie again on October 10, saying I wanted to check that he had received my message. He asked what I meant by "decline?" I said not to accept the offer. Binnie said the judge had ruled that I was to return to a general "supervisor's" position, apparently assuming any job titled "supervisor" was acceptable whether I was actually supervising anyone or not. I said, no, Judge Evans had said to return me to a *specific* job: Supervisor of Industrial Arts and Industrial Education. The judge ordered what the board was to do. Now I had to defend his ruling against assistant superintendent Binnie.

During the evening of October 10, I returned a call to Augie Martinez. He said it was really bothering him that no permanent teacher had been put in the wood shop at Gaither. It was taking a toll on him: he had to work up lesson plans for the substitute teacher each day. The substitute teacher wasn't certified in industrial arts, and for safety reasons, no hand tools could be used or machine work be done. Those poor kids.

Augie said that his principal, Ron Allen, had called downtown to the School Administration Building to request that he either get a teacher or permission to close the class. Allen had been told to keep it open until the end of the nine week grading period, for another three weeks. Augie remarked: the Board doesn't care about the students; they just do what they want to. Ron Allen said the same thing to him, he said. Augie said they should transfer Mike Grego, who had taken my place, to Gaither at supervisor's pay and put me back into the supervisor's job.

Bob McKee called me on October 16 to tell me we had a hearing before Judge Steinberg on October 30 on the Board's contempt of court. He reviewed with me the sections in the summary judgement that said I was to be reinstated in the position as supervisor and not removed until such time that cause had been shown as defined in the tenure law. It was very clear to me.

Cammaratta called on October 16 and wanted to meet me for lunch so we could talk. He had breakfast with Sam Rampello at this board member's request at a restaurant called Pach's Place. This was a small cafe in an exclusive part of old south Tampa. Cammaratta couldn't wait to tell me what Rampello had said. My notes summarize what Cammaratta told me:

1. Smouse screwed up twice, and Shelton had to support Smouse.

2. Smouse should not have taken over the year-end evaluation of Bill Wieser—it was Camm's job.
3. About the teaching job at Gaither—is Wieser going to sue us?
4. Rampello asked Cammaratta for his help in his re-election campaign for the School Board.

Here is proof, Cammaratta said, that Smouse was wrong, Cammaratta was right, and Rampello did nothing about it. Why?

Smouse screwed up and Shelton *had* to support him? No he didn't, Shelton *chose* to support him. Why(?), to save his own face? Was I expendable to allow Shelton to reach the pinnacle of his career in the position of president of AASA? Was there some other reason he didn't want attention drawn to the school system then?

On October 19, I received a call from Denis Binder, an industrial arts teacher and Department Chairman at East Bay High. I have known him as a good friend for almost twenty years. He had just got home from a yacht club race, and recently had spoken with Earl Lennard. Denis wanted to know why I didn't put an end to all of this. I told him I was trying to. He said he just wouldn't have the patience that I had. I said I wasn't a man of patience, but a man of principles. He said Lennard had told him that if the judge put me back in my original job, he knew the Board would fire me on the spot. It will use this as a test case. Lennard had told Denis to talk to me.

Was Lennard using Denis to deliver a threat to me, in an attempt to stop me from pushing the issue? Seemingly in an effort to soften the blow, Lennard told Denis that he thought I got a rotten deal. "I like Bill. He is my friend," Lennard told Dennis. "I will try to find him another position."

I didn't put any trust in what Lennard had told Denis about being my friend. I believe it was all a matter of poppycock. I let Denis talk, and I didn't argue extensively with him. They must think I'm a real dummy to believe stuff like that. It also told me the Board is leaving no stone unturned to stop me from getting reinstated into my job. I must be very careful.

On October 20, at an Ybor City Optimist dinner meeting, Cammaratta told me Lennard had asked him to lunch during Professional Study Day. They had gone to Valencia Gardens. Lennard had told him to "go easy" on lunch when he meets with me, to take shorter lunch breaks. He told Lennard that he gets to the office very early and puts in more time than is required. It sounded to me that they were trying to cut the communication between Cammaratta and me. Who was keeping tabs on Cammaratta? This made me wonder if someone was following us? Was the school system security in action again?

Lennard said that he thought Cammaratta was upset because Lennard got the job as assistant superintendent. Cammaratta said yes. He told Lennard that he had called the Superintendent, long distance, out in Kansas or somewhere in the mid-west, and talked to him about applying for Smouse's job. And then Cammaratta had met personally with the Superintendent when he returned. Cammaratta had asked if he should apply for the job and Shelton had said yes. Cammaratta took that as a green light that it was an "open" job, meaning that no one had been secretly selected before the interviewing began.

Then Cammaratta ended his questions with a comment about the vocational funding formula (see Chapter 38—"Money Means Power"). He told Lennard that everyone, all the vocational supervisors (including Lennard), had approved using it and then Smouse had decided to change it. Lennard continued to give one-third of the total funding to the three vo-tech centers, slighting the other forty-odd secondary schools. Cammaratta asked Lennard why? Cammaratta said Lennard had no response.

When Cammaratta and Lennard left the restaurant, Cammaratta told me he pointed out to Lennard that his invitation to lunch, by the way, had taken two hours. Lennard responded by saying this was business. I guess that means that when Cammaratta meets with me, it doesn't qualify as business. It sounds discriminatory to me. We all know that administrators do take long lunches from time to time.

October 20, 1989, was a very busy day. At 11:15 a.m., I happened to pass Denis Binder on Interstate 275. He saw me and we pulled off at the exit to talk. He said he had just come from the Professional Study Day activities and he had talked to Lennard. Lennard told Denis not to mention to me what he said the other day. Denis said they were standing right in front of Superintendent Sickles at the time. Denis told me again that if the judge puts me back into my job as Supervisor of Industrial Arts, the next day I would be fired; he warned me, "the board will take this all the way and it will cost you more money than you can afford, your legal case may only have just begun."

I clearly saw these statements as continued threats.

I wasn't afraid of Lennard's threats. If I were reinstated to my original position and the Board decided to fire me based upon Smouse's documentation, I knew they would have a difficult time. Smouse's documentation of me was weak, had holes in it, and could even have been self incriminatory, showing a conspiracy between Smouse and my office staff—Hair and Lakes.

I was sure the Board would manipulate whatever was necessary to keep me from being "reinstated." Therefore, they wouldn't have to rely on Smouse's documentation in a public forum.

Then Denis wondered out loud: "Why didn't Lennard call and speak to you since he is your good friend just like he said?" I guess that Denis couldn't see the forest for the trees.

Denis said he would like to see me teaching at East Bay with him, rather than at Gaither. I said that wasn't the point. Supervising was the point. He felt I should give in. He couldn't understand how I lasted so long. We both had places to go. Our short roadside conference ended.

On the same day, October 20, I had a luncheon meeting of my own with several colleagues at JD's restaurant in Ybor City. Pete LaBruzzo, assistant director at Brewster, was there. He told me that he had spoken to School Board member Glenn Barrington at the Downtown Lion's Club luncheon that week. Glenn had said that he was upset with School Board attorney Gonzalez. Glenn felt this thing with Bill Wieser could have been over long ago. The Board isn't informed, Glenn complained. Gonzalez had got them into a big mess. I remember Pete LaBruzzo saying that Barrington had been upset with the handling of my case before this date. It wasn't a one-time comment. About a year later, Pete became President of the Downtown Lion's Club, where Barrington is a member. Congratulations to Pete.

This was interesting information to say the least. It made my wheels turn faster in trying to decipher who was pulling the strings within the school system. Apparently, the new school board members didn't have much authority. I have been told that Sam Rampello is the power on the board. If you ask me, I would say this board sounds like an example of education out of control.

Later the same day, October 20, Denis Binder came to my home after a meeting with Earl Lennard. He had decided to go and see Lennard on his own. He said Lennard had changed some of his thinking.

Lennard had originally said that if the judge put me back as supervisor, the next day the Board would fire me. Now Lennard told Denis that firing me is "one of the options," because my case has widespread implications and it may affect others on tenure in Tampa and Florida.

It makes me wonder where Lennard got this information in the first place. Now he had changed the threat into an "optional consideration." Did Lennard commit a professional blunder by stating I would be fired if I was reinstated? Was he really the best choice for the position of assistant superintendent?

When Lennard told Denis, "I could work my way back up, if I returned to the classroom," Denis laughed out loud and told Lennard it wasn't true. "You can't fool me," Denis said, "Bill would be locked in that position." Then Lennard agreed. Lennard had said again that he was my friend. And it would be okay with him if I taught at East Bay High in Denis' department.

Lennard had told Denis that the judge would make a decision in two weeks about me returning to my job. Lennard was apparently worried about what they would do with Mike Grego, who had taken my job.

Denis had a question for me about what specifically the judge had said. He asked, did the judge say return me to *my* job or *a* job. I told him precisely that I was to be reinstated to the exact same job and *it* was spelled out by the judge in the summary judgement!

Lennard's son attends East Bay High. Denis told me he has helped Lennard several times with problems he had between his son and an agriculture teacher there named Timmons who had been under Lennard's supervision when Lennard was Supervisor of Agriculture.

Let's move up to October 22, 1989. A phone call from Augie Martinez came in. He said that parents of students in the wood shop had complained to Dr. Orlan Briant, area director in charge of principals, about the substitute in the wood shop. He also told me that during Professional Study Day, some people told him that "they" were trying to make me take the job at Gaither. He said news travels fast. Then he said something eye opening. The principal at Gaither, Ron Allen, wanted to ask the School Board to lift the freeze on hiring an industrial arts teacher for his school only. The freeze could have been a tool used by the board to put the Gaither job on hold until they saw what the judge was going to do. There was some underlying significant reason why this job at Gaither looked as if it was being held for me. What was their plan? Who was calling the shots? Did the position at Gaither solve their problem of placing me back at the county office? I guess even modern morality plays aren't complete without a deus ex machina.

Augie said they just don't care about kids. He had said so before.

I don't think any of the decisions in my case were based upon what was good for the students or programs. The administration and the board must think that it's all right if the voting public isn't made aware of it. If so, this is a public charade.

As this rolls on, my financial status has come to a critical stage. I received a "past due" notice from the "friendly teacher's credit union" that my mortgage payment was not received. Well, I hadn't sent it; the cupboard was bare. The notice says "prompt payment is the basis for good credit." I needed money; I needed to settle this case. It has created a hardship for me.

57

ATTORNEY NUMBER 3³/₄

I didn't think my third attorney, Robert McKee, foresaw any validity in any criminal charges against the Board, Shelton or his administration. McKee had joined my case after many things had happened and his area of practice was labor relations. My suit only concerned the tenure law of Hillsborough County and my wrongful termination. I needed to reach for an additional remedy to prevent the Board from hassling me again, should I be returned to the job.

With all this time off, I watched a lot of TV talk shows and lately saw one particular attorney named Ellis Rubin. He had taken a wide variety of cases and was known for challenging the establishment and defending the underdog. He was from outside of Tampa, yet nearby in Miami and he had experience in criminal matters. He was controversial and called a brilliant maverick lawyer because of his unusual approach to cases. He appeared to be just what I needed.

The appointment was set for Friday the 13 of October, 1989. There was a $500.00 consultation fee for the initial meeting. I met with Ellis Rubin and his associate Hinda Klein. I gave an overview of what had happened to me in the school system and summarized the status of my court case. I explained that I came to them to examine the possibility of filing criminal charges against the Board, Shelton, Smouse and/or others. We talked about topics like conspiracy, fraud, civil rights, due process and others. They gave me some good feedback. It was difficult for them to give me specifics on any action to take because they needed more information. I had the feeling they knew what they were doing.

I asked about the possibility of writing a book about my true experiences in the school system. Hinda said the best defense in writing a book is to "tell the truth" and have the documentation to back it up. Then she asked if I had the documentation in a safe place. That second query cautioned me and scared me a bit about writing the book. My documentation was valuable and it needed protection. Her question about my documentation being in a safe place caused me to take extra precautions.

I was told Ellis Rubin doesn't take cases on a contingency basis and his consulting fee was $250 per hour. And at this point, I still didn't know for sure that I had a case to pursue, but I didn't want to drop it yet. I left the meeting after a little more than an hour. I indicated that copies of all my court action would be forthcoming for their perusal.

Later that month, I send copies of the court activities and several other documents. I indicated I would wait until the upcoming court action in December before I contacted them again.

Meanwhile, things became busy back in Tampa and McKee started talking about the possibility of filing another suit of some type. I didn't make any further contact with Rubin Ellis mainly because I knew I just couldn't afford him. But I had tried.

Ever since Hinda Klein had warned me about keeping my book documentation in a safe place, I have taken extra precautions. I believe there are a number of people who would not want this book to be printed. I just don't know where their hankering would go. So, I needed some insurance. I erased all of my written documentation on my computer hard disk drive and transferred it to a floppy disk which is easily removable. Each time I would shut down my computer, I took out the disk and hid it. If I would go away for the weekend, I would hide the disc and boxes of documentation in a safe place. If I was gone for more than a weekend, I would take my documentation over to a neighbors for safety. And then I would have to bring it all back to continue my writing. A real pain in the lower back.

My writing continued with a new regard for risk and seriousness.

58

HEARING NUMBER FIVE:
CONTEMPT OF COURT

Attorney McKee wanted to meet with me the day before the Hearing. We reviewed the details of the case. He said we were filing a "Motion to Enforce" because we believed the School Board was in contempt of Court by not putting me back into my original job as the circuit court's Summary Judgement stated. I was supposed to be made "whole" according to Judge Evans.

McKee reminded me that there was going to be a change in judges in my continuing case. Judge Evans, who ruled in my favor, was retiring soon and another judge would fill in for him because Evans would be using up his accumulated vacation time. The new circuit court Judge that would hear my case now was the Honorable Ralph Steinberg. It appeared that we were changing our horses in the middle of the stream. I sensed a slippery slope here.

I checked with McKee to be sure that we were ready for the hearing and that a court reporter was scheduled the next day, October 24, 1989. He said it was done. McKee and I showed up early for our 8:45 am hearing in the chambers of Judge Steinberg in the same courthouse where Judge Evans had his chambers in downtown Tampa. We waited in the conference room. Soon, attorney Thomas Gonzalez showed up to represent the Board with two witnesses. They were Dr. David Binnie, Assistant Superintendent for Personnel and Mrs. Marilyn Wittner, Director of Personnel, both with the school board. The three of them waited out in the hall. The five of us entered the judge's chambers and the hearing started with McKee summarizing my case and explaining our motion to enforce.

I need to point out now that the court reporter never showed up. Therefore, I'm using my own brief notes to summarize the hearing.

I can remember Gonzalez challenging some of the statements McKee made about what Judge Evans ordered a year ago in my hearing for a temporary injunction. Judge Evans had said he wouldn't give me an injunction, but he told the school board to tell the new supervisor, who takes my place, that he will have to move over if I am reinstated by the court. Gonzalez argued that Evans never addressed this topic. Gonzalez's statement was false. But how did the new Judge know if this was true or not? Gonzalez went on to argue additional items about Evans' comments during that first hearing.

You may now recall that there was no court reporter at my first hearing and therefore no transcript to document what the judge said. However, you may also recall that there were several extra witnesses there like Shelton, Sickles and Smouse. They were witnesses to what was said, but what could I do? It was their word against ours.

McKee argued that I was not placed back into a "supervisory" position, but I was placed into a classroom teaching position without any supervisory duties.

Gonzalez argued back and said I was placed back in my job as Supervisor of Industrial Arts and Industrial Education, but my duties were different. He then said that supervisors and teachers were the same job. I guess he was referring to the Tenure Law and its definition of "teacher."

McKee pointed out that, essentially, I was demoted into the classroom. Then Gonzalez quoted the Tenure Law and said it is not a demotion if the person is paid the same pay rate.

I don't remember Binnie or Wittner saying anything at all except possibly a comment about a copy of the supervisor's job description.

Judge Steinberg must have seen this argument flip-flopping back and forth, because he said there must be some case law on this topic and told the two attorneys to continue this hearing on Friday, later this week. The hearing lasted about fifteen minutes.

I met with McKee after the meeting. He seemed somewhat tormented. I asked if we could call Sickles as a witness to what Judge Evans said about putting me back into my specific job. He didn't think that was a good idea. On second thought I agreed. Then he said the best witness to call would be Judge Evans himself. We could wait until he retires and then he would just be a regular "citizen," not a member of the court, and we could call him as a witness. That would be better than a court transcript. Then attorney Kelly suggested to McKee to call me as a witness because I was at the first hearing and heard everything.

McKee said he needed a copy of a teacher's job description so he could show the judge a comparison of the two. McKee went on to say that we would meet with Steinberg on Friday and act upon his decision.

Some time later, I went down to the courthouse and checked on the court reporter. The secretary in the court reporter's office showed me the schedule book for reporters and a reporter was listed and scheduled for my hearing. For some reason the reporter didn't show up. I once tried to have a court reporter from a private agency take the transcript at one of my hearings. The private agency told me that only Betty M. Lauria, Official Court Reporter for the Circuit Court in and for Hillsborough County, or her designated Deputy was authorized to report on proceedings. This appeared to be some type of monopoly and it smelled fishy. If you don't like the service, then that's just too bad.

Looking back at this hearing now, I can see that it seems like we were trying my case all over again because there was no transcript to rely on. Was the Board's strategy now to demote me since they weren't successful in firing me?

My best witness would be Judge Evans himself.

CONTINUATION OF HEARING NUMBER FIVE

McKee called me before the hearing and gave me an update. He proclaimed that there is only one job in Hillsborough County as the Supervisor of Industrial Arts and Industrial Education. He went on to say there was only one when I was there, only one during my court case, and only one now after the rulings of the courts. However, there were presently two people working in the job as Supervisor of Industrial Arts and Industrial Education and they were Mike Grego and me.

McKee said that Judge Evans knew exactly what he was doing when he ruled he could make me whole.

He added that attorney Gonzalez was the one who drafted the Summary Judgement document for Evans to sign and the School Board had no objection to it. But, now the Board is fighting it because I have come a long way and proved them wrong. Then, McKee said they even filled my position after they knew of the contents of the Summary Judgement from Evans, knowing I may return.

The hearing was scheduled for 2:00 pm in the Chambers of Judge Steinberg. Gonzalez was there for the Board and McKee for me. Dr. Binnie was a witness. The court reporter did show up and her name was Patty Zajkowski.

Judge Steinberg began the proceedings by saying he continued this matter because he saw it would take more time than was originally scheduled. Claiming he remembered all the issues involved in my case, Judge Steinberg directed Gonzalez to present his case law, apparently to rebut facts already in evidence. Even though the judge instructed the lawyers *not* to review the issues of the case because he was familiar with them, McKee quickly summarized why we were here:

> ...As Your Honor knows, this case has been around since 1988 and was originally with Judge Evans who entered a final judgement in Mr. Wieser's favor ordering, among other things, that he be reinstated to the Supervisor of Industrial Arts and Industrial Education.
>
> The School Board has made an offer of re-employment, but in our view, it does not comply either with the letter or the spirit of the final summary judgement entered by Judge Evans.

The Judge interrupted:

> Excuse me right there. I was under the impression that the School Board had already reinstated him to the position of Supervisor of Industrial Arts, et cetera.

After responding, "No," McKee asked if Judge Steinberg had a copy of our attached motion; the Judge said no, he still didn't have the court file. McKee handed him a copy and went on to say that I was offered re-employment as an "Instructional Supervisor" with an assignment as a classroom teacher. McKee explained our view: the final summary judgement clearly and specifically directed that I be reinstated to my former position, a unique position of which there is only one in the county. McKee referred to the duties and responsibilities of the supervisory job, none of which included classroom teaching. He said, for example, the supervisor assists in curriculum planning, assists principals in planning, develops programs, prepares budgets and conducts meetings.

McKee emphasized a point by stating that if the Court permits the School Board to comply with the order of Judge Evans with some other employment, then in effect it would be "compounding the deprivation of due process that led us here today in the first place."

Finally, McKee asked the Court for consideration on the impact that this classroom assignment would have on my career. I would be expected to take several steps backwards after I had worked my way up from the classroom teacher. He went on to say the following:

> ...We think that this would have a devastating impact on his career, inasmuch as it would damage his professional reputation among his col-

leagues, and it will also impinge upon his chances for advancement, both within this school system and perhaps outside of the school system in another district.

As his replacement is gaining valuable experience in the supervisor's position, Mr. Wieser is expected to go back and languish in the classroom.

The Judge stopped McKee and asked Gonzalez if he could respond. After looking at the reinstatement letter from Binnie, the Judge said the letter indicated that my assignment would be that of a classroom teacher, but that I would be paid as a supervisor. Then the Judge stated that Judge Evans' order directed that I should be reinstated to the position of Supervisor of Industrial Arts and Industrial Education, but that Binnie's letter did not say that.

Gonzalez argued that the letter did say that. He said:

> ...he is being re-employed as an instructional supervisor, which is what he was before, the Supervisor of.... His assignment of duties is as a teacher. Even the thing that Mr. McKee is relying on now, the position description down in number 20, the School Board always retains the right to assign other duties, "perform other duties as assigned."

Gonzalez emphasized this point by adding that "there is nothing in this Tenure Act that prevents the School Board from assigning Mr. Wieser different duties than what he had before." He went on to state that there were three promises in the Tenure Act: "you will not be discharged, you will not be demoted, and you will not have your compensation reduced."

Possibly anticipating an argument, Gonzalez defined the term "demotion," concluding that it is determined by a reduction in salary.

Addressing McKee's earlier point about the uniqueness of the position of Supervisor of Industrial Arts and Industrial Education, Gonzalez said there was an innocent person in that position now who is capable and well thought of, and doing a great job." He added "that person should not be any concern to the Court."

I agree that the school board can assign additional job duties to my job description, but not in lieu of eliminating all the original duties. When Gonzalez defined the term "demotion," he didn't explain that a demotion was also defined as a transfer to a position which carries a lower salary. A classroom teaching assignment carries a lower salary than a supervisor.

Attorney Gonzalez's last statement is most misleading. That person in my position should be of the utmost concern to the Court because Judge Evans ordered that he *must* move over if the court rules in my favor so I could be made whole. And now the School Board has a problem of what to do with my replacement. Did it react too quickly in permanently filling my "vacant" position? Did the Board inform my replacement about moving over like the Judge said? Consequently, it might as well fight a law suit with me now, rather than fight one later against the person who filled my position? Was the strategy to make me the target because I was identified as the "black sheep" who would stand up for what was right and defend my performance, even if it may be contrary to the intentions of the administration?

Gonzalez went on to talk about my chances of being promoted. I ask you to take a short moment and view these statements from my perspective. Speaking for the School Board, Gonzalez said:

> In terms of his ability to be promoted, it has nothing to do, Judge, with what position that he is in. Being a classroom teacher will not stop him one bit from being promoted to a position above supervisor: although, I will be candid with you, I do not think that it is a surprise to anyone that the School Board does not believe that Mr. Wieser should be in any position higher than supervisor.

I was shocked when I heard Gonzalez say this for the record. I now have received information that tells me the School Board is totally against me progressing above the level of supervisor if I ever get back to that position. This reminds me of the time when Earl Lennard said I could work my way back up within the system and when Binnie said he could not predict my chances for a promotion in the future. (It also makes me look again at the events in Chapter 49—"What Right to Work," when I was denied the right to even apply for a position.)

McKee asked for a few moments of rebuttal and argued:

> We have established there is only one such position. It does not say reinstate to a similar position. It does not say reinstate to any supervisor's position. It does not say reinstate to a classroom teacher's position and call him a supervisor.
>
> It says reinstate to that particular position. The School Board had the opportunity if it felt that this order was too narrowly drawn, to take it up with the Second DCA. They did not, because the order is clear and unambiguous that they are stuck with what Judge Evans has said.
>
> There is a person in that job right now. He is an individual that was hired after Judge Evans told the School Board that it was going to—that the Court was going to enter judgement in favor of Mr. Wieser.
>
> The School Board went ahead and hired this person anyway, knowing full well that summary judgement would be entered.

We had a hearing on September 20, 1988 and Judge Evans said. "I am going to give summary judgement to Mr. Wieser." The order was not signed for several weeks thereafter since we had to go around about what the order would contain, but they knew full well when that man was hired that this very real possibility existed: that they would be stuck with two people.

Between the two—Mr. Wieser was denied due process, whether the School Board wants to admit it or not, because he did have tenure, and that position was taken away from him.

To this day, the School Board has never accused him of any wrong doing or given him the opportunity to respond. Here we are with the School Board trying to get in through the back door what they could not get in through Judge Evans, and that is that this man should be taken out of a job that he has interest in by virtue of having earned tenure as the Supervisor of Industrial Arts and Industrial Education.

The Court has to abide by its order.

Gonzalez, McKee and the Court exchanged *L. A. Law*–type arguments for another six pages in the court transcript. Then the Court said the following:

All right. I think that the Court has heard everything. All right. You have come here and presented this matter to me on a Motion for Contempt. You are saying that the School Board is in contempt because of what their plans are for the future and not what they've done.

I think that the most that I could do today is to order them to comply with the order entered by Judge Evans, and that is to reinstate Mr. Wieser to the position—I hate to keep repeating it—Supervisor of Industrial Arts and Industrial Education.

Now, what they do after that may bring about further contempt proceedings...

McKee said that the contempt ruling would develop another and separate law suit. The Court said he didn't think it could go any further than what he already said. The Judge offered that "what we have here is anticipatory violations of the Court's order. They did not violate it yet."

Judge Steinberg said he would not make any ruling as to the duties of the supervisor's job because Judge Evans didn't. Gonzalez asked if the Court was ruling that the Board can only have one Supervisor of Industrial Arts and Industrial Education and the Judge responded "No, I am not ruling that."

The hearing lasted thirty minutes.

I had the feeling that we were back to square one again. I disagree with the Judge's reading of "anticipatory violations." We already had the letter from

Binnie, three weeks earlier, directing that I would be placed in the classroom as a teacher. I clearly believe the Board *already* had violated Judge Evans' ruling.

Since arguments presented by both sides in this case were so critical to the interpretation of Judge Evans' ruling, I think that Judge Steinberg should have asked Judge Evans himself to rearrange his vacation schedule and hear this case so it could be finalized with the same disposition as when it started!

I had hoped that Steinberg would have ruled in the same understanding that Evans did, but he didn't even come close.

Changing judges in the middle of a case was like changing horses in the middle of the stream. The result was an inarticulate flow of information in enforcing Judge Evans' ruling.

The only hope for finding a fair remedy for both parties was in the hands of Judge Evans. He originally denied my request for an injunction, but in the residue he said he could make me whole. I won in the court, but I lost on the job. I wasn't made whole. This was wrong. I feel embarrassed for Judge Evans and the circuit court of Hillsborough County.

Supposedly, I have had my day in court, but I really didn't think the day had ended yet. My intuition tells me that in the long run, my day in court may not actually come in the form of a courtroom.

It ain't over till it's over. Right Yogi?

59

REINSTATEMENT ?

On Monday morning, October 30, 1989, I showed up for reinstatement in Binnie's office in the Personnel Department. I was told that Binnie was out of the office and that Marilyn Wittner, Director of Personnel, was in a staff meeting. Another meeting was set up for 1:30 that afternoon with Binnie. The secretary said Binnie did want to talk to me.

I returned for the 1:30 meeting and waited for an hour and twenty minutes. Still, Binnie did not return to his office and his staff couldn't tell me how long he would be. I was a bit on edge just sitting there with everyone staring at me, so I told the secretary to reschedule my appointment for the next morning.

The meeting with Binnie was brief. He gave me a Pre-Contract Binder for Teachers that gave my assignment as a Supervisor; typed in was "classroom assignment." I told him that I wanted to pass this contract by my attorney before I signed it. He said fine, but added that it needed to be signed soon. I told him that I would be back the next day after I finished the school day at Gaither High School.

I immediately took the Pre-Contract Binder to McKee. He said it was Okay, but I should sign it under protest with an attached letter stating so.

I was ready to report to Gaither High School for my first day of work. As an introduction to this chapter, let me review the philosophy of Gaither High. The 1989/90 philosophy states, in part, the following:

> We at Gaither recognize the difference in each student's abilities, talents, and needs. Identifying the student's strengths and weaknesses and guiding them into the appropriate programs is a priority. The successful total school program is one which is broad enough to meet every student's needs, structured enough to provide each student with the necessary tools to learn, and versatile enough to create an atmosphere which promotes creative self-expression and development.

The philosophy seems to stress the student's welfare. If this were actually true, then how come this program that I was assigned to wasn't closed after the eight day enrollment report because of the lack of a certified teacher. If I had been acting supervisor, I would never have allowed it to reside in limbo so long. The eighth day of the new school year marks the point of adjusting the final class enrollment to determine if there is sufficient interest to offer the course taught by a certified teacher. Why wasn't this program closed and the students guided into another "appropriate program" to meet their development needs? The school year starts toward the end of August, so there was plenty of time—two months!—to help these students and give them the appropriate and "necessary tools to learn." Was this program singled out for me and put on hold at the consequence of the 100 plus students in the six class periods? While I was supervisor, I never saw or heard of a program or the student's right to an education being postponed like this. Let me speak for the students and their parents and ask the School Board one simple question: why?!?

The Hillsborough County Faculty Handbook for 1989–90 outlines areas of supervision for high schools. The number-one position listed is the Principal and it reads:

> The principal is the administrative and supervisory head of the school. The principal is responsible for the operation of the entire school unit and is the final authority on all matters relating to school personnel, financial affairs, equipment, building and grounds. The Principal recommends the appointment of faculty and staff members, guides and supervises instructional units, office procedures, and the athletic program. The principal represents the school in professional meetings, locally and on the state and national levels. All organizations and activities are subject to the principal's approval. The principal has power to delegate authority as seen fit, but is responsible for seeing that instructions are carried out. The principal works closely with the county superintendent and the staff, and sees that policies adopted by the Board of Public Instruction are carried out within the school.

The principal of Gaither High School was Ron Allen. The school was about six years old and was called the "ivy league" school because of its location in the "upwardly mobile" section of town. Allen has been its principal since it opened.

Allen was one of the principals that wrote a letter to Dr. Cammaratta in support of his yearly evaluation of me back in April, 1987. Allen wrote about the "fine job" I was doing and said that I had "been more than willing" to give of myself and aid the school in his every request.

It will be interesting to see how he changes as the school year advances now that I have been reinstated as a "teacher" at his school.

REINSTATEMENT?

I arrived at Gaither to begin my reinstatement. To start off, Principal Allen didn't greet or welcomed me to "his" school until several days after I arrived. Then he did say Hello one morning in the teacher's lounge and shook my hand; that was it. It was short, but not sweet. I would have preferred a brief meeting in his office to show me some respect. The scenario was set. Instead, I was directed to see Augie Martinez, the Department Head of Vocational Programs, for my orientation to the school, classroom and all procedures. You should recall that, as county supervisor, I supervised Augie as one of the industrial arts teachers and now, after my "reinstatement," he supervised me. Holy demotion Batman, where is Judge Evans now? I just got zapped and I don't think I'm "whole?"

Augie took me down to the shop to meet the substitute teacher that had been there for the last two months. The sub would remain with me on my first day since it was the last day of the nine-week grading period and he was finalizing grades for report cards. The students were out of control. There was no discipline and little sign of any classroom management.

This wood shop has a school program title of Industrial Materials and Processes. For reason of convenience, I will continue to refer to the class as a "wood shop" because it is common language to other school personnel and to the community. However, when I say "wood shop," I do give this program all the respect that it deserves in its design to provide today's youth with a knowledge of industry and the materials and the processes applied to manufacture useful products. It's not just make-a-tie-rack-shop anymore.

The normal workday for a teacher includes five class periods of student contact. Under certain circumstances, teachers may teach a sixth class period which is considered an overload. Of course there is extra pay for this extra teaching.

Upon arrival at Gaither, I was assigned six class periods, an overload. During the second week I was there, I was told my schedule would be reduced by one class period. They chose to eliminate my one class of exceptional education students. The "academically slow" or low I.Q. students were my best students. They had no discipline problems, and these kids, male and female, loved to work in the shop. This was the one class I didn't want canceled. As a supervisor, I have observed other shop teachers that have said they get the biggest reward as a teacher by teaching exceptional education kids. I agree.

Instead of cancelling this class, why didn't the principal offer an overload schedule to one of the other three industrial arts teachers in the school? All three had previously taught in this same shop. I felt sorry for these academically slow students. The school's actions didn't match its philosophy for these students.

Now, I was teaching a normal load of five class periods except for one minor point. Of the five classes, there should be no more than three different courses because of the amount of preparation. I was teaching four different courses, meaning I had to do greater preparation than most other teachers, a situation which is contrary to Board policy.

The first day I started teaching the class, the students asked me if I was a "real" industrial arts teacher. I said yes and then they asked "when are we going to do real work on machines?"

During that first full day, the most obvious thing I saw was that the behavior of the students was overwhelmingly out of control. Students would blatantly break school rules right in front of me without a second thought. They had lost any sense of restraint. Because of this dangerous situation, I decided to use a new classroom management technique. There must be discipline before any learning can take place.

The technique I used was rather basic. When a student would break a rule, and I caught him doing it, I would ask him to take out a piece of paper and write down what he did. He was to sign it and include the date. Most students would follow my directions and write it down. However, some did not. Then I would stop the class and write it down myself. It turned out to be a good example for all the students as to what I expected from them. Plus, it gave me a written record to keep for each student in case an in-school parent conference became necessary.

Some students thought this technique was ridiculous; some made fun of it, while others thought I was treating them like kindergarten children. But, some saw the need for it to put control back into the classroom. The bottom line was it worked!

To give you a sense for the student behavior that confronted me, I have assembled a sample of the papers I collected shortly after I started:

I will not leave the classroom without permission.
I will not arm wrestle in class.
I will not horseplay in the shop.
Wearing my head set in class is wrong.
I will not make noise under my arm anymore.
I will not twirl my book on my finger.
I will not kick the trash can and spit in it.
I will not saw the table.
The ruler is not a sword.

I will not bang on the desk with a wrench.
I will not ignore the pledge to the flag.
I will not talk during the "moment of silence."
Cussing in class is wrong.
I will not get out of my seat after told not to.
I will not eat in class.
I will not go out the back door when told not to.
Hammering a screwdriver into the work bench is wrong.
I will not use a machine unless I ask.
I went into the teacher's desk.
I will not look in the teacher's grade book anymore.
I will not play with the glue.
Making unauthorized shop project.
I will not throw the safety glasses.
I will not talk while the teacher is talking.
I didn't mean to put the screwdriver in the machine.
I will not hammer nails into the table.
I will not throw plastic beans around.
I will not pass gas in class.
I will not play with the emergency shut-off switch.
I will not go into the project room without permission.
I will not juggle hammers.
I will not cut coins in half again.
I will not stick bubble gum in the hole in the wall.
I won't hit Mike with my Spanish II folder.

Again, this list was just a sample. So tell me, what lessons did the School Board teach these students over the last nine weeks of school?

One of the principles of vocational education is that it enhances other parts of education. Many students remain in school because of the vocational programs. Vocational education can be the catalyst to cause a student to graduate. I'm sorry, but the above classroom situation that was given to me was *not* a good example of these principles.

After my first full day back at work in the classroom, I returned to the Personnel office with the contract. One of the many clerks behind the counter in the personnel department asked if she could help me. I identified myself and said I was here to sign my contract. She looked startled and said to me "You ARE (?) going to sign the contract? I calmly and proudly said yes. She gave me a pen and said that she had to show it to Binnie. I told her to also show a letter to him which stated that I was signing this contract under protest because I was not given supervisor duties. The contract was approved by Binnie; I was given a copy and set to work the next day. The personnel clerk's reaction to my signing of the contract told me that office gossip was predicting I would quit after one day in the classroom. I can understand them thinking that for some of the administrators they work with downtown; but, obviously, they didn't know me that well. I took the clerk's startled reaction as a professional compliment. If they give you lemons, you make lemonade, right?

It is interesting to note that, during the very first week of the school year in August, this wood shop program was taught by B. H. Blankenbecler, who had retired four years earlier as the Supervisor of Industrial Arts and Industrial Education. That's right; he retired after about 38 years with the system and I took over his vacated supervisory job. Now he wanted to work full-time again. So, he was in this shop from the start of school. However, he resigned his teaching position after one week and ended up teaching wood shop part-time nights at another school in the Adult Evening Program.

One of the other vocational teachers at Gaither came to me and told me his opinion about why Blankenbecler left after only one week of classes. He said that Blankenbecler couldn't handle the kids; discipline was a big problem. The kids told me the same thing about Blankenbecler.

I now understand the reaction the clerk in the personnel department had when she asked me if I was going to sign my contract and I proudly said yes. Presumably, she heard that the past supervisor (Blankenbecler) couldn't handle the high school kids there and she expected the same out of me.

I returned to Gaither the next day. It was my first time teaching high school since I was promoted out of the classroom over ten years ago. But, let me tell you, one of the reasons I was promoted was that I was a good teacher. I knew I could take the worst program in the county and turn it around in the right direction. How many administrators do you know that could and would return to the classroom and survive in today's high school settings. If it sounds like I'm bragging a bit, then you hear me correctly. I care most sincerely about the students' interests.

The total chaos I saw in the classroom the day before continued. I had to dig down to the deepest of my classroom management skills bag to apply the concept of emergency control in these classes. First of all, the class roll given to me by the substitute had a red line through the names of students that already had withdrawn from class. With just a glance at the class periods, it was evident that about one forth of the students had already withdrawn. I had no idea of how many students transferred to another class, moved out of town or just dropped out, or were, should I say, "pushed out?" There was a possibility that 130 students could be enrolled in the five classes with an additional fifteen in the overload class which was made up of exceptional students. That would be a possible enrollment of about 145 students; yet, only about 100 remained.

According to a U.S. Department of Education report, Florida ranks highest in the nation in dropouts. Is this a coincidence? I know this was an exceptional situation, but the people that made this decision to put this class on "hold" for one forth of the school year are the same people that make *all* the other decisions in the school system.

Take a minute to look at the shop facility with me. This wood shop had thirteen pieces of stationary machinery. Of these, if safety wasn't followed, six could cause serious arm injuries, eleven could cause serious finger injuries and all could cause serious eye injuries. There are also portable power tools like routers, drills, saws and sanders that could cause harm if strict safety wasn't followed. This gives you a good picture of the concerns facing me on the first day that I took over this potentially dangerous class. It wasn't fair for me or the students to be placed into a situation like this. In spite of the odds against a successful year, I knew what I had to do. I ran a safe shop. I was cut out for this job.

The only way I could see teaching this class was to start at the beginning as though it were a new school year. I took a copy of the old shop rules and regulations and added some rules of my own. I reviewed these rules with each class and had all students sign to signify that they understood them. I also developed a five-page safety test. They had to get 100% accuracy on this exam. If they got any answers wrong, they had to correct the question and then sign this test too.

One of the first rules of classroom management I had to enforce was to require that all shop projects be approved by me on a three part Project Plan, important because it gave students organizational skills in project designing, drawing, listing materials and calculating cost. When the project was finished, it would be evaluated by the student first on a nine part Project Evaluation Plan, then evaluated by me.

The administration was well aware of the problems in the shop. The first week I was at Gaither, I visited with Assistant Principal Jeff Vardo. He was one of three assistant principals at Gaither in charge of student discipline. He asked me how things were going in the classroom. Because Gaither students took the name "Cowboys" for their nickname, I responded to Vardo by saying that "The cattle are out on the range; and I am rounding them up; and bringing them into the barn." He said that he visited the shop several times while the substitute was there, and he understood. I also told him I wrote six referrals on student discipline problems that day. I invited him to visit me in the shop anytime: announced or unannounced, stop in for ten seconds or stay for twenty minutes. He said okay. Unfortunately, he only came in when he was picking up a student to take to his office. Shortly thereafter, Augie told me that Vardo said to him that I "Hit the nail on the head" with those six discipline referrals I wrote. Vardo said these six were definitely trouble makers.

But not all students were trouble makers; I did have some good students. When they did something right, I complemented them. I made some complementary phone calls to parents too. Boy, were the parents surprised. I also gave extra credit to those students who helped out in some special way.

During the first week of school, I parked alongside Roseanne Miller, who taught graphic arts, a program I had supervised. She welcomed me and said that she was glad to see that I was at Gaither, but she was sorry for all that they had done to me. I said it wasn't over yet. Then she smiled and said "I didn't think you would just roll-over." I said that I'm teaching an overload of six periods and her response was "An overload (?) . . . on top of all this!"

Home economics teacher Becky Burgue welcomed me and said she was glad that I made the decision to come to Gaither. I told her that it was not my decision to come here; it was the Superintendent's. She was surprised and said she didn't know. When I added that I was still technically the Supervisor of Industrial Arts and Industrial Education, she commented that she couldn't understand that. It may be interesting to know that her county supervisor is Rhonda Trainor, Supervisor of Home Economics. I worked with Trainor, as she was a member of Cammaratta's staff. What is interesting is that Trainor hired Smouse's daughter to be a secretary in the home economics county office. It was common knowledge that Trainor was to help Smouse's daughter stick to a diet and lose weight because of a weight problem.

Several teachers suggested that I join the CTA (Classroom Teacher's Association) so the union could fight for my rights. I was a bit leery, but I contacted them about joining, since I did feel more like a teacher, and they said they had to check on it. When the CTA returned my call, I was told I could not join because I technically was a supervisor.

Augie came to me during the first week I was there and said that "the word" got around fast about me, disclosing that it was "sad" that my situation had happened and that I was put back at Gaither. Augie also told me that I was to work an 8 hour day. Even though I was teaching and all other teachers worked a 7 hour 35 minute day, I was a supervisor; therefore, I had to work longer. I asked him for it in writing and never got it. There were times when teachers were off and I was required to be there because the school administration said I was on a 12 month schedule even though the letter from Personnel (Binnie) said I was on a 10 month schedule. Was I fish or fouled?

An interesting thing happened during this first week of school. One of the three assistant principals for student affairs (Paul Durso) came into my second period class in the middle of a lecture to see how I was doing. My class lecture was put on hold while he asked me questions in front of the class. He said these kids needed "hands-on experience," I said I agreed, but I said they weren't ready for it yet because of safety reasons. What appalled me was the fact that he wanted to see what lesson I was teaching at the moment. I showed him the two-page list of shop rules that I was explaining to the students. He stopped me dead in my tracks and stood there reading over the twenty-one rules while the students waited. When he finished, he said to me that these were acceptable rules, but he wanted me to explain rule number 16, "No coinage allowed in the shop." I pointed out to him that the shop was about sixty feet long and that it had become a "game" to throw a coin from one side of the room to the other. By the time I heard the coin ricochet off a couple of machines, the student had time to return to a neutral posture. It was impossible to catch anyone doing this. Therefore, my rule of "coinage" prohibited any student from having coins out of his pocket while in the shop. The only time they needed money was when they were paying me for a shop project.

This situation appalled me for several reasons. First of all, I don't like an unannounced interruption in the middle of a class lesson as important as this one on class rules. Second, I don't like being professionally insulted in front of my students by being challenged and having my safety rules reviewed in front of my class. I'm sure it made me look foolish in the eyes of the students. I didn't feel that I was getting the appropriate support from the administration in solving a problem that it created. Third, it was not the Assistant Principal of

Student Affairs' job to review my curriculum. There was another assistant principal specifically for "curriculum" at the school. He was over-stepping his boundaries in a most unprofessional manner.

I speculated if Durso decided to do this on his own or if he was told to do it. Which ever it was, I considered it detrimental to the learning process. Another term for it was harassment, both for me and the students. I could tell already it was going to be a long school year.

During an in-school parent conference among a trouble-making student, his mother, Assistant Principal for Student Affairs Delaney and myself, the parent was blaming her son's problems on me and the lack of shop work during the first two months of school when the substitute was there. She asked her son, "what did you all do in class for the first nine weeks?" Her son responded, "annnnnnything we wanted." That simple statement told the whole story of why I found things like I did. I place the blame on the school administration, the Superintendent and the School Board. However, *I* have the job to correct it.

Many of these specific behavioral problems of students spawned phone calls home and/or written referrals to the assistant principal's office for student affairs. It was an unbelievable task. I even made several "home" visits. Some parents were supportive and some were not. I made an extensive and comprehensive record of these calls and visits and gave a copy to all three assistant principals in charge of student affairs. I feel these assistant principals at the school didn't put enough teeth into the referrals that I sent to them. I needed total support from the school administration due to the conditions I found. I believe they gave less than they could.

In spite of the behavior problems, I tried to make strides toward positive things. I asked for interested students to apply to be my shop assistant, one for each class, each semester. I wanted to encourage eager students to excel. Plus, this assistant would also help as an authority figure from within the student population. I didn't want it to look like it was me "against" the students. I wanted some control from within. I sent home "Congratulations" letters, complete with gold seals, about their selection as my shop assistants. I call these "refrigerator" letters, because that's where they end up.

Another positive approach open to each student was my policy of supporting their language skills class in the shop. I told them if they caught me misspelling a word, I would give them extra credit. Then, I went to the library and checked out a dictionary. There were none in the shop. When a student asked me how to spell a word, I would point to the dictionary; if he looked up the word, I would give him an extra credit check in my grade book. I was disappointed to see that only about one dozen kids took advantage of this "piece of cake" extra credit. However, I hope I made the impression that language is important, even in the shop.

The agriculture classrooms adjoined my classroom. One of the two agriculture teachers said she couldn't teach for the last couple of months because the noise coming from the wood shop was too loud. I said that I hoped that the decibels had been reduced. She said they definitely were and then said thanks.

Consider my immediate concern for the students and their predicted success for this school year. The number-one concern for any shop teacher is student safety. Classroom discipline was less than satisfactory. Much less. All the students wanted to do when they signed up for this class was to work on projects. Now, for one forth of the year they were restricted from doing this. They were climbing the walls to go to work in the shop and that is understandable. But, because of their behavior which had grown worse each week, they were in no condition to even go near a machine because of safety. That was problem number one. I'm not sure they realized this.

By the second week at Gaither, I had sent fifteen discipline referrals to the assistant principals' offices. Augie came to me and said that Paul Durso, assistant principal for student affairs, complained to him that I was sending too many referrals. The school discipline procedure states that a teacher is to call parents before writing a referral about a student. Augie told me that he explained to Durso that my class was out of control because of the last nine weeks and that I didn't need to call parents, but that I needed immediate administrative help.

Later in the week, Durso visited my class, unannounced. I was in the middle of reprimanding a student for walking around three minutes after I assigned seats. I then showed him several referrals that I was writing *that* period on a student for using the word "bullshit" and two others for giving false identification during roll call, pretending to be other students. Durso said "be careful not to back anyone into a corner." I told him I knew that and could handle it. His comment made me wonder if he could? Why didn't he do something about their misconduct right then and there? What did this incident teach the students?

Problem number two came up when the new Supervisor of Industrial Arts and Industrial Education, Mike Grego, came out to visit me and said that all of the "book work" that was done by the substitute teacher over the last two months had to be done all over again because that teacher wasn't certified in Industrial Arts.

Grego also said to call on him any time if I needed help. The help I needed was for him to have closed this class after the eight day enrollment report. Or, he could have indicated to the School Board that the longer this wood shop program was kept on hold, the more detrimental it would be to the students who were counting on the School Board for a quality education. The question is, why didn't Grego do his job as supervisor and close this class (program) after the eight day report. That would have been the help I needed from the new supervisor. Couldn't he foresee the problems that would develop such as redoing two months of book work that he just informed me about (not to mention the abuse of the students' education)? I speculated if he was influenced by some administrators downtown.

Another thing Grego told me was that he heard that I was having discipline problems and he wanted to help me with my problem. I didn't like the way he presented this situation. So, I told him, as directly as I could, that *I* was not having a discipline problem; the *students* were having discipline problems because they had no shop work to do for the last several months and the substitute teacher did not successfully apply the appropriate classroom management expected in a shop. Since Grego was rather new, I also told him that it was not his job to help me with "discipline problems" unless the principal had called him in for assistance. Discipline is first the responsibility of the teacher; if the teacher needs help, one of the three full-time Assistant Principals at Gaither responsible for student affairs is called in. All student discipline referrals are requested on a specific county form and are sent to the assistant principals at that school. This form is not sent to the county program Supervisor.

All I could picture in my mind was a rumor in the wind that I was having discipline problems at Gaither, when in fact it was the problem of the principal who let this thing get out of hand in the first place. I have already seen what rumors of disinformation can do within a large school system. By the way, who told Grego that I was having discipline problems in the first place? And did someone tell him to specifically visit with me to nail down the obvious fact that I was not the supervisor anymore, but that he was? He supervises about 150 teachers; why did he "choose" to visit me during my second week on the job? Was this a form of intimidation?

I told Grego that I could use some help with curriculum. I had come into the class in the middle of the term and there was no set curriculum available from the previous teacher, Augie Martinez. I had to schedule my daily, weekly, and monthly lesson plans on my own, in a last minute situation. Assistance in immediate curriculum from Grego never came. I was on my own like a new teacher.

Grego did not look good when he visited me. He looked worn down. I was told that, later in the year, he had an attack or something while on the job. His speech became slurred; he almost passed out. He was taken to the hospital in an emergency vehicle. I never found out exactly what happened. I wondered if it had anything to do with the stress of the job.

Problem number three came. For several years, the school board had required that uniform semester exams be given to all students in the county. Augie told me that the Assistant Principal for Curriculum, Betty Wilson, said that I would have to write my own exams for the upcoming required semester exams period for my classes because the students had missed half of the semester. I would not have the pleasure of using the standard county confidential exam that would be sent out to the schools just before exam time. For the sake of the students, I agreed, knowing that it would be additional work for me. Then, during the second semester in the spring, it was also agreed upon that I would write the year-end exam for the same reason. It too was an additional burden, of course.

I remember the nine-week substitute teacher telling me that he recommended that all the tests be done over because "the kids were not really receptive or enthusiastic." Obviously, the complete county-required confidential exams as they existed were useless.

On top of all this extra work I had to do, I had to concern myself with security in the shop. I often sent notes to Augie telling him about the misuse of the wood shop by outsiders. I told him of the times I came into class in the morning and saw sawdust or wood chips where someone had worked in the shop the evening before, when there was no night class. Numerous times, custodians would bring tools back to me which they borrowed when I was out of the shop. One morning I found a "push stick" broken. The push stick is used on the table saw, the most dangerous machine in the shop. This broken stick told me that someone was using the equipment without authorization and was doing it unsafely.

Once, a $3/8$ inch electric hand drill was missing for a week. After I reported it missing, it happened to show up in the tool cabinet. I guessed that someone had a project at home to do. Often, I found the padlock on the tool cabinet open, telling me more about tool misuse. Nothing that I'm aware of was done to stop it. I knew of at least a dozen people that had keys, and access—both day and night—to the shop: custodians, teachers, and administrators.

On December 11, 1989, Betty Castor, State Commissioner of Education, wrote a letter to Superintendent Walt Sickles. She spoke about recent budget cuts and said "Therefore, I am urging you to carefully review your current spending plans to identify ways you can reduce administrative expenses and eliminate non-essential activities." I could see in my crystal ball that the fact that a supervisor was being paid to do the job of a teacher would eventually become an issue before the School Board even without a letter like this one from the Commissioner. Somebody would make this a campaign issue. Even if I wanted to stay in the classroom, with supervisor's pay, I could forecast that my days were numbered. A slow death?

On December 12, 1989, I received a letter from Constance Delaney, assistant principal for student affairs; it advised me that one of my students was "seizure prone but has not had any problems thus far." With all those machines in the shop, why wasn't I told on October 30, when I took over the class? Why was he put into the class in the first place? Was I placed in jeopardy?

The daily bulletin gave various student and faculty information. One day there was some information about Florida public schools. It said Florida will need 38,000 new teachers and 600 new schools in the next ten years. It was impressive. It showed the tremendous growth in the state as well as the opportunities for students to become teachers. I hope it encouraged some kids to be teachers.

What if I decided not to accept the position at Gaither and resign? What would the Board have done with the six shop classes: look for a certified shop teacher in the middle of the school year?; close the classes and transfer the students?; keep a substitute for the remainder of the year? If the Board's classroom teaching threat *had* worked, if I had quit as I think I was expected to, would it have been at the cost of the students' education? Some Boards have more leverage than they can comprehend.

My "reinstatement" by the Board turned out to be quite a "statement" about education in Hillsborough County.

Donna continued to call. I kept my distance and didn't return her calls.

60

UNITED STATES COURT

The Circuit Court directed that I be reinstated back into my original position as Supervisor of Industrial Arts and Industrial Education. I was reinstated with this title, but not with the duties of the job.

The personnel office classified me as a supervisor, but repeatedly I was treated like a teacher. First of all, I was teaching and had no supervising duties. I had no office, no budget, and no secretary.

The supervisor who took my place, Mike Grego, treated me like a teacher too. He would hold an industrial department head meeting and I wasn't asked to help plan nor attend the meeting. Whenever he sent me a communication, it was addressed to "Technology Education Teachers." Once he sent an application for me to join the county vocational association under the category of "teacher," so that he would have 100% industrial teacher membership countywide. There also was a category for "supervisors;" why didn't he send me an application for supervisor? Then Grego sent me his published roster of industrial teachers in Hillsborough County. My name was listed as a teacher at Gaither High School and the courses that I taught were itemized. This list is commonly given to outside sources like vendors who sent teachers literature on equipment and supplies for sale. Many of these vendors knew me from previous contacts in the supervisor's office.

Another interesting event served to prove I was a teacher and not a supervisor. During the first week, when I began teaching at Gaither High, I was teaching an extra class period. I asked the personnel department if I would be paid for this "overload schedule." I didn't expect to be paid because supervisors are hired on a yearly contract and do not, have not, and cannot, to my knowledge, be paid for "overtime." Traditionally, supervisors just did the job until it got done no matter how long it took. To my surprise, I received a check from payroll for this "overtime." For one week I was placed on the "T" payroll for this extra class period, a payroll usually reserved for teachers who teach the overload. So, now it appears by their actions that the personnel and payroll departments deem me to be a "teacher." Paychecks don't lie.

Here is one last comment to unmask the teacher or supervisor "to be or not to be" quandary. I left a note on the chalk board, about some classroom supplies, for the night school teacher that I knew rather well. At the end of the note, I signed my name and then in a fun way, I put the title of Supervisor after it. The next morning I saw an answer to my question on the chalk board. It was addressed to me, but the title after my name read "Stupidvisor." It was just a joke because of my position in the classroom, but it did hit home and told me that my supervisor title was hollow and ridiculous.

With all of these things happening, I felt under duress. Heavy stuff. I could see that I was between a rock and a hard place. I called a meeting with attorney McKee and updated him on the latest happenings with me as a teacher. Earlier, I had already concluded with him that I was dissatisfied with the way the school system put me back into the classroom, contrary to the Judge's order. The thinking then was to file suit in federal court. Hello Uncle Sam.

On November 7, 1989, I filed a Complaint and Demand for Jury Trial in the United States District Court, Middle District of Florida, Tampa Division. The Judge selected to hear my case was Elizabeth A. Kovachevich.

I was in the middle of finalizing the Circuit Court judgement; I just ended the Appeal Court run and now I was starting in United States Court. I had too many irons in the fire. Things were getting hotter and more expensive by the hour.

The style of the case had changed to Wieser vs. The School Board and Walter Sickles, Superintendent. The first section of the Complaint states the following:

1. This is an action for damages and equitable relief to redress the abridgement, under color of state law, of the plaintiff's due process rights protected under the United States Constitution....

The Complaint went on to tell about my story; I was an employee, then terminated and then reinstated by Judge Evans' ruling. Sections 10 through 13 detailed what had happened to me after reinstatement and said that I had a "property interest" and a "liberty interest" in my job. The following quotations help explain these conditions.

10. ...Although he was given the title Supervisor of Industrial Arts and Industrial Education and placed on the supervisor's salary scale, Wieser was

not assigned any of the duties or responsibilities of the position nor has he been accorded any of the rights and privileges traditionally associated with such position as are outlined in the School Board's job description....

11. Since his reinstatement, Wieser has been assigned duties as a classroom teacher. Such action was punitive in nature and was carried out by the School Board and the Superintendent without just cause and without according Wieser procedural due process.

12. Wieser has a property interest in his continued employment by the School Board in the position Supervisor....Such property interest encompasses not only the Supervisor's title and salary, but also the duties, responsibilities, rights and privileges traditionally associated with the position....

13. Wieser also has a liberty interest in his ability to work and earn a living and to be free from actions taken under color of law which damage his standing in his profession and in the community or which otherwise stigmatize him. By stripping Wieser of all of the duties, responsibilities, rights and privileges traditionally associated with the Supervisor's position, and by requiring Wieser to assume the duties of a classroom teacher, the School Board and the Superintendent have impaired Wieser's prospects for professional advancement both within the Hillsborough County school system and with other prospective employers. Wieser's forced return to the classroom has also stigmatized him in the eyes of his co-workers and the School Board's administrative cadre.

14. As a direct and proximate result of the defendants' conduct as outlined in paragraphs 10-13, above, Wieser has suffered injuries to his personal and professional reputation and has been publicly embarrassed and humiliated.

Therefore, I prayed that the Court would take jurisdiction over this action and award me compensatory damages, reinstate me as Supervisor of IA and IE with all the rights, et cetera and reasonable attorney's fees.

Finally, I asked for a trial by jury on all issues so triable.

I thought McKee did a great job describing what happened to me and in asking for a legal remedy. I had the feeling this was finally going to end my four-year nightmare once and for all.

To be sure that all Board members were informed as to my case, personal copies were hand delivered to each Board member at the start of the next Tuesday's regular Board meeting. It was signed, sealed, and delivered. Okay school board, the ball's in your "court." No pun intended. Yeah,...it was intended.

Guess what the School Board did next: it filed a Motion To Dismiss. Well, deja vu. I say green; it says red. I say yes; it says no. Let's call the "whole" thing off. What else did I expect. It was a legal tug-of-war.

The Motion To Dismiss was filed on December 12, 1989, and it moved for dismissal because it claimed the School Board was "within the sphere of discretionary decision making" when it assigned me teaching job responsibilities. It went on to say "...the School Board fears the administrative upheaval which would occur if a protectable interest is recognized as a limitation against the power and right of school authorities to assign 'teachers' particular duties." The Motion went on for another fourteen pages explaining the reasons for dismissal. The Board quoted many other cases of law. Often, I didn't understand the legal jargon and I will not try to explain it now.

Now, it was our turn to file a Memorandum Of Law In Opposition To Defendants' Motion To Dismiss.

My Memorandum started with this statement: "The defendant's motion raises questions requiring the interpretation and application of federal and state law which cannot properly be undertaken without an understanding of the facts which underline this dispute." McKee went on to generally summarize what happened up to this point and then became specific with the following observations:

> ...Thus, Wieser has not been assigned a secretary or coordinator to assist him, he has no office from which to conduct the business of the supervisor, and he is not scheduled to attend administrative functions normally attended by supervisors. Rather, Wieser has been indefinitely assigned duties as a shop teacher at an area high school. Such assignment was made by the Superintendent as a punitive measure inasmuch as Wieser was told upon his re-employment that, in the Superintendent's view, he was unfit to assume the duties of a supervisor. At no time has Wieser been given the opportunity to respond to such allegations in a setting which comports with even the most basic notion of due process.

McKee went on to quote other cases in response to the Board's Motion. Nine pages later, my memo concludes with this statement:

> ...Wieser will prove that his situation is unique, that supervisors are not assigned to classroom teaching duties and that this assignment was unjustly imposed by the superintendent as a punitive measure to damage Wieser's career and to encourage him to leave the defendants' employment. Wieser should be permitted to develop his proofs through discovery and to prove his claims at trial.

The facts and opinions were submitted in writing. It was time to wait for a decision from the Judge and to try to have a Merry Christmas and a Happy New Year's celebration. My birthday was on January 4, so, I made a wish.

Extreme stress and depression over all the holidays seems to always have an over-emphasizing effect. I pretended to have a good time.

My birthday wish didn't come true. Judge Kovachevich ordered that the defendant's motion to dismiss be granted.

Basically, my suit asked for two things, property interest and liberty interest. Essentially, the property interest, where I requested damages and a jury trial because I was demoted, was denied. The second part, liberty interest, was accepted as a claim if I would file an amended complaint within twenty days for that part only.

The property interest was denied because I didn't show that Florida law grants me "legitimate claim of entitlement" of job responsibilities. Plus, the Board alleged that the Tenure Act "does not limit the inherent power of the School Board to assign job responsibilities." In addition, the word "demotion" was said to be narrowly defined in the Tenure Act; It means a "reduction in salary or transfer to a position which carries a lower salary, without the teacher's consent." Since I'm paid on the supervisory scale (except for that one week that I was paid overtime on the teacher's T payroll), I was not "demoted" according to the Tenure Act. The Judge concluded that I had no legitimate claim.

The liberty interest claim would allow me to have a hearing, not a jury trial, but a hearing before a state officer to prove that Smouse's claims of my poor performance were false. Now, this would provide me with an opportunity to prove my claim, but I wouldn't receive any damages; it would just "clear my name" as to my overall job performance.

McKee explained to me the above-mentioned order. As I read the order, I had to express that I disagreed with the Judge's decision because her interpretation of "demotion" and mine were different. I told him that I took logic in college, but it didn't take as much as it would take to understand what the Tenure Act said about the term demotion. Demotion was identified as a "reduction in salary or transfer to a position which carries a lower salary." I said to McKee that the key word in that definition is OR. I didn't receive a reduction in salary, but I was transferred to a position. What kind of position? A teaching position. A teaching position is a position that is described as having a lower salary; therefore it is a "demotion." I emphasized that "salary" was the issue in the first part of the definition and "position" was the issue in the second part. I guess that any loser would find fault with a judge's ruling. But, I guess that's why we have the appeal process. I couldn't understand the judge's logic or thinking.

I told McKee that I was interested in appealing. What could be done? He suggested that we file a Motion For Reconsideration, which was done two weeks later on February 13, 1990.

In the Motion For Reconsideration, McKee emphasized the same part of the Tenure Act that I had a complaint about, the definition of demotion. He pointed out the difference in a supervisor's salary and a classroom teacher's salary. Then, he stated the following:

> Thus, under the second prong of the Act's definition it is evident that the plaintiff has been demoted, inasmuch as he has been involuntarily transferred to a position which carries a lower salary. To hold, as the Court seems to have done in its January 30 order, that a reduction of salary is the linchpin of a demotion under the Act, would have the effect of eviscerating a portion of the statute. Florida's courts have long recognized a "cardinal rule" of statutory construction, *to wit*, statutes should be construed so as to give effect to all of their provisions.

To no avail, my Motion For Reconsideration came back on February 28, 1990, and it simply said "Denied and So Ordered." There was no written language about her opinion, just the original motion stamped Denied and signed. Her signature, with all the extra lines for emphasis, was six and one half inches long. When I saw the Motion, I got the feeling that I had insulted the court by asking for reconsideration.

I asked McKee to explain to me where I was now. He said we could appeal the property interest claim, but only after I had gone through the procedures of the liberty interest part of the claim. That included a hearing on all the documentation that Smouse had compiled in my file. If I came out successful, I couldn't claim any damages or attorney's fees. He said it could get very costly because of the volume of documentation and we didn't know what the Board might do to slow things down or drag things out. The only guarantee is that it would cost me a lot in attorney's fees and time.

The other option was to try and work out some "political" solution to clear my name with the Board. I hadn't seen any inviting prospects here, even after I had worked on their campaigns, so I chose not to pursue this route.

The next to last option was to continue teaching in the classroom at supervisory pay, because McKee said it really wasn't a bad gig for now. Although, he said that eventually my supervisory salary would become an issue for the Board to address.

We did not talk about the very last option. I wasn't ready to resign from the school system yet.

For some unknown reason, my case was still stopped from appearing before the public. It didn't make it in front of the school board in a public hearing when I filed my Grievance against Smouse. It didn't make it in a hearing before the State Educational Standards Commission, because of the Commissioner's decision. The news media, electronic and print, chose not to go with a full story of my wrongful termination. This time I missed out on a jury trial in front of my peers and the public.

I never was a strong believer in the concept of Tenure, because I saw it could prevent a system from getting rid of someone who was actually deadwood. However, I do believe that a competent and quality administration can still work within the Tenure Law if it follows all policies and procedures.

The legal tug-of-war was over; they ended up having more "pull" than me. Good bye Uncle Sam. And now, federally speaking, all I can cry is…"uncle."

61

HEARING NUMBER SIX:
FINAL JUDGEMENT

Soon after the Appeal Hearing, McKee wrote a letter on August 30, 1989, to school board attorney Gonzalez about Gonzalez's concern for me to mitigate my damages. McKee sent him documentation regarding my efforts in searching for employment. McKee went on to say he felt Judge Evans would rule in my favor for back-pay. He also pointed out that my back-pay calculations, prejudgment interest, request for medical expenses incurred after my termination, restoration of sick and vacation days and credit on the salary scale for experience were issues to be finalized.

Earlier, I had alerted McKee to the gossip that I heard about the Board firing me under the Tenure Act the moment I was reinstated because of the documentation Smouse accumulated. You may remember that Gonzalez had said this to McKee too, right after the summary judgement given by Evans. To head off any of this, he included this last paragraph in his letter:

> If your client has any interest in resolving this matter informally, please let me know. Mr. Wieser is prepared to put this matter behind him and to continue his career with the School Board. If the School Board chooses to escalate this dispute by seeking to terminate Wieser's continued contract, it should know that he is absolutely committed to exhausting all of his legal remedies in response to such an action. I trust such a confrontation can be avoided.

No, no, no. The board didn't want to resolve this informally; it wanted to go back to court and take another shot at eliminating any back-pay or at least, reducing my payment by claiming I didn't mitigate my damages. This thing was going right down to the wire.

I know this must be a tough time for a losing attorney, because now we begin to seriously talk about how much money the Board is going to pay me. This amount of the settlement is a reflection upon the losing attorney. Nobody likes losing especially when it includes big bucks. This told me that the Superintendent and the Board didn't want to see me with a big check either. The amount of the settlement would be a reflection against them too.

The Final Judgement Hearing was set for December 4, 1989, in the Chambers of Judge Ralph Steinberg again. The court transcript says that attorney Gonzalez represented the school system, but that wasn't correct. It was another attorney, the one that accompanied Sizemore at the Appeal Hearing. I didn't get this attorney's name. It makes you wonder why they sent a new attorney to the Final Judgement Hearing. McKee represented me and I was there as the only witness. The court reporter was Donald R. Salvog.

I must point out that to my knowledge, the School Board never requested a court reporter; it was only McKee that did. If this issue of the Tenure Law was so critical to the Board's operations that it would be appealed, then why didn't the Board ensure that a court record would be established?

There are some interesting happenings in this hearing and therefore I will spend some time on it. You need to remember that McKee will be speaking for me because he knows what we have previously discussed and what I want out of this case. On the other hand, their attorney will be speaking for the Superintendent and the School Board. Try to picture them in court as their attorney presents their side.

Attorney McKee began by briefly giving the background of the case and the reason why we were here, to establish the back-pay and attorney fees that the court ordered the defendants to pay me. McKee started to read into the record the issues which were included in my case like back-pay, social security contributions, vacation and sick leave accounts, retirement contribution and such.

The Board attorney said the amounts of these issues were not in dispute, but whether or not I had a right to these was.

"The first issue that has to be resolved is this back-pay issue," the Board's attorney said before citing a case which suggested I had a duty to mitigate my damages. He went on to say that I was offered a job with the school board and failed to take it. He felt that the School Board was entitled to an offset in back-pay for that year of probation that they offered me. He said there could have been an "avoidable consequence" if I took the job under probation, because now the Board wouldn't have to pay for something it had offered to me already. He thought that I had a duty to take the job for the extra year.

McKee jumped in then, saying he was frankly surprised that this matter was being raised again, since it was raised before Judge Evans and rejected and then rejected again by the Second DCA.

The Board attorney continued his point;

> And your Honor, I have come in this case in some—you know, on the brief writings and other points. I was not involved within the hearing. I have read this to say that the Court was not going to terminate his right to back-pay by— because of him not taking that job.
>
> But what I am saying is that there is another whole body of law that says that we are entitled to an offset if like or similar employment was rejected for the amounts that could have been earned during that one-year period.

He continued to say that the Board was still trying to figure out what amounts were to be subtracted from my back-pay.

I now had a good idea why Gonzalez didn't show up. This attorney sounded like he was drawing on his ignorance of the case, saying he read it as saying this and that. It seemed like their strategy was to try this case over again in front of a new Judge and see if they could get any consolation prizes. It ain't over until it's over.

Now we got to the part of the discussion where I had to show that I acted like a reasonable person in seeking out reasonable employment. The Board attorney then said:

> I want to show that he sent out certain resumés in kind of a shotgun manner and was actually sent back requests for interviews. And I don't know at this point if he followed up, whether he actually contacted these people and set up the interviews. That, again, goes to the duty to mitigate the damages which means he acts as a reasonable person and tried to get other employment during that period.

I'm not sure where he got his information, but the statement was incorrect. I was never requested for an interview.

The "offset" issue for the Board still continued. Then the Judge said my testimony should be taken. I was sworn in. Judge Steinberg wanted to be sure both attorneys were in agreement on how much I was entitled to if the court found that I did everything possible to find work. Again the Board attorney said there was no problem with the amounts, only if they were entitled to any offset.

I couldn't believe that they wouldn't give in on this part. I guess they saw it as their only chance to sooth their losses.

The examination began with McKee questioning me. Among other questions, he asked me if I applied for unemployment compensation benefits and if I received those benefits. I said I applied but I was turned down because the Florida Department of Labor determined, through information from the School Board, that I had quit my job for personal reasons and, therefore, I wasn't entitled to any benefits. He asked me if I secured employment after my discharge or if I earned any money since then. My answer to both questions was no.

McKee then asked me to describe for the Judge the steps I took in attempting to find employment. I said I *did not* use a shotgun approach, but I used a scientific method which parallels the system used with the Florida Unemployment Division which requires three contacts to be made each week. Sending out a resume' was considered a contact. My two-page resumé was on expensive paper and it included a cover letter indicating I was available for employment immediately. I stated that I was interested in supervisory or administrative type of employment.

I went on to say that I mailed a resumé package to all but one school district in Florida which was sixty-six total. Then I mailed copies to all the community colleges and all nine state universities. Then McKee asked about out of state contacts. I said I applied in twelve different states, mostly to vocational and technical schools.

I said that I had sent out a total of about 205 resumés. McKee asked if I received any job offers for administrative or supervisory positions. I had not, but I received one call to interview for a teaching position. He asked if any of my 205 resumés were follow-ups or repeats; I said yes. After one year of sending out three resumés per week, I decided to send a fourth resume to one of the school districts that I had contacted over one year before, because they may have purged their files. This would keep my application current in more school districts. McKee ended his questioning. His questioning of me under oath was covered in five pages in the court transcript. Now it was the Board's attorney's turn to cross-examine me on my job search.

The Board's attorney's cross-examination of me encompassed the next thirty-five pages in the transcript. At one point, the Board attorney asked me if I rejected the offer of probation " as a matter of principle" and I said it was a "matter of Florida State law." Later, he asked again if it was a matter of principle. Then he asked if there was any hostility. I said no; I couldn't understand how come my evaluations were all satisfactory and I was being offered probation. What does "hostility" have to do with my mitigation of damages, I wondered? There were a lot of questions about me running as a candidate for the School Board too.

The Board's attorney finished his cross-examination and what we had left was the Judge's ruling on the issues of my efforts to mitigate my damages and the prejudgment interest.

After some summarizing dialogue back and forth between the two attorneys, Judge Steinberg was able to say I did act like a reasonable person in seeking employment by stating "the evidence does show me that the plaintiff had done every reasonable, possible thing to mitigate the damages under the circumstances." He then ruled in my favor for back-pay, and in the defendant's favor against my request for prejudgment interest.

I didn't have to ask McKee to explain what happened this time. I knew we won. I was relieved. However, I didn't have my check yet.

The Final Judgement Order was signed by Judge Steinberg eleven days later on December 15, 1989. It was two pages long and it listed the amounts for back-pay and attorney's fees for the circuit court.

I met shortly thereafter with McKee. He reviewed the two-page Final Judgement and added that as of December 15, the School Board was obligated in paying me 12% interest on the total amount in the judgement. He estimated it would be about $600.00 a month. He wasn't sure how long they would take to pay me. We would wait patiently for the check. I was on pins and needles waiting to hold that check in my hands. I had waited a year and a half since I was wrongfully terminated, so, a few more days of patience wouldn't be too much to ask.

Later, McKee told me that he spoke to attorney Gonzalez on Wednesday, December 27. He told Gonzalez that the School Board already owed me $300 in interest. He went further and said that if the Board paid me by Friday, December 29, I would charge no interest. McKee said that Gonzalez's answer was that "I wasn't fishing with very big bait." Come December 29, there was no check. I guess they didn't want me to have a Merry Christmas or a Happy New Year's celebration. They were just hurting themselves, I thought.

The check came into McKee's office on January 12, 1990. He called me immediately and I went to his office. The check from the School Board was made out for the amount of $69,753.40. It was dated January 11, 1990. The signatures on the check were Joe Newsome, School Board Chairman and Walter Sickles, Superintendent.

You may remember that Kelly and McKee did not push me to pay their monthly fee in full, because they were aware of my unemployed situation. So, before I left the office, their bill was paid. It totaled a little more than $22,000 at that time, not including the amounts I had already paid over the last two years, nor all of the fees for the on-going suit in Federal Court.

McKee pointed out that the school board didn't take out any taxes. So, I should be prepared to pay that amount. I wondered if the Board waited on purpose until January, the new tax year, to issue the check because it would give me a windfall in income along with my current salary that I was earning by teaching at Gaither?

I asked McKee if I was going to be paid interest for the delay in sending payment. He said they had some leeway and the interest would not be as much as we expected. I wanted to get whatever they owed me. For some reason, McKee didn't follow up on this. I never received any interest. I'm still thinking about asking the Board for it myself. Every dollar adds up. During these hearings, I saw that I was never able to ask for more than I was entitled to, but they were able to present arguments that might end up giving me less. It didn't seem fair. And they fought hard and often were rewarded with a reduction in some of the payments to me.

Easy come, and easy go was the thought I had on the way home from McKee's office. I had no income for one and one half years; therefore I had some bills to pay. The two key words in that sentence were "SOOOOOOME BILLS." I made a photo copy of the original check for my continued viewing and pleasure. I thought it would be great to hang it in my classroom. But, I was cool; I didn't. I just kept it with my other records. After I did pay off my loans from family, friends and credit cards, there wasn't much left. But, I did have some fun or therapy as I call it; I bought a brand new motorcycle. You know that bumper sticker "When the going gets tough, the tough go to the mall." Well, what would you do?

This now ended Hearing Number Six. Looking back at all of the court hearings, I can remember them having four different attorneys representing the Superintendent and the School Board. And during the hearings, I had two attorneys representing me, Kelly and McKee. I'm waiting to see a new bumper sticker that says "He who dies with the most attorneys representing him, wins." Some day when this is all over, I want to see an itemized accounting of how much it cost the taxpayers of Hillsborough County for my back-pay, my attorney's fees and their multiple attorney's fees. I estimate that it would far exceed $100,000.00. Plus, how many man-hours of administrative time were consumed by the Superintendent and his administrative staff on my case. Time will tell if this information ever gets to the public.

FINAL JUDGEMENT

A couple of weeks after the Final Judgement Hearing, Cammaratta and I had breakfast in "the nick of time." It was New Year's Day 1990, and Cammaratta told me that he saw Elba Garcia, a supervisor in the school system's Personnel Department, at the friendly credit union. He considered her to be a friend in the system for a long time. She came to him and said "don't let them move you out, you stay right where you are."

Over the last year, Cammaratta had also told me of incidents that he felt were signals to get him to retire. This comment from Elba told me that either office gossip was alive and well or that she knew of a plan to put the pressure on Cammaratta to get him out. I'm sure he was perceived as a thorn in their side because he stood up for his principles in general and for me in specific.

The word was out and the pressure was on.

INTERCOM, the Hillsborough County Public Schools newsletter, spring 1990 edition, reported that Dr. Raymond O. Shelton, recently retired Superintendent of Schools, was recently recognized for his leadership. The American Association of School Administrators (AASA) honored him with a Distinguished Service Award during a presentation in San Francisco. "Each winner must have made significant contributions to education and educational administration. In the performance of their duties as school administrators or college professors, recipients must have brought honor to themselves, their colleagues, and their profession."

At first, when I read the news, knowing what I know now, I concluded that his award, in my eyes, was meaningless. And then I opened my eyes farther and saw there *was* a great deal of meaning in this award.

62

CAMMARATTA RETIRES

Cammaratta almost had forty years of service with the Hillsborough County School System. For some time he had been considering a change of lifestyle to the "good life" of retirement.

I can remember talking with him over the last year since he was turned down for the promotion to Assistant Superintendent. As you remember in Chapter 49—"What Right to Work," Earl Lennard was promoted to that position over Cammaratta. He told me numerous times that Earl was putting the pressure on him to retire. Earl even spoke to Cammaratta on several occasions about his future with the school system. Cammaratta told me that he always interrupted Earl and told him as directly as he could that it would be *his* decision when to retire, and not Earl's. Cammaratta also told me that Earl was putting the pressure on others to retire too.

In December of 1989, Cammaratta told me that he had financially calculated that it wouldn't really pay him anymore to continue to work since his retirement pay would be based upon his last five years of service. It could be said that he was working for free. With this explanation of his status, I could see he was worn down by the treatment given to him by Lennard on top of all the upsets to do with my situation over the last few years.

I knew that he had bought a small old cottage that could become a perfect retirement project to fix up for his family. I knew he enjoyed carpentry work, but I also knew there were possibilities for him to be an Adjunct Professor at USF or do consulting work in school systems in the southeastern states. All the benefits of retirement were at his door step. The stage was set, but a difficult decision had to be made.

On February 28, 1990, Cammaratta retired. He told me that it was the hardest decision he ever had to make in his long career. He was born and raised in Tampa. His Baccalaureate degree was earned at the University of

Tampa and he received his Ph. D. here at the University of South Florida. All of his years of educational service were in the Hillsborough School System. He had a most full and respected career. A home town boy makes good. I salute him for what he accomplished in his career. He was and will remain one of my mentors and role models.

Six months into his retirement, he was inducted into the three-year-old Florida Vocational Association Hall of Fame. The yearly handful of inductees are selected from the business and industry community as well as all levels of the educational system. It certainly was an honor for him to enjoy during his retirement years. No other administrator from Hillsborough County has ever been inducted.

Cammaratta was elected president of the Ybor City Optimist Club. It was a great chance for him to remain active and participate in civic duties. I'd like to see him run for the School Board.

Oh, by the way, on April 4, 1990, RoseAnne Bowers was appointed Director of Vocational Technical Education, the job that Cammaratta vacated. I was told that not many people applied for this position. This Director's position was one of the reasons I returned to Hillsborough County. Obviously, I would have applied for the promotion. I believe my credentials on paper were better than those of Bowers, and I know I would have the support of the principals, but I didn't have the political connections that she had. I was told that RoseAnne had a cousin on the Hillsborough County School Board and his name was Sam Rampello. Bowers said, in an article in the Florida Vocational Journal, August/September 1990, "...I look forward to many new challenges as Director of Vocational Education and to working with Earl Lennard, Assistant Superintendent for Vocational, Technical, Adult and Community Education...."

63

LESSONS IN CLASS

To avoid any misinterpretations of the title of this chapter, its meaning concerns lessons that I learned while I was teaching in the classroom at Gaither High School.

Shortly after my reinstatement at Gaither, *The St. Petersburg Times* printed a brief article about my case. The article was titled "Employee sues School Board a 2nd time." The short article briefly summarized my first suit back in 1988 and said I was suing the School Board this time because it was paying me as a supervisor but making me work as a classroom teacher.

The school system produces a "Press Summary" every several weeks and distributes it to schools and administrators. The summary is a collection of photocopies of newspaper articles about the school system. Dean Fox Holland, Supervisor of Public Information/Public Relations is in charge of its production.

The Press Summary for the period of November 1st to the 22nd did not include the article about my case. The summary had 41 pages with articles "cut and pasted" on each side of the page, making a total of 82 pages. I knew a lot of teachers and administrators didn't know about what had happened to me; therefore I was sure there was an interest to see it included in the next issue. I called Dean Holland and asked her, if I sent her a copy of the article, would it be printed. I also told her of several administrators who said that hadn't seen the article. She told me to send it and she would see if there was room. She also said that there were other articles in the Press Summary from *The St. Petersburg Times* .

My article did not appear in the next issue of the Press Summary, nor any future issue. I didn't think that "space" was the deciding factor.

Subsequently, on January 3, 1990, a memo was sent from Dean Holland to Walt Sickles, Superintendent. The subject of the memo was "December Press

Summary—Goal #6: Enhance Positive Image." Copies were sent to the School Board, Superintendent's Staff and Principals. A blind copy was enclosed in my copy of the next Press Summary.

The memo said, in part, the following:

> I thought you would be pleased to know that at least 87 of our schools had positive press coverage in December! ....
> We do not always print all articles from the community papers....
> Not all articles are of equal importance, of course....
> *Every inch* of positive news about student or staff accomplishments, programs that work; or the many wonderful "photo-stories" serves to enhance the image of public education in Hillsborough County and thereby makes the job of education a little easier.
> Our personnel continue to demonstrate their commitment to quality education.

It is interesting that this letter was written soon after my request to print the article about me.

I'm glad 87 schools had positive coverage, but what about the other 63 schools? I'm not sure that only printing positive articles is the way to demonstrate a commitment to quality education? A statement on the document says "These news articles are compiled for the employees of Hillsborough County Public Schools as an information resource making readers aware of news and opinions about our school system."

However, the above memo and the rejection of my article told me that the Press Summary was a self-serving venture at the taxpayers' expense. Was it a suppression of information? For some reason the progress in my case against the Board or my total story was not to be told. Perhaps the title of the Press Summary should be changed to PRAVDA—American Style. I never received a reply to my letter to Dean Holland about printing my article. I think the above memo to the superintendent was really a memo to me.

Back to the classroom.

Discipline continued to be my number-one priority for some time. I wasn't always looked at by the students as the "nice guy" teacher. But, it wasn't my job to be their buddy. I often told them this wasn't a beauty contest for me. Later in the year there were situations: one student called me a jerk; and one used the "F" word toward me. Several students threatened to burn my car and one student said he wanted to kill me. After I wrote a discipline referral for the student who said he wanted to kill me, the assistant principal interviewed several students who heard him say it. The assistant principal confirmed what was said, but told me he didn't think the kid really meant it; what I should do, he advised, is call the mother, a single parent. The student was back in my class several days later. I knew for a fact this student knew exactly where I lived; previously, he had lived on the same street. I wonder if the assistant principal would have responded differently if *his* life was threatened.

Another student, one who threatened to burn my car, also described details about my second floor condo, the hanging plants on my terrace, and exactly where and how I park my car, which I backed into the reserved space in front of the garage. He must have followed me home. I hoped he wasn't a habitual stalker. I told the resource police officer assigned to Gaither; he said I should buy a gun and make the student aware of it. I thought his advice was sarcastic and useless.

On January 5, 1990, Augie brought a 28" x 48" x 1" black walnut board to me. He said it belonged to the principal's wife. He said I was to plane it from 1" down to $3/8$ of an inch in thickness on the surfacer machine. A week later, when I had time to work on this special project, I verified the size with Augie. He checked with Allen and reported back to me that Allen said he needed it that day. After it was cut, I had a student take it up to the principal that afternoon; when he returned, he said the principal sent a thank you. Talk about misuse of equipment. Perhaps he didn't know that Smouse reprimanded me for using the upholstery sewing machine, and now the principal is directing me to surface some wood for his wife. I know that misuse of school equipment is common, but this was rather bold of principal Allen. I guess that he didn't want to "get into the middle of this thing," so he sent his department head to me.

County policy requires that industrial shop teachers be responsible for repairing their equipment and tools. My teaching schedule had the last period of the day as my planning period, with no students. I would often sign-out of school during that last period to go to the county warehouse or to a supply store for repairs or to pick up shop supplies that couldn't be ordered through the warehouse. The night-school shop teacher would also leave broken tools for me to take in for repairs. When signing out, I would first clear it with the department head (Augie), and then the principal or one of his assistants in his absence.

I was directed several times to come down to the county administration office, on business, and I used the signing-out procedure for that too. The school administration kept challenging whatever I did. In February, Betty Wilson, assistant principal for curriculum, asked Augie if all my sign-outs were necessary. Augie said they were. She asked who did all these jobs before I came there? Augie said he did. (This tells me that Augie didn't seek her permission when he left school, if indeed he had to request permission at all.)

He went on to tell her the trips for tool repair were authorized by the county industrial supervisor (Grego) and paid for from the county office. The next month Augie said that Allen questioned him on the same topic about me.

The Administrative Bulletin, a weekly communication type of newsletter produced by the Assistant Superintendent for Administration, announced an upcoming county-wide joint meeting for principals and supervisors. These are held about every other month or when necessary and *all* principals and supervisors attend. The superintendent and his staff speak, plus others who have current information to be shared. The meeting opens with live entertainment from the band or orchestra at the school where the meeting takes place. Often times, Board members and news reporters are there, along with the several hundred county administrators. As supervisor in the past, I never missed these meetings no matter how busy my office was. It was expected that all attend. On January 3, 1990, I requested from principal Allen permission to attend the next "joint principal/supervisor" meeting. He responded by saying that he "checked this out, and I need not go because he needed me at the school." Later, he was told to give me a summary of the meeting, since he would be there. Of course, I never received a verbal or written summary, no handouts, no nothing, except the cold shoulder.

I will chuckle and tell you the next joint principal/supervisor's meeting, January 11, was announced as the annual meeting "where School Board members are present for an interchange with principals and supervisors." In past years, Board members took questions on 3x5 cards and responded to the group. Were Board members embarrassed to be seen with me or afraid of me asking intriguing questions in public? I was professionally insulted that I was not allowed to go. I hate dirty politics.

Round two. I requested to attend the Supervisor's Council meeting. There are about 80 county supervisors in the system and we elect officers and have about five meetings per year, like other county councils do. I was a current dues-paying member and our next council meeting was our "Annual Breakfast" for school board members and it usually lasted about an hour and a half. As in the past, each Board member would sit at a different table to interact with supervisors, and then comment to the total group at the end of the meal. They would always say how important the supervisors were. My request to attend was denied. Here, I was not even allowed to be visible with my fellow supervisors. I'll bet my name was there in some conversations. What message do you think the supervisors received when they heard I had returned to the system, but obviously wasn't attending their meetings? Was I a supervisor or a teacher? Judge Evans, where are you?

Round three. I applied for two week's vacation time in January. I had over a month of vacation time earned as a supervisor. I needed some rest and relaxation. I had planned a ski trip. The request went to Cammaratta since he supervises all vocational supervisors and signed all my vacation requests in the past. Cammaratta told me that he approved my leave form, but when he passed it up the ladder to Earl Lennard, Lennard refused to sign it, saying that because I was at a different work site, the principal, Allen, should sign it. Allen denied it, saying I should take vacation time when students aren't in school. Essentially, that means summer. I was getting upset.

Time was short, and not sure who was my supervisor, Cammaratta or Allen, I wrote a joint letter to both. My letter requested that I take a combination of "personal days" (from accrued sick leave) and vacation days for the two weeks. Personal days are taken at any time, for any reason, and are not to be questioned at all by the administration. I stated that I had previously committed to a vacation trip and would lose a substantial amount of money if I had to shorten my trip and lose a greater amount, plus penalties, if I were unable to go. Cammaratta informed me it was okay with him. I personally handed this letter of leave request to Allen as he was leaving the main school office, telling him it was a request for release time. He said "Bill, I ain't gonna get into the middle of this thing,...we need to sit down and talk about it, probably Friday." I told him that I needed to know by the next day and that I was acting on the advice of my attorney; Friday was too late. He took the letter and then walked out of the building. I knew he was already in the middle of things when the superintendent transferred me to his school. It seemed that he wasn't going to claim me as a supervisor or even a teacher. He ignored my letter and gave me no response at all. He never did "call me in to talk about it." That was it; I knew I wasn't able to go. I called my trip contact person and indicated I would not be going. I was depressed more than you could imagine.

Here are some additional details about my ski trip. During the time the school board was appealing my ruling to return to work, and I was out of a job, I joined the Tampa Bay Snow Skiers. I had skied for 20 years and I enjoyed group travel. The club had over 2,000 members and sponsored about 22 group trips per year. Each trip had a trip leader and a co-leader. I applied to be a co-leader and was selected for the two-week Austria trip. I had skied in Europe before. When I made arrangements for the trip a year earlier, I was certain that I would have the two weeks free to go: if I won the court appeal, I would be placed back on the job with sufficient vacation time already in place; if I lost my case and was not reappointed, I would be unemployed and have all the time in the world. I worked with the club for ten months promoting the trip and signing up 50 skiers to attend.

As co-leader, the club paid half of my trip expenses because it got a discount on big group rates. Therefore, two weeks in Europe would "cost" me one week. I paid $760.00 up front. I poured most of my personal life style into the ski club. My social life revolved around the club activities because of all the fun friends I made. Of course, many teachers were members, as were other professionals, but skiing was the topic of our conversations, not education. After I indicated that I couldn't go, the ski club sent me a bill for the other half of the trip. I didn't go, lost $760.00, and now had to pay an additional $730.00. I withdrew from the ski club and away from my friends I made there because of my embarrassment from not being able to follow through on a commitment. The school system had torn my professional life apart, and now my personal life was under their attack. Can you guess the level of respect I had for Principal Allen, Earl Lennard and others in the school system? This professional nightmare just had a direct hit (pin-point bombing) on my most personal social life. The school system, and many of the people who ran it, had infiltrated my remaining well-being. There was no escape from "them."

More and more, I was viewing myself as a teacher rather than a supervisor. Whenever it was to the school board's advantage for me to be a supervisor, then I was a supervisor; whenever it was to its advantage for me to be a teacher, then I was a teacher. Damned if you do and damned if you don't.

On February 15, 1990, Earl Lennard came into my classroom, unannounced. He said it was National Vocational Education week. He didn't come close enough for a hand shake; he kept his distance. I'm sure his posture—dark suit, white shirt, and bright red tie gave a message to the students—said that he was in a position of authority. He walked around the far end of the shop. I asked if I could help him with anything. He said no and kept walking. He seemed to be looking for something. There are about 600 teachers in his division, why did he choose to visit me? After a few minutes of browsing, he went to the door to leave and he asked me if these students were energetic. I said "some days yes, some days less." Then he left and never returned. Was he playing brain games?

Teacher Becky Burgue told me that her supervisor, Rhonda Trainor, asked her about me and how I was doing. Trainor said she wished this whole situation would end because it was putting pressure on Mike Grego. I told Becky that it sounds like it was my fault that Mike is under pressure. I stated that I understand Trainor's concerns, but where was she and the other supervisors when the pressure was on me. Why didn't she and the other vocational supervisors stand up and support me back then? Then I added, for that matter, where were the other 80 supervisors from the entire county, who were fellow members of the county Supervisor's Council, when I needed their ethical support. You can't say they didn't know about it. Becky said I was right. She also said that she told Trainor that I was doing a good job at Gaither. I thanked her for her comments.

To show my dedication to the students, faculty and administration at Gaither, I purchased a sweat shirt and a golf-type shirt, with the blue and white Gaither "Cowboy" logo, from the parent's booster club for $20.00 each. Those who purchased the shirts wore them on "spirit Fridays" to promote a winning team spirit in the weekend football or basketball games. I tried hard to fit in.

In spite of all the hassle with the "system," my basic character kept coming through. I was asked for "shop" help by other teachers and staff. To name a few examples, I made several chemical troughs for the science department, sharpened tools for the custodians, gave small book racks to the library and fixed a wooden chair. I made a custom mop rack for the lunchroom workers (they said they were waiting two years for it), and a special cutting board for the long loafs of Cuban bread. The lunchroom manager brought the wood in for that one and there was some left over, so I made a small cutting board too. The coaches asked me to repair some track and field equipment; I made flag poles for the driver education traffic cones, plastic key holders for the auto shop, frames for silk screen printing in the graphics lab, and a wedding arch for the family living class because they had a mock wedding each year. Whenever possible, I assigned students to do the work and gave them credit when they completed the required project plan, evaluation sheet, etc.

On February 7, 1990, Binnie called me in for a conference in his office. I wondered what he was up to this time. With him were Earl Lennard and Marilyn Wittner. Wittner gave me a letter pointing out specific do's and don'ts concerning my "teaching assignment." Shouldn't I have received this letter back in October. She also said that, although I was teaching, I would be evaluated on the new, regular "short" supervisor evaluation form twice a year just like had been done before.

Earl Lennard didn't say much, but he did say that "we are family and we must work together." He sincerely tried to convince me that I could "progress and advance in the vocational division." I told you he didn't say much. As sincere as he tried to be, I saw his comment about my possibilities to advance as a big bunch of baloney! He wasn't fooling me.

According to Board policy, supervisors are to be evaluated twice a year: formative evaluation in December and the summative in April. Allen had to use the same evaluation form and procedure for his six assistant principals. He did walk through my classroom, unannounced and during class several times during the year. His "walk through" visits would last less than three minutes. However, he broke policy and never evaluated me. Since my previous performance was so profoundly scrutinized by Smouse, and was used as a basis for my termination, then why wasn't I evaluated at all once I returned to the system? Didn't they want to give me the credit for doing a good job under preposterous conditions? It's difficult to discover any sanity in the system's actions on evaluation.

The handling of contracts didn't make much sense either. When all the other teachers had received their contracts for the following year, the only thing I got was the contract "binder" that I signed at my reinstatement. So, not only was I never evaluated; I also did not receive my contract. Was the Board trying to erase my existence? Were they caught in the "Perceiving, Behaving, Becoming" syndrome I spoke about back in Chapter 12?

But the problems didn't end there. In the middle of the school year, a problem developed concerning my pay check. I was under the direct deposit system where the School Board would electronically deposit my bi-weekly check into my credit union's checking account. Suddenly, my account was over-drawn. I called the credit union to check on my deposits and was told that the school system's computer had put my check into my savings account, odd since the direct deposit had always worked with no hitches. When I called the school system payroll department, I was told I would have to wait several pay periods for the situation to be corrected. In the meantime I would receive a regular check and have to deposit it myself. I saw this as an inconvenience and a form of continued harassment by the school system.

Alas, the problems kept coming. As a part of the court settlement, I was awarded back sick days for the time I was terminated. Of the yearly number of earned sick leave days, four are "personal days." They can be used at any time, for any reason, without justification, and the administration is not to question the use of these. When used, they are subtracted from accrued sick leave. Toward the end of the school year, in June, I had already used my four days for the current year. I took several more personal days' leave and charged these to the sick leave awarded to me in the court settlement from last year when I was terminated.

The Personnel Department docked my pay check saying I didn't have the use of these "personal days" from the last year because they don't accrue. I explained that I wasn't employed last year because I was wrongfully terminated and therefore I was awarded back sick days which *included* the four personal days. I specifically called Binnie on this and he said he would check on it. It was never resolved. My paycheck was *docked* several days even though

I had a balance of "regular" sick days left. I feel the school system still owes me a few day's pay. Some day when I find attorney #4, I will pursue this and other matters left unfinished with the school system. I viewed this docking of my pay, while I had a balance of sick days, as a form of embezzlement of my lawful wages by the school system. Insult was added to injury.

Looking back when I started at Gaither, I never received the enthusiastic welcome from Augie that I expected. One of the first things that I needed was some curriculum and specific lesson plans for the several courses that I was required to teach. I was generally aware of the curriculum, because of my experience as supervisor, but I never taught in a wood shop before and I needed immediate and specific assistance. I needed his experience. He gave me a curriculum guide that was ten years old, but no organized lesson plans. He did suggest a couple of projects, but no year-long plan for the shop. A few weeks later, I found all his old lesson plans in a file cabinet and selected previous lessons that would fit in the reorganized class year.

After the first semester, Augie told me to take an inventory of the shop equipment, power tools, hand tools and supplies. I told him, in no uncertain terms, that I'd rather not do it and suggested that he do it as department head, especially since he was a previous teacher in that classroom. I also noted that no inventory was done when I first came into the shop. I wasn't going to set myself up for an incomplete inventory when so many people had shop keys and so many tools were being borrowed without my knowledge. I smelled something fishy. He never did the inventory while I was there.

Another time Augie came to me and said another teacher, who was black, told Augie that I might be prejudice because of the way I treat students. I told Augie I treat all students the same. If a student breaks shop rules, I take the appropriate action. I run an ethical and proper classroom and am proud of it. I told Augie that if a student or another teacher felt I did something wrong, he or she should go to the principal; I was confident he would follow up on anything like that. Nothing was ever said again about my relationship with minority students.

A week later, Augie came to me again. He took me outside the building and said that the same teacher came to him about me again. She told Augie one of her students thought he smelled alcohol on my breath in the morning. Augie wanted to know my reaction. I was "humorously insulted," because I laughed and was offended at the same time. I told him there wasn't anything to it and I would volunteer to be tested at anytime. He said he just wanted to tell me. I said thanks.

At the end of the school year, June 4, Supervisor Mike Grego and Augie stopped in my shop with a newly-graduated teacher from Ball State. The teacher was interviewing for a job. They walked around the shop, avoiding me, and then went outside. I could hear them talking outside of the open door. Augie said to the new teacher "we need new blood in this shop" and "we plan to update and renovate the entire place." I felt Augie was cutting me down as an excuse to show how they would welcome a new and enthusiastic teacher in a shop that was going to be all "new." Augie's comments, in front of Grego too, cut deep into our "friendship."

This next part is very difficult for me to convey. I have known Augie Martinez, department head at Gaither, for about fifteen years. It has been a tradition in the supervisor's office to hire a teacher as a consultant during the summer to assist in up-dating the shop safety manual and to work on curriculum. When I became supervisor, I hired Augie for the summer. It helped my office and it was good training and experience for him, should he be interested in a promotion in the future. We had a good line of communication and common interests. We would talk about race cars, the Indy 500 and drag racing, in addition to school talk. I remember him asking me for my opinion of his design of a new deck with a jacuzzi that he was building.

I respected him because I saw, first-hand, the quality of the programs he taught when I would visit his school. As friends, we would always talk about, in detail, my problems with Smouse and the Board. His experience in my office gave him an understanding of some of the ridiculous procedures we had to follow. When I was running in the school board election, he came over and helped me assemble some of my campaign signs. I helped him shop for a new truck; he wanted one like my full-sized Chevy Blazer. We were at each other's homes frequently. During the Christmas holidays, after I was terminated from the system, he invited me to spend the day with his entire family. He knew I was going to be alone. I enjoyed the warm holiday visit. I surely didn't want to be out of work, depressed, and alone during the holidays.

After I was terminated and as the months went on, I remember telling him that he was the only teacher that kept up a regular dialogue with me. He told me that he frequently tried to defend my actions in talking to his assistant principal, Danny Valdez, at Gaither. I told him not to defend me because it would reflect on him and he would be labeled like I was. He said not to worry. Later, Danny Valdez was promoted to Director of Adult Education. I confided in Augie about my desire to write a book on what happened to me. I showed him some pages that I had written to get some feedback and to see if this was a feasible thing to do.

Sometime later, I remember Augie asking me about my book. I said that I had extensive documentation and I was currently writing the truth about what happened. I specifically remember him stating that he hoped that I had all this documentation in a safe place. I took that statement to mean that someone might want to get that documentation away from me, thus preventing me from writing the book. Then, I wondered if he was really asking me *if* the papers were in a safe place, or where the papers were? That made me think defensively and I told him they were safe. But, they weren't. They were in my condo, in a few folders on the dining room table. From then on, I decided to say that I gave up on writing the book because it was hopeless. However, I continued to write confidentially. I told many of my very close friends that I gave up too. I grew more concerned; a few months later, when Augie mentioned again that he hoped that my papers were in a safe place, to protect myself I told him that my attorney had copies of *all* my documentation.

Augie's questioning about my documentation reminded me of the caution that Hinda Klein, an associate of attorney Ellis Rubin, gave me about keeping my documentation in a safe place. Augie's comments turned out to be a second warning about the value of my papers.

Another incident caused me to ponder the "sanctity" of our friendship. Augie came over, without calling first, and I invited him in. He usually sat in my barber chair near the sliding glass door. We talked for awhile and then he asked for some bubble gum. I collect antique gum ball machines and they were across the room in the dining area next to my computer. They were full of gum and needed no coins. When he went over to get the gum, it was obvious to me that he was really looking and shuffling through my book chapters and newspaper articles that I was working on. My chapter outlines, in chart form, were hanging from the chandelier at his eye level. It was apparent, to anyone inside my condo, to see that I *was* writing something. My confidentiality was exposed. That was the last straw for Augie's visits. The next time he came by, I met him outside and said that I was advised to change my lifestyle and I'd rather that he not come in. I told him I was sorry. He accepted what I said and left. He never visited again.

The highlight of my year was on May 5, 1990. The officers of the Technology Student Association (TSA), previously called the American Industrial Arts Student Association, came to me and asked if I would be their club advisor for the next school year. I told them I was honored and I would be glad to, *if* I was returned to Gaither next year. I said I hadn't heard about my assignment for next year yet. I had previously worked with several of these students over the years when I was Supervisor. We already had a positive working relationship. My picture appears twice in the Gaither year book, once in the faculty section and again in the TSA Club picture.

On May 28, 1990, School Board Chairman Joe Newsome sent a letter to Ron Allen, signed by every Board member, expressing how pleased they were about his school being awarded a "Red Carpet School" by Commissioner Betty Castor. The letter said "It is the hard work, dedication, and leadership of our school principals, teachers, staff, parents, and members from our community, that make events such as the Red Carpet Schools program possible." The letter also indicated that Castor announced that Hillsborough County was leading the State in the number of Red Carpet School recipients. When I read the letter, I almost threw-up. Enough is enough.

Moving ahead to the end of the school year, I had submitted a request for reimbursement for in-county travel mileage. All supervisors have automatic in-county travel budgets. I used the same form and procedure that I had for three years as supervisor at the county office, except that I submitted it to Allen for his approval instead of Cammaratta, and asked him, in writing, to forward it to Earl Lennard. The $70.00 claim for mileage to the county office and for tool repair, all school business, was never paid. I never found out who stopped its processing.

On the last day of school for teachers, June 11, Augie put the icing on the cake for this chapter. His department, about ten vocational people, had a small party for one of the agriculture teachers who was transferring to another school because of low enrollment at Gaither. Augie baked a home-made cake for her party. It was in the shape of a horseshoe for good luck. We all signed her card, including me, wishing her the best. Augie already knew that I was being transferred. He said he knew some time before I did. However, there wasn't any cake for me, not even a fake cake, nor even a card to wish me well. I felt professionally and personally empty. When the cake was gone and everyone was leaving, Crimm, the electronics teacher, asked me where I was going next year. When I told him, everyone was immediately silent. Then, Crimm said my experience at Gaither would be useful training for my next teaching assignment. No one else commented, not even Augie, my department head.

Looking back at the classroom, I feel I was thrown into a snake pit and was expected to die an agonizing death. Nonetheless, the Phoenix rose from the ashes. Once a teacher, always a teacher, I'm proud to say. The Superintendent and School Board have taught me several "lessons in class" when it comes to their class act on how to provide students with the best possible education they deserve. Shame, shame.

In conclusion, I look at the situation that the Superintendent put me in at Gaither. Consider if this was a trial by fire?: I was demoted back into the classroom without any due process; my morale was down because of the court's decision on contempt; I hadn't taught in the classroom for over ten years; even though I had experience in teaching small gas engines and metal shop; I was placed in a course that I had never taught before—a wood shop; I was placed on the job with an extra class period, making me teach an overload from day one; I was placed on the job in the middle of the term; the students had a substitute teacher, not certified in industrial arts, for the last two months; students were restricted from doing any machine or bench work and were required to do "book work" because of safety; there had been a lack of appropriate discipline and management in the class. This was a set-up for a disaster. But the biggest challenge was still to come.

64

GO DIRECTLY TO JAIL

Is there a monopoly going on here between the school system and me?

Allow me to set the scene for this chapter. In Chapter 56—"Degrade Charade," the Board said to me, in a letter from Dr. Binnie, that I would be administratively transferred to a twelve-month classroom position when one became vacant. This meant that I could be transferred any time during the year. Well, it was the last week of school and I was still at Gaither High in a ten-month position. All the other teachers knew a month before what their job placements for next year would be, all except me. My teacher friends would ask me at lunch if I was coming back to Gaither next year or going somewhere else. I felt like a professional dummy telling them I didn't know. I truly had the perception I was like a game piece in a Monopoly game, if that's possible. It was obvious to me the other teachers pictured me as being used and abused.

I was willing to stay at Gaither and teach during the summer session if that would help make me a twelve-month employee.

Then finally, on June 4, 1990, Marilyn T. Wittner, Director of Instructional Personnel, called and wanted to meet with me. We set up a meeting for the next day. She said for some reason "they" stopped her from having our meeting two weeks before. I didn't ask any questions about that issue. She didn't tell me what the meeting was about. I didn't ask either because I'm conditioned to surprises with the school system. However, I had a good hunch it was about my assignment for next year.

The next day I met with Wittner and she presented me with a letter that was written a week earlier on May 29. She told me this was my assignment for next year, starting next week. She said the decision for this assignment was made by Earl Lennard. I considered him to be a "stepper-upper." Remember, he took Smouse's place. She made it clear that it was not her idea to transfer me. Her one paragraph letter started with this sentence:

Effective June 13, 1990, you will be administratively assigned to our educational unit located at Hillsborough County Jail East, where your assignment will be in the area of ABE/GED. Mr. Allen Rogers will be the person to whom you report....

The letter went on to say I should meet with Rogers, who would explain my new job. I have known Allen Rogers for almost twenty years. His position level is Supervisor, the same I'm supposed to be. Since when does a Supervisor supervise a Supervisor? Is this Board policy, or just another "board game?" Their move moved me. Was this being done as an example of consequences, to show all others what will happen to you if you stand up against the Superintendent and the Board?

According to Wittner, Lennard recommended that I be transferred to the jail, but all administrative assignments (transfers by the superintendent) must be recommended to the Board for approval by Sickles. I thought all this crap would be over after Smouse and Shelton retired; however, the momentum continues. The news media has told me that New York hotel queen Leona Helmsley was called the "Queen of Mean" by her employees. In my small world, I have a vote for the candidate known as the "King of Mean," and his last name begins with S. Take your pick, you need not limit you choice to only one.

The meeting with Wittner continued with her explaining that the new $68 million County Jail East was just built and dedicated. It was a state of the art concept in detention centers and she said there was an article in the paper the week before. I remembered seeing it on the TV news but I didn't see the newspaper article. So I went to the newspaper's main office and got a back issue. I was interested in knowing all about where I was going to work. The article made the new jail sound like a great place to work, if you can overlook the principle fact that I thought I should be working at the county office as a Supervisor in my previous position like the Circuit Court ordered.

I was up all that night after I learned I would be teaching at the jail. I just couldn't sleep. This wasn't fair; I didn't deserve to be treated like this. I'm a man of principle. This made it look like this "whole" thing was my fault. I was so mentally and physically exhausted the next morning, I called in sick at Gaither High.

Let me take a moment to explain the abbreviation ABE/GED in Wittner's letter. ABE means Adult Basic Education and GED means General Educational Development. Adult Basic Education is a program that is separate from Vocational Education where I previously worked. Adult Education has different goals, principles, philosophy, strategies and certification than Vocational Education. They are as different as English and Science programs. Perhaps, you can see what had just happened here. I had been transferred from one program area to another. I have no experience in adult education. I've never taught, administered or supervised Adult Education programs. All my experience has been in vocational education. My first teaching job after college was in vocational education in Hillsborough County, twenty years ago. I did take courses in Adult Education Administration to become certified as to enhance future promotions, but I'm not experienced.

Can you imagine what Lennard's decision did to me. It cut my legs off, my educational and experiential legs. All my vocational educational roots were useless. I have to build up all new relationships in adult education like those I built up in vocational education over the last twenty years in the state and in the nation. Now, I must start with zero experience. How long would it take me to qualify for a promotion in this county or have the experience to apply for a better job elsewhere in Adult Education? What about all the trade organizations and professional associations that I have joined. One decision wipes it all away. Not only do I just "Go Directly to Jail," but I also go back to "GO" and "don't collect $200.00." I have to start all over again. If this were a monopoly game, I guess I got the boot.

If this was Lennard's decision, it's difficult for me to understand why. He and I worked together under Cammaratta for over eight years. He had first-hand experience of my performance and capabilities as his colleague. If he thought I was so lacking in my performance, then why didn't he take Smouse's documentation of me and discharge me under the procedures in the Hillsborough Tenure Act? Did his decision possibly have anything to do with the fact that I also applied for the job that he now occupies? Was I Lennard's competition within the school system? Was this his opportunity to knock me down? Hmmm. Was a deal made when he was promoted that he would "take care of me" when and if he had to? Was politics a factor? These were actual questions raised by my family and friends.

I considered writing Lennard a letter asking him to justify his criteria for recommending to transfer me to a different program area from vocational. Then I thought to myself, do I really expect he would write back and say he was prejudiced against me and they put me in the jail to insult me and hoped that I would quit? I decided not to waste my time. I didn't write.

Let me test your memory. Remember back in Chapter 56—"Degrade Charade" when Binnie told me that I was reinstated and assigned to Gaither, but would be transferred to a twelve-month position like Seffner. At that time, I considered it to be a threat. Well, now that threat has come true by placing me at the County Jail which is like Seffner.

Don't get me wrong about Adult Education. I know the value of education at all levels. My very first teaching job was at a juvenile home with lock-up. I know I could do an excellent job in a jail setting like this one and it could be very rewarding. However, that's not the point. What about my future career in education; what are the realistic opportunities compared to what they could be in Vocational Education if I was still a practicing supervisor.

One last thought about Adult Education. The county Director of Adult and Community Education is Daniel J. Valdez. He was promoted from Gaither High School to this position and reported to Earl Lennard. I specifically remember watching the School Board meeting on Government access TV when Superintendent Shelton announced Valdez's promotion. There was a bit of laughter because someone commented that Valdez got the job because he played golf with Shelton. Shelton implied that it wasn't true because one of the second place candidates also had played golf with him, but he didn't get the job. Nonetheless, that year, 1990, that second place person, was promoted to Director of The Erwin Vo-Tech Center. But, Shelton was gone and he couldn't have any influence on someone who played golf with him being promoted to Director,...could he? All I can do now is to yell..."fore." Watch out everyone.

As per Wittner's instructions, I called Adult Education Supervisor Allen Rogers for an appointment. I met with him on June 12, 1990. He was very friendly and opened the discussion by saying he didn't know all about the things that happened between Smouse and me over the last several years, but it didn't matter to him. He said we knew each other before and he sees no problem working with me again. I think he was most professional and sincere in what he said. Consequently, my thoughts were that I wished he, and all others, *did* know what happened between Smouse and me, because I probably wouldn't have been in this situation if they had. How do I know what rumors he has heard. Don't forget, I am instructed to report to him. Would he be able to evaluate me in an unbiased manner? Supervisor supervising Supervisor? Adult Education Director Danny Valdez came over to Allen's office area and greeted me. He came through as *plastic*. I wasn't impressed. You can't fool me.

He went on to explain that I would attend a two-week workshop there at the Adult Center and I would be developing Adult Education curriculum to be used in their programs. This was confirmed in his Duty Assignment letter of June 19. Then he said I would spend some orientation time with Manuel Benitez, the teacher at County Jail Central and Ernie Diaz at County Jail West. Then, they said I should be ready to accept the full-time teaching position. It looked like a good orientation plan. He also indicated the new County Jail East wasn't quite ready yet and all of the prisoners hadn't been transferred. He finished with some general information and asked me for questions.

The orientation started with Manuel at Jail Central. He was most helpful. Of course, at first I had to explain where I came from and that I sued the Board and all the rest of the story. I told Manuel I would be teaching at the new County Jail East. He said that must be a newly-created teaching position. The orientation continued the following week with my afternoons at County Jail West with Ernie. The same introductions took place and he was most helpful too. Moreover, during our talks I found out that I wasn't going to the new jail; I was going to the old Jail Central to be the second teacher there. Someone had suddenly retired. It was downtown and was considered the maximum security jail of the three in the County. I was to teach high school diploma preparation to the juveniles that were housed on the third floor. While I had worked with Manuel at Jail Central, he did take me up to the third floor to see the juveniles area and the teaching room. It was the worst setting I've ever seen in which to teach. It was small, poorly lighted, very noisy, no cabinets or shelving and had benches like picnic tables. It had been used to feed the inmates, but now they eat in their cells. It was a disgrace to the concept of education.

In the middle of all this chaos with my transfer and my career, I'm usually able to find something that strikes me funny. In the Inmate Handbook at the jail there is a list of 51 Prohibited Acts that are in accordance with the Florida Administrative Code. Prohibited Act number 8 is "Escape." I couldn't figure why escape is listed at all. I thought prisoners should know they shouldn't escape. And if it should be listed, why wasn't it Prohibited Act number 1? I guess it just goes to show that some educators and some corrections administrators must think alike. Please remember I said some.

As the orientation continued, I began the Adult Education Workshop and began to develop the Adult Education curriculum from oral instructions. I felt a bit lost because of my lack of experience in Adult curriculum, but I commenced writing. The next day, I received written instructions as to what I was to develop. The letter, dated June 19, 1990, from supervisor G. H. McBride to Allen Rogers, outlined my responsibilities. In part the responsibilities read like this:

> ...It will be the task of Mr. Wieser to develop two activities per career development competency and three outcome test questions for each activity. Therefore, in English Skills IV the nine career development competencies will

be represented by a total of 18 activities and 54 outcome test questions. Using the same nine career competencies, 18 different activities and 54 outcome test questions will be needed to be developed for Life Management Skills.

The above needs to be completed and submitted to me by Monday, June 25 at 1:30 PM....

So, what do think I would be doing on Saturday, June 23 and Sunday, June 24? I was told that I was to work alone, because others would be doing work in different groups, although, adult supervisors would help me if I needed it. I did believe that I needed professional help now, but it wasn't the kind they could provide.

The third day into the workshop I became sick and remained at home for the rest of the week. I had a touch of a head cold, a ten ton headache and found myself taking deep breaths often. But more so, I found myself in a deep reactionary depression because of the way Hillsborough County Schools have treated me as a professional and as a person. I could sleep for only a few hours at a time to ease my pain. I went to sleep thinking about my problems with the system and woke up in the middle of the night thinking the same way. Thank God that I had Cable TV. I was in a nose dive and a tail spin. I wasn't sure which way was up. I wasn't even sure of upside down. I got worse and remained out sick the following week. My daily schedule and bodily functions were all mixed up. To feel better I would eat a big meal of my favorite food and then I would end up with diarrhea. Easy come, easy go. Damned if you do and damned if you don't.

I had to do something.

BEGINNING OF SCHOOL YEAR 1990–91

65

HEALTHY TIME-OUT

The years of frustration were taking a toll on me; I was near my limit. The assignment to the jail knocked my principles all to hell. I believed beyond any doubt that this was a political and punitive move and I clearly saw it as cruel and unusual punishment. It caused me to experience extreme stress. I finally looked for the easy way out. I decided to quit.

As a courtesy, I called attorney McKee, on June 29, 1990, to tell him that I was seriously planning to quit the school system. In our brief conversation, I remember him saying that if I quit, they win. And then he said it wasn't a bad job, teaching with supervisor's pay. He went on to say that I should consider a leave of absence; that would give me time to think things over. He added that nothing legal or binding would be affected by me leaving.

Pondering McKee's suggestion of leave as a viable option, I called a close colleague that I hadn't seen for sometime. After I told him of my present situation, he asked me who wins if I quit. Then he too suggested a leave of absence. That sold me on the idea of a health leave.

I made an appointment with my doctor for a check up on my stressed condition. I had been a patient of his on a regular basis for over a year. He diagnosed me of having chronic fatigue and experiencing a major depression. He placed me on the drug Buspar, a tranquilizer, for my stress. He commented about me being over-weight. I explained that when under stress, I don't do drugs or alcohol; I do refrigerators. I asked him for a letter to my employer so that I could request a leave of absence.

I contacted the school system's personnel office to inquire about the application and procedures for a leave. According to Mr. Gardner, Supervisor of Personnel, I had to submit the request through my work location; then it went through channels and on to the School Board for its approval. He told me that I would also need a letter of approval from my doctor to return to work. That was the least of my worries. I requested a six month leave that would start on the second week of July, 1990, two weeks into the new school calendar year. I claimed sick days until then.

The best thing for me now was to get as far away from the school system as possible. Recently, I had purchased a BMW motorcycle and joined a bike club in St. Petersburg. The bike, a "Beemer," was a rally-touring model and I was primed to travel cross-country with club members. It always had been a dream of mine to see this beautiful country by motorcycle like my grandfather did. Everything was right; I needed a get-away, had the time, had a reliable bike, club members to ride with and the money to go. Motorcycle travel can be rather inexpensive because you use little gas and we planned to tent camp rather than motel it.

My first big trip took me out to Wyoming, then Wisconsin, back out west to South Dakota and home to Florida. Later, I made several short trips along the east coast.

The bike trips were helpful in putting distance between the school system and me; however, I soon realized that I did carry some blind baggage. This turned out to be my unavoidable job experiences. I just couldn't escape them. For example, when in Oconomowoc, Wisconsin, visiting friends, we started talking about education. My friends just had their third child graduate from the local high school and problems with school systems became a dinner topic. After relating some of my experiences and saying that I had begun to write a book on the problems within education, they said that someone needed to enlighten them about the "goings on deep inside of education." This was encouragement for me to write; I even felt obligated, but I couldn't write. It was like being hungry with no appetite. The stomach says yes and the mouth says no.

I looked for an "out" from my job situation and decided to work with my hands and build a camping trailer to pull behind my motorcycle. This is the same type of therapy I used when my Dad passed away. Then, I did some life-size wood carvings of Florida pelicans. It was hard work creating the pattern with all the details, lots of concentration and sweat. A cleaning time away. When I finished the trailer in a couple of months, club members said it did not look homemade.

The trailer project helped me cope, but it wasn't enough. I had seen shows on TV where some Vietnam veterans were having a difficult time adjusting to regular life after the war. They were diagnosed as having a "post-traumatic stress disorder." With all the respect to the veterans, I believe that I was suffering from something similar if that could be true in a non-war setting. I was just coasting along, bouncing off of this and into that and not really caring about anything except that I wished it would be over so I could be something or someone. I was lonely, hopeless, had guilt about something, and preferred isolation.

As a matter of trust, I limited people who could get close to me. Since my experience with Donna, I had difficulty trusting any female who wanted to get close. Right away they would ask about my personal life and my job. This was restricted information for now. I was too vulnerable. Therefore, no personal relationships. Paranoid, if you wish. Job number one, protect thyself.

Around town I would be careful where I shopped. I'd wear a baseball hat and sunglasses when I went out. I'd look down store aisles before I went. I would avoid public places most of the time. If I saw someone I knew, what would we say after we said Hello?; would I be questioned about my job situation? I needed space. Later, I found out this was a form of agoraphobia, a fear of public places. I started to let my hair grow. I looked different. I was different.

My eyes tear when the little old lady is pulled from the twisted car wreck on *Rescue 911*. My mother always said I had sympathetic eyes, eyes that respond to pain and suffering. I think they've become even more sensitive since my ordeal began.

The majority of my personal exposure was in the motorcycle club over in St. Petersburg, away from Tampa. We didn't talk about the school system even though there were several teachers in the club. We talked about motorcycles and trips, mostly. I ran for office and was elected as president. All of my personal life was put into this club. I started to come out of my protective shell when I crossed the bridge from Tampa into Pinellas county. It was my only rewarding and fulfilling activity.

After my long bike touring trips were over, I bought a parrot. I remember seeing a number of shows on TV on how therapeutic pets were to people in the hospitals and nursing homes. I had a couple of dogs while a kid, but not pets as an adult. Now, I have a "friend" at home to talk to and play with. I named him Beemer because he was the same color as my motorcycle. I guess I could have given him the name Rex, but spelled Rx, because he turned out to be a real therapeutic pill. He was messier than I; he bites and I don't, but I love him.

A while back, I had made this commitment to a community volunteer and friend to be in charge of putting up signs to help celebrate Earth Day. Consequently, I was unable to do it now because I couldn't face the public. I didn't return her phone calls and knew that I betrayed her trust in me. Things like this were tearing me apart.

In August, 1990, an article was run in *The Tampa Tribune* about a teacher who criticized the administration of his school. He is now being transferred over his objections. The article says Superintendent Sickles is running the risk of creating a martyr of the teacher which would send a signal to others that if you speak out you'll get the same. A union representative said, "And if people can't speak out when they know there's a problem, what you're going to have is a powder keg that's going to blow up at some point down the road." In the end the principal was transferred. I still wonder what happened to my due process rights.

September, 1990, Sam Rampello, a fourteen-year veteran, won his re-election race to the school board with 54% of the vote. A *Tribune* article quotes Rampello saying "I look forward to an additional four years and working on behalf of the teachers and employees to make this the best school district in the country and the state of Florida." Marion Rodgers and Joe Newsome were both re-elected because they were uncontested. Business as usual.

A grass-roots petition is distributed in Tampa, by resident Jack Gargan called T.H.R.O. (Throw the Hypocritical Rascals Out). It asks Americans to vote every incumbent out of office. His petition attracted the eye of several national TV shows. Go Jack!

Lawton Chiles was elected as Governor of Florida. My fingers are crossed and I wish him the best.

Governor Bob Martinez gave raises to several high-level employees in the waning days of his administration, a *Tribune* article reported in November, 1990. The article explained that, if they lose their jobs when the new governor takes over, their severance pay will be calculated at a higher rate.

November, 1990, Betty Castor defeats former Gov. Claude Kirk, for a second term of state Commissioner of Education.

November 12 to 19, I try to comfort myself because I'm proud to be an educator during American Education Week.

December, 1990, former Tennessee Gov. Lamar Alexander is selected to be the next secretary of education for the Bush administration. My fingers are crossed on both of my hands.

Cammaratta tells me about his attendance at a graduation dinner at Tampa Palms. He saw Walter Sickles, Earl Lennard and other administrators there. Sickles said hello and shook hands and he said Earl just walked by with no hello, no handshake. Cammaratta said he was embarrassed for Lennard.

In November, 1990, a detective from the school system's security department called me at home. I practice screening all my calls as a part of my right to privacy and for my own protection. After his second call, I spoke with him and he said he had a letter to deliver to me and he wanted to bring it to my home.

This was totally suspicious to me. I surely didn't want anyone from school security at or near my home. I have been taught that the security department works unethically. I said that I would meet him at the Tampa Stadium parking lot. He could give me the letter there. He said I had to sign for it. I was leery, but I went. I took my gun.

The letter turned out to be from the Supervisor of Payroll. It was about my taxes for 1990. The letter said that I received a Final Judgement of $69,753.00 for back pay and taxes were not deducted by the school board and therefore a "problem exists." I was informed that the IRS recommended that I make an estimated tax payment on the $69,000 next month, using Form 1040-ES which the school system enclosed for my convenience; they forgot to enclose it, no convenience. The letter went on to say that I had to pay the school system $1,769.00 now for Social Security Tax. The letter ended with "Please note that this is a very important and vital issue and adverse IRS judgements could affect you personally." That wasn't a threat was it? I contacted my CPA and did what I had to. I called the supervisor of payroll and discussed the matter with her during the first week of December.

On a second issue, I don't believe that it is efficient for the school system to have a detective hand deliver a letter to an employee's home. A phone call to pick it up, or a post office signed receipt would be sufficient and cheaper.

About a month later, another school detective tried to contact me by phone. I returned his call, but he could not be reached by radio. Shortly thereafter, I came home and found a detective's business card on my front door. I felt violated. The card had no message on it. Then my neighbor across the street said he saw a policemen, in uniform and wearing a gun, park in my space and go up to my condo when I was out. I was angry. I consider this to be a form of harassment, a violation of privacy and a waste of taxpayer's money. I called the security office and told them I would pick up the second letter at the security office. I was convinced that they were trying to get me to quit.

The second letter, December 21, again from the Supervisor of Payroll, simply summarized our phone call earlier in the month and repeated what taxes I owed and to whom. Oh yes, she did acknowledge that she "failed" to send me the tax form for my convenience. She didn't wish me a Merry Christmas.

I was apprehensive about an article in *The St. Petersburg Times* two weeks later on January 9, 1991. A man impersonating a police officer in Little Rock, Arkansas, handcuffed and abducted a person, drove him out of town, stabbed him six times, dragged him to the edge of a pond and left him to die. Police reports said that he confessed to killing two people in Oklahoma and is a suspect in two other murders in North Carolina. You never know what can happen, even from a man in uniform.

I was sure that I was a prime candidate for a heart attack. I heard news reports that said a study showed that if you take simple aspirin daily, you will reduce the possibility of a heart attack. I took one a day.

During this health leave my weight increased. I ate and ate my troubles away. My weight peaked at 271 pounds on my 5'9" frame. I looked and felt obese.

I kept seeing negative information about my chosen profession as a teacher. The Baywinds Learning Centers, a popular, private group in the Tampa Bay area, offers non-credit courses for adults. Their 1990 catalog advertises a course called "Alternative Careers for Teachers." It insults me and my profession, but I can understand the long-term career needs of teachers.

The frustrating times just keep coming. I still want to fight for what is right. I don't really want to leave education.

66

ATTORNEY NUMBER 3⅞

As strong as anything that I believe in, I believe I have been wronged by the school system and I must continue to work toward making things right.

I haven't found attorney number 4 yet; that's why these others have received fractional identity.

Television, newspapers and all of the media has some impact on what I do and how I think. So often I have seen noteworthy and reputable attorneys on television or in the print media who took on and defended justice in a landmark case.

One of several of these dynamic attorneys was Gerry Spence from Jackson, Wyoming. You may recall his work on the Karen Silkwood case and more recently representing former Philippine first lady Imelda Marcos. I decided to contact him because there was an unexplainable feeling I had about his projection of truth and justice. Perhaps it had to do with the time I traveled through Wyoming and the west. I acquire a mental image of people with an unbiased good ol' cowboy demeanor. I was told that in many small towns the people don't lock their cars or houses. All of that enticed me and my principles of life.

If he concludes that I had some kind of case to bring to justice, I was sure he would be interested in representing me because my case was one where the little guy ends up fighting the big system. It could be an all-American grass roots feature.

I called on Halloween, October 31, 1990. He was out of the office and would be back around 3:00 p.m., Tampa time. On my second call, I spoke to one of his associates named Rosemary. After I explained that I was interested in obtaining Gerry Spence's services, I summarized what had happened to me in the school system. She said I might have a defamation case; however, I should consult with an attorney in Florida who is familiar with Florida law. I asked for a recommendation for a Florida attorney. She said they were working on a medical malpractice case here, but she couldn't even recommend anyone. I had hoped to be able to share some of my documentation with him, but it wasn't meant to be. I wasn't able to get through to speak with Spence. I was dejected.

Sure, I was relatively disillusioned. I was starting to believe I may not have a case in the court system to right my perceived wrongs. Only two options came to light: first, just say "uncle" and give up or change my philosophy of life, philosophy of education and what I believed in or secondly, write a book and seek to clear my name and career through the public domain.

The ball was in my court. I was still searching for the justice that Gerry Spence talked about in his book titled *With Justice For None*.

67

184/120 HYPERTENSION

My six month health leave was up and I needed a release from my doctor to return to work. I knew I had anxiety about my return, but I had no other practical option. My friends urged me to return because I needed the money; they said I should hold my head high.

It was January, 1991; I was sitting in my Doctor's reception room reading the last month's *Reader's Digest*. I happened to turn to a story written by Dr. Joyce Brothers. Her story told about her husband, who, in his early 50's, developed hypertension, and then other complications; he died a few years later. It was sad. I always enjoyed hearing her speak on TV.

I felt relaxed when the nurse took my blood pressure until she took it three times to be sure of the reading. Dr. Ciliberto came in and examined me. I asked him if he would release me to go to work. He told me that I definitely wasn't going back to work; in fact, he was contemplating whether he should put me in the hospital immediately. He explained that my blood pressure, of 184/120, was at the "explosion" level. This was serious. It was hypertension. He indicated that my heart couldn't rest even when I was asleep. He directed me to immediately change my diet and be aware of any pain in my chest or arm; if I had any, I should call him immediately, day or night. I was given literature about my condition. He suggested that I apply for disability. I was to report back for another office visit in two days.

I was 48 at the time, but this diagnosis made me feel very old and frail.

I was placed on Verelan for my blood pressure and Buspar for my nerves and anxiety, double dosage. I didn't expect this result; it scared the Hell out of me because my dad died of a massive heart attack. I'm now aware that high blood pressure is called the "silent killer."

I applied for an extended health leave for another three months. When I filled out the forms at the Adult Education Center, I saw several of the other "real" supervisors there. I spoke to Joe Perez and told him that I had seen him on TV the week before on a continuing education show at USF. He commented on my weight gain and said he heard that I was grooming myself for another job. I mentioned that I had planned to come back, but I developed hypertension. "It makes you think about what's important in life," he reflected.

After the usual red tape, my health leave was approved. When my leave was over, I was told I would be assigned to my former school.

Several weeks later, my blood pressure was "down" to a still life-threatening 172/110. Dr. Ciliberto told me to be aware of "mini" stroke symptoms: I should be alert to sudden changes of my face muscles, slurred speech, and a crooked tongue. I had to stay away from salt. He sent me to a specialists to check my red eyes for blood clots. I also had a chest x-ray to check for an enlarged heart and an EKG to check heart rhythm. All were okay. I settled into a new routine of awareness.

The war broke out in the Gulf and Americans developed an immediate and unified patriotic surge. The chronicle of the 100-hour ground war is well known. However, some specific details about the Tampa Bay area brought the war closer to home. Operation Desert Shield had its U. S. Central Command headquarters here at MacDill AFB. The country's very first concern, after the announcement of war, was what to tell the children; how do we tell them that mommy's going to fight and she might not come back? What about the kid's stress about their teachers and principals going off to fight? How do you explain death of a teacher to a third grader? There was much talk about the wellness of the children during the war. I was glad to see that our basic instincts came to life for the importance of our children.

The nation's eyes were on Tampa during the 25th Silver Anniversary Super Bowl. Tampa was put on alert. People were buying gas masks at the local Army/Navy store. Security was at a pinnacle: land, air, and sea. The pre-game and half-time shows were performed by youngsters of central Florida; a number of them were children of soldiers in Desert Storm. The children gave a salute, choreographed by Disney, to their "heroes" in the Arabian desert. It was very patriotic to say the least, of the kids. When our country is at war, we think of the kids first and they respond. We need to do the same thing when we think about our children's education. The children's future is dependent upon us and our future is dependent upon our children. E Pluribus Unum.

When the Gulf War ended, *The Tampa Tribune* published an article entitled, "School chief calls gulf victory a credit to U.S. public education." The article began with the following:

> Walter Sickles, superintendent of Hillsborough County schools, sees the American victory in the Mideast war as a vindication not only of the military, but of the U. S. public education system as well....
> "Our education supports our culture in this particular country. It is an education that stands up to the test," he said.

In the spring of 1991, I was given a copy of an NCLA Lettergram. You may remember this was the National Council of Local Administrator's (vocational) that Ralph Smouse went to work for. The ten-page newsletter was sent by Smouse. One page listed the directory of national and regional officers. Smouse was listed as Executive Director with address, home phone and FAX access. The FAX was indicated to be at the Erwin Vo-Tech Center, which is part of the Hillsborough Public School System.

I couldn't help but to remember that Smouse had once reprimanded me because I used a sewing machine in the upholstery class. Although this use of school equipment was common-place, it was a misuse of school equipment and he was right; I was wrong for using it. I decided to look into this suspected misuse of school equipment by a retired employee. I sent a FAX letter to Smouse through his printed national FAX number with the school system. I used a fictitious name, a friend's address in Pinellas County and said I was interested in joining NCLA. Sure enough, two weeks later, I received a letter and application from Smouse. Later, I also received a letter from the Pasco County School Board with an application for the Florida affiliate (FCLA) of NCLA.

Please explain to me why was I reprimanded for misuse of school equipment by Smouse, who then turns around and does the same thing? Is there a double standard here, or is it because his daughter is an administrator at the Erwin Vo-Tech Center? Things like this prevented my recovery from job stress and hypertension. I began to write this book again to help my mental health.

You never know when two-cents worth of meaningful encouragement will appear. I purchased take-out Chinese food and the fortune cookie said "Depart not from the path which fate has you assigned." I took this as a requisite to finish my book.

A Canadian researcher reported that taking blood pressure medication with grapefruit juice boosts the amount of drug that gets into the blood. I immediately switched from daily orange juice.

Newspaper reports emphasized another disappointing fact that I was already aware of. The Industrial Arts programs in Florida were undergoing a radical update in program philosophy. The new name would be "Technology Education" and it would emphasize high-technology trends in conjunction with Florida Education Commissioner Betty Castor's "Blueprint for Career Preparation." The newspapers spotlighted several schools that were changing to the new technology and they interviewed the supervisor that replaced me. The door was slammed in my face to be a leader in this technology change on a local and state basis when I was wrongfully terminated and then involuntarily transferred to teach at the jail. I felt like an outcast; I missed the boat to the future.

My three-month leave was over. Dr. Ciliberto told me that I wasn't ready to return to work and recommended that I take the rest of the school year off (three more months). He asked me if I could afford to; I replied that I would have to. His letter to the school board indicated I had erratic hypertension which was unstable and uncontrolled. Ciliberto did some additional testing because there was question if I was becoming diabetic.

My application for another extended leave was approved.

In May, Tampa was in the international spotlight again when Queen Elizabeth II of England visited and made Tampa resident General H. Norman Schwarzkopf an honorary knight for his leadership in the Gulf War. The School Board, too, honored him by naming a new elementary school after him. Speculation about Schwarzkopf running for political office in Tampa or Florida ran high. I wish he would have run for the school board. He didn't.

The topic of ethics at local, state, and national levels kept appearing in the media. It attracted, or should I say distracted, my attention regarding my job of writing my story. A sample of these follows:

The local news told about a principal who, after numerous parental complaints, was found guilty of six out of sixteen charges made against him. These included "promoting children without proper procedures; ordering an employee to falsify records; grouping children by racial and ethnic backgrounds and intimidating students, parents and employees," according to *The Tampa Tribune*. The principal requested a transfer to the county office in the position of supervisor and it was approved. I want to know why he wasn't fired as I was or at least transferred to the jail to teach?

On June 13, 1991, *The St. Petersburg Times* reported that at least 24 legislators had been hauled into court in an investigation of failing to report free trips they accepted from lobbyists. The state Ethics Commission said it had cleared some legislators, while others admitted it was an error. These are the same legislators who govern the education legislation and education budget.

Also on June 11, 1991, the *Times* ran an article by Rep. George Miller, D-Calif., with a dateline in Washington. The article began like this:

> The sleaze factor is slipping back into the White House.
>
> During the Reagan administration the number of ethical transgressions by high-ranking presidential advisors created a sleaze factor that resulted in dozens of resignations, dismissals and indictments.
>
> Bush administration repudiated such conduct, vowing it would tolerate no impropriety in the behavior and finances of its high officials.

Miller went on to talk about John Sununu and his personal use of military aircraft, and Attorney General Richard Thornburgh's involvement in the settlement of the oil spill in Alaska. Ethics and government kept popping up wherever I looked or listened.

I was so glad to see that a course titled "Ethics in Government" was being offered during the 1991 summer at the University of South Florida in the Continuing Education program. The course description stated "Recent scandals and allegations of wrongdoing in the U.S. Congress and Florida Legislature and increasing numbers of ethics complaints filed against local government officials have made ethics in government an issue that will not disappear." I paid my fee for the non-credit course, and then found out that it had been cancelled because of lack of enrollment.

At this time, my credit cards were my financial life blood. I was going deeper in debt, but I really didn't want to return to the school system. Perhaps, I could get an advance on my book which would allow me to pay my bills while I finished writing. Then I could look for another job, something I could do from my home, since moving was financially out of the question.

On the first approach to sell my book, I sent information to nine selected agents, trying to secure their services. All rejected it. Plan B, go directly to the publishers. Again, I selected what I considered to be the top sixteen publishers which included companies in New York, San Francisco and Boston. Twelve rejected it; four didn't respond.

Now, I was dejected and broke. I had to go back to work to be able to afford to live and self-publish my book, if I could only finish writing it. I wondered if it was worth it. Was I too stubborn to admit that writing the book could be a lost cause or that it might create more harm for me than good? What if...?

I was still experiencing sleeping and eating disorders. I would get severe headaches more often, especially when I would awaken. Luckily, I didn't have much of a desire for alcohol, even though my doctor recommended that I have a glass of wine occasionally to relax.

July, 1991, break time was over; still on medication and with Dr. Ciliberto's approval, and with no other convenient form of income, I returned to teaching in the Hillsborough County school system under tension.

BEGINNING OF SCHOOL YEAR 1991–92

68

ATTORNEY NUMBER 3[15/16]

A friend and neighbor of my brother and school teacher mother back in Wayne, New Jersey, Joe Afflitto, was generally aware of my situation here and he recommended that I contact internationally-known attorney F. Lee Bailey. Afflitto was a well-known attorney in his own right in New Jersey, and had worked with Bailey before. My brother called and told me that Joe recommended that I contact Bailey's office, in West Palm Beach, Florida, because Bailey was looking for a big case to give some PR to his new Florida office. It sounded great to me. I was well aware of F. Lee Bailey's reputation. My brother told me that I should mention Joe Afflitto's name because the office would be expecting my call. It was June, 1991 and my brother said that Bailey was currently in New York working on a criminal case. It was on all the TV stations.

When I called the office, I first spoke with Arvis, Bailey's secretary. When I mentioned that I wanted to set up an appointment with Bailey, she asked me what the case was about. "Wrongful termination and defamation of character for starters," I said. I explained that I wanted to meet with Bailey to see whether he felt that his office could be of assistance to me. I saw that it would be very difficult to explain the depth of my case over the phone. She asked me if I was ready to pay a $5,000 retainer. I knew then that my inside connection wasn't as clear as I had hoped. I mentioned Joe Afflitto's name and she did recognize him.

Arvis then said that I had to first speak to an associate of Bailey's, David Schultz. I tried four times to contact him over the following couple of weeks. Finally, I wrote him a letter, outlining seventeen points of my case. When I did get to speak to him several weeks later, he told me he didn't have my letter, but that it might be in the pile of mail he received while he was gone. He then asked me to explain my case over the phone. Again I tried to summarize. But I got the feeling as I was telling him about a school teacher who was fired that my case just didn't have the sizzle he was looking for. Then, I dropped the bomb. I inquired about Bailey taking my case on a contingency basis.

Schultz clearly told me that Bailey doesn't take cases on a contingency basis. However, if I wanted to hire Bailey, I would need to pay a $25,000 retainer, plus $10,000 for expenses. An hourly rate of $250 to $350 per hour would then be applied to the retainer. Schultz did say that Bailey was planning a trip to Tampa in two months. I knew then that my chances of meeting with Bailey, even in Tampa, were remote.

One of my neighbors in Tampa told me that he just heard Bailey speak at an insurance conference in Orlando. He said Bailey was top notch, the best there is. He said Bailey really did his homework, knew his stuff, and knew how to present it. I was drooling on my crossed fingers.

I called my brother again in New Jersey. I told him of my failure to set up a meeting with Bailey. When I told him about the letter to Schultz, he said I should have written directly to Bailey. That was the inside tract that was given to us. I then wrote another letter directly to Bailey giving additional information and sent it certified mail with a return receipt.

Just two days later, I received a letter from Bailey's law office written by Schultz. It was obvious that he did not get my last letter. Schultz's letter explained that Bailey regrets that he cannot take on the representation of my interest because he must limit the number of cases in order to adequately meet the demands of each case and the needs of the client. He went on to say that their firm knows of no one in my area who handles this type of law. The letter went on to say that he hoped I would be able to reach some type of resolution.

The letter was no surprise to me; I saw that the fact that I was asking their law firm to consider taking my case on a contingency basis was a stumbling block. I certainly can understand them having enough work, paid up front, and not take a gamble on a case that might not pay off in the end.

All in all, I was thankful to Joe Afflitto for his recommendation. My only disappointment was the fact that I couldn't present more extensive documentation to Bailey in a short, one on one meeting.

But, it just wasn't meant to be.

I continue to search for attorney number 4, so that I can finally set this albatross free, have a normal career and return to a normal lifestyle. I don't need a lot.

In June, 1991, *The Tampa Tribune* reported on some Florida school district discrepancies in vocational reports. The article, titled "Report says schools padded jobs data," began with the following:

"To keep their programs from losing state money, school districts have inflated the number of vocational school graduates who found jobs," a state report says.

Dozens of vocational school programs have failed to meet state standards for employment rates, records show, but only a handful have lost funding as the law requires....

The local district's numbers are "impossibly high," a state Senate report says....

Hillsborough County, for instance, reported placement rates of 96 percent for high school vocational programs and 97 percent for adult programs. The state computer showed 76 percent and 72 percent of these students were in jobs, not taking into account whether the jobs were related to the training.

What this means, according to the Senate report, is that when schools face penalties for inefficient programs, they'll focus on changing their statistics to make the programs look better.

That's what Dade County officials did when they lost money for some of their programs last year because the placement rates reported by some of their schools were too low....

The article went on to say that it was difficult to follow-up on some students and...one solution was to do away with the threat of cutting off the money. It also said they were looking for a way to check on these programs.

69

JAILBIRD

While still under my doctor's care, I returned to work with the school system. In some distant way, I think I can understand why repeatedly abused wives return to their husbands. I returned to the school system for the same reasons: I love education; I can't afford to move; I probably couldn't get a better job somewhere else right now; I was far into debt; I needed an immediate and convenient paycheck, (well up on the pay scale); I believed that the worst had passed and things probably would get better. Could they get worse?

In July, 1991, I reported to Mr. Allen Rogers, Supervisor of Adult Special Programs, at the Adult Education Center. I wondered if I would be placed back at the old county jail to teach the juveniles. He said I would be assigned to the new county jail to teach GED to adult inmates. He indicated they had a position there for me that was newly created.

I would be the sixth full-time teacher at County Jail Central. There were three vocational teachers with programs in agriculture, sewing and culinary arts. The culinary arts program was previously under my supervision when I had been the real supervisor. Also, there was a teacher of GED, a teacher conducting a vocational assessment program, and several part-time people teaching days and/or evening GED classes. There was one full-time education counselor who had an office at the jail. He was the "contact" person at our work site.

The culinary arts instructor, Bill Taniguchi, and I had worked together since 1979. He ran an exceptional, well-balanced food service program. His previous experience was that of chef on Air Force One. He "served" four presidents, but always wanted to be a teacher. He asked what had happened to me because he wanted to clarify the different rumors he heard. I summarized what happened over the last few years and then we exchanged some detailed stories about other people in my previous office. In the end, he complimented me several times for supporting his program back then at a different correctional prison. He was sorry that all this happened to me.

Rogers told me to report to Ed Wickham, the school system's counselor at the jail, and instructed me to follow any direction that Wickham gave me as though it came from him. I felt degraded even more because Rogers and I were both "supervisors" and now I was supposed to take directions from someone subordinate to us. I keep getting "demoted" in this system, contrary to what the courts declared.

Roger's supervisor was Danny Valdez, Director of Adult Education. You may remember that he was assistant principal at Gaither (before I was there) and Augie Martines told me that he often spoke to Valdez about my problems with the system. Valdez did *not* give me a welcome back to Adult Education.

Wickham assigned me to Housing Unit 6. The one-year-old jail, a state-of-the-art facility, had seven housing units with room for about 250 inmates in each unit, thus, a total of 1,700 inmates. Wickham instructed me to spend a week with Ernie Diaz, GED teacher in Housing Unit 5, before teaching on my own, so Diaz could orientate me to the school's procedures in the jail. Ernie had taught in the prison system for 22 years. Ernie and I quickly became friends. He helped me a lot and I assisted him whenever I could.

Ernie talked rather straightforwardly to me. He told me the biggest problem that I would find at the jail was the difficulty in keeping class enrollment up to a minimum of 18. He said that keeping enrollment up results in being left alone by the administration. I wasn't too sure about that in my case. The GED educational program was voluntary, except for several court-ordered students. He emphasized the reality of "turn-over" of students, saying the *average* stay of an inmate in the jail was 15 days. The average enrollment for a student on his class roll was 7 days with 3 days of actual "show up" time. He said that last year he only had one student long enough to pass the GED exam.

For the most part, I immediately saw this job as a challenge to interest inmates in the GED concept (rather than try to complete it) and encourage them to finish the GED when they were released back onto the street or if they were transferred to one of Florida's state prisons.

The enrollment, testing and attendance paper work turned out to be horrendous, to say the least. I had to recruit, orientate, and test each student, evaluate the results of the tests, register the inmates in my class, counsel them, and assign class work, as well as TEACH, and review the daily work of each student. So often, a student was gone in one or two days. You hardly ever knew if he was transferred to another unit of the jail, made trusty status, was sentenced to state time, was released or what. The few days of intense paper work went in a folder and had to be kept on file for two years.

My overall orientation to my job at the jail was terrible. I was never introduced to the sheriff's administration, I was not given a tour of the facility (even when I asked for one), was never introduced to the civilian workers (case workers, library, secretaries, custodians) or to the deputies in my unit. I introduced myself whenever I could. However, what limited orientation that I did receive came from Ernie.

The first week I began teaching on my own, Wickham assigned me to teach six hours of class time. It is a county rule that teachers have a maximum of five hours of contact time with students per day. My computerized teaching schedule came out from Rogers and it had six hours of daily classes. Everyone else was teaching five. When questioned, Wickham said the mandate for my six-hour schedule came from Earl Lennard through Rogers.

I thought to myself, Lennard is testing me to see if I "faded" while I was on my health leave. I decided unless I showed Lennard my true colors, I would be black-and-blue all year long. I told Wickham, as directly as I could, that he was to inform Lennard that I would be teaching a five-hour schedule, unless I was to be paid overtime. Period! A few weeks later, Wickham came down to my classroom and said that "Mr. Lennard feels that I should remain on my current schedule for now (5 hours)." They blinked. I only ask that they follow the rules. I don't ask for any special favors.

To keep abreast of news within the school system, I called the downtown administration office and asked that I be sent a copy of the "Administrative Bulletin," a weekly newsletter from downtown. The secretary asked who I was. I gave my name and said I was a supervisor. Then, she asked "supervisor of what?" I didn't know what to say, I wasn't in industrial arts anymore, so I said "supervisor of adult education?" The rustling of paper I heard over the phone indicated to me that she was looking at a list. She said she would have to do some research on my request. The message was coming through loud and clear; I was a supervisor of *nothing*, and I was a supervisor who received directives from a position (counselor) several steps subordinate to mine.

Meanwhile, my classroom tribulations continued. Ordering supplies turned out to be a trial by fire. I shared an office with the evening part-time GED teacher. She came into my class one day and we introduced ourselves, exchanging the usual pleasantries: "we looked forward to working together." She was using a number of her own office supplies brought from home and requested that I order supplies for her too. I wasn't given a budget for the year, as I did for my teachers when I was supervisor. Nonetheless, Wickham told me to just fill out a supply request form. I was ultra conservative in ordering only what the two of us needed for the school year. I ordered 38 line items.

A few days later, a few supplies were in my mailbox as was a copy of my request. Wickham must have wanted to play "King for a Day" because he cut my order to pieces. There were no chalkboard erasers, so I ordered three. He allowed me two. I requested a name plate for my desk because the new students kept asking for my name. The name plate was rejected. I requested five rolls of scotch tape; he gave me one. Requested five reams of paper, got one. Requested two tape recorders for non-English speaking students like the two recorders that Ernie had. Denied. Requested three boxes (not cases) of paper clips. Received one box, one little box of (illegal) metal paper clips. (A jail rule requires that we are to use plastic paper clips because inmates are not to have access to metal ones.) Ordered five *boxes* of pencils for the year, got one *package* of twelve pencils. Requested a calculator for computing the results of the Test of Adult Basic Education (TABE) like the one Ernie used. The state requires that the TABE be given to every student upon entering the class. Calculator denied. A sponge to wash the chalk board. Denied. Five yellow hi-lite markers, got one. Five blue hi-lite markers, got zero. Two pair of plastic (legal) scissors, got one in metal (illegal). And requested a calendar. Denied. (Wickham sent me refills for it in January, but I still didn't have the holder!) Management at its best? I was well aware of county budget restraints, but this nickel/dime confrontation bordered on intimidation and harassment, not dollars and *sense*.

The class provided pencils and paper for the inmate's class work. To keep my sanity, I purchased pencils with my own money at the flea market, ten for a dollar, rather than go pleading to Wickham. For Thanksgiving, I got orange pencils. In December, I needed more pencils, so I bought red ones and green ones: Merry Christmas. In January, I got the ones with sparkles. Happy New Year everyone.

I had two inmates in their sixties and they needed glasses to read the tests or workbooks. They were in jail for the long haul. They said the jail gave them a hard time about getting glasses. I didn't even bother to ask Wickham. Ernie told me he bought some basic reading glasses for his students to borrow. I decided to do the same. I bought two new pairs of generic reading glasses at the flea market. The glasses worked great and so did the two inmates.

One of these older inmates, Craig, had trouble with writing the number 8. His number was slanted, open at the top and flat like a pancake. He asked for assistance. I always had a theory about teaching children how to write their letters and numbers. I thought this would be a good chance to try out my theory and see if it would work for an adult. I used the chalk board to draw a three-foot-tall number 8. I had Craig trace over it slowly and told him to be sure to put his entire body into the motion of tracing it. I pointed out to him where he was taking a "short cut" across the roundness of the number and made him correct his line. Then, I had him slowly draw his own number next to mine, still three foot tall. When it was satisfactory, I had him practice drawing the same size number down the rest of the board increasing his speed naturally and then stepping back to study and admire his work. He smiled and said they looked good.

In the next step, I drew a one-foot-tall number and had him trace it using only his arm for the tracing movement. Then, he drew his own again and practiced on the rest of the board space. The next step was a four-inch number, using only his wrist for movement, then following the same procedures as before. At last, we were ready to move to paper. I drew a one-inch number 8 on paper for him to trace and said he was only to move his fingers for the tracing; then, draw his own and practice.

Finally, I drew a "normal" size number 8, about a quarter of an inch, and he followed my steps again, increasing his speed to a natural rate. From a population of one, I "proved" my theory to myself or at least to Craig who said: you *can* teach an old dog new tricks! I didn't consider him an old dog because he was also teaching me things about adults and education, especially in a correctional facility setting. I was proud to see this positive event come out of my experience in the jail.

I always went into work early to read the newspaper before class. I would then give the paper to the inmates to read. They were grateful for the access. In August, 1991, I noticed an article in *The Tampa Tribune*, dateline Washington, which said the following about the state of education as a nation:

> Scholastic Aptitude Test (SAT) scores of high school seniors fell to a record low this year in verbal skills while mathematical scores declined for the first time since 1980, the College Board announced....
>
> ...Florida students continue to post slightly lower average scores on the verbal and mathematical portions compared to the rest of the country....

Recently, my interest in the prison system has heightened. On September 27, 1991, a news report said that money is the problem that is preventing Florida from having a prison system that doesn't quickly recycle criminals onto the street. State corrections officials said the state budget shortfall is the main problem in managing the correctional system. Officials also said it is now up to the taxpayers and the lawmakers to correct this problem.

My assigned teaching area, Housing Unit 6, was divided into four "pods" A,B,C and D, as are other housing units. Each pod had a deputy in charge, except pod C (Charlie); it had four deputies because it was maximum security. Pod 6 - Charlie was divided into five "mods." All cells were isolated (1 person). Inmates were placed in there for various reasons, but mainly because they were not to have contact with other inmates. These inmates were not allowed to come out of 6 - Charlie to participate in any jail programs. This meant that I had to draw my enrollment from the remaining three pods, while Ernie in unit 5 and part-time teachers could draw from four pods to meet their enrollment quotas. The part-time evening teacher sharing my office drew from the same population as I did, thus reducing my potential source even more. Ernie had no part-time teacher sharing his assigned unit 5 to draw students away from his enrollment. He still complained about the continuous concern to maintain the required class size. I thought of a good way to increase my chances of maintaining the required class size was to eliminate the evening part-time GED program because both of our programs were drawing from the same inmate population. The evening program wasn't needed since I returned. However, it was kept in place nonetheless.

Ernie had introduced me to a civilian employee who worked in the administration offices up front. She asked where I worked and I said in Unit 6. She exclaimed; "Oh, your down there with the crazies!" I was a bit surprised, but I said yes. Inmate Danny Rolling, who was indicted for the 1990 grisly mutilation murders of five University of Florida students, was housed in 6 - Charlie. He was in Tampa on trial for robbery, burglary and a gun battle with police. Everyone, inmates and sheriff deputies knew about "6 - Charlie."

In September, Chris Reed, a civilian case worker with the sheriff's department assigned to unit 6, told me of an inmate from 6 - Charlie who would be attending my regular class, because "we" couldn't discriminate with those in lock-up. I had blind trust in her, so I didn't challenge her directive. She was blond, thin, attractive, a "ten," a real girl-next-door. Whenever I was ready to start class, I was to notify the Sergeant's office across the hall and the deputy there would call the pod deputy and request that the GED students be escorted to my class. The reverse procedure was used at the end of the two-and-a-half hour class session in the morning and afternoon.

The next day I called the sergeant to send out the GED students. I specified that I also had one inmate coming out of 6 - Charlie. He asked who said so? When I told him that Chris Reed informed me about it, he said "she can't do that." I was a bit apprehensive. However, fifteen minutes later, the sergeant brought the inmate to me and said it was okay.

The first week of class went well. The inmate, Kevin, was a black 19-year-old, with no high school diploma. He said he was placed in 6 - Charlie because he beat up another inmate with a telephone when he was taken to appear in court. I worked closely with him. He was a hard worker and was no problem to me. I was still apprehensive, not with the inmate, but with the administration and their procedures with 6 - Charlie.

The next week, the day before an announced visit by Earl Lennard and Superintendent Sickles, Chris Reed told me the 6 - Charlie inmate would not be coming out anymore. What a coincidence? However, she said that I should tutor him inside of 6 - Charlie, in his maximum security cell. I knew I could fight this if I wanted because it was student contact beyond the maximum five hours per day. Yet, I had developed a rapport with this student because he really wanted to learn. I decided to follow the directive given to me through the sheriff's office.

By the way, I was told by Rogers that Lennard and Sickles had never been to the jail. How could Lennard ethically recommend that I be administratively transferred to a place like this when he had never witnessed this program? Coincidentally (?), now that I was there, they're making a visit. What would I say to them after I said Hello?; would I look at my two chalk board erasers, my one roll of scotch tape, my lack of tape recorders for Spanish speaking inmates, my one box of illegal "metal" paper clips? I called in sick the next day because I couldn't face Lennard or Sickles; my irony level was too high. I'm sure my blood pressure went up a few notches too.

Continuously, Wickham gave me written directives to go into 6 - Charlie to tutor court-ordered inmates and to sign up specifically named new students. Also, he had me give GED test results to a student who failed and to one who passed his test that he took before he was arrested. Clearly, this paper work was *his* duty as program counselor, the administrative liaison between us and the jail and the Adult Education district office. Why was I always asked to do it, especially since I had to do it during my lunch hour or planning time. It was assigned overtime (student contact) that I was never compensated for in wages *or* gratitude.

I must say that I *did* agree to tutoring Kevin in 6 - Charlie on my own time, but that one case should not have been taken as blanket approval. I didn't like being abused.

I am pleased to say that it became very rewarding to teach Kevin, even in maximum security. Whatever work I assigned, he took full advantage of it.

The deputies in 6 - Charlie couldn't understand why I kept coming in on my own time because Kevin was one of their worst behavior problems. He would argue and fight with the deputies, throw food all over and clog up his toilet to flood his cell. His cell was on the second floor and of course water runs downhill, so it would flood the first floor too. Whenever I would enter his cell, I would have to step over an opened Bible that he put on the floor by the door. He opened the Bible to certain passages to keep the bad spirits from entering his cell. During my lessons, he often wanted to talk about the problems with the deputies. I always said that a teacher was a counselor first and a teacher second. I made three home visits to talk with his mother and aunt.

The news media quoted President Bush on September 4, 1991. *The Tampa Tribune* article with a dateline from Lewiston, Maine, said:

> Bush, delivering a troubling back-to-school message, said Tuesday that America's education system is failing and "we must blame ourselves for betraying our children."
> "The ringing school bell sounds an alarm, a warning to all of us who care about the state of American education..." [Bush said] . "Every day brings new evidence of crisis...."

More news. In the September 1991, *HVA Highlights*, the newsletter of the Hillsborough Vocational Association, an announcement said that Ralph L. Smouse, Jr., was inducted into the Florida Vocational Association's Hall of Fame during a ceremony in August. The article, written by his daughter, summarized his background and listed his other awards. I have no further comment.

October 1, 1991, Lake Buena Vista, Florida, a *Tampa Tribune* article reports on a speech given by President Bush at Disney World. It was reported that Bush honored 575 "Points of Light" (volunteers) from across the nation for their community service. The article reported:

> "If, as president, I had the power to give just one thing to this country, it would be the return of an inner moral compass, nurtured by the family and valued by society," Bush said. "It would show us that each life lost to despair devalues us all. It would remind us that caring and conscience make us human and make us free...."

October 18, 1991, an article in *The Tampa Tribune* said, in part, that a Blake Junior High teacher, who is the wife of Hillsborough County School Board member Glenn Barrington, had been warned by school officials not to strike students in her classroom. The article goes on to report that the police records indicate Barrington hit the 13-year-old boy after he laughed at her while she was disciplining another student. The School Board reportedly responded to this incident and sent a letter to Barrington which warned that any repetition of her behavior could have "serious consequences."

Teachers, under Rogers' supervision of Adult Special Programs, met for Professional Study Day in October. Danny Valdez, Director of Adult Education addressed the group. He said because of budget cut backs, the minimum class size of 18 may be raised to 19 or 20 depending on what the Board might do. I have heard, over and over again, about the minimum class size, but I wondered about the maximum size. When I asked Valdez about the max, he said that is determined by each individual administrator. That sounded like a bunch of baloney; why would the Board set one limit but not the other. I raised this question because by this time, I had surpassed the minimum 18 required students signed up and currently had 47 on my October FTE list used to claim reimbursement from the state. My program was so strong that I felt I was "carrying" other programs in the county that couldn't make the minimum limit. Overall and on an average, this would still make Valdez look good, at my expense, in the eyes of his superiors—Lennard and Sickles. I know the games that the administration plays with class size; I used to work at the county office.

My classes were going so well that inmates would bring other inmates with them and I didn't have to go into the pods anymore and recruit during my lunch time. My enrollment was now "self-generating." I felt proud. Ernie said that Wickham told him to cut the enrollment off when he reached 18. Wickham never told me, even when he saw my unusually high enrollment sheets. On a daily basis, we had to place our enrollment sheets in our mailbox on the way out of the building and then pick them up in the morning, a new procedure that began the day I arrived at the jail, Ernie told me. I must clarify that all the inmates enrolled in class did not show up each day: some were in court; others met with the public defender; some saw family visitors; some were transferred to another jail; some were sick and some *pretended* to be sick, but were just lazy.

I began to question the job that Wickham was doing. His title was counselor, but I never saw or heard of him doing any counseling. None of my students knew who he was or even knew that there was a counselor at the jail. I did a lot of counseling with my students. It appeared to me that he was "playing" his job more as an administrator or supervisor. He seemed more connected to the county Adult Education office than to the jail, teachers and inmates. Apparently, he was getting approval and support from Rogers and Valdez. It made me wonder how the state prison accreditation board viewed his position of "counselor." I know the School Board's educational programs at the jail were helpful, if not required, in state accreditation of the jail. Was someone pulling the wool over someone else's eyes? Were inmates receiving less than they deserved?

The last day of September, Jan Bates, inmate program supervisor with the sheriff's office, called me and said I was now to recruit inmates out of the clinic in Housing Unit 7. Those who requested GED school would be sent to me. If they were Spanish speaking, then they would be sent to Ernie Diaz's class. My present enrollment was about 30 students, 12 above the minimum standard. Why were additional students being assigned to me?

I called Rogers later that day and asked him if it was true that I would be getting students from the clinic. He said "Why not?" I complained, saying the order came from within the sheriff's department instead of from the school board. Was I now supposed to be a servant of two masters? That was fine with him. He also said he heard that Ernie's class was overloaded. I told him so was mine. Rogers directed me to call Wickham to check on this. I knew if Rogers thought it was okay to get directives from sheriff's personnel, then Wickham wasn't going to disagree with his boss.

The best thing that I saw to do was to get these directives in writing. My management training had told me that being employed by one agency and taking directives from another agency make for poor management. I also wanted to show that my class enrollment exceeded the standards and now an additional overload of students was being assigned to me. Why didn't the school system place an additional teacher in Housing Unit 4 which had no full-time day teacher? This new position could handle the overload I was getting. There were enough students to pay for the cost of the additional teacher.

The next day I went to Wickham and requested that he provide me with a memo of my assignment of students from the clinic. This documentation would show the "overload" of students assigned to me. Two days later, Wickham sent me the following hand-written letter:

> This note is to explain that students are assigned to each class through the inmate program's supervisor, Jan Bates.
>
> I'm not going to get into a position of writing a memo each time you have a question and feel that you need something-in-writing. If I did as you requested, I'd do nothing but write memos all day! I've never had to do that with other instructors assigned to the jail and I'm not going to start now. If you have

a problem with the students that are assigned to your class by the inmate program's supervisor, this clearly is a problem you should take to our county's personnel office.

Should you require further clarification about this matter, feel free to call Allen Rogers....

In a way, I was surprised with Wickham's slovenly response. It clearly told me I wasn't going to get the documentation I requested.

When I originally called Rogers about the clinic assignment, I also asked him to send me information on the school system's policy concerning students who have communicable diseases, specifically AIDS. He said he just gave a policy to Wickham and I could get a copy from him. He added, that "It is our policy not to discriminate." He said this information came from Mary Ellen Gillette, Supervisor of School Health Services.

Recently, Ernie and I spoke about the topic of communicable diseases, specifically AIDS. He never got a straight answer from the school system or the jail when he inquired about it over the years he had been teaching in the prison system. He too, wondered about the policy about inmates who were known to be HIV positive and then were assigned to our class. We didn't know what was happening, if anything. We knew we were in a high-risk environment at the jail and were concerned about injury falling on us.

In the meantime, Ernie had called the teacher's union about the policy on AIDS. He was sent a copy of a memo from Marilyn Wittner, Director of Instructional Personnel, to Carl Crosson, HCTA President, with the topic of "Working with Students with AIDS." The letter gave four statements about the school system's approach to AIDS. Item number 2 stated in part:

> 2. The school system cannot justify disclosing the fact that a person has AIDS in order to protect the health and safety of the workplace, because such disclosure would be an invasion of the AIDS-infected person's privacy....

Ernie and I both reacted the same way: wondering about discrimination against the teacher who has contact with known HIV positive student but is not made aware of it.

I received a copy of the AIDS policy from Wickham, sent by Rogers. The policy was two pages in length with two pages of general information about AIDS attached. Basically, the policy dealt with determining if a student had AIDS or not. This was different from Ernie's memo which said if the system knew of HIV positive students, we couldn't invade their privacy. The two sources of information didn't correlate. I decided to call Mary Ellen Gillette for some clarification.

When I called her, things were rather busy and I asked if I could visit with her to answer some of our questions rather than try to do it over the phone. She said fine; we were to meet the next day.

Ernie and I joined Manuel, the GED teacher from County Jail West, at Gillette's district office. The first thing that Gillette said to us was that she was going to talk "straight" to us. She said that the AIDS policy given to us yesterday by Rogers was old, out-of-date and had already been revised. We were shocked. We also knew something was up because of the tone of her conversation. We explained our concerns of teaching in a high-risk environment and our potential exposure to communicable diseases. She fully understood our concerns. She then stated the superintendent's policy on AIDS. She said that Sickles feels that if the system knows a student is HIV positive, then the teacher should know. Then she gave us copies of the new, revised AIDS policy. She said the school system's first concern about HIV positive students is if they are considered to be "biters." We said our first concern would to be to determine if they were "fighters." Gillette referred to the "universal procedures" when in contact with people with AIDS. I didn't even know what all of the procedures were. I've never had this kind of training.

It became obvious that we were ignorant to a number of facts. She said that she had conducted in-service workshops for teachers and other personnel. She suggested that we contact Rogers and recommend a workshop for us that would include him. She gave us a county-produced video tape on AIDS education and we left, thanking her for the information and her openness.

I didn't like being ignorant about the topic of AIDS, since it was a life and death matter. I decided to write a letter directly to the Superintendent (instead of Allen Rogers) with a copy to Marion Rodgers, School Board Chairman, October 7, 1991. The letter said:

Dear Dr. Sickles:

As you know, as of last July, you administratively transferred me to teach in Adult Education at the Hillsborough County Jail. I was assigned to teach in Housing Unit 6. In addition, I am now directed to recruit students from the jail infirmary in Housing Unit 7. This move alerted me to the overall concern about health and the educational environment in a detention facility. In addition to my classroom, I supervise and secure two adjoining rest rooms.

I checked with fellow teachers about health procedures and school and jail policies related to pupils and teachers. To my surprise, there was very little information available. The most information I received was that there was no information. Therefore, still concerned about communicable diseases, with and among inmates, I requested information from the Adult Education Department on the School Board's policy on AIDS. AIDS is a matter of life and death. Shortly after I received this written information, I found out it was old, out-of-date and already had been revised.

I'm not just concerned about AIDS, but *all* communicable diseases. A fellow teacher told me about an inmate that died three years ago from spinal meningitis. The teacher wasn't told about this until a deputy came into his classroom and inquired why he was in the room when it was quarantined. Why wasn't the teacher informed? He did have to go through a series of medical shots as a preventative treatment because of his exposure. He was also exposed to hepatitis at another time.

I believe the jail teaching environment is, potentially, a very volatile setting where fights among inmates in the classroom can happen rather quickly and therefore the possibility of open wounds and bleeding becomes a reality. Another teacher told me of being splattered with blood several times from previous inmates fights. Last month, one of my students came to class with a fresh wound over his eye from a fight the night before.

Most recently, an inmate was taking a test in my class, had a seizure and "swallowed" his tongue. Other inmates immediately cleared the area when he started coughing up fluids. The only thing I could do was to phone for assistance. This makes me question what my legal, professional and moral responsibilities are as a supervising teacher in this type of educational environment, especially, should a fight break out.

I need to inform you that I do teach in a locked room with no teaching assistant or deputy in the room. I have no key to get out. I must call a deputy if I want or need to leave the room.

I need to know my legal and medical responsibilities according to Board policies and state law and am requesting this specific inservice training for myself as soon as possible to properly do my job and reduce my risk of infection. I have been told that teachers in contact with known AIDS pupils have received training from Mary Ellen Gillette, Supervisor of

School Health Services. I would like to request the same. It has been said that the best prevention against AIDS is education.

I'm also requesting that I receive school issued disposable rubber gloves, a supply of USEA approved spray disinfectant and a copy of the School Health Services Manual.

Your consideration in this matter would be greatly appreciated.

Sincerely,

William Wieser

While I waited for a response, the news media accented my concern with AIDS. There was a report that the life expectancy of Americans has gone up another notch; however, fatalities among persons between 25 and 44 were up because of a 31-percent increase in AIDS deaths. Another article said that a survey showed that primary care physicians are more concerned with protecting themselves than with treating AIDS patients.

Kimberly Bergalis, a Florida resident who contracted the AIDS virus from her dentist, had recently testified before Congress about requirements for health care professionals. Her condition was worsening and, sadly, she died two months later. There was news about an inmate, said to have AIDS, who bit a deputy. There was a report about a man, claimed to be infected with the HIV virus, who resisted arrest by spitting in the face of an officer. Another newspaper article said that three years ago AIDS was the 11th leading cause of death in Florida; now it is 7th. Then, Magic Johnson, National Basketball Association player of the decade for the 1980's, announced that he had tested positive for the HIV virus and would retire from the sport.

Ernie told me that, when he was in one of the pods, he saw an attorney interviewing an inmate in one of the conference rooms. The attorney was writing on a legal pad and was wearing rubber gloves. We both thought this prevention was a bit extreme; regardless, there was a message there.

It had been over a month since I sent my letter to the Superintendent and I had heard *nothing* at all. He didn't even contact me to acknowledge he had received my letter and/or was working on it. I believe that I was placed into a situation characterized as "reckless endangerment." When I told my doctor about the lack of response, Ciliberto suggested I write a second letter to the Superintendent with a copy to the Hillsborough County Director of Public Health. That second letter, dated November 10, 1991, was as follows:

Dear Dr. Sickles:

Due to recent events in the national news media concerning NBA player Magic Johnson and his new role as an educational ambassador for AIDS, I was forced to write a second letter to you concerning communicable diseases and my risk of infection as a Hillsborough County Public School teacher assigned to teach in the county jail.

I still feel I'm in a vulnerable situation and in a high risk position subject to infection. Why have you failed to acknowledge the requests in my letter for my desperate need of inservice training concerning communicable diseases and specifically AIDS education. Why haven't I been issued disposable rubber gloves and a supply of USEA approved spray disinfectant that I had also requested in my original letter of over one month ago. Furthermore, why wasn't all of this taken care of *before* I was placed on the job last year.

I would like to give you another example to emphasize my "at risk" situation at my job site. I am told by several of the inmates, in my class, that there are inmates who masturbate in the rest room adjoining the classroom in which I teach. (The rest room door locks from the inside.) They say that the inmates would rather not chance being caught masturbating back in the pod in the shower or in their cell, especially if two inmates were housed in one cell. I have to lock and secure this rest room four times a day. I worry about what the inmates have told me since semen can carry the AIDS virus and masturbation is accomplished through hand manipulation. I touch the same door knob, light switch and fixture handles as these inmates when I secure this room.

I have been told that other county employees, even in other agencies, receive training, on a regular basis, about AIDS and other communicable diseases.

I ask again to receive immediate inservice training about these diseases and receive the appropriate protection equipment.

Desperately,

William Wieser
pc: Marion Rodgers, Chairman, School Board
    Dr. Joyner Sims, Director
    Public Health of Hillsborough County
    Dr. Thomas Weinberg, District 6 Administrator
    Public Health, Hillsborough County
    Robert Williams, Secretary
    Department of HRS, Tallahassee

Well, well, well, letter number two must have lit a fuse. Two days later, at the end of the workday, I found some rubber gloves and spray disinfectant in my school mailbox. I thought it was funny because there were nine rubber gloves that were just loose. That means that I had four-and-one-half pair of gloves. Talk about being cheap? There was no letter, note or anything saying who they came from or why I got them. Why didn't "they" give me a full box of 100 gloves, which is the same size as a tissue box, that the school system stocks in the county warehouse? What did "they" do, order one box and divide it up among the teachers? Ernie said he got ten gloves; that's a full five pair. For practice, I wanted to try on a pair, clean something, and then remove them without getting my hands contaminated. But, I didn't want to waste a pair, because then I would only have three pair, and *one* "handful" left. Was this rubber glove frolic by the school system stupid, or was I stupid to think so?

The next week was American Education Week. I didn't celebrate.

Then on November 11, 1991, I was called into Wickham's office. He wanted me to sign that I received a memo. The memo was to all staff, Adult Special Programs, and was from Rogers. The memo announced a one hour inservice training session on communicable diseases conducted by Gillette. It said that attendance was extremely important and expected.

Before the inservice training, the part-time evening GED teacher that shares my classroom sent me her weekly communication note. I had told her that I had received rubber gloves and I put them in the file cabinet. Her note said: "We got rubber gloves at my day school a couple of years ago. You are right, I hope we never have a problem, but we can't be too careful. Thanks for letting me know where they are... Ed (Wickham) was just here and he gave me the memo on the communicable disease inservice program. He told me to call Rogers and tell him I had the presentation already."

I was angry at Rogers and more so at Valdez and Lennard for not previously educating their adult special programs staff in communicable diseases. I felt violated in a most personal way! This reinforces what I've heard so often before; the administration really doesn't care about the teachers in the classroom.

The one-hour-and-ten-minute inservice training session had 18 teachers and four supervisors in attendance. Lennard and Valdez did not attend. Gillette covered universal precautions, disease transmittal, classroom protection, seizures, health supplies and the wearing of rubber gloves. The session was good, but too short to completely cover those of us in the classroom who are on the front side of contact. However, I guess it did cover the backside of the administration.

I never did get my copy of the School Health Services Manual.

As soon as this problem was addressed, another scam arose. Each school year has ten work days when teachers work, but students do not come to school.

These have traditionally been called non-pupil days. They typically include four days of preparation before the first day of school in August, conference days, professional planning days and post-planning days (after the last day of school for students in June). These days were part of the school calendar that was negotiated in the previous year between the teacher's union and the Board. I have memos, from as far back as 1984, when Sickles was assistant superintendent for personnel, that show it was routine for the personnel department to announce the specific dates of non-pupil days. Attached to it was a "question and answer" sheet to "clarify any questions that might arise."

On October 1, 1991, Marilyn Wittner, Director of Instructional Personnel, sent a memo to all principals about the length of the workday for non-pupil days. It explained that teachers like Ernie, who worked a 7 hour and 35 minute day, are to be on duty for 6 hours, including lunch. Those employees who worked a regular 8-hour day (such as principals, assistants and me) were not eligible for the 6 hour day. Many principals did allow teachers to leave the school after 5 hours if they didn't eat lunch.

The very next day, a "revised copy" of Wittner's memo came out, but was still dated October 1. In the question and answer section, there were some modifications. Next to the question "which teachers will be excused at the end of 6 hours?" appeared the answer "All teachers who normally work a 7 hour and 35 minute day...." On this revised sheet was "...and do not have students in attendance on those days." This was oxymoronic. How could you have students "in attendance" on non-student days? This reminds me of comedian George Carlin's list of "unrelated terms" like "jumbo shrimp" and "military intelligence." They didn't fit together.

The next day, Rogers visited my classroom. He needed to clarify the non-pupil day. He said that I was to have students on the non-student day. I expressed the fact that during my ten years at the county office, I never heard of any teacher having students on those days. As a matter of fact, I often planned inservice activities months ahead of time for my teachers on non-pupil days. All of the other vocational supervisors did the same. He looked at me and bluntly said "You *will* have students that day!" He also specified that Ernie would be able to go after 6 hours; however, I was to stay the full 8-hour day.

I compared notes with Ernie and he said Rogers gave him the same information and stressed that he too "*will* have students that day." I couldn't understand how 8,000 other teachers in the system would not have students, but those of us at the jail would. Our teaching contract was the same as theirs. We didn't get extra "combat pay" to be out here. Having students on these days meant that we would record it on our class rolls and therefore the school system would earn "extra" funding reimbursement for these non-pupil days. The extra FTE would make the Adult Education office shine, at our expense.

I called several administrators at the school administration center and asked for clarification on this directive to have students on a non-pupil day. I got the typical administrative run-around and they started to challenge my thinking rather than Rogers'.

Incidentally, contrary to the vacation policy at Gaither High School, in the adult education department I was permitted to take vacation anytime during the year except during the four different FTE weeks. Students in session had nothing to do with it. Therefore, why I couldn't go on the ski trip while at Gaither? *Someone* chose for me to lose my money and the trip and gain frustration and harassment.

Ernie had contacted the union (CTA). At first they were supportive, then the CTA said they might not be able to win this one. Ernie was shocked; he wondered what he was paying his dues for. Because of the lack of support from the CTA, Ernie said he would not file a grievance. I considered filing a grievance on this issue, in which I saw a "cut and dry" conclusion in my favor. But then I remembered that the system had demonstrated that they manipulate the procedures when they want to. If they are saying "no" to me now, they will say "no," somehow, during the grievance process. I decided not to file. No faith.

On October 1, 1991, while President Bush was giving his speech in Disney World, The National Education Goals Panel, back in Washington, gave U.S. students a failing grade. The report card compared student to "world-class standards" rather than state to state and concluded that U.S. students were at or near the bottom in mathematics and science. Commenting about the report, Education Secretary Lamar Alexander said, "Today's children seem to know about as much math and about as much science and read about as well as their parents did at that age about 20 years ago." The report, finally, made a dismaying observation: "The performance gap is real; it is a threat to our future, and it cannot be attributed to others...."

The teacher in the vocational assessment program at the jail passed away after a bout with cancer. His position was being advertised in the Administrative Bulletin. A November, 1991 issue listed the position and the qualifications. The last sentence stated: "Should be computer literate and be willing to work in a county correctional facility." Valdez, Lennard or Sickles never asked me if I was willing to work in a correctional facility. Lennard and Sickles didn't even *visit* this jail before they put me out there.

November, 1991, the School Board voted to name a new elementary school after board member Rev. A. Leon Lowry Sr.. He was in his 16th year on the board. He was quoted in *The Tampa Tribune* saying: "It's a unique and rare honor. It came as a total surprise. I never had the remotest idea."

I received my work contract from the school system in December, 1991. The position was Supervisor, with Tenure, but the salary was exactly the same that I was earning, to the penny, since the first day I was reinstated and assigned to Gaither High School. I called the payroll department and after a few minutes of exchange, they said I had to speak to Dr. Marilyn Hall, Compensation Supervisor. Her explanation of my pay rate was confusing. She said there was a new salary scale design. I asked her to send me a copy of her explanation to me for my study. Strangely, the letter came from Marilyn Wittner, Director of instructional Personnel, with reference to information from Hall. The attached information sheet didn't resolve my confusion. I can't understand why I haven't received a step or a cost of living raise in the last several years. No increase whatsoever. This was another battle that I didn't have the energy to fight.

A strange coincidence continues. My job performance was never evaluated at Gaither High School, and now at the jail, the required Formative evaluation for me in mid-year (December) was never done by Allen Rogers or Danny Valdez. I wonder why they failed to do this? I wonder if it had to do anything with the fact that I received no pay raise, not even a cost of living increase? In the meantime, I designed a "student evaluation of the teacher" form and asked about forty inmates to evaluate me. This, along with my high enrollment, would be positive data on my side should the system ever decide to evaluate my performance according to Board policy.

An editorial in *The Tampa Tribune*, on January 3, 1992, talks about the exodus of key university professors because of drastic cuts in funding over the last several years. In part, the editorial said:

> State university officials say Florida's institutions of higher learning are suffering from a brain drain -- an exodus of many of our finest teachers from a system that can ill afford to lose them. In most cases, the departed teachers say they left Florida reluctantly.

For no specific reason, I finally got "around to" making out my Last Will and Testament. It was a basic process and simple to do, just difficult to start. Witnesses and the notary signed it and I sent copies to the appropriate persons. My family had urged me to do this for years.

In December 1991, the Administrative Bulletin announced a retirement reception "In Honor of Richard H. Hair," Coordinator of Technology/Industrial

Education, with 34 years of service. The date/time of the reception was announced. I did not attend. In spite of the "concerns" Cammaratta had about Hair's actions, he still retires in fame (Honor) and I'm still in shame.

Also retiring was Steve Cannella (Chapter 7—"The Cryptic Memo") with 32 years of service. Plus, James Randall, Deputy Superintendent, was calling it quits with 36 years. He played a role in my grievance procedures. The newspaper said he was earning $88,000 a year. And Harold Clark, Assistant Superintendent for Supportive Services, was retiring. The newspaper reported his salary to be $83,000 a year. He was one of three people on my grievance Review Board.

December 15, 1991, *The Tampa Tribune* reported:

> A Hillsborough County educator is among five people chosen by Gov. Lawton Chiles for the state Board of Correctional Education.
>
> Pending Florida Senate confirmation, Daniel Valdez, 45, the county's director of adult and community education, will join the nine-member board that manages and operates the state's prison education program.

The report went on to say that two of the other board members were: the labor secretary, whose department denied my unemployment compensation appeal when I was terminated by the school system (Chapter 42—"Don't Beat a Dead Horse"); and Betty Castor, Education Commissioner, who dismissed my ethics complaint against Smouse (Chapter 31—"The Commissioner's Ethics"). I'm disgusted by the way Valdez manages his correctional staff here in Tampa. What kind of quality leadership can he provide to the state Board of Correctional Education in Tallahassee? I'm not sure that the make-up of this state Board will be the best approach to prevent recidivism in Florida.

One day I found a new Inmate Handbook in my school mail box. I surmised that it was just for my information. I read the first sentence in the handbook which said: "This handbook is provided to help answer any questions you may have during your stay in the Hillsborough County Jail System." I'm not incarcerated, am I?

70

ATTORNEY NUMBER 3[31/32]

During the latter part of the Summer of 1991, I decided to try to pursue the services of another attorney. Cammaratta had recently seen a St. Petersburg attorney in the news and it reminded him of my desire to obtain an attorney, outside of Hillsborough County, to take my case to a conclusion. Cammaratta mentioned the name of Anthony Battaglia; I recognized the name but I couldn't remember any specifics. He said Battaglia was the best in Pinellas County and a real "go-getter." I said I would check into his suggestion.

At the next meeting of my bike club in Pinellas County, I asked a couple of members standing in a group if they had heard of an attorney named Battaglia. They all reacted enthusiastically, saying that he was the best, top notch. I didn't need any more convincing, but I got it in an article in the *Tampa Bay Business Journal*.

The article was about the names of the best lawyers in the Tampa Bay area. Battaglia was one of the lawyers mentioned because he was also one mentioned in the ninth edition of *The Best Lawyers in America*. The article listed him under the category of business litigation and real estate.

I was convinced to try and secure Battaglia's representation. I called for an appointment and asked for a consultation with Anthony Battaglia. The secretary asked if I wanted senior or junior; I quickly thought that it must be senior. She inquired about my case topic. When I said wrongful termination, she said that Battaglia didn't do labor cases anymore. I pressed forward and asked for an initial meeting anyway. And I got it. So far so good.

I asked Cammaratta to join me at my meeting. We drove over to St. Peterburg together and when we entered the law office building we noticed the sign outside that indicated that Battaglia had sixteen associates. His reception area was very impressive, lots of wood and some antiques. Classy for sure. I could handle it; I wasn't scared.

When we met with Battaglia, I introduced myself and then Cammaratta. They exchanged a couple of words in Italian. I thought that was a good sign. I started by saying that I wanted to see if he could be of service to me. Next, I questioned him concerning any possible conflict of interest he might have with the School Board of Hillsborough County. He said no. I felt confident to go ahead with my facts.

I had prepared a two-page letter to him outlining my case and specifying seventeen critical events over the last several years. I summarized my job with the school system and answered his questions as we went along. He seemed very interested. I also told him that I had kept a journal and I had extensive documentation on my job experience. He said that I definitely had a good case.

He did have a question about the status of my Federal suit. He asked if the judge was Elizabeth Kovachevich and I smiled and said yes. That told me he was current with the United States District Court located in Tampa. My confidence grew. His question of concern about the federal suit centered around the fact that the ruling was given over a year ago. I explained that McKee told me that we could put the case on hold if we responded within the twenty days of the order by Kovachevich. I indicated that, indeed, I did instruct McKee to put a hold on it because I had run out of money and I wanted time to think it over to decide what to do. However, I also said that I never got back to McKee to confirm that this had been done. I just was pretty certain that it was.

He then stated that I probably wanted him to take my case on a contingency basis. Ever so gently, I said that was a consideration. But first, I wanted to see if he felt I had a case, then we would talk about finances. Battaglia said he would take my case to the committee, but in the meantime, he would get into his car and drive over to Tampa and personally check on my status in Federal Court. I left several pieces of documentation with him including my original letter. I was totally energized. Cammaratta and he dropped a few names of people that they both new in the educational community. I was sure these points helped to encourage Battaglia's interest.

Cammaratta and I stopped for dinner at the Red Lobster in St. Peterburg because we wanted to talk over the meeting without having to drive in traffic. We both agreed that Battaglia definitely sounded interested in my case. We both agreed that we must have caught him at the right time, meaning he didn't have any other demanding cases just then.

At the next bike club meeting another club member and close friend asked me about my case. I asked if he had heard of Battaglia and he said that his father, a well-to-do businessman, had tried to hire Battaglia and had to settle for one of his associates. He then asked how I was able to obtain his services. I explained that he wasn't secured yet, but we had a good session and things looked promising. This added to my speculation that I had found attorney number four.

About two weeks later, a letter from Battaglia arrived. I was hoping for a phone call. The letter briefly said that he looked over my material and his office did not wish to undertake my representation.

The letter didn't tell me why he didn't want to take my case, nor did it give the status of my Federal suit, if he knew. I called him and spoke with his secretary, asking why he decided not to take my case. She returned my call and simply said that he gave no specific reason. She then said I should try to contact the Hillsborough Lawyer Referral Service for an attorney.

I sent one more letter to him asking if he had made any copies of the documentation that he had sent back to me. His return letter simply indicated that his firm did not wish to undertake my representation and they did not retain any copies of my documentation.

A short time later Cammaratta and I saw several TV news reports about a scandal in the sale of an expensive government building. We believe that Battaglia was the defending attorney. A busy man in the spotlight again.

So close, yet so far from number four. It might as well have been four million.

The University of South Florida School of Continuing Education offered a two-day course titled Doing the Right Thing: Revolutions in Professional Ethics. The details of the course revolve around the obligations of Florida's public service professions and appeal to the humanistic values of community, individual human dignity and the obligation of government to the governed. The course description states "The conference has national significance because Florida is the first to attempt an ethics-based redirection of professional life."

I recently saw one of those little yellow diamond shaped signs in the side window of a teenager's car. I chuckled, but it was bittersweet. It read: "This year I'm going to get something out of school...me!"

71

CUT! THAT'S A PRINT

CUT!

For the longest time, I had hoped that my story would have reached a conclusion with justice being served. Now, I don't believe my story will ever end, so I'll just stop writing about it. This will be my "cut and print."

My attention was drawn to news about recent violence in area schools in March. Two junior high schools in Hillsborough county and a high school in neighboring Pinellas county experienced student violence. Specifically, a student leaving a Tampa junior high school was reportedly beaten by a group of classmates on the way home; five students were arrested. The school—which had a population of 1,442 students—had registered 995 suspensions in only seven months (200 related to fighting or assaults) according to the principal, a figure up from "400 or 500 suspensions" the year before. Parents volunteered to patrol the school hallways. The violence, which spread like a virus to other schools over the following weeks, involved knives and guns.

The news gives me the impression that, no matter what, life goes on and it will be business as usual in the Tampa Bay community, the state of Florida, our nation, and the world. In a random ordering, these are stories recently reported in the news that set the scene as I "cut:"

> Local media cover student unrest as hundreds of students in the Tampa Bay area junior and senior high schools have walked out of class to protest education budget cuts proposed by the Florida legislature. They assembled on the ball fields and carried posters such as: "Education Cuts Don't Heal."

> It is generally agreed that the Florida Lottery has not been the educational system enhancement that it was promoted to be. While it does bring in revenue, state Education Commissioner Betty Castor said that over one billion

dollars was cut from the regular education budget over the last several years, making it a replacement rather than an enhancement.

Children's advocates accuse Florida's politicians of putting children "last instead of first because voters let them get away with it" and rally the faithful to put the heat on state legislators. The Florida Children's Campaign launched its 'Vote Kids '92' campaign with vows to increase public awareness of children's needs . . . and vote unsupportive politicians out of office. "Florida simply cannot afford to endanger its most priceless treasure—its children," Governor Lawton Chiles told the conference.

A Census Bureau report, entitled *School Enrollment—Social and Economic Characteristics of Students*, states "one-third of high school-age Americans have either dropped behind their class level or dropped out entirely..." in reference to 1990 school enrollment.

A controversial study from the University of Chicago finds that the General Education Development (GED) high school equivalency certificate graduates "fare no better than dropouts and much worse than graduates in the job market."

There have been numerous protests by Florida students at all levels against state budget cuts in education. In February, 1992, more than a thousand college students crowded onto the steps of the Capitol in Tallahassee. Responding to a challenge made by Governor Chiles four months before to get involved in the political process, they chant "We're off our duffs."

Proposed legislation in Florida would reduce the number of required credits for a high school diploma from 24 to 22 to save money.

In September, 1991, Governor Lawton Chiles, using a University of Tampa ethics seminar as a backdrop, criticized the "corrupting influence" of money on judges and called for trial judges to be appointed the way appeals and Supreme Court justices are. "The outcome of judicial elections too often is determined by the size of a candidate's war chest," Chiles said of lower court judicial elections.

In February, 1992, a defense lawyer accused of being the middle man in a 1991 bribery case boasted privately of corruption within Hillsborough County courts. Reports also indicated that in February, 1992, the U.S. Attorney's office unsealed a federal indictment against two persons, charging them with extortion and bribery. Later, an ex-prosecutor pleads guilty in case fixing. The federal investigation continues.

The Tampa Tribune collected two of three top newspaper awards given by the Florida Teaching Profession - National Education Association for excellence in news coverage. Bay area stations won in the television competition. Gov.

Lawton Chiles addressed the FTP-NEA group during the awards presentation and vowed to win a tax increase to help education.

In February, 1992, a five-alarm fire ripped through the Hillsborough County school system's Raymond O. Shelton school administration building destroying computer equipment and valuable records. Investigators concluded that the estimated $7 million blaze was caused by "an overloaded extension cord." There were no sprinklers or smoke detectors in the main building which was built in 1979; there were sprinklers in the parking garage.

According to James Petterson and Peter Kim, authors of *The Day America Told the Truth* (Prentice Hall, 1991), the number-one cause of our world business decline is "low ethics by executives."

In March, 1992, an alarming article about Florida's kids cites a study, financed by the philanthropic Annie E. Casey Foundation and conducted by the nonprofit Center for the Study of Social Policy in Washington, D.C., which determined that: "Florida's children are more likely to be born dangerously small, grow up poor, quit school or die violently than those in most states...." Additionally, the national Kids Count project ranks Florida 43rd among the states and Washington, D.C., on nine key measures of child well-being. Florida's poor showing doesn't surprise Bob Williams, the secretary of the state Department of Health and Rehabilitative Services (HRS) who commented, "I think they are good indicators of the fact we are failing the children of Florida miserably." Jack Levine, executive director of the Florida Center for Children and Youth, a Tallahassee-based advocacy organization, and co-director of the newly-formed Florida Kids Count project, warns that, because the study mainly used 1989 data, the most recent available, to rate the states, Florida's true ranking might be even lower after two years of budget cuts.

One alarming finding in the study was that Florida's graduation rate dropped 6 percent between 1982 and 1989. Florida's 56.5 percent rate puts it last among the states; only children in the District of Columbia fared worse.

Even though Hillsborough county leads the state in trying children as adults, critics say the juvenile justice system is crowded and outdated. Gov. Lawton Chiles lamented that Florida will remain the most crime-ridden state in the nation unless it curbs juvenile delinquency; he proposes spending $30 million for more treatment programs.

More than 1,000 teachers, parents and students representing primary and secondary schools from around the state urged lawmakers to boost educational spending during a rally at the Capitol in Tallahassee.

Riots in Los Angles after the acquittal of four police officers in the videotaped beating of motorist Rodney King again bring to the forefront our commitment to civil rights, justice and ethics.

In *The Next Century* (Morrow, 1991) David Halberstam discusses why this country's economic power is sliding in the world community and draws concerns to several topics, one of them education. Halberstam states "The President says that he is an education president, but there is no real sign that he makes a connection between education and the malaise in our country....

Work demands ever-higher levels of education and competency. That is true not only here but around the world. But as it happens, we are not responding to it."

Our nation hears Japan's prime minister say that Americans lack a work ethic.

In a July 2, 1992 editorial concerning the 1992 Florida Legislative Session, *The Tampa Tribune* asserts that the Legislature "will live in shame." It states:

A disgrace. That's the best that can be said of the 1992 Legislature. Devoid of political courage, subservient to special interests, unwilling to confront the plain truth about Florida's needs, this Legislature may be the worst of the modern era.

After months of gyrations, the Legislature produced a budget that leaves the state's schools and universities among the most poorly funded in the nation, keeps the criminal justice system languishing, neglects environmental responsibilities and all but abandons the elderly, the disabled, and the needy.

...It failed to revamp the lottery so that revenue would be spent on enhancing education, as voters intended....

...What do lawmakers think will occur when the best and brightest professors and college students continue to flee the state because its universities are crumbling? When school classrooms are jammed and beleaguered teachers demoralized? When teen-age hoodlums run amok because there is no place to incarcerate them? When no company will relocate to Florida because of its unskilled work force?

What makes all this so sickening is that most lawmakers understand the state's desperate needs. They simply didn't trust the people enough to tell them the truth....

In a similarly critical editorial published July 3, 1992, *The St. Petersburg Times* bids "Good riddance" to the Legislature: "The worst legislative session in memory can now fade into history."

After hearing nothing from School Board member Yvonne McKitrick since I worked on her campaign four years ago, even though she earlier promised to "talk to me about my job situation," I receive a form letter requesting a contribution to her re-election campaign. The letter, which in part, read "I have encouraged open lines of communication.... I need your help..." was sent to my home address, not my work location address at the jail.

Its all A's for Hillsborough County school Superintendent Walter L. Sickles who received a "spectacular" yearly evaluation by the School Board according to *The Tampa Tribune*.

There is explosive growth of education in Russia. Hundreds of private schools and colleges have spawned in Russia since President Boris Yeltsin signed a law allowing non-government schools in the post-Cold War period. The vast majority of students who have paid sky-high tuition (more than eight times what a typical Russian earns in a year) want business degrees (M.B.A.), according to a *Cox News Service* report in *The Tampa Tribune*. Don't count Russia out!

Politically, Florida has been considered "Bush Country." The week before "Super Tuesday" in 1992 (the day more delegates are selected than any other day of the election primaries), President George Bush made a political visit to Tampa at a $1,000-a-plate fund-raising luncheon attended by Gulf War hero Gen. H. Norman Schwarzkopf, who introduced the President to the 450 people in attendance. The president managed to visit the Florida Strawberry Festival in Hillsborough County which was covered live on television. It was speculated that he would make a visit to one of the two public schools adjoining the festival grounds. He did not. However, the next day a color picture appeared in *The Tampa Tribune* showing the "education" President seated beside and enjoying strawberry shortcake with School Board member Joe Newsome. Such priorities? Later that day, Bush went on to make a visit in Miami where his son Jeb lives; Jeb Bush is said to be running the re-election campaign in Florida.

A promotional spot on WTVT Channel 13 endorsing "One For The Children" in the Tampa Bay area features first lady Barbara Bush. She thanks the business community for their involvement and encourages others to support "One For The Children."

On March 9, 1991, Barbara Bush wrote a letter, on behalf of the President and herself, to Hillsborough County public schools and the Educational Partnership Foundation, complimenting them on recognizing special teachers.

President Bush signed a letter supporting Republican candidate Buddy Johnson, who was running for a vacated state representative seat in 1991 in Hillsborough County. Johnson won the special election. Nonetheless, Johnson "bemoans the state of public education" and sends his son to private kindergarten to expose him to more "traditional values," according to a report in *The Tampa Tribune*. Johnson became a member of the state House committees on public schools and vocational/technical education. Later, in the Fall of 1992, Johnson was removed from the House education committee because of allegations of an incident of sexual harassment involving an education committee lawyer. "I thought it was in the best interest of the House to move him," said House speaker T.K. Wetherell, according to *The Tampa Tribune*.

With President Bush's speaking engagements at Disney World, vacation fishing trips in the Keys and campaign swings throughout Florida, Floridians might conclude that we are meaningful (recreationally) and essential (politically) to the success of our President. Nonetheless, the anguish of education here is eluding him. Or is he eluding it? What else can we do? Aren't education values a part of family values?

President Bush's far-reaching America 2000 initiative has set excellent National Education Goals, but it will not cure the disease that has prevented us from reaching similar goals long ago. Simply putting up a newly designed target doesn't make one a better marksman.

As I search for the end of my story, the wheels of the establishment continue their radial-power-thrust into the future. The local school systems are the foundation of this nation, and this country is failing in educational competition among industrial nations. But this problem is not new, nor is it without solution. Yet still we grapple. Perhaps John Locke, in 1690, crystalized the essence of our struggle most clearly:

> The great question which, in all ages, has disturbed mankind, and brought on them the greatest part of those mischiefs which have ruined cities, depopulated countries, and disordered the peace of the world, has been, not whether there be power in the world, nor whence it came, but who should have it.

EPILOGUE

In February, 1992, I went for another checkup. My blood pressure was up again to 168/118 and I gained back the twenty-five pounds that I had lost last Fall. Dr. Ciliberto stressed that I select a careful diet and give him back fifteen pounds. He also prescribed the drug Prozac for my stress. I told him that I needed time away from the job. He recommended several months of health leave based upon job stress and hypertension; it was approved by the School Board.

The accumulated pressures from the job had been mounting. I still couldn't get it straight in my mind that justice had been served and I was in the educational position I should be. I wrestled daily with what I should do with the rest of my career. I wasn't writing the book for the last seven months; I experienced "writer's block." My efforts had gone towards learning my new job at the jail, and trying to secure a publisher for this book. I realized that I had to discipline myself and finish writing it.

Two years ago, I met a person on the road when I was on a bike trip headed to New Jersey. I had stopped at a rest area in Maryland and an older gentleman in a full-sized Buick pulled in next to me. He appeared to be an executive type with a expensive white shirt and nice conservative tie. He walked over and commented on my bike and asked about my trip. I could tell that he wished that he was on my bike and I was in his Buick. He asked what type of business I was in; I told him that I was a school teacher. He said that he admired me for that. I added that I was also writing a book about what was wrong with the educational system. He responded by saying that I could write volumes about that, and that I should. Our meeting was brief; he wished me luck on my book. All I could think of, on the remainder of the trip, was his encouragement to write.

Donna (Chapter — 45 "No Fury") called me again in March, 1992. Her recorded message said "call as soon as possible, I need to talk to you." She said to call her at home or work. I debated what to do for a few days and then decided to call her because it was almost four years now that she was trying to get close to me.

I called her at work, early in the morning. She surely was surprised to hear my voice. She was worried about me because I had not returned her calls, but, she was glad that I was still alive. She wanted to get together at her home and talk. I said I was starting a new lifestyle and I had new friends. Donna asked again to get together sometime. She indicated that she had driven by my condo, but forgot the code for the security gate. She said she was going to come up to my door and ring the bell. I was relieved that she didn't get the chance. Since I haven't dated for awhile, my desire for an intimate relationship was high. Nonetheless, I said to myself "no thank you." I was still leery about her intentions and persistence, as well as her connections to the school system. As a matter of fact, I was scared even though I didn't think she was stalking me.

With the information I have now, it is speculated that the Professor was a double agent. His ties were too close to the Commissioner and the Superintendent's office. By way of Cammaratta, the Professor's recommendation of attorney number two was attractive because of the lure of contacting a "headhunter." In the end, attorney number two recommended that I cancel the Level II grievance hearing and then declined to file suit against the School Board. Post attorney number two, the Professor faded away.

It is speculated that additional school officials were involved in the Textbook Scam. It is also speculated that school officials, even at the tippy top, made rendezvous to the four beach front condominiums that were purchased with textbook funds. What happened to the unaccounted-for $700,000.00? The textbook supervisor has been released from prison.

It is also speculated that the $7 million fire that struck the Raymond O. Shelton school administration building may not have been caused by an "overloaded extension cord." The fire, which started at 6 p.m. on a Thursday, miraculously waited just over an hour after the end of the work day to do its damage. It was estimated that about 20 people were in the building at the time. Media announcements told clerical and secretarial workers not to report to work the next day. And administrators and supervisors were told to report to another school site, leaving only the top school officials to survey the damage. Officials said they would not have a damage report until the next morning (Friday). However, Superintendent Sickles was quoted saying "I'm sure there are records in there that have been destroyed. All this stuff is very valuable," in Friday morning's *Tampa Tribune*. (Employee paychecks were recovered.) Was the "overloaded extension cord" overloaded all day? Could the fire have been a way to destroy or cover-up documents? I have already been told of an incident in which a teacher had subpoenaed some documents for a law suit. The School Board responded by saying the documents were "lost in the fire." It will be interesting to observe how many times this response will be given to other serious inquiries in the future.

As I look back at my story, I ponder some questions that probably will never be answered. Was Smouse engaged in a premeditated crusade to ensure that I was terminated? Why did the Superintendent of Schools refuse my witnesses access to my formal grievance hearing that he himself recommended? What was the real reason a tainted school system security investigation was conducted? Why did the security report end up as a part of Smouse's response to my ethics complaint with the Commissioner of Education? Was a deal cut in Tallahassee to overlook my Code of Ethics complaint against Smouse if he would retire? Was there a suppression of the news by the print and electronic media concerning the "people's right to know" about my law suit against the school system for wrongful termination? Which school official told the Florida Unemployment Bureau that I quit my job, therefore disqualifying me from receiving unemployment compensation benefits even after I made two appeals? What force played havoc in the systematic removal and destruction of my campaign signs in the School Board election? By what authority could the school system refuse to accept my application for the position of Assistant Superintendent for Vocational Education? Why did the School Board fail to resolve my situation with Smouse before it cost the taxpayers so much money? Why did the Circuit Court fail to see that I was reinstated to my original position as it stated in its summary judgement? What was the real reason the Circuit Court Judge was changed in the middle of my case? What was the real reason the Federal Court refused to allow my right to a public trial by jury on the violation of my civil rights? Why didn't the local print and electronic media consider my total story to be newsworthy and inform the voting public when I was a candidate for the school board? Why was I (a Supervisor) placed in the classroom at the county jail after I was reinstated? Why do Florida students rank at the bottom of the scale in national dropout rates? Why are student's performances so low in the United States as compared to world standards? Why would George Bush wish to proclaim himself the "education" President and then turn his back on the nation's schools? What will be the fate of American education, and consequently, the fate of the country itself? And life goes on.

The usefulness of this book was not to assign blame, but to uncover ignorance. Nor was it the design to take anything away from anyone, but to give to all a prompting that even what appears to be quality education management still needs its checks and balances.

I pray the telling of my story will be a successful catharsis for me and, in part, be beneficial to my profession, community, state and country.

The children's future depends upon us and our future depends upon the children. We must ask God to bless America and then *we* must stand behind her and try to guide her.

Amen.

On October 1, 1992, after an eight month health leave of absence recommended by my doctor, I returned to work with the Hillsborough County Public School system. Still classified and paid as a Supervisor, I was directed to teach GED to juvenile inmates at the county jail under the supervision of a Coordinator, a position subordinate to that of a Supervisor.

George Bush is defeated in his reelection bid as President. Bill Clinton is elected and appoints Richard Riley as Secretary of Education. Janet Reno is nominated as Attorney General. I bet she'll keep one eye on the management of American education because the Miami, Florida resident has been known for her diligence in pursuing cases in political corruption.

My clasped hands commence an optimistic prayer for our school kids and America's future stature in the forever changing world society.

EPITAPH

Over the years, the field of education has seen the exit of many of its best professionals because of the frustration with the lack of adherence to ethics within the educational bureaucracy.

Allow this story, *Death by Education: An American Autopsy*, to act as a red flag for all to query the local school system and make an ethical commitment to put the pursuit of knowledge and happiness back into the educational process.

Now, more so than ever before, to ensure domestic tranquility, education needs creative professional leaders with the principles, foresight, dedication and endurance to purge the local educational systems and give our youth the means to establish the future of this country's intellectual ranking at the top of a world society.

In the quest for creative education reform, may we all heed the words of Sir Winston Churchill during the arduous times of World War II: "Never give in, never give in, never, never, never, never—in nothing, great or small, large or petty—never give in except to convictions of honor and good sense."

May the problems in American Education be put to a peaceful rest.

APPENDIX

1. The Code of Ethics of the Education Profession in Florida and The Principles of Professional Conduct for the Education Profession in Florida.
2. The American Association of School Administrator's Statement of Ethics for School Administrators.

1

The Code of Ethics of the Education Profession in Florida Florida State Board of Education
June 15, 1982

(1) The educator values the worth and dignity of every person, the pursuit of truth, devotion to excellence, acquisition of knowledge, and the nurture of democratic citizenship. Essential to the achievement of these standards are the freedom to learn and to teach and the guarantee of equal opportunity for all.

(2) The educator's primary professional concern will always be for the student and for the development of the student's potential. The educator will therefore strive for professional growth and will seek to exercise the best professional judgment and integrity.

(3) Aware of the importance of maintaining the respect and confidence of one's colleagues, of students, of parents, and of other members of the community, the educator strives to achieve and sustain the highest degree of ethical conduct.

Principles of Professional Conduct for the Education Profession in Florida

(1) The following disciplinary rule shall constitute the Principles of Professional Conduct for the Education Profession in Florida and shall apply to any individual holding a valid Florida teacher's certificate.

(2) Violation of any of these principles shall subject the individual to revocation or suspension of the individual teacher's certificate, or the other penalties as provided by law.

(3) Obligation to the student requires that the individual:

    (a) Shall make reasonable effort to protect the student from conditions harmful to learning or to health or safety.

    (b) Shall not unreasonably restrain a student from independent action in pursuit of learning.

    (c) Shall not unreasonably deny a student access to diverse points of view.

    (d) Shall not intentionally suppress or distort subject matter relevant to a student's academic program.

    (e) Shall not intentionally expose a student to unnecessary embarrassment or disparagement.

    (f) Shall not intentionally violate or deny a student's legal rights.

    (g) Shall not on the basis of race, color, religion, sex, age, national or ethnic origin, political beliefs, martial status, handicapping condition if otherwise qualified, or social and family background exclude a student from participation in a program; deny a student benefits; or grant a student advantages.

    (h) Shall not exploit professional relationship with a student for personal gain or advantage.

    (i) Shall keep in confidence personally identifiable information obtained in the course of professional services, unless disclosure serves professional purposes or is required by law.

(4) Obligation to the public requires that the individual:

    (a) Shall take reasonable precautions to distinguish between personal views and those of any educational institution or organization with which the individual is affiliated.

    (b) Shall not intentionally distort or misrepresent facts concerning an educational matter in direct or indirect public expression.

    (c) Shall not use institutional privileges for personal gain or advantage.

    (d) Shall accept no gratuity, gift, or favor that might influence professional judgement.

    (e) Shall offer no gratuity, gift, or favor to obtain special advantages.

(5) Obligation to the profession of education requires that the individual:

(a) Shall maintain honesty in all professional dealings.

(b) Shall not on the basis of race, color, religion, sex, age, national or ethnic origin, political beliefs, martial status, handicapping condition if otherwise qualified, or social and family background deny to a colleague professional benefits or advantages or participation in any professional organization.

(c) Shall not interfere with a colleague's exercise of political or civil rights and responsibilities.

(d) Shall not intentionally make false or malicious statements about a colleague.

(e) Shall not use coercive means or promise special treatment to influence professional judgements of colleagues.

(f) Shall not misrepresent one's own professional qualification.

(g) Shall not submit fraudulent information on any document in connection with professional activities.

(h) Shall not make any fraudulent statement or fail to disclose a material fact in one's own or another's application for a professional position.

(i) Shall not knowingly withhold information regarding a position from an applicant or misrepresent an assignment or conditions of employment.

(j) Shall provide upon the request of the certificated individual a written statement of specific reason for recommendations that lead to the denial of increments, significant changes in employment, or termination of employment.

(k) Shall not assist entry into or continuance in the profession of any person known to be unqualified in accordance with these Principles of Professional Conduct for the Education Profession in Florida and other applicable Florida Statutes and State Board of Education Rules.

(l) Shall report to appropriate authorities any known violation of Florida School Code or State Board of Education Rules as defined in Section 231.28(1), Florida Statutes.

(m) Shall seek no reprisal against any individual who has reported a violation of Florida School Code or State Board of Education Rules as defined in Section 231.28(1), Florida Statutes.

(n) Shall comply with the conditions of an order of the Education Practices Commission imposing probation, imposing a fine, or restricting the authorized scope of practice.

(o) Shall, as the supervising administrator, cooperate with the Education Practices Commission in monitoring the probation of a subordinate.

A Note of Interest:

The Florida Department of Education, Betty Castor, Commissioner, published the above Code of Ethics and Principles of Professional Conduct in a brochure format. The back of the brochure, received in 1987, stated:

FLORIDA: A STATE OF EDUCATIONAL DISTINCTION.

On a statewide average, educational achievement in the State of Florida will equal that of the upper quartile of states within five years, as indicated by commonly accepted criteria of attainment.

This publication was produced at an annual cost of $1,805.12 or $.0185 per copy to implement Section 231.546(2), Florida Statutes by providing to members of the Florida educational community revised copies of State Board of Education Rules 6B-1.01 and 6B-1.06 FAC.

The achievement of this "upper quartile" goal has not been commonly accepted. However, the state of Florida did attain the dubious achievement of having the highest dropout rate in the nation.

Commissioner Betty Castor preached this "upper quartile" goal during her 1986 campaign. If you round off the per copy price of the brochure ($.0185) to the nearest penny, it equals two cents. We now know the value of that stated pledge and the State Board of Education Rules themselves.

2

American Association of School Administrators Statement of Ethics for School Administrators May 1, 1981

An educational administrator's professional behavior must conform to an ethical code. The code must be idealistic and at the same time practical, so that it can apply reasonably to all educational administrators. The administrator acknowledges that the schools belong to the public they serve for the purpose of providing educational opportunities to all. However, the administrator assumes responsibility for providing professional leadership in the school and community. The responsibility requires the administrator to maintain standards of exemplary professional conduct. It must be recognized that the administrator's actions will be viewed and appraised by the community, professional associates, and students. To these ends, the administrator subscribes to the following statements of standards.

The educational administrator:

1. Makes the well-being of students the fundamental value of all decision-making and actions.
2. Fulfills professional responsibilities with honesty and integrity.
3. Supports the principle of due process and protects the civil and human rights of all individuals.
4. Obeys local, state, and national laws and does not knowingly join or support organizations that advocate, directly or indirectly, the overthrow of the government.
5. Implements the governing board of education's policies and administrative rules and regulations.
6. Pursues appropriate measures to correct those laws, policies, and regulations that are not consistent with sound educational goals.
7. Avoids using positions for personal gain through political, social, religious, economic, or other influences.
8. Accepts academic degrees or professional certification only from duly accredited institutions.
9. Maintains the standards and seeks to improve the effectiveness of the profession through research and continuing professional development.
10. Honors all contracts until fulfillment, release, or dissolution mutually agreed upon by all parties to contract.

Reprinted with permission from the American Association of School Administrators.